Critical Rhetorics of Race

CRITICAL CULTURAL COMMUNICATION

General Editors: Sarah Banet-Weiser and Kent A. Ono

Critical Rhetorics of Race

Edited by

Michael G. Lacy and Kent A. Ono

NEW YORK UNIVERSITY PRESS

New York and London

NEW YORK UNIVERSITY PRESS
New York and London
www.nyupress.org

References to Internet websites (URLs) were accurate at the time of writing.
Neither the author nor New York University Press is responsible for URLs that
may have expired or changed since the manuscript was prepared.

Library of Congress Cataloging-in-Publication Data
Critical rhetorics of race / edited by Michael G. Lacy and Kent A. Ono.
p. cm.   (Critical cultural communication)
Includes bibliographical references and index.
ISBN 978-0-8147-6222-6 (cl : acid-free paper)
ISBN 978-0-8147-6223-3 (pb : acid-free paper)
ISBN 978-0-8147-6236-3 (e-book)
1. Racism—United States.   2. United States—Race relations.
3. Racism in popular culture.   4. Racism in mass media.
5. Racism in motion pictures.   6. Racism in sports.
I. Lacy, Michael G.   II. Ono, Kent A., 1964–
E185.8.C88   2011
305.800973—dc22   2011003830

New York University Press books are printed on acid-free paper, and their binding
materials are chosen for strength and durability. We strive to use environmentally
responsible suppliers and materials to the greatest extent possible in publishing our
books.

Manufactured in the United States of America

c 10 9 8 7 6 5 4 3 2 1
p 10 9 8 7 6 5 4 3 2 1

Contents

Acknowledgments

This book benefited greatly from the generous spirit of many people. From the outset, we would like to thank Dana Cloud, who introduced us to each other. Since first meeting, we have had many wonderful conversations about communication, race, politics, and life. We sent each other email messages, talked via phone, sent drafts of ideas back and forth, and, from time to time, picked one another up when the other was down. During that time, we developed an idea for a book. We sought out contributors, pored over book chapters, convened convention panels, and carefully revised and edited each other's work. This book is the end result.

We could not have sustained a book project without the help and support of our families, friends, colleagues, librarians, and editorial staff. We therefore thank our families for their endless love and support (especially Michael's mother, Margaret P. Lacy), even in difficult and trying times. We especially thank our partners (Michael's) Kathleen Haspel and (Kent's) Sarah Projansky, who created a loving space, listened to us talk, read our work, and urged us on, with humor and grace. Completing a book like this makes you think a lot about time. Mina and Daniel (Kent's children) grew significantly over the time it took to complete the book; Daniel is now talking in complete sentences, and Mina has almost finished the Harry Potter series! Kent thanks them for their patience and love.

We thank those who advised us on the early stages of the book, including Joe Marconi of DePaul University. We thank New York University Press editor Eric Zinner and editorial assistant Ciara McLaughlin for their patience, advice, and support. Series editor Sarah-Banet Weiser supported the concept of the book unflaggingly. Despina Papazoglou Gimbel and our copyeditor, Karen Verde, did remarkable work in the production phase. We also thank the anonymous reviewers for their thoughtful suggestions and detailed advice, which we tried to address carefully. Though they go unnamed, their generous ideas have significantly improved this work. We also greatly appreciate the works that were submitted to us that we ultimately could not include, because of space limitations. We feel lucky to have had the opportunity to read and review such exciting work in the field. These pieces have already begun to be published elsewhere, and we plan to read them and teach them in our classes.

We offer special thanks to our research assistant, Sayuri Arai, who worked diligently and arduously making needed editorial changes and also making the book stylistically consistent, a tall order indeed. Thanks also to our additional research assistants, Kapil Mathur, Nina Li, and Robert Mejia, for helping out when we were overwhelmed. Kapil and Nina entered changes, and Sayuri and Nina produced the index. All of these contributed tremendously to the book's quality. We are greatly indebted to the DePaul University librarians, and the librarians at Chatham Library in New Jersey (especially Diane and Mary), who always made time to help us. We also want to thank all of the students in our critical rhetoric and race courses, especially Rya Butterfield, who helped Michael and Kathleen during the early stages of their chapter.

Others who directly or indirectly inspired us to write this book include: Aaron Gresson, Dexter Gordon, Joe Marconi, Roderick Hart, Molefi Asante, Carole Stabile, Eric Watts, Kirt Wilson, Gus Friedrich, Pat Sullivan, Steven Goldzwig, Barry Brummett, Henry Louis Gates Jr., Karlyn Kohrs Campbell, Herman Gray, Carole Blair, John Nerone, Robert Hariman, Radha Hegde, Mark McPhail, Ronald L. Jackson II, Tom Nakayama, Cameron McCarthy, Karen Tracy, Robert Craig, Curt LeBaron, Robert Weiss, John Sloop, Bruce Gronbeck, Michael McGee, James Hay, Angharad Valdivia, Lisa Nakamura, Kal Alston, Cara Finnegan, John Murphy, Ned O'Gormann, Debby Hawhee, Fernando Delgado, Ben Attias, Lisa Flores, Dreama Moon, Raka Shome, Isabel Molina-Guzmán, Lucy Xiang Lu, and our many other colleagues with whom we work and have worked.

Special thanks are reserved for Raymie McKerrow, who waited patiently for us to finish the book before kindly writing the guest preface for it, using his 2010 spring break to do so.

Finally, we thank the contributors to this volume for sticking with us through thick and thin, for responding to (too many) requests for revision and information, for their collegiality and friendship, and for believing in the project. Without them, there would be no book at all.

Foreword

Raymie E. McKerrow

Critical Rhetorics of Race advances our understanding of the ever-present nature of racism, whether in its malevolent overt expression, or in its more insidious covert guise, often masquerading via claims of its absence. Taking a stand against racism, as these chapters do, requires a clear understanding of its presence within culture. In establishing its presence, the chapters offer a thematic unity while examining the effectivity of racism within and across divergent arenas. As a consequence, they challenge the grounds for claiming we are in a post-racism era.

Considered collectively, the chapters evince a clear understanding of what it means to assume a critical perspective on the ways symbols *perform* in addressing publics, while at the same time they represent their own work as a rhetorical *performance*. Adopting a transdisciplinary stance, they are highly sophisticated, analytical, and methodical; their methodological approaches service analysis rather than overtake it. Critical terms, when utilized, are on point in illuminating or punctuating insights into how racism functions. A singular focus that unites the chapters is a critique of domination—particularly as it is represented via an unpacking of relations of power. One lesson drawn from the works is that it is not necessary to overtheorize power to understand its influence; nor is it necessary in all cases to mention the term while recognizing its presence. Noting the absence of a claim ("you would not say that to . . .") is a clear implication of the presence of a power differential containing as well as constraining discursive possibilities.

Essentializing race, as the editors note in their introduction, is a temporary and strategic move that is, well, essential. Fixing race, while recognizing its fluid, multivalent, contingent, and ever-changing nature as a social construction, is a move that allows the critic the opportunity to show its oppressive as well as potentially productive impact. From a critical rhetoric perspective, this move is unproblematic. The sense of recursivity that accompanies critique does not end the possibility of criticism, but rather ensures its continual examination of power relations, lest they go unchallenged. That said, each present becomes a potentially different future, given an effective critique of power relations in the moment. These chapters present such a critique and thus offer the possibility of change as we move forward. Recognizing the futility of post-racism in our present time does not mean that we will never see a post-racist future (though it does raise the question of whether such is in fact a possibility). Should that future arrive, it also does not mean we have reached nirvana and no further improvement in our lives is needed.

The most important question these chapters raise is "where do we go from here?" The task of unmasking relations of domination within the context of race relations is not finished. There is more to be said—if only to strengthen further the case for an anti-racism stance. Nevertheless, seeking "freedom from" oppression is only part of the story. There is a further obligation to focus on a "freedom to" become something other than we are at present. While the critique of freedom is not premised solely on a critique of domination, such critiques do begin to suggest sites of intervention, wherein the possibility of a productive sense of power—what it can do for us beyond oppression—opens up new avenues for exploration. What would a rhetoric free of racism be? One thing it would not be is color-neutral. A rhetoric that simply values difference for the difference it makes restores the possibility that power can be used productively to initiate social change. The challenge before us, as this text so admirably elucidates, is to create the conditions for a rhetoric that constructs a racism-free world. At the very least, if that proves an impossible dream, the challenge is one of fashioning a rhetoric that diminishes the effectivity of racism as a material force.

Introduction

Michael G. Lacy and Kent A. Ono

Contemporary U.S. media culture represents race in ambivalent, contradictory, and paradoxical ways. Media tell us that the United States is a *post-racial* society, in which race and racism are passé relics of a bygone era. Yet, those same media bombard us daily with spectacles of racial violence and disturbing racist images that serve as evidence that race and racism are alive and well in the United States. Witness the euphoria and great ballyhoo about a "post-race" era ushered in by the 2008 presidential election and inauguration of America's first "black" president, Barack Obama. Recurring media storylines described Obama as a *mixed-race*[1] man who spent his formative years in Hawai'i and his early childhood in Indonesia, whose black father was born in Alego, Kenya, and whose white mother was born in Fort Leavenworth, Kansas. Yet, soon after the election, a *New York Post* cartoon featured two white police officers, one of them pointing a gun at a dark ape lying dead on the ground, in a pool of blood with three bullet holes in its back and its tongue hanging out of its mouth. In a dialogue bubble, one of the police officers says to the other: "They'll have to find someone else to write the next stimulus bill," implying that President Obama is the dead ape. The cartoon generated controversy, outrage, protest, and denials of and apologies for racism. Such paradoxes disturb our cultural psyche, but they also remind us that race and racism remain stable fixtures in U.S. American life, expressing cultural anxieties, fears, and material inequalities.

Contemporary U.S. culture produces, circulates, and reproduces contradictory images of race, which creates problems for scholars, critics, educators, and those who aim to expose and eliminate oppression and promote social justice. How do we respond to claims that race and racism are simply historical artifacts of yesteryear? How do we respond to the paradoxical jubilation of and celebration (which first began with neoconservative commentators over a decade ago) by media reporters, politicians, pundits, and others globally, all proclaiming the end of racism, while also witnessing media spectacles, such as the cartoon that depicts President Obama as an ape and dramatizes his murder by police officers?

Critical Rhetorics of Race shows that race and racism (and intersections of sexism, heterosexism, classism, and neocolonialism) are very much part of contemporary daily life in the United States. Racism, of course, ranges from everyday racism experienced by individuals in private contexts to longstanding structural inequalities and conditions. This book focuses on racism, both explicit and inferential, that appears prominently within public spaces. It offers examinations, descriptions, analyses, interpretations, explanations, and evaluations of racial practices, problems, and phenomena. Furthermore, it provides tools to deconstruct and interpret representations of race and racism, while explaining how and why race and racism function for people in everyday life and across time.

We offer ways of intervening, contesting, challenging, and perhaps changing race and racism in the process. We show how people use media to produce obvious, subtle, and ambiguous representations of race and racism. Cultural studies scholar and theorist Stuart Hall observed that some racist discourse is overt, clear, and virtually indisputable; but, some racism operates in less obvious, subtle, and "inferential" ways. He writes: "By inferential racism I mean those apparently naturalized representations of events and situations relating to race, whether 'factual' or 'fictional,' which have racist premises and propositions inscribed in them as a set of *unquestioned assumptions.*"[2] Critical rhetorical scholars who examine racial discourse propose case studies and analyze representations of racist acts and violence, such as stories of police beatings, shootings, or the killing of black men in major U.S. cities (e.g., Amadou Diallo in New York City in chapter 8 of this volume). We do so because such images and stories form the basis of our knowledge and perspective of race, which helps us to see how we perceive and define ourselves, others, and our material lives, as well as the ways others perceive us globally. In contemporary life, when white supremacists brutally beat and kill a black male, a media ritual occurs: the news media cover it; people watch it or read about it; people protest the beating; a public trial ensues; people publicly express outrage, guilt, or denial; and consequently, institutional policies and practices may change. All of these practices are ritualized and memorialized by media. While spectacles of overt racist acts warrant scholarly attention, we believe that inferential and figural dimensions of race and racism require further discussion, illumination, theorization, and response, especially from scholars and educators concerned about social justice.[3] Even with the most overtly racist acts, inferential forms of race and racism are also at work (e.g., see Williamson 2002).

Moreover, in today's discursive milieu, race and racism are often difficult to isolate, interpret, and explain. Race and racism are deflected, denied, disavowed, minimized, and excused. Stories of racialized victims claiming institutional racism are routinely followed by white and black conservatives charging "reverse racism," "playing the race card," or "political correctness." Such a milieu suggests that inferential race and racism are only recognizable when we carefully seek them out, treat them as interconnected fragments, and examine their role in producing and maintaining power and its real, material, social, and cultural outcomes.

Not only are race and racism difficult for contemporary critics to locate and isolate without focusing on power relationships, but because of changing cultural conditions and new technologies, discourses and logics of race and racism are always transforming themselves to fit new contexts and situations. This means that any effective critique must be able to change perspectives to see and appreciate the shifting historical contexts and racial formations, while being sturdy enough to unearth its rhetorical residue. Today, for example, with a mixed race African American president and efforts to dismantle progressive social welfare policies (e.g., affirmative action), we are seeing a new *racial formation*[4] and new ways to represent that formation. This formation connects to a legacy of racial projects from the past (e.g., white supremacy), but also contains novel, updated logics and characteristics adapted to the present time, circumstances, and conditions.

Arguably, contemporary race and racism function more subtly and inferentially than overtly; in fact, some might argue that race and racism are most effective that way. Therefore, looking for inferential forms of race and racism is a particular kind of political act. When racialized discourse does not call attention to itself, responses to it become easily misunderstood or formulaic. We can overcome such misinterpretations and ideological scripts and begin to understand different perspectives only if we question, challenge, interpret, and critically analyze cultural practices. While loud charges of race and racism have become media spectacles, we argue that the mundane, everyday, and routine cultural practices perhaps have the greatest potential to survive, work in tandem with overt racism, and affect us in their commonplace and taken-for-granted forms.

In a world in which race and racism are discussed, described, displayed, performed, and filmed, they are always in the process of being transformed and appear in a veiled manner, flying under the radar of ordinary global citizens. Therefore, what is necessary is a critical model, or educational apparatus and heuristic, that aims for broad knowledge about how race and racism emerge and function in their various guises and conditions. With such a model, we might be able not only to understand and navigate such a world but ultimately change it. This is a high calling, but one we believe is necessary.

A Critical Approach

We begin with a critical perspective that recognizes, names, and exposes racism when it appears, however diffuse, inferential, and subtle. This critical approach presupposes that racism is a discursive, residual, and material part of the historical and contemporary reality of the United States and other colonial contexts. Such an endeavor requires critical methods, tools, and vocabularies to unearth, analyze, and interpret complex media images, however explicit or implicit their declarations of a post-racial reality may be, and however vigilantly race and racism are denied. We offer an approach to the study of cultural discourse that responds to everyday life's situations, one that aims to make people keenly aware of theories, histories, and modes of rhetorical critique. This project requires a sophisticated understanding how rhetoric has been used historically, as well as how rhetoric is used in the contemporary world.

Our project is a *critical* one. That is, it seeks to understand discourse and its effectivity, especially the way power operates to constitute subjects through discourse. Such an orientation is designed to help scholars and educators analyze and expose overt and inferential forms of racism, while highlighting and interpreting complex relationships and intersections that, at first glance, might not appear to be about race and racism. For example, while the dominant media hail Barack Obama as the "first black President," few see Republicans John McCain and Sarah Palin's presidential and vice presidential campaign as part of a rhetorical project to recover white masculine heroism in a neocolonial context. The media's story of McCain and Palin is recognizable in mythical form, reaffirming a succession of white male presidents who adopted personae of rugged western individualists, or mavericks, who confronted dangerous, dark, subversive enemies and forces with extreme militarism and laissez-faire economic policies (see Lacy 2010b). A critical approach seeks out, examines, and brings forth such discourse, thereby highlighting the dominant media's production of Obama's race as a relevant marker, while simultaneously rendering McCain's and Palin's whiteness as unremarkable, irrelevant, or natural. Such criticism shows how whiteness discourse, for example, conceals and obfuscates power relationships,[5] while preempting critique, analysis, interpretation, and change.[6]

Our critical orientation emphasizes plural *rhetorics*, because we think the most useful rhetorical work is done with many voices and in many modes. We acknowledge that there are myriad ways to approach and analyze discourses of race, and that such approaches, whether discursive or rhetorical in focus, whether historical or contemporary, whether social scientific or humanistic, are attempts to make sense of race and racist discourse. Thus, by using the term *rhetorics*, we mean a multiplicity of different perspectives, approaches, and rigorous methods used to analyze discourse in diverse sites where racialization and racial logics become reified, including the forms such discourse takes. Therefore, this anthology includes a variety of humanistic, interpretive, and social science critiques and studies that interrogate public and media discourse, offering a way for us to understand how race and racism function both to oppress and to liberate people. Hopefully, these insightful approaches will inspire others to deconstruct, dismantle, alter, and expose racial hegemonies and control, as well as show how cultural knowledge is produced, always allowing for new possibilities and ways of seeing and imagining the world.

A Transdisciplinary Commitment

We borrow from many disciplines, creating a transdisciplinary approach that uses a variety of relevant and useful methods and approaches. Forging methodologies together to expose overt and inferential race and racism in our contemporary public and media environment is part of our critical and political praxes. A transdisciplinary approach crosses multiple social scientific and humanistic approaches, bringing together useful critical tools from different disciplines (e.g., rhetorical theory and criticism, history, political science, sociology, psychology, postcolonial criticism, feminism, black feminist thought, critical race theory, queer theory, literature studies, film theory, and transnational and diaspora studies). Once ideas from different disciplines are considered, understood, synthesized, and integrated, transdisciplinary approaches are possible.

While still viewing communication as central to human activity and our critical orientation, a transdisciplinary commitment requires that we learn how race functions in fields other than communication. Such an approach is necessary to comprehend educational, economic, government, and media culture industries—indeed, every institution; therefore, the development of transdisciplinary critical skills enlivens and increases our consciousness across levels and layers of society. There are fruitful and wonderful possibilities for conceiving of things differently, and responding to them insightfully is perhaps multiplied by working across intellectual fields and structures. We believe that examining discourses of race and racism need not be limited by disciplinary myopia, perspectives, approaches, and questions, but augmented by insights from other fields of study, methods, approaches, and assumptions that emerge at the interstices of fields. In this way, a transdisciplinary commitment shows and tells us something new and possibly surprising. Multiple methods and approaches must be sampled, used, and recast to study contemporary manifestations of race and racism, because they are represented in ways that are ever-changing to fit new situations and conditions. Critical methodology therefore has to be able to change, too, in order to appreciate the richness, complexity, and nuances of discourse as it changes, as well as historic discourse about which scholars (now armed with new theories and methods) can begin asking new questions.

The study of rhetoric is well suited for such a project. The history of rhetorical theory and criticism tells us that the scope of rhetoric is broad, with no specific or stable objects of analysis, and which requires critics to propose genres or types of rhetoric in a variety of ways. Rhetoric can be found in public speeches, novels, in newspapers, on television, on the radio, in movies, in day-to-day conversation, and thus in the mundane performances of everyday life. A critical rhetorical approach that examines race and racialized or racist discourse draws upon multiple methodologies to examine the changing landscape of racial formation. By doing so, scholars in this volume attempt to address the most intellectually challenging and compelling issues and topics of the day, revealing insights about culture. Such analyses have a multiplicity of potential effects, including shaping public policy that affects the quality and value of human life. By exposing these effects, we recognize new, recurring, and taken for granted cultural practices and phenomena, thereby generating the possibility for transforming social realities and producing social change.

Critical scholars have argued that discourses of race and racism are cannibalistic and vampiric, feeding off of cultural changes and one another, transforming themselves to fit every situation or context. In doing so, discourses reify racial identities and logics while effacing their own existence, thereby remaining elusive, going underground, and defying detection. Therefore, a critical apparatus that can expose and interrogate racialized discourse as it changes and adapts to new cultural conditions is necessary. For example, media images and caricatures of African Americans as apes in contemporary society would be something one might expect to see on a white supremacist website, and we often do.[7] We might expect public outcry and an apology as in the case of the *New York Post* cartoon discussed earlier. While such images offend liberal, progressive, and egalitarian sensibilities, they continue to appear in dominant mainstream popular media. Moreover, the dominant and popular media make regular use of such images beyond white supremacist fora. From a critical perspective, we are skeptical about the changing nature of these shopworn racist images, while inquisitively remaining open to changing forms and functions of such discourse. In this light, it is not surprising that the long-standing racist representation equating African Americans with apes emerged again when the April 2008 Cover of *Vogue* magazine pictured basketball great LeBron James holding supermodel Gisele Bundchen. A media meleé broke out over the publication of this image because of its similarity to a famous H. R. Hopps recruitment poster published during World War I, in which the man holding a woman dressed similarly and in a comparable pose was figured as a King Kong–like ape with a baseball bat as a bludgeon with the word "kultur" written on it.[8]

A critical approach is especially well suited to examining racial discourse, because it helps to explain how it is that, in a society that often memorializes abolitionists and African American civil rights protestors, the production of representations equating African Americans with apes is still possible, indeed commonplace. Making dark "colored people" appear as dangerous apes or brutish animals still persists in popular culture discourse and crime news stories. Yet, such artifacts are not immediately understood as fragments of historical/contemporary, intentional/latent, and domestic/international relations and ideologies of white supremacy or colonialism. Critical rhetorics of race scholars use rigorous and flexible critical methods to unearth the historical dimensions and significance of these discourses, while showing how contemporary media deflect, deny, and disavow racism. Critical scholars explain the relationship between racism at home and racism abroad to show precisely how race and racism persist, while the cultural environment conceals and discourages such critique with familiar storylines, mythic (meta) narratives, and archetypal characters.

Critical Rhetorics of Race

In offering a critical rhetorics of race perspective, we acknowledge that our work is built upon pioneering work within the communication field. We foreground the term rhetoric in our book because it has significant historical meaning dating back to classical Greek society and, as Asante has shown, to Africa before that.[9] Communication scholarship has produced: (1) studies that show how communication reifies race and racism;[10] (2) foundational rhetorical studies on race and racism that uncover hidden white supremacist ideologies, complicity, and cultural fears;[11] (3) anthologies that have inspired integrative communication studies of race;[12] (4) discourse theories of race;[13] and (5) studies of language and race in the broader humanities[14] and social sciences.[15]

Our project uses *critical rhetoric* as a springboard to theorize race and racism, not unlike how critical race studies emerged in part as a response to critical legal studies.[16] Our project attempts to move the scholarly discussion from critical rhetoric to critical rhetorics of race. In 1989, McKerrow's classic essay, "Critical Rhetoric: Theory and Praxis," introduced rhetorical scholarship to key poststructural, theoretical ideas and scholars, particularly the work of Michel Foucault. In doing so, McKerrow defined critical rhetoric as critical practices and performances that demystify power, knowledge, and universal theories (e.g., "truth"), producing critiques of *domination* or *freedom*. Scholarship following McKerrow's opening gambit: (1) adopts a skeptical and self-reflexive attitude about universal or utopian claims and uses of power; (2) examines and reconstructs discourse and diffuse discourse fragments from mundane discursive sites, including those found in a variety of everyday communication media contexts; (3) analyzes discourse produced by elites, public intellectuals, citizens, and vernacular communities; (4) commits to a critical orientation or perspective about power, rather than erecting a sacred singular methodology; and (5) models, practices, and performs new meanings, or at least circumscribes new struggles for meaning and cultural knowledge.[17]

McKerrow's project was premised on a formulation of *critical rhetoric* as a non-essentialist, perhaps anti-essentialist, performative rhetoric; yet, we emphasize effectivity and materiality of race (i.e., practices and policies affecting real people's lives) to focus on the paradoxes of culture and race at this moment. To do otherwise would mean adopting a post-structural position premised on a *telos* of never-ending critique (one without ends, one without effectivity, one that never stands up, takes a position, or challenges oppression). This is not to suggest that other dimensions of social life and living are less important or relevant than race. Indeed, at other times and in other contexts, for the sake of effectivity and materiality, other foci may necessarily be front and center in a given critical project. But the critical focus on communication and race might offer new insights. For instance, in *The Terror Dream*, journalist and feminist author Susan Faludi observed that in response to the terrorist attacks on 9/11, U.S. politicians' and media discourse offered masculine archetypes of tough, rugged, individualist heroes that required weak women needing to be saved.[18] Lacy and Haspel (in chapter 1) add that this mythic narrative implies that heroic *white* males are needed to combat dangerous *dark* masculine brutes bent on raping, killing, and destroying our civilization. Perhaps, the authors argue, this accounts for the multitude and prominence of dangerous black looters in the major press coverage, raping, killing, and taking over New Orleans in Hurricane Katrina's wake. Examinations of discourse and race, such as this one, reveal the presence of an old mythic race narrative that expresses apocalyptic cultural fears, loss, white paternalism, and colonial motives, even in these heady "post-racial" days.

Critical Rhetorics of Race is intersectional, premised on the multiplicity of cultural identities. This collection strategically essentializes[19] race in its particularity, but we do so in order to tell novel stories, with reflexivity and self-critical awareness of essentialism, while we strategically employ it to understand how and why race works. Such critical awareness includes at times centering race, while also examining issues of gender, sexuality, class, and nation. Critical rhetorics' methodologies and perspectives adapt to postmodern conditions and highlight the challenges of particular cultural environments. Such an approach necessarily requires rethinking and readapting to existing cultural conditions.

The chapters provide careful and thoughtful analyses of discourse within contexts, while being keenly aware of the political and economic conditions in which discourses arise and operate. Thus, for instance, using Ono and Sloop's concept of "vernacular discourse,"[20] scholars in this volume (e.g., Bacon and Huspek) retrieve archival discourses generated by people who are not traditional rhetors (nor elite) and show how marginalized people create discursive spaces within their own communities to reshape their own identities. In doing so, critical rhetorical scholars take seriously the meaning of discourse that marginalized people produce, and thus provide a more self-conscious, detailed, and nuanced critique. In reading vernacular histories, the authors of the chapters in this book acknowledge and highlight the complexities and intersections that exist.

The Chapters and Structure of the Book

To help readers access and comprehend the vectors of critical rhetorics of race, and hopefully to inspire scholarly projects, we have divided the book into four sections; they are: (1) racialized masculinities, (2) whiteness, (3) vernacular resistances, and (4) racialized complexities and neocolonialism.

Racialized Masculinities

The chapters in Part I discuss the persistence of racialized masculine villains (especially black males) in dominant news coverage. In "Apocalypse: The Media's Framing of Black Looters, Shooters, and Brutes in Hurricane Katrina's Aftermath," Michael G. Lacy and Kathleen C. Haspel show how dominant news stories featured dangerous black male brutes who took over New Orleans in Hurricane Katrina's aftermath. This apocalyptic narrative enabled public officials and police officers to justify violence and extreme policies against the black looters and to criminalize the evacuees, while absolving themselves (especially the Bush administration) of delays and inaction. The authors conclude that the narrative expresses deep cultural fears that the government can no longer resolve national crises and rescue people, while mourning the loss of mythic white western heroes.

Cynthia Willis-Chun explores intersections of race, nationality, class, and heterosexuality in news coverage of the Virginia Tech and Columbine school shootings. In "Tales of Tragedy: Strategic Rhetoric in News Coverage of the Columbine and Virginia Tech Massacres," she finds that media discourse constructs the killers as socially deviant, using race, nationality, and sexuality to do so. By aligning violence with urban cities, depicting suburban college campuses as idyllic, and rendering the racialized masculine killers as out of place, media discourse draws attention away from examination of the social and cultural basis for violence and distress.

In "N-word vs. F-word, Black vs. Gay: Uncovering *Pendejo* Games to Recover Intersections," Catherine Squires shows how dominant media stories pitted and ranked one marginalized group (blacks) against another (LGBTQ) by highlighting the anti-gay epithets made by black male celebrities, who served as culpable exemplars for the larger black U.S. culture. Such logics reduced all gays to being white males and all blacks (especially black males) to being straight and homophobic. Squires challenges scholars to study intersectionally, across social groups, in an effort to find common ground to build coalition, and produce identification versus what she calls "de-intersectioning."

Whiteness

Whiteness studies have become one of the most vibrant areas of communication research. Whiteness scholars use critical or post-structural frameworks to expose white racial identities in discourse (especially popular media discourse) that reproduces white power and privilege, while simultaneously denying its existence, especially in post–civil rights, postcolonial, and neocolonial contexts.

In "Quentin Tarantino in Black and White," Sean Tierney examines strategies of whiteness in the discourse of the popular film producer and director Quentin Tarantino. Tierney shows how Tarantino claims an authorial position of "being black" in order to justify using the word "nigger" in his public statements and popular films. Doing so helps Tarantino establish white artistic privilege while simultaneously subverting the moral authority of black filmmakers, such as Spike Lee. Tierney finds Tarantino's rhetorical tactic of appropriating black culture and identity employs a postmodern discourse that reinforces whiteness's hegemonic power and privilege through its appeal to uncritical white publics.

In "Patrolling National Identity, Masking White Supremacy: The Minuteman Project," Michelle A. Holling analyzes the Minuteman Project's (MMP) website and discovers that the MMP recovers mythic fragments and historical linkages to the revolutionary American minutemen (e.g., Paul Revere). MMP members recast their vigilante-style militarism and nativism into a patriotic mission to save the American body politic from invasion by "invisible" Mexican immigrants who enter the United States by crossing the southern U.S. border. By doing so, Holling argues that the MMP's rhetoric transforms undocumented immigrants into would-be colonizers and oppressors, while denying and remaking histories of colonization in the Southwest United States.

In "Control, Discipline, and Punish: Black Masculinity and (In)visible Whiteness in the NBA," Rachel Alicia Griffin and Bernadette Marie Calafell argue that media discourse about the NBA commissioner David Stern as well as his public statements help to reify white paternalism. In a popular sport in which 75 percent of the players are black but virtually all of the corporate owners and commissioner are white, Stern's enforcement of extreme penalties and policies (e.g., anti–hip-hop dress codes) affecting primarily black players visibly reproduces a spectacle of the white father figure and black slave child relationship found on plantations during the antebellum South. Such policies became particularly evident after the 2004 brawl in Detroit, featuring riveting images of black players engaging with white (male) fans in the stands.

Vernacular Resistances

Vernacular discourses are produced in local contexts, often by people who are socially marginalized. They construct cultural identities and syncretic cultures that are independent of, different from, or resistant to the dominant culture. Ono and Sloop observe that very little has been written about vernacular discourse in the field of communication. The chapters in this section address this shortfall in new and creative ways.

Jacqueline Bacon offers a fascinating exploration of black abolitionists who argued for emancipation and liberation on their own terms. In "Declarations of Independence: African American Abolitionists and the Struggle for Racial and Rhetorical Self-Determination," Bacon examines the rhetoric and critiques of slavery by black abolitionists who were constrained by white abolitionists who held white supremacist beliefs that blacks lacked the intellectual capacity to marshal persuasive rational arguments. Bacon's riveting study unearths heretofore unexamined rhetoric generated by black abolitionists, who created their own fora to address black audiences while eloquently critiquing their white abolitionist colleagues.

In "Transgressive Rhetoric in Deliberative Democracy: The Black Press," Michael Huspek argues that modern conceptions of rhetoric in liberal democracies tend to be limited on account of unacknowledged ideological biases that favor restrictive norms of rationality and that at the same time condemn as irrational rhetoric that appears to violate such norms. Huspek's analysis of black press rhetoric reveals that some forms of rhetoric do indeed transgress norms of rationality, but do so in ways that are intentionally made visible to readers in order to expose the ideologically freighted idea of what counts as rational discourse in the public sphere.

In "Bling Fling: Commodity Consumption and the Politics of the 'Post-Racial,'" Roopali Mukherjee describes how images of conspicuous black consumption ("ghetto fabulous" and "bling") constitute a "post-soul" reality that is marked by equivocations and ambivalence. She draws a connection between contemporary and earlier expressions of images of conspicuous black consumption, showing that the present moment evolves from earlier meanings of consumption within black culture—both as a way to manage access to needed goods and as a potential cause of racist violence. She ends with an analysis of hip-hop artist Kanye West's challenge of the Bush administration to provide economic aid following Hurriane Katrina, placing it in the large context of black consumption in contemporary neoliberal culture.

Racialized Complexities and Neocolonialism

The authors of the chapters in Part IV examine rhetoric that purports to move beyond the traditional black-white racial binaries found in the United States. They reveal media constructions of race and racism working in service of neocolonialism, or inferential colonial narratives that conceal violent white European economic and global expansion (see Ono 2009). The authors also examine standard white-black binaries and hierarchies hidden among "diverse" racial, or "mixed-race" ethnic characters, situated in major California cities, for example.

In "The Rhythm of Ambition: Power Temporalities and the Production of the Call Center Agent in Documentary Film and Reality Television," Aimee Carrillo Rowe, Sheena Malhotra, and Kimberlee Pérez show how documentaries help westerners overcome their anxieties about globalization and outsourcing. They do so by featuring a white male narrator who visits, describes, and then leaves the lowly social conditions of Indian subjects (especially Indian women), while highlighting the Indian subjects' negotiation between their premodern realities and ideologies and the neoliberal present. The documentaries position Indian transnational subjects as inferior to western U.S. viewers through time/space ambivalences that, in an attempt to conceal anxieties about the changing landscape of transnational employment, thereby acknowledge and then protect U.S. workers from worries over the loss of their jobs at home.

In "Inscribing Racial Bodies and Relieving Responsibility: Examining the Racial Politics in *Crash*," Jamie Moshin and Ronald L. Jackson II study the film *Crash*, examining its racial politics and providing a challenging view of a film widely hailed as racially progressive. Los Angeles, California, serves as an interesting site because it ultimately disguises and reifies racial binaries and white privilege. Moshin and Jackson argue that, in spite of its racially diverse characters, *Crash* induces audiences to feel hopeless and indifferent about the persistence of racial stereotypes and conflicts, reflecting a broader cultural paralysis about the United States. In doing so, the film redeems the white racist cop by making him the hero who rescues a black woman he molested earlier in the film, while the black male characters devolve into emasculation, rage, helplessness, criminality, and violence. By suggesting race is either everyone's problem equally or no problem at all, the film avoids discussion of white responsibility for racism, while simultaneously portraying white characters as largely heroic.

Marouf Hasian, Jr., Carol W. Anderson, and Rulon Wood uncover an old colonial narrative present in a "progressive" contemporary popular film. In

"Cinematic Representation and Cultural Critique: The Deracialization and Denationalization of the African Conflict Diamond Crises in Zwick's *Blood Diamond*," the authors show that, in spite of the filmmakers' noble intentions to raise public consciousness about the oppressive diamond trade in Sierra Leone, the film reproduces a colonial narrative formula (and neocolonial in the United States) of a rugged white masculine hero who learns to change his racist ways and saves an infantilized noble black man and his son by confronting brutal black villains. This white savior narrative redeems whites who express anti-black sentiments, while reproducing ideologies of black and African inferiority. While the film calls for U.S. audiences to take action about the diamond trade, as the authors' interviews in Sierra Leone illustrate, it forsakes realistic depictions of black Africans and the conditions they face in Sierra Leone.

In "Abstracting and De-Racializing Diversity: The Articulation of Diversity in the Post-Race Era," Rona Tamiko Halualani argues that regional newspaper stories in Silicon Valley, California, create the appearance of a *raceless* society, bolstering legislative efforts in California (e.g., Proposition 209) to eliminate affirmative action, multiculturalism, and other racialized policies. The newspapers do this, Halualani argues, by constantly featuring "empirical" surveys predicting a *majority minority* in northern California cities and by reporting personal testimonies about the positive effects of "diversity," such as interacting with people from all over the world.

This book describes and illuminates multiple vectors of critical rhetorics of race to explain the persistence of race and racism in a context in which media constantly presage the end of racism, while nevertheless producing texts documenting overt racist acts, images, and media spectacles that affect our material lives. Our project seeks to intervene and contest stories of such ambivalence by warning institutional policymakers and publics about the persistence of seemingly outdated colonial narratives and racialized villains (especially black males) and by explaining some of their meanings. By doing so, we hope to encourage scholarly inquiry and social change.

Our book begins with remarks from Raymie McKerrow, whose seminal article has spawned critical communication scholarship that exposes and explains how discourse (1) masks and mystifies power to oppress or liberate people; (2) produces cultural knowledge about places and peoples (especially about others); (3) legitimates, sustains, resists, or disrupts hegemonic interests; and (4) forms, transforms, and adapts to changing historical conditions. The authors in this collection answer McKerrow's call by offering insightful critical analyses of race and racism from a variety of communication studies contexts, sites, approaches, methodologies, and perspectives. We do so as media circulate contradictory messages and images about race and racism in this critical moment. We offer our best efforts to inspire more critical thinking and scholarly inquiry along these lines.

NOTES

1. We are aware that historically the phrase "mixed race" has negative connotations in the United States because, even as it proves such purity untrue, it implies "blood purity" that reflects biological determinism, which is a biological fallacy. "Race" is a social and political construct. We use the phrase "mixed race," as do film and media scholars, to connote the visual and inferential signs or logics people use to define ambiguous and multiracial subjects, exposing the unstable categories of "race." See Mary Beltrán and Camilla Fojas, *Mixed Race Hollywood* (New York: New York University Press, 2008), 2–4.

2. See Stuart Hall, "The Whites of Their Eyes: Racist Ideologies and the Media," in *Silver Lining: Some Strategies for the Eighties*, edited by George Bridges and Rosalind Brunt, 28–52 (London: Lawrence and Wishart, 1981).

3. As Williamson concluded about the verdict sentencing two white supremacists to death for dragging James Byrd to death with their pickup truck: The "dragging trial" served to purge the ancestral ghost of whites terrorizing and lynching blacks in the South, and allowed whites and blacks to express tolerance, but, it also left everyday racism experienced by blacks unnoticed and unacknowledged.

4. See Michael Omi and Howard Winant, *Racial Formation in the United States: from the 1960s to the 1990s* (New York: Routledge, 1994).

5. If one imagines comprehensively the sum total of all of the instances in which racial power relations are not made obvious, this exercise comes close to being able to identify the much broader dimension of race and racism that functions to structure social relations at the macro level of society and micro level of day-to-day interaction.

6. One vein of scholarship that has addressed racial ineffability has looked at whiteness, specifically. Thomas Nakayama and Robert Krizek (1995) imported conceptions to whiteness from various disciplines into communication studies to expose the dominance, complexity, and ubiquitous nature of whiteness in discursive cultural practices that shape and control people's lives and reproduce white privilege, without their knowledge or consent. Following Nakayama's early work, Nakayama and Judith Martin's (1999) edited volume *Whiteness: The Communication of Social Identity*, provides a rich and diverse collection of communication studies of whiteness. For more on scholarship on whiteness in communication, see work by Raka Shome, Carrie Crenshaw, Ronald L. Jackson II, Lisa Flores and Dreama Moon, and Michael Lacy.

7. On *Stormfront*, discussions of African Americans as apes or ape-like is common. See, for instance, http://www.stormfront.org/forum/showthread.php?s=4d11da9a1f1479fca51a4eeddee3cad5&t=609089. Accessed June 12, 2009.

8. The Hopps poster preceded the release of the film *King Kong* and may have been an inspiration for the film itself.

9. See, for instance, Molefe Asante, *The Afrocentric Idea* (Philadelphia: Temple University Press, 1987), 182.

10. With apologies to the many significant scholars we leave out of this endnote, we offer some venerable examples here, albeit not in any way a comprehensive list. Such figures as Jack Daniel, Molefi Asante, and Melbourne Cummings played a leadership role in centering race in communication scholarship historically. Jack L. Daniel's *Changing the Players and the Game: A*

Personal Account of the Speech Communication Association Black Caucus Origins (Speech Communication Association, 1995) tells an institutional history of the emergence of the Black Caucus within the Speech Communication Association, and discusses the efforts of many people, including Lucia S. Hawthorne, Dorthy L. Pennington, Melbourne S. Cummings, Carolyn Calloway-Thomas, and Venita Kelley, who all have afterwords in the book. As well, the book mentions the work of, among others, Molefi Asante, Lyndrey Niles, and Orlando Taylor. For more information about the role of the contribution of black communication scholars, see Ronald L. Jackson II and Sonja M. Brown Givens, eds., *Black Pioneers in Communication Research* (Thousand Oaks, CA: Sage, 2006). Other early work includes Karlyn Kohrs Campbell (1971), Richard B. Gregg, A. Jackson McCormack, and Douglas J. Pedersen (1969), John W. Bowers and Donovan J. Ochs (1971), Gronbeck (1973), Van Graber (1973).

11. Rhetorical work such as Celeste Condit and John Lucaites's (1993) *Crafting Equality* has explored "ideographs," or culturally contingent abstractions or phrases (e.g., "equality," "liberty," and "property"), found in public arguments that provide motivations or justifications for public action. Mark McPhail's *The Rhetoric of Racism* (1994) and later his *The Rhetoric of Racism Revisited* (2002) are notable works that address rhetoric's role in constructing race and racism, stressing both that actors (e.g., whites and blacks) are complicit in the existence of ideas of race and that racism itself is akin to a psychological disease. Rhetorical scholar Aaron David Gresson has authored two highly important and influential books: *The Recovery of Race in America* (1995) and *America's Atonement* (2004). Gresson's work, which has not been given the prominence it richly deserves, is much discussed by scholars in this volume. Gresson responds to conventional (post-structuralist) interpretations for discourse in the United States by offering (social) psychological interpretations of competing and cannibalizing race narratives. Gresson (2004) argues that contemporary racial discourse in the United States reflects "racial pain," or the identification with a damaged racial identity or ego. The most dominant form of racial pain is "white masculine pain," or a damaged white identity or ego that has been forced to see itself as "oppressor." Gresson contends that recovery rhetoric and rhetorical acts of atonement found in a wide range of nationalistic discourses and cultural practices (e.g., the Yellow Ribbon Movement), films (e.g., *Forrest Gump*), and public debates (e.g., multiculturalism), serve to redeem white masculinity and nationalism by using women and minorities as props or supporting characters.

12. Anthologies primarily published in the 1990s on communication and race, especially media, have often taken an approach that attempts to do justice to each racial group: Asian Americans, African Americans, Latina/os, Native Americans, and Whites (e.g., Wilson and Gutierrez). Clint C. Wilson II and Felix Gutierrez, eds., *Minorities and the Media: Diversity and the End of Mass Communication* (Beverly Hills: Sage, 1985); the second edition entitled *Race, Multiculturalism, and the Media: From Mass to Class Communication* (Thousand Oaks, CA: Sage, 1995); the third edition (with Lena M. Chao) entitled *Racism, Sexism, and the Media: The Rise of Class Communication in Multicultural America* (Thousand Oaks, CA: Sage, 2003). Other examples include: Gail Dines and Jean M. Humez, eds., *Gender, Race and Class in Media: A Text-Reader* (Thousand Oaks, CA: Sage, 1994); second edition 2003; Angharad Valdivia, ed., *Feminism, Multiculturalism, and the Media: Global Diversities* (Thousand Oaks, CA: Sage, 1995); Stephanie Greco Larson, *Media and Minorities: The Politics of Race in News and Entertainment* (Lanham, MD: Rowman & Littlefield, 2006); and Alberto Gonzalez, Marsha Houston, and Victoria Chen, eds., *Our Voices: Essays in Culture, Ethnicity, and Communication* (Los Angeles: Roxbury Press, 1994).

13. Some scholars studying race and communication have approached the subject using a discourse analytic approach. Chief among them is Teun Van Dijk's *Communicating Racism* and

Elite Discourse and Racism (1987, 1993). Reisigl and Wodak's (2001) *Discourse and Discrimination* offers a comprehensive discourse analytic study of race. Van Dijk uses discourse analyses to show how European and U.S. lay people and elites reproduce anti-black racism in overt and subtle ways. Van Dijk integrates the cognitive and ideological aspects of racism by showing how media and white elites produce anti-black images, while denying racism (e.g., "I'm not racist, but . . ."), blaming the victim, and accusing marginalized groups of being racists. The ambivalence found in such strategies, van Dijk argues, reflects the cognitive complexity of expressing racist views, while conforming to contemporary standards of politeness and egalitarianism. They provide a rich and complex framework to analyze racism, anti-Semitism, and ethnicism reflected in discourse (political speeches, legal documents, newspaper articles, television broadcasts, and conversations). The authors develop a critical discourse analytic framework that provides interpretation of racism and discrimination in three case studies, revealing a whole range of linguistic devices used by politicians and media productions to code racist, anti-Semitic, and xenophobic beliefs and ideologies. Other social scientific works include Michael Hecht's edited volume, *Communicating Prejudice* (1998). In *Communicating Prejudice*, Hecht views racial prejudice found in public and private discourse as a component of the broader form of prejudice and discrimination. Also significant is Michael Billig, Susan Condor, Derek Edwards, and others, *Ideological Dilemmas: A Social Psychology of Everyday Thinking* (Beverly Hills: Sage, 1988). In the book, Billig challenges psychological analyses of modern racism as conversational gambits, and argues that the ambivalence and denials found in the discourse reflects commitments to Enlightenment ideals and bourgeois Liberalism ("reasonableness" and "rationality").

14. In literary studies, for instance, is Carl Gutierrez-Jones's (2001) *Critical Race Narratives*. Gutierrez-Jones adopts a post-structuralist perspective to study "knowledge" people produce about racial "injury" in U.S. popular culture, legal, and academic discourse. Gutierrez-Jones does so by collecting a diffuse array of narratives of elite and influential texts on race (e.g., *The Bell Curve, The Alchemy of Race and Rights, The Mismeasure of Man*) that challenge extant models for analyzing race. Gutierrez-Jones concludes that racialized injury claims have produced a sense of impasse, resentment, and interdisciplinary cannibalism.

15. Omi and Winant, for example.

16. For a brief discussion of their relationship, see Richard Delgado and Jean Stefancic, *Critical Race Theory: An Introduction* (New York: New York University Press, 2001), 4–5. Also see Patricia Williams, "Alchemical Notes: Reconstructing Ideals from Deconstructed Rights." *Harvard Civil Rights—Civil Liberties Law Review* 22, no. 1 (1987): 401.

17. For a broad sampling of McKerrow's influence, see the following articles: Carole Blair, Julie R. Brown, and Leslie A. Baxter, "Disciplining the Feminine," *Quarterly Journal of Speech* 80 (1994): 383–409; Stephen O. Gencarella, "Constituting Folklore: A Case for Critical Folklore Studies," *Journal of American Folklore* 122, no. 484 (2009): 172–96; Ronald W. Greene, "Another Materialist Rhetoric," *Critical Studies in Mass Communication* 15, no. 1 (1998): 21–40; Thomas K. Nakayama and Robert Krizek, "Whiteness: A Strategic Rhetoric," *Quarterly Journal of Speech* 81, no. 3 (1995): 291–309; Kent A. Ono and John M. Sloop, "The Critique of Vernacular Discourse," *Communication Monographs* 62, no. 1 (1995): 19–46; Kent A. Ono and John M. Sloop, "Commitment to *Telos*—A Sustained Critical Rhetoric," *Communication Monographs* 59, no. 1 (1992): 48–60.

18. Susan Faludi, *The Terror Dream: Myth and Misogyny in an Insecure America* (New York: Picador, 2007).

19. See Gayatri Spivak's (1988) early use of the term. Also, see Ono and Sloop (1992) for an argument favoring strategic essentialism in the field of rhetorical studies.

20. Ono and Sloop's work built from McKerrow's and advanced the concept of vernacular rhetoric as discourse that emerges from local communities and forms in resistance to dominant ideologies or for group constitution, and that may take the form of anti-racist, anti-sexist critiques. Ono and Sloop (2002) developed their theory further in *Shifting Borders*, a study of public discourse surrounding the California anti-immigrant ballot initiative that attempted to eliminate health, education, and welfare benefits for undocumented migrants in the state. The authors expose the rhetorical constructions of nationalism and nativism found in the *Los Angeles Times* and the complicity and resistance in vernacular discourse, produced by self-identified members outside the dominant community. By doing so, they expose how shifting constructions of nations, borders, and migration alter the way people perceive nations, borders, and peoples and influence public policies concerning citizenship, immigration, and national identity. There, they made distinction between civic and outlaw discourse as well as dominant discourse and vernacular discourse, arguing that it is necessary to consider the amount of publicity and the degree to which logics of discourse actually challenge the status quo.

I Racialized Masculinities

1 Apocalypse

The Media's Framing of Black Looters, Shooters, and Brutes in Hurricane Katrina's Aftermath

Michael G. Lacy and Kathleen C. Haspel

In late August 2005, the United States was exposed. Hurricane Katrina hit the Gulf Coast and became the most lethal and destructive hurricane in U.S. history,[1] causing 1,836 deaths, destroying 300,000 homes,[2] and costing $150 billion in damages across three states.[3] Media coverage of the storm's aftermath was marked by crime news reports that New Orleans had descended into chaos, anarchy, and lawlessness. However, further investigation revealed that almost all news media reports of looting, shooting, rapes, murders, and mayhem were unsubstantiated, exaggerated, or false.[4] Federal and state government officials now believe that the erroneous news reports "slowed the response to the disaster and tarnish[ed] the image of the victims."[5]

Critical rhetorical scholars argue that popular culture discourse constitutes a *diffuse text*, embodied by discursive signs, fragments, and recurring storylines that tap into, invoke, and activate larger meta-narratives or cultural myths that extend over time and space,[6] yet are independently experienced by people.[7] The deep formal structures of news discourse create audience expectations based on previous or similar texts, forms, and experiences, offering mythic storylines and motivations that resolve cultural problems in familiar and nostalgic ways,[8] while concealing ideologies and cultural fears or anxieties.[9]

In this chapter, we argue that Katrina's aftermath became a great human catastrophe, because dominant U.S. news media produced a diffuse mythic narrative, transforming New Orleans into a primitive swamp that unleashed primordial and sinful creatures in the form of dangerous black brutes who looted, raped, murdered, and took over the city. The narrative implied that large militaristic forces, harnessed by white paternalistic heroes, were necessary to rescue New Orleans' women, children, and elderly from the black beasts. But, mythic heroes never arrived in Katrina's aftermath. Instead, institutional officials demonized black looters, absolved themselves of failures, lionized local white civil servants and John Wayne lookalikes, and vilified the hurricane victims as "third world" racial Others and criminals. The narrative expresses deep cultural fears that our democratic government and institutions will not save us in times of trial, and our sacred white western heroes are simply relics of a time gone by.

Paradoxically, such conditions provide an opportunity for critical scholars and nimble politicians to face these problems, identify with human suffering, and become heroic.

In this chapter, we describe Hurricane Katrina's impact; the critical methods and procedures we used to reconstruct the narrative embodied by major news stories; and the structural features and functions of the narrative, which are (1) an apocalyptic scene comprised of brutish black looters and tainted evacuees and (2) fallen heroes, which include failed institutional leaders and local civil servant heroes. We also consider the implications of the media's reproduction of archetypal black villains and white western heroes in contemporary contexts.

Brief History

The National Hurricane Center (hereafter NHC) reported that Hurricane Katrina landed in New Orleans as a Category 4 storm, with driving rain and sustained winds of 125 miles per hour and a storm surge with 30-foot-high waves that crashed, topped, and breached the Lake Pontchartrain levees within minutes.[10] Eighty percent of the Crescent City was flooded, some parts under 20 feet of water. Dead bodies were seen floating in the water.[11]

Two days earlier (on August 27), NHC Director Dr. Max Mayfield warned President Bush, FEMA Director Michael Brown, Department of Homeland Security Secretary Michael Chertoff, Louisiana Governor Kathleen Babineaux Blanco, and New Orleans Mayor C. Ray Nagin that the levees could fail, and there could be a large loss of life.[12]

Mayor Nagin ordered a voluntary evacuation on August 27, a mandatory evacuation on August 28 (the first time in the city's history), and a total evacuation on August 31. About 300,000 people got out of the city through the only available route, westbound via the I-10 span bridge, while about 90,000 did not.[13] For the remaining residents, Mayor Nagin designated the New Orleans Superdome the "refuge of last resort."[14] Once the Superdome reached its capacity (about 30,000 people), rescue workers sent people to the Convention Center; that number swelled to 20,000 people who waited to be rescued for three days under squalid conditions. FEMA ordered 18 medical disaster and rescue teams, along with supplies, equipment, water, and MREs (Meals Ready to Eat) for 15,000 people.[15] On August 31, FEMA staff members told director Brown that people were dying at the Superdome. On September 2, 6,500 National Guard troops arrived in New Orleans, providing food and water to the evacuees and restoring order. On September 3 and September 4, 42,000 evacuees were bused to other U.S. cities.[16] About 2,000 people remained trapped in hotels, hospitals, schools, and homes,[17] most of whom were airlifted off rooftops over the next two days.

In one week, 1,577 people lost their lives in Louisiana; 200 bodies were unidentified; over 5,000 children were reported missing (all were accounted for); and New Orleans' population was reduced from 450,000 to 316,000 residents.[18]

Critical Methods and Procedures

We collected 323 news stories[19] about Hurricane Katrina published between August 29 and September 6, 2005, using the *ProQuest National Newspaper Index*, which provides access to national and regional newspapers in the United States (ProQuest.com).[20] We analyzed the news stories' content, isolated the discourses' formal narrative structures, and aligned them with their corresponding dramatistic metaphors (scene, act, agent, agency, and purpose) to reconstruct a coherent narrative.[21] We found that the news discourse produced a mythic narrative featuring an apocalyptic scene filled with dangerous black brutes and chaos, which implied that a great white militaristic force (e.g., a cavalry) should restore order and rescue the culture. Tragically, the apocalyptic scene enabled government officials to excuse their delays, absolve them of their failure to save New Orleans' poor and black evacuees, and taint victims as dangerous criminals. The formal structural features of this dystopian narrative are (1) the apocalyptic scene and (2) fallen heroes.

Apocalyptic Scene

Apocalyptic narratives reveal a dystopian vision of a final great catastrophe that unleashes monstrous beasts reaping total destruction onto a sinful culture, reordering life as we know it.[22] During Hurricane Katrina's aftermath, major news discourse produced a diffuse apocalyptic narrative, filled with brutish black looters and racial Others, reducing New Orleans to lawlessness, anarchy, and chaos.

Apocalyptic Looters

Kenneth Burke observes that narratives consisting of multiple agents often blur into a scene that externalizes human action and objectifies and dehumanizes human beings,[23] especially black victims, notes Martha Solomon.[24] The most distinctive scenic feature of Hurricane Katrina news coverage during the aftermath was, collectively, the looters. Looters appeared 369 times in our sample of major news stories. Although most news reports did not name the looters' racial identity,[25] they were depicted as archetypal racial villains: subhuman, irrational, criminal, immoral, and demonic beings.[26] Such rhetoric served to justify extreme actions and policies against New Orleanians, including shooting and killing them.[27]

Looters as Subhuman

Major press coverage depicted the looters as subhuman beings who emerged from apocalyptic conditions[28] by using archetypal and primordial symbols, objects, and images (e.g., fire, smoke, dark skies, gas, water, and putrid smells[29]). The primordial images suggested that the storm reduced New Orleans to a primitive swamp, unfit for human life or existence. The only surviving creatures in New Orleans' toxic waters were the demonic symbols of biblical sin: snakes and insects. The *Los Angeles Times* reported: "The water is the enemy. . . . It hides snakes, dead, bloated rats and, in the areas with the worst flooding, untold numbers of bloated bodies."[30] The *Chicago Tribune* offered eyewitness testimony: "'We saw dead alligators,' said James Swanson, a rescue crew member trained as a swimmer . . . 'four of them, belly up. If [they] can't survive in their own waters, you know it was bad.'"[31]

Out of these base conditions, the "Looters . . . emerged, as if from some dark corner of the civic soul . . . savages," wrote a *Wall Street Journal* columnist.[32] "Looters are among the lowest form of life," echoed a citizen in the *Washington Post*.[33] The *Boston Globe*, The *Atlanta Journal-Constitution*, and *Los Angeles Times* depicted the looters as aggressive predators (emphasis added): "[A] restaurant . . . in New Orleans's Warehouse District . . . has fallen *prey* to looters."[34] "[L]ooters appeared, *roaming* the streets and *preying* at will."[35] "[A]bout 30 looters *descended* on the general store in east New Orleans."[36] Major columnists from the *Washington Post* and *Los Angeles Times* described the looters as "*scavengers*,"[37] "*wilding*" on innocent victims.[38] Some news reports likened looters to insects: "'The looters, they're like cockroaches,' H. J. Bosworth said."[39]

Looters as Irrational and Immature

Media reports depicted looters as irrational, which was most vividly displayed in accounts of them "stealing guns, TV sets, beer, and other non-essential items."[40] The *Boston Globe* reported:

> One man was packing his van so full of computers, televisions, and DVD players that he had trouble closing the rear doors. One woman was carrying three jugs of laundry detergent in a city with no power to run a washer . . . "Is everything free?" asked a woman who pulled up in a red car. Hearing "yes," she started to chant, "TV! TV! TV!" . . . A little girl balanced atop a cart filled with cases of beer . . . They're getting chainsaws and fishing poles, anything they can get for free.[41]

The *Chicago Tribune* further depicted the looters' irrationality through descriptions of their emotional states: "the thieves seemed ecstatic";[42] they were "laughing," "smiling," and "cheering."[43] The *Atlanta Journal-Constitution* cited reports from NOLA.com (The *Times-Picayune*'s website), which suggested that the looters knew one another, and displayed a perverse looters' code:

> Some looters were seen smiling and greeting each other with pleasantries as they passed, ... Another group was seen riding in the back of a pickup truck, honking the horn and cheering.[44]

Looters as Dangerous Criminals

Major press reports also depicted the looters as urban brutes, who were aggressive, dangerous, and primarily hyper-masculine criminals: "Huge dudes muscle into an abandoned store and hustle out with stolen TVs and boom boxes."[45] A *Boston Globe* columnist narrated: "A Wal-Mart was one of the first stores broken into; its inventory of guns promptly disappeared."[46] Two other *Boston Globe* reporters wrote: "The police are on the lookout for looters, many of whom are reportedly armed and dangerous."[47] The deadly looters were also mobile (via carjacking), especially at night.[48] *USA Today* reported: "Michael Mansion said carjackers held a knife to his throat Wednesday and stole his red Nissan pickup."[49] A *Boston Globe* columnist wrote: "Carjackers stole a vehicle from a nursing home bus driver."[50]

Looters as Rapists

During Katrina's wake, major press reports stylistically strung rapes and murders together with other crimes (e.g., looting and carjacking), enlarging the sense of lawlessness, danger, and chaos in New Orleans.[51] On September 1, The *Times-Picayune* reported: "Rumors of murder, rape and deplorable conditions were circulating."[52] The Associated Press (AP) relied on police officers to confirm reports: "And the rumors of rapes," New Orleans Police Officer Joe "Pollard added, are not rumors anymore. 'It's true,' he said."[53] The *New York Times* offered Police Chief Eddie Compass's account of crimes occurring on New Orleans' streets:

> [T]hugs repelled eight squads of 11 officers each he had sent to secure the place and ... rapes and assaults were occurring unimpeded in the neighboring streets as criminals "preyed upon" passers-by, including stranded tourists.[54]

The AP also reported the rapes and violence as fact: "Storm victims were raped and beaten, fights and fires broke out, corpses lay out in the open, and rescue helicopters and law enforcement officers were shot at as flooded-out New Orleans descended into anarchy Thursday."[55]

Rape and Murder in the Superdome and Convention Center

The most brutal and disturbing scenic images in Hurricane Katrina's aftermath took place in the Louisiana Superdome, which sheltered an estimated 30,000 New Orleans residents and visitors who waited to be evacuated to the Houston Astrodome. Major press coverage portrayed the Superdome and Convention Center as sites of revulsion by featuring the evacuees (mostly mothers with children, carrying diapers) surrounded by feces, urine, blood, and sweat.[56] Such imagery effectively worked to brutalize and demonize the evacuees.[57] Under such conditions, rapes and murders allegedly occurred. The *Los Angeles Times* reported: "At least two people, including a child, have been raped."[58] Several major newspapers cited Police Chief Compass's allegations of rape: "'We have individuals who are getting raped, we have individuals who are getting beaten,' said Compass."[59] The *Times-Picayune* offered ear- and eyewitness accounts of rape and murder: "Several times a day, witnesses said, gunshots rang out, prompting stampedes that they said had killed at least one child. Others said a girl—age estimates ranged from 10 to 14—had been raped in a bathroom, her throat cut."[60] The *New York Times* reported unconfirmed accounts of children being raped: "Several residents said they had heard of children being raped, though it was not clear whether anyone reported such incidents to the authorities, and no officials could be found who could confirm the accounts."[61] The *Times* quoted one eyewitness, Darcel Monroe, who "'stammered hysterically as she recounted seeing two young girls being raped in one of the women's bathrooms'" in the Superdome. "'A lot of people saw it but they were afraid to do anything,' she said. 'He ran out past all of us.'"[62]

Such portrayals dehumanized and demonized New Orleans' residents and evacuees, thereby implying that extreme measures were necessary to eliminate them and save the body politic. St. Bernard Parish Sheriff Jack Stephens "authorized his haggard deputies to shoot to kill the looters," reported the *Times-Picayune* on two consecutive days (September 4 and 5).[63] Louisiana Governor Blanco announced (reported The *New York Times*): "'I have one message for these hoodlums: These troops know how to shoot and kill, and they are more than willing to do so if necessary.'"[64]

Denials and Inferential Racism

Major newspaper columnists and citizens' letters offered denials of race and racism during Katrina's aftermath, which worked to contain and deflect charges of racism,[65] while universalizing the looters' motives. Two *Washington Post* letter-writers denied that race and racism were factors in the looting: "Skin color has nothing to do with the urge to take what doesn't belong to you. Poverty also isn't the reason liquor gets stolen in a storm-ravaged city."[66] "Life, as the week's events show all too graphically, can be more than unfair, but misfortune is an equal-opportunity business. Blaming racism just won't wash."[67] In the *Atlanta Journal-Constitution*, a woman from Lawrenceville, Louisiana, viewed blacks and whites in equally pejorative terms: "'You got white trash, and you got black trash,' Weinberg said. 'There is bad in any race. It is sad this happened, but it has nothing to do with race.'"[68]

Tainted Others: The Evacuees

Major media depicted the storm's victims as primitive racial Others, non-American refugees, threatening aliens, and criminals. By doing so, the media discourse distanced, objectified, and criminalized the evacuees, forestalling broad (modern, progressive, racial, national, class, and neoliberal) audience identification with the evacuees and their plight.

Exodus: Evacuees as Premodernist Subjects

Major news coverage commonly described the New Orleans evacuation in biblical terms, as an "exodus," transforming the evacuees into emancipated biblical slaves or premodernist subjects. For example, the *Times-Picayune* reported:

> The mile-long trail of suffering on the interstate underscored the biblical proportions of Hurricane Katrina. "This is the Red Sea—that's what we're trying to cross," said Earl Miller, 57. "This is a mass exodus, like the Israelites fleeing from Egypt. One key difference: the flood victims could see no promised land."[69]

Evacuees as Non-American Others

The media also suggested that the evacuees were not Americans by referring to them as "refugees"[70] and offering metonymies (i.e., reductive personal stories and markers) of evacuees' plight that reinforced the image of New Orleans as a chaotic, disorderly, and foreign "third world" cultural space (e.g., "Just like Haiti,"[71] or "Baghdad"[72]). Orientalist tropes of chaos and disorder offer a panoramic view of impoverished cultural spaces, ideologically distancing progressive and civilized western spectators from a chaos of brown and black people frozen in time and place.[73] The *Washington Post* captured this view of hurricane victims:

> Those left behind in the Crescent City, including many with diabetes and other worsening health conditions, clung to rooftops, gathered on overpasses and bridges, and huddled on islands of dry ground, waiting for help that never came. Parents carried small children, and grown children carried their elderly parents through the flotsam. Corpses floated in fetid waters and lay amid the crowds of refugees.[74]

The frozen metonymies of desperate and poor black women, children, and elderly (men are noticeably absent from these portrayals) living in chaos and disorder in major urban cities is a recurring trope in U.S. news discourse, but one that does not necessarily invite empathy from U.S. citizens.[75] The metonymic narratives imply that blacks (especially women and children, absent black men) constantly need federal government assistance, Brummett argues, producing white and middle-class resentment and blaming poor black victims.[76] Moreover, depicting U.S. blacks as "third world" "natural" disaster victims positions media consumers as spectators, which facilitates blaming the victims for not embracing (and perhaps rejecting) "first world" capitalism and neoliberal and neocolonial logics of the American Dream.

Evacuees as Alien Threat

The media used pseudo-quantifications to reinforce the epic scale and magnitude of the evacuees' exodus, but the discourse also objectified and depersonalized the evacuees. For instance, *USA Today* reported: "*More than 500,000 evacuees from Hurricane Katrina are on the move. It is a storm surge of the disposed, an exodus on an historical scale in the USA.*"[77] Two reporters from The *New York Times* wrote: "Four days after the massive storm devastated New Orleans . . . *thousands upon thousands* of people wanting to leave, the unprecedented exodus could take days to complete."[78]

More perniciously, major news reports combined the quantitative expressions with water metaphors to suggest that the evacuees were a large, unmanageable, and amorphous blob moving to distant locations, producing an alien threat. Crime news stories and U.S. government reports during the nineteenth and early twentieth centuries commonly used water metaphors to describe "waves" of "not-yet-white" people migrating to the United States to compete for employment, resources, and opportunities.[79] The metaphors signified an external threat by "aliens."[80] Similarly, press reports used water metaphors to describe New Orleans' evacuees, implying that they were a large alien force that would be competing against residents from other U.S. cities and states for resources. For example, *USA Today* reported: "The forced migration from flooded Gulf Coast homes is *swamping* cities in Louisiana and Texas. The *waves* are *rolling* to Michigan, New Mexico, Arizona and as far as Oregon and New York."[81] The *Washington Post* and *USA Today* chronicled the exodus to Baton Rouge: "A *stream* of people from New Orleans, 75 miles away, continues to arrive."[82] "Thousands of others (refugees) were already *streaming* into Baton Rouge" (emphasis added). [83]

In addition, major newspapers cited experts' observations and citizens' complaints that raised fears about competition for scarce resources owing to New Orleans' black evacuees' migration to other cities. *USA Today* cited UCLA Adjunct Professor of Social Welfare Jorja Leap's assessment: "No violence has been reported in any city, but it remains a potential problem." "I don't think they're [the black evacuees] going to be absorbed seamlessly in American life . . . [due to] competitive pressure on resources."[84] Such competition surfaced in Baton Rouge between middle- and lower-class blacks, the *Washington Post* reported: "We don't mind sharing, but there's going to be competition for jobs," said Tara Williams, a medical transcriber and black Baton Rouge resident.[85]

Evacuees as Criminals

In one of the most alarming recurrences, the media featured law enforcement and public officials' statements (including those from neighboring cities and communities) that vilified and criminalized the New Orleans evacuees. These official statements justified police surveillance, threats, incarceration, and violence against the evacuees, while deflecting attention from the victims' plight. The *Chicago Tribune* reported:

> Even though dry land exists leading out of the city, emergency officials continued to prevent able-bodied storm victims from trying to walk across the Crescent City Bridge, citing the dangers they said would be posed by an uncontrolled exit from the city . . . "We don't know if they're lawless going out of the town and we don't want them to be walking around wreaking havoc," [said Louisiana State Lt. Lawrence Mcleary].[86]

Similarly, the *Washington Post* quoted Baton Rouge's black Mayor Melvin "Kip" Holden's warning "that he would not tolerate 'lawlessness' from the arriving Hurricane Katrina evacuees," because he "has a place for them": the Baton Rouge jails.[87] The *Post* also featured a black woman from Baton Rouge who predicted a violent outcome for New Orleans' evacuees, whom she viewed (in contrast to survivalists) as criminals: "'I can understand trying to survive. But the element coming here, well, they might try to rob stores,' or 'break into people's houses.' Mosby said she envisioned 'shoot to kill' orders if break-ins do occur . . . They gonna let these people know, 'You ain't in New Orleans. You in Baton Rouge.'"[88]

However, NAACP President Bruce Gordon claimed that "the news media has [sic] overblown the amount of crime" and "demonized many of its victims, who are disproportionately African American."[89] A "lucky" woman from New Orleans urged privileged Americans to stop blaming and condemning "those people," "living below the poverty level," "without transportation," and "faced with evacuating their homes" forever.[90] Some educated and middle-class blacks believed that their class achievements should insulate them from being tainted as criminals. New Orleans school teacher Barbra Martin said "she has been made to feel 'uncomfortable' in Baton Rouge. 'I am a middle-class black person, and I'm being treated by the color of my skin.'"[91]

In sum, major media stories depicted New Orleans' evacuees as racial Others, non-American ("third world") aliens, and dangerous criminals, deemed unworthy and undeserving of being saved. Such rhetoric justified the control, mistreatment, and even violence against the black evacuees. The legacy of these frozen images has far-reaching implications for natural disaster victims, especially black victims.[92]

Fallen Heroes

In mythic stories, the greater the problem facing the culture, the greater the hero must be.[93] In Katrina's wake, major press coverage featured an apocalyptic scene filled with archetypal black villains and chaos, requiring heroes capable of defeating the dangerous black brutes, rescuing women, children, and the elderly, and restoring order. Instead, the media exposed institutional failures of mythic proportions, which include: (1) failed government leaders, (2) absolution, and (3) local civil servant heroes.

Failed Government Leaders

The media depicted the Bush administration and FEMA (Federal Emergency Management Agency) officials as failed leaders who acted too slowly and brought inadequate resources to deal with the national crisis. In a radio interview-turned-global media spectacle, "the mayor [Nagin] of New Orleans angrily accused [the Federal government] of responding slowly and with inadequate resources—charges echoed by other political leaders, including the Congressional Black Caucus and Louisiana's Republican senator."[94]

The *New York Times* and other media highlighted Nagin's insurgent style of attack (describing him as "incensed," "exploded," "lashing out," and using "scathing language"), while President Bush and FEMA officials conceded that the government's response was slow and inadequate. "A day after Bush acknowledged the federal response to the hurricane was inadequate, [FEMA chief] Brown agreed. 'Everyone at FEMA agrees that it is unacceptable,'" The *Boston Globe* reported.[95] After hearing Bush's assessment, FEMA coordinating officer William Lokey was mortified: "I'll probably be lying awake for quite a long time second-guessing about how we might have done things different ramping up," adding, "Well, I tried my best with what I had." [96]

In reporting institutional failures, the media explained that the Bush administration and FEMA suffered from three tragic character flaws: ignorance, distraction, and structural racism and classism.

1. *Bush administration as ignorant.* A *Washington Post* editorial reported: "Mr. Bush said yesterday, that nobody 'anticipated the breach of the levees.'"[97] The *Los Angeles Times* reported: "When Homeland Security Secretary Michael Chertoff was asked on National Public Radio why no help had been sent, he said he was 'unaware of the problem.'"[98] FEMA Director Michael D. Brown "acknowledged that he had not known about perilous conditions around the city's convention center until Thursday morning.'" "'That shows how difficult communications are,' he explained."[99]

However, the press refuted the Bush administration's claims that they were unaware of potential problems posed by hurricanes by citing experts who complained that government officials ignored the problems: "They did anticipate breaching of the levees, that the pumps wouldn't work," said Natural Hazards Center Director Kathleen Tierney in The *Los Angeles Times*. Louisiana and New Orleans "couldn't get the federal assistance they needed. They knew they were living on a time bomb."[100] The *Times* also cited disaster expert and Florida International University Political Scientist Richard Stuart Olson, who said "None of this can be a surprise." Olson suggested that the federal government adopt an extreme all-out warlike posture to rescue New Orleans, like that of mythic American western heroes: "Where the hell's the cavalry?"[101]

2. *Bush administration as distracted after 9/11.* The second reason the media offered for FEMA and the Bush administration's failure was that they diverted, restructured, or mismanaged government resources after the September 11, 2001, terrorist attacks and Iraq War. The *Boston Globe* explained that, following the 2001 terrorist attacks, "FEMA became part of homeland security," but its "preparedness function" was changed to "counterterrorism, not national disasters."[102] Former Clinton administration Director of Emergency Management James Lee Witt observed that the Bush administration "minimized FEMA" and made it disappear under the Department of Homeland Security. In The *Los Angeles Times*, Witt continued: "'You can't report up through three different chains of people and make things go fast. . . .' 'FEMA needs to be put back as an independent agency with the people and resources to do its job well.'"[103] Even former President Bill Clinton chimed in: "It has something to do with how they reorganized after I left."[104]

The media also revealed tensions between Louisiana Governor Blanco and President Bush. According to the *Los Angeles Times*, Blanco feared being blamed by the Bush White House for the "slow moving government disaster operations."[105] She repeatedly requested more National Guard troops and authority over them, but claimed that the troops were unavailable to help Louisianans because they were in Iraq.[106] Yet in the *New York Times* and other media, Secretary Chertoff responded that "the issue was not the numbers, but logistics."[107]

3. *Bush administration as racist and classist.* The media *ambivalently* suggested that the Bush administration's and FEMA's slow and inadequate response was the result of structural racism and classism. The media featured the explicit racist charges made by black and white celebrities, citizens, and evacuees, and implicit racist accusations made by elected black officials and civic leaders. The chorus of black (and white celebrity) voices produced a moral and counter-hegemonic challenge to the Bush administration's image as white, conservative, western mythic heroes, exposing them to be hegemonic white elitists.

Celebrities, citizens, and evacuees explicitly charged the Bush administration with racism, classism, and indifference. For example, during "A Concert for Hurricane Relief," simulcast on NBC, MSNBC, CNBC, and Pax, popular rapper Kanye West accused President Bush of reproducing America's most foundational exclusions: "America was set up to help the poor, the black people, the less well-off as slow as possible."[108] West broadened his attack to include the media:

> "I hate the way they portray us in the media. If you see a black family, it says they're
> looting. See a white family, it says they're looking for food" . . . "[West] declared
> that government authorities are intentionally dragging their feet on aid to the Gulf
> Coast." After which he stated, "George Bush doesn't care about black people."[109]

In response, the media struck back. In a widely circulated AP report, the press undermined West's attack as an illegitimate and immature "rant," coming from a sore loser who was "snubbed" at the American Music Awards one week before his "emotional outburst."[110]

While registering their complaints, major media productions presented black intellectuals, leaders, and elites as the culture's emotional surrogates by featuring their reactions to the "multitude of news media images" of "dead, dying and crying blacks," and "their desperate pleas for help, stirring a "national discussion in living rooms, chat rooms and radio talk shows."[111] In a statement "broadcast on hundreds of [radio] stations," Xavier University administrator Beverly Wright stated: "'I am very angry, and I really, really believe that [the crisis] is driven by race . . . 'People can say what they want, but when you look at who is left behind, it is very disturbing to me.'"[112]

The media also presented implicit racist accusations made by members of the Congressional Black Caucus and African American citizens, who used rhetorical questions to sharpen their counter-hegemonic attacks on the government. U.S. Congressman David Scott complained: "'Many people in the African-American community are saying the reason why this government did not respond as quickly as it should is because those were black people in New Orleans.'" In the *Chicago Tribune*, Scott asked, "'If they were white, would this be happening? Would it have taken this long to respond?'"[113] Similarly, an African American evacuee Yvette Brown pointedly asked: "'You know why all those black people stuck down there are dying?' 'If they were white, they'd be gone. They'd be sending in an army of helicopters, jets and boats.'"[114]

The White House responded to the racist accusations by deploying African American and Secretary of State Condoleezza Rice to the media to defend Bush and his administration. In a widely reported interview, Rice stated: "Nobody, especially the president, would have left people unattended on the basis of race."[115] Moreover, Rice deflected charges of racism behind government delays by suggesting that media images adversely affected all Americans, not just the African Americans accusers: "I think everybody's very emotional. It's hard to watch pictures of any American going through this," yet she acknowledged that "the African-American community has obviously been very heavily affected."[116] Black conservatives defended the Bush administration and deflected charges of racism by accusing the congressional black leadership of "racially politicizing a natural catastrophe."[117] Ward Connerly stated that it was "simply a coincidence that most of the hurricane victims on television are black," dismissing African American leaders' and white celebrities' charges of structural racism as merely "looking for someone to blame."[118] Connerly scolded them: "black leaders who are blaming racism, shame on them."[119]

Absolution

People absolve themselves of blame by stressing the scenic or external motivations that reduce human actions to simple motion, which makes their actions and choices seem merely responsive to the environment.[120] In spite of the news media's implicit call for mythic heroes (e.g., cavalry) to defeat the apocalyptic scene (comprised of looters and chaos) and rescue Katrina's victims, federal government officials attempted to absolve themselves of blame by gaining lexical control over it.[121] President Bush and conservatives repeatedly referred to the storm and government actions as a "natural disaster."[122] "Under fire" for his inexperience, FEMA director Brown stated: "We're still dealing with a catastrophe."[123] In newspapers and television news programs, Secretary Chertoff called the storm and aftermath "an 'ultra-catastrophe,' that exceeded the foresight of planners," shifting responsibility from Bush administration officials back onto nameless planners.[124] Chertoff prophesied: "'We need to prepare the country for what's coming . . . it's going to be as ugly a scene as you an imagine.'"[125]

Absolving Rescue Officials

One of the most tragic features of Hurricane Katrina's aftermath was the multitude of government and rescue officials who absolved themselves for not saving evacuees, allegedly keeping their workers out of harm's way. (At least 12 types of rescue workers aborted their mission to save the hurricane victims because of alleged reports of gunfire.)[126] To illustrate the scope and dimensions of aborted rescue missions, we present the reports of danger in spatial terms: air, water, ground operations (law enforcement and levee repair), and evacuation sites.

1. *Hospital rescue helicopters.* The *Boston Globe* reported: "'Hospitals are trying to evacuate,' said Coast Guard Lt. Cdr. Cheri Ben-Iesan at the city emergency operations center. 'At every one of them, there are reports that as the helicopters come in people are shooting at them.'"[127]

2. *Hospital rescue boats.* The *Washington Post* quoted chief executive of Acadian Ambulance Services Richard Zuschlag: "Both mornings, we have tried to go to Charity Hospital by boat and each time we have been shot at, so we determined it wasn't safe. The doctor there has 500 people inside his hospital and he is going berserk."[128]

3. *Local Police.* The *New York Times* reported Police Chief Compass's assessment: "200 of the 1,500 officers on his force had walked off the job, citing the perils of fighting armed and menacing refugees, and he reported that two officers had committed suicide."[129]

4. *Contractors sent to repair the levees.* The *Atlanta Journal-Constitution* reported: "14 contractors on their way to help plug the breach in the 17th Street Canal levee were traveling across the Danziger Bridge under police escort when they came under fire," yet "[n]one of the contractors was injured."[130]

5. *Evacuation ambulances and buses.* The *Christian Science Monitor* reported: "Fights and trash fires marred the exodus from the Superdome, in addition to the shots and brandished guns that halted ambulance service and evacuation convoys Thursday."[131] The *Washington Post* reported that even the buses leaving the Superdome for the Houston Astrodome were allegedly under attack: "At the storm-damaged Superdome, faltering efforts to transport as many as 23,000 refugees to the Astrodome in Houston were temporarily halted after a gunshot was reportedly fired at a military helicopter."[132]

Local Heroes: Civil Servants

The media's apocalyptic narrative in Hurricane Katrina's wake implied that grand, mobile, militaristic, and moral mythic heroes were necessary to rescue New Orleans and its people. However, against the backdrop of government failures, major media stories lionized local civil servants as heroes, even while their rescue missions were limited, delayed, and at times aborted. Still, in death-defying rescue missions, local and national civil servants were depicted as saving stranded and desperate New Orleans residents, tourists, and evacuees. The Coast Guard, in particular, was praised for rescuing more than 15,000 people.[133] In doing so, the major dailies cast them and the National Guard as superheroes who "plucked" "a twisting column of refugees" off rooftops with helicopters and cutter boats,[134] "clawed through roofs with bare hands,"[135] and broke through rooftops with axes, pulling individual residents out of harm's way. A *Washington Post* editorial compared the heroism in New Orleans to that of "New York after September 11, 2001."[136]

In addition to providing basic needs (safety, food, and water), the National Guard members were depicted as civilizing agents, restoring law and order to New Orleans, yet with overwhelming and deadly force. For example, The *Chicago Tribune* reported:

> At least 7,000 of the guard troops, many of them veterans of the Iraq war and, their general said, proficient in the use of lethal force, headed into New Orleans, along with a contingent of military police assigned to restore order . . . "The cavalry is and will continue to arrive," said Lt. Gen. Steven Blum of the National Guard.[137]

The National Guard's presence was also depicted as psychologically restorative for Louisianans. "They brought a sense of order and peace, and it was a beautiful sight to see that we're ramping up," Governor Blanco said in the *Los Angeles Times*. "We are seeing a show of force. It's putting confidence back in our hearts and in the minds of our people. We're going to make it through."[138]

The most colorful hero in the press coverage was Lt. Gen. Russel L. Honoré. As commander of Joint Task Force Katrina, Honoré led the National Guard troops into New Orleans. In doing so, Honoré was depicted as an archetypal Western hero. "'That's one John Wayne dude down here that can get some stuff done,' [Mayor] Nagin said admiringly. 'He came off the doggone chopper and he started cussing and people started moving.'"[139] Like John Wayne in *The Searchers*, Honoré was (1) rugged and obscene ("cussing," "barking," "gruff," "terse," and "cigar-chomping"[140]); (2) colloquial (referring to troop strength as "boots on the ground," and commanding "let's get it on!"[141]); and (3) pragmatic, patriotic, and optimistic ("Worse things have happened to America. We're going to overcome this too," announced Honoré[142]).

However, the allusions to classic Western heroes could not be sustained. The local civil servants' rescue missions were aborted, delayed, or limited. The National Guard did not arrive until Friday, four days after the storm landed. Once they arrived, Arkansas National Guard Sgt. Mike Chenault acknowledged their limitations: "You can get them some water and an MRE [packaged meal], but other than that there's not much you can do."[143] Hurricane Katrina's apocalyptic conditions demanded a greater heroic force; but none was forthcoming.

Cultural Implications

Major media news stories during Katrina's aftermath produced a diffuse mythic narrative, in which black brutes looted, raped, and took over New Orleans.[144] The news coverage suggested that New Orleans was out of control and desperately needed federal government help. In doing so, the media coverage dehumanized and demonized black looters, which justified extreme government policies, including the shooting and killing of looters, evacuees, and residents.[145] Furthermore, media's apocalyptic scene enabled multiple government officials to absolve themselves for delays and failures, or led them to abort their missions completely, primarily by citing anonymous reports and rumors of shooting and dangerous crime.

Black U.S. Congress members, leaders, officials, columnists, citizens, and (black and white) celebrities contested the negative images of blacks. The black leaders and celebrities served as emotional surrogates monitoring the disturbing images of poor and desperate blacks waiting for government help; but they were also depicted as emotional, "angry," or immature, thereby undermining their moral authority to accuse the government of structural racism. By contrast, the media trumpeted and elevated the voices of black conservatives, whose lightning-fast refutation to charges of structural racism have become their raison d'être. Black looters and evacuees were depicted as irrational, barbaric, damaged, and criminal, thereby reproducing Manichean dualities found in imperialistic colonial narratives. Such discourse reproduces Enlightenment ideologies of white western superiority and domestic Orientalism, in which blacks are viewed as primitive, barbaric, immoral, and threatening, rather than as American citizens or innocent hurricane victims.

Major media news discourse produced an apocalyptic narrative, in which the chosen were those who could get out of New Orleans or passively (and perhaps helplessly) watch the media spectacle from afar. The unforgiven (poor, residents, tourists constructed as blacks) were transformed into dangerous criminals even before evacuating New Orleans. The deep structures of the narrative reveal a dystopian nightmare, which expresses unconscious fears that the government forces cannot manage or solve large national crises and save the culture, much less rescue its most vulnerable victims. Our cultural agencies, institutions, and leaders are no longer heroic. Therefore, we celebrate civil servant heroes.

Our study shows that white civil servants emerged as local heroes as federal government leaders failed to solve the national cultural crisis. Aaron David Gresson III argues that the media's lionizing of white civil servants is part of an ongoing project to recover a heroic identity for white males constructed as oppressors by egalitarian and liberation discourses.[146] Susan Faludi contends that the media's lionizing of white civil servants (especially working-class New York City firefighters) in the wake of 9-11, served to restore a rugged, tough, John Wayne-style of masculinity for white males suffering from feelings of failure, fear, and vulnerability following the terrorist attacks.[147] Yet, Faludi warns that the cultural embrace of mythic Western heroes requires weak and vulnerable women and the subversion of feminine archetypes.[148]

We would add that these archetypal Western heroes are white, and they rescue women and children from the clutches of dangerous and demonic, dark masculine brutes. Perhaps this accounts for the multitude and prominence of brutish black looters in the news stories during Katrina's aftermath. The formal structures of the discourse imply that extreme militarism deployed by paternalistic white Western heroes en masse (a cavalry) was necessary to rescue New Orleans' women, children, and elderly. Carol Stabile observes that U.S. crime news narratives that foreground black criminals render black victims invisible.[149] Our study shows more clearly that the media depicted the evacuees as possessing many of the same characteristics as the looters (e.g., black, irrational, and criminal), thereby equating the evacuees with the looters. Furthermore, the news media depicted the evacuees as historical, geographic, and "third world" others, forestalling racial, national, middle-class, and modernist identification with the hurricane victims. The speed (within six days) with which media transformed innocent victims and evacuees into dangerous black criminals and the global reach of such media demonstrate the power that demonic racial villains have on our cultural psyche in times of fear and distress; it also justifies and excuses extreme actions in response to cultural crises, no matter how erroneous and damaging.

The media's recurrent call (through public officials and experts) for the government to become mythic Western heroes in order to rescue Hurricane Katrina's victims is problematic. Conservative U.S. politicians who have adopted a Western persona (e.g., Ronald Reagan and George W. Bush) have also embraced rugged individualism and laissez-faire government policies.[150] Such conceptions of government become problematic when large, swift, and efficient government forces are necessary to manage and resolve national and cultural crises, in order to save people. The failures of FEMA and the Bush administration fuel beliefs that their ideological commitments to rugged individualism and neocolonialism (based on Social Darwinism) left them ill-equipped to handle a large human catastrophe and complex cultural problems. Katrina's aftermath required insightful cultural heroes: (1) scholars capable of exposing hidden structural problems and illuminating pathways to change regarding institutional policies and practices; and (2) political heroes capable of harnessing government power and moving swiftly and efficiently to defeat large enemies, while identifying with and saving all people (including poor and black people), thereby confronting cultural shadows, or nightmares filled with vengeful racial monsters, created by cultural leaders and people who remain asleep to structural racism.

NOTES

Versions of this chapter were presented at the 2006 International Communication Association Conference in Dresden, Germany, the 2009 National Communication Association Convention in Chicago, IL and at the 2010 International Communication Association Conference in Singapore. The authors thank Kent Ono, Carol Stabile, Rya Butterfield, and the anonymous reviewers for their advice and support. The authors dedicate their work to all victims of Hurricane Katrina.

1. "Facts about Katrina," *Surviving Katrina*. The Discovery Channel, 2008.

2. Michael Chertoff, "Written statement of Secretary Michael Chertoff, Department of Homeland Security, for the U.S. Senate, Committee on Homeland Security and Governmental Affairs." *Hurricane Katrina: The Homeland Security Department's Preparation and Response* [Hearing], February 15, 2006.

3. Federal Deposit Insurance Corporation, "Bank Performance After Natural Disasters: A Historical Perspective," January 16, 2006.

4. *Washington Post* reporters Robert E. Pierre and Ann Gerhart write that local, state, and federal officials now believe that "unsubstantiated reports of violence" and "exaggerations of mayhem by officials and rumors repeated uncritically in the news media helped slow the response to the disaster and tarnish the image of many of its victims." See "News of Pandemonium May Have Slowed Aid: Unsubstantiated Reports of Violence Were Confirmed by Some Officials, Spread by News Media," *Washington Post*, October 5, 2005, A8. In addition, the *New York Times* investigation found that reports of armed robbers looting the Acadian Ambulance Company's ambulances and Covington's firehouse "proved totally untrue." Jim Dwyer and Christopher Drew, "Fear Exceeded Crime's Reality in New Orleans," *New York Times*, September 29, 2005, A1. The *Times* also found the story of "400 to 500 armed looters . . . advancing on the town of Westwego" to be false; "the looters never appeared, said the Westwego police chief, Dwayne Munch." Ibid. As for the reported rapes, news outlets confirmed that there were "no official reports of rape and no eyewitness to sexual assault" anywhere in the city. CNN, "Reports Exaggerated"; *USA Today*, "After Review"; Angela Tuck, "Katrina Blew Journalists' Skepticism out the Window," *Atlanta Journal-Constitution*, October 1, 2005, A15; Christopher Shea, "Up for Grabs: Sociologists Question How Much Looting and Mayhem Really Took Place in New Orleans," *Boston Globe*, September 11; 2005, E1; Robert E. Pierre and Ann Gerhart, "News of Pandemonium," *Atlanta Journal-Constitution* reported that "the worst stories . . . [about] the beheading of a baby [and] the systematic rape of white women" were false. See Tuck, "Katrina Blew Journalists' Skepticism out the Window." As for shooting, the *Washington Post* reported that "Louisiana National Guard officials on the ground at the time now say that no helicopters came under attack and the evacuations were never stopped because of gunfire." Pierre and Gerhart, "News of Pandemonium." The Civil Air Patrol, Air National Guard, and U.S. Coast Guard officials agreed that there was "no official confirmation that a single military helicopter over New Orleans . . . was fired upon." Matt Welch, "They Shoot Helicopters, Don't They? How Journalists Spread Rumors During Katrina," *Reason* 37, no. 7 (2005): 16–18. See also Gary Younge, "Murder and Rape—Fact or Fiction?" *The Guardian*, September 6, 2005. http://www.guardian.co.uk/world/2005/sep/06/hurricanekatrina.usa3 (July 29, 2007).

5. Pierre and Gerhart, "News of Pandemonium."

6. Most critical rhetoric scholars who propose mythic criticisms are influenced by Kenneth Burke's theories and criticisms. See Barry Brummett, *Rhetoric in Popular Culture*, 2nd ed. (Thousand Oaks, CA: Sage, 2006), 86; *Rhetorical Homologies: Form, Culture, Experience* (Tuscaloosa: University of Alabama Press, 2004); "How to Propose a Discourse," *Communication Studies* 41, no. 2 (1990): 131; Janice H. Rushing, "On Saving Mythic Criticism—A Reply to Rowland's Rejoinder," *Communication Studies* 41, no. 2 (1990): 147; Janice H. Rushing, and Thomas S. Frentz, "The Frankenstein Myth, in Contemporary Cinema," *Critical Studies in Mass Communication* 6 (1989): 61–80; Michael G. Lacy, "White Innocence Heroes: Recovery, Reversals, Paternalism, and David Duke," *Journal of International and Intercultural Communication* 3, no. 3 (2010); "White Innocence Myths in Citizen Discourse, The Progressive Era (1974–1988)," *Howard Journal of Communications* 21 (2010): 20–39; Abhik Roy and Robert C. Rowland, "The Rhetoric of Hindu Nationalism: A Narrative of Mythic Redefinition," *Western Journal of Communication* (2003): 225–48. In addition to Burkean theories, critical rhetoric scholars proposing mythic criticisms also use post-structuralist theories (especially those introduced by Frederic Jameson, Mikhail Bakhtin, and Antonio Gramsci), who argue that meta-narratives in postmodern contexts exist in fragmented form; see "Rushing, "On Saving Mythic Criticism," 147; Janice H. Rushing and Thomas S. Frentz, "Integrating Ideology and Archetype in Rhetorical criticism," *Quarterly Journal of Speech* 77 (1991): 385–406; Brummett, *Rhetorical Homologies*, 76.

7. Rushing, "On Saving Mythic Criticism," 147.

8. Brummett, *Rhetorical Homologies*, 29; "How to Propose," 130; Rushing and Frentz, "The Frankenstein Myth," 63–65; Rushing and Frentz, "Integrating," 388.

9. Rushing, "Mythic Criticism,"146–47; Rushing and Frentz, "Integrating," 406.

10. NOAA, National Climatic Data Center, "Climate of 2005: Summary of Hurricane Katrina," December, 29, 2005. http://www.ncdc.noaa.gov/oa/climate/research/2005/katrina.html (Feb. 17, 2006).

11. Ibid. See also Charles M. Madigan, "Bearing Witness to a Catastrophe," *Chicago Tribune*, September 4,

12. Reported by the *Times-Picayune*, *St. Petersburg Times*, and Associated Press in "Katrina Timeline." http:..thinkprogress.org/2005/09/07/the-katrina-timeline/ (July 29, 2007).

13. See note 12.

14. Joseph B. Treaster and Abby Goodnough, "Powerful Storm Threatens Havoc Along Gulf Coast," *New York Times*, August 29, 2005, A1.

15. Kris Axtman, "Big Relief Effort Meets Katrina," *Christian Science Monitor*, August 30, 2005. http://www.csmonitor.com (accessed August 4, 2009).

16. Wil Haygood and Ann Scott Tyson, "It Was as If All of Us Were Already Pronounced Dead," *Washington Post*, September 15, 2005, A1.

17. "House-to-House Rescues Under Way in New Orleans," CNN.com, September 5, 2005.

18. "Facts about Katrina," The Discovery Channel, 2008; Michelle Hunter, "Death of Evacuees Push Toll to 1,577, *Times Picayune*, May 19, 2006, 1.

19. We chose to examine major daily newspaper discourse because: (1) newspapers chronicle events on a daily, unfolding, timetable, in contrast to the so-called 24-hour news cycle of broadcast and electronic media; (2) newspapers provide crime news narratives of depth and granularity, especially when compared to news media that deliver immediate, sound-bite-driven reporting; and (3) other news media rely on newspapers and news services as primary sources.

20. The major dailies include: *Atlanta-Journal Constitution*, *Boston Globe*, *Chicago Tribune*, *Christian Science Monitor*, *Los Angeles Times*, *New York Times*, *Seattle Post-Intelligencer*, *USA*

TODAY, Wall Street Journal, and *Washington Post.* Our sample also included 81 stories from the *New Orleans Times-Picayune* because of its proximity to the events. The *Times* earned a Pulitzer Prize for reporting on Hurricane Katrina and its aftermath.

21. Brummett, "How to Propose," 130; Michael Osborn, "In Defense of Broad Mythic Criticism," *Communication Studies* 41 (1990): 121–27; Rushing, "On Saving," 140; Rushing and Frentz, "Integrating Ideology," 390–93; "The Frankenstein Myth," 63.

22. Edward F. Edinger, *Archetype of the Apocalypse: Divine, Vengeance, Terrorism, and the End of the World* (Chicago: Open Court, 1999).

23. Burke, *A Grammar of Motives* (Berkeley: University of California Press, 1969), 9, 12–13, 18, 28.

24. Martha Solomon, "The Rhetoric of Dehumanization: An Analysis of Medical Reports of the Tuskegee Syphilis Project," *Western Journal of Speech Communication* 49 (1985): 233–47.

25. Columnists, editorialists, scholars (especially sociologists), and citizens explicitly referred to the looters as "black" primarily to expose the material effects of being black and poor in the United States, thereby offering a sociological critique of the institutional and government policies that produced the looters. A *Washington Post* columnist even cited sociologist Gunnar Myrdal's description of black oppression in America as the nation's "original sin." See David Ignatius, "Time to Mend the Safety Net," Editorial, *Washington Post,* September 2, A29.

26. See Cal Logue, "Rhetorical Ridicule of Reconstruction," *Quarterly Journal of Speech* 62 (1976): 400–409.

27. Five years after the storm, the PBS television news documentary program, *Frontline,* revealed a number of incidents in which police officers shot civilians in Katrina's wake. *Frontline* reports that a New Orleans police captain told a group of officers: "We have the authority by martial law to shoot looters." See "Law & Disorder." *Frontline* television program. Produced and Directed by Thomas Jennings. Written by Thomas Jennings and Seth Bomse. Boston: WGBH, August 25, 2010.

28. President Bush viewed all looters as criminals. Bush stated: "There ought to be zero tolerance for people breaking the law . . . If people need water and food, we're going to do everything we can to get them water or food." See Judy Keen, "Bush Recruits his Father, Clinton for Fundraising," *USA Today,* September 2, 2005, A6. However, most reporters and columnists were sympathetic to the looters who were trying to survive in contrast with criminal looters. The *Washington Post* quoted University of Delaware Professor Benigno Aguirre: "'It may look from the outside as if they are stealing or breaking the law, when in fact some of them are trying to survive.'" See Jeff Jacoby, "The Looting Instinct," *Boston Globe,* September, 4, 2005, E11. In fact, the *Times-Picayune* reported that "In the first few days after the storm, police largely turned a blind eye or even supervised looting for basics such as food and water. See Jacoby, "The Looting Instinct"; Matthew Brown, "The Ice Trucks Cometh to Relief of Many; For Those in homes, The cubes are "Like Gold," *Times Picayune,* September 6, 2005, A6. A *Chicago Tribune* reporter explained that "Nobody would begrudge a desperate family from lifting food or bottled water." See John Kass, "In Storm's Wake, There's More than 1 Way to Plunder," *Chicago Tribune,* September 1, 2005, 1.2.

29. "New Orleans in Chaos; Fights and Gunfire Break out as City Slips into Anarchy," *Chicago Tribune,* September 2, 2005, 3; "'It's Insane,' New Orleans in Crisis with Water still Rising, Looters, and Despair Setting in," *Chicago Tribune,* August 31, 2005, 3; Scott Gold, "In Katrina's Aftermath: Chaos and Survival. [Column One]. A City's Open Wounds; A Walk through New Orleans Is an Assault on the Senses: Distressing Sights and Smells, an Odd Quiet in a Water-

Choked Urban Wasteland," *Los Angeles Times*, September 2, 2005, A1; Chris Kirkham, "Violet Family Tells of Harrowing Tale of Survival: Stench of Death Filled St. Bernard Parish," *Times-Picayune*, September 6, A11.

30. Gold, "In Katrina's Aftermath."

31. Stephen J. Hedges, "Navy Pilot Says 'a Lot of People' Still Trapped," *Chicago Tribune*, September 2, 2005, 1.6.

32. Tunku Varadarajan, "Taste—de gustibus: In New Orleans, Moral Levees are Inundated Too," Weekend Journal, *Wall Street Journal*, September 2, 2005, W11.

33. David W. Owen, letter to the editor, *Washington Post*, September 3, 2005, A30.

34. Carol Beggy and Mark Shanahan, "A Friend to Pats Fans Copes with Katrina," *Boston Globe*, September 3, 2005, D2.

35. Mark Davis, "Katrina: the Aftermath: Dad Takes Rescue into Own Hands," *Atlanta Journal-Constitution*, September 6, 2005, F1.

36. Scott Gold and Ellen Barry, "Katrina Hits the Gulf Coast; Dozens Killed, Damage Heavy as Katrina Roars In; New Orleans Is Hit Hard, but Mississippi Feels Category 4 Hurricane's Full Force," *Los Angeles Times*, August 30, 2005, A1.

37. Linton Weeks, "Carried Away; Looting Has its Roots in the Chaos of Catastrophe," *Washington Post*, September 1, 2005, C1.

38. P. J. Huffstutter, "Column one: Making Good on a Promise; Hurricane Veterans, the Flints Vow to Stick Close," *Los Angeles Times*, September 3, 2005, A1.

39. Patrick O'Driscoll, "'The Looters, They're Like Cockroaches'; New Orleans Neighbors Guard against Encroaching Mayhem," *USA Today*, September 2, 2005, A3.

40. Jimmy Greenfield, "Looters Fail Ultimate Character Test," *Chicago Tribune*, September 2, 2005, 2.

41. Natalie Pompilio, "Stores Invaded, Stripped of Merchandise in Beleaguered City," *Boston Globe*, August 31, 2005, A16.

42. John Kass, "In Storm's Wake."

43. "Looters Laugh. Hurricane Katrina: When it Rains, it Roars," News Brief, *Atlanta Journal-Constitution*, August 30, 2005, A7.

44. Ibid.

45. Weeks, "Carried Away."

46. Jeff Jacoby, "The Looting Instinct."

47. Michael Levenson and Raja Mishra, "Troops Just Back from Iraq to Head South," *Boston Globe*, September 3, 2005, A8.

48. Shankar Vedantam and Christopher Lee, "Patience Thin as Supplies Run Low; Residents Criticize Speed of Delivery; Cleanup Continues," *Washington Post*, September 2, 2005, A9.

49. O'Driscoll, "Like Cockroaches."

50. Jacoby, "Looting Instinct."

51. The term "chaos" appeared 40 times in our database.

52. Trymaine D. Lee, "Nightmare in the 9th Ward All Too Real for One Woman," *Times-Picayune* [National Web Edition], September 1, 2005. http://www.nola.com.

53. Keith O'Brien, "Big Easy Struggling to Regain its Swagger," *Boston Globe*, September 4, 2005, A27.

54. Joseph Treaster and Deborah Sontag, "Despair and Lawlessness Grip New Orleans as Thousands Remain Stranded in Squalor," *New York Times*, September 2, 2005, A1.

55. "'It's Insane'"; See also Tribune News Services: "Armed Against a City in Chaos," September, 4, 2005, 5.

56. Scott Gold, Ellen Barry, and Stephen Braun, "Katrina's Rising Toll; Trapped in an Arena of Suffering; 'We Are Like Animals,' A Mother Says inside the Louisiana Superdome, Where Hope and Supplies Are Sparse," *Los Angeles Times*, September 1, 2005, A1.

57. See Burke, *A Grammar*, 9, 300–303.

58. Gold, "Katrina's Rising."

59. "New Orleans in Chaos." Michael Martinez and Howard Witt, "'A Desperate SOS'; New Orleans Mayor Pleads for Help from Washington as Rescuers, Survivors Face Gunfire, Anarchy," *Chicago Tribune*, September 2, 2005, 1.1.

60. Brian Thevenot, "Amid Chaos, a Rare Voice of Strength," *Times-Picayune*, September 3, 2005, A1.

61. Joseph B. Treaster and Maureen Balleza, "At Stadium, a Haven Quickly Becomes an Ordeal," *New York Times*, September 1, 2005, A1.

62. Ibid.

63. Paul Rioux and Manuel Torres, "St. Bernard Rescuers Find Horrific Scenes; Stephen King Couldn't Write a Script Like This' 31 Dead in Nursing Home; Man Found with Dead Family," *Times-Picayune*, September 4, 2005, A12; Ron Thibodeaux and Gordon Russell, "7th Day of Hell; A Week of Horror Ends with More Evacuations and Uncertainty, *Times-Picayune*, September 5, 2005, A1.

64. Robert D. McFadden and others, "Bush Pledges More Troops as Evacuation Grows," *New York Times*, September 4, 2005, 1.1. Notably, the press primarily depicted the police as weak, while the looters operated like vampires, seducing the local police, security guards, and National Guardsmen, and transforming them into criminals. For example, the *Washington Post* reported: "A pair of cops joins the thievery, pushing a basket of stolen goods through a Wal-Mart in New Orleans, which according to a TV reporter is on the verge of becoming 'a city of outlaws.'" See Weeks, "Carried Away." A *Boston Globe* columnist complained: [E]ven police or National Guardsmen looters hauled cases of stolen beer through hip-deep water, filled trash barrels with clothes, shoes, and jewelry, and crammed car trunks with computers and DVD players. . . . Police officers looted, too." See Jacoby, "Looting Instinct."

65. Stuart Hall observes that denials of race and racism in contemporary liberal contexts signify an inferential form of racism because such discourse implies that blacks created the problems. See "The Whites of Their Eyes: Racist Ideologies and the Mass Media," edited by Gail Dines and Jean M. Humez, *Gender, Race, and Class in Media*, 2nd ed. London: Sage, 2003, 89–93.

66. Colbert I. King, "Time for Action, Not Outrage," *Washington Post*, September 3, 2005, A31.

67. Sandra Kashdan, "Letter to the Editor," *Washington Post*, September 3, 2005, A30.

68. Rich Badie, "Katrina: The Aftermath: Public Opinion: Accusations Spark Race-Tinged Debate Activists, Lawmakers Blast Administration," *Atlanta Journal-Constitution*, September 3, 2005, A16.

69. Brian Thevenot, "Trek Seems Endless for Exhausted Survivors; Waits, Worry Only Adds to Horror," *Times-Picayune*, September 3, 2005, A7.

70. The term "refugees" appeared 46 times in our sample.

71. Hector Tobar, "Katrina's Aftermath; Katrina Elicits Sympathy, Jeers Worldwide; Even as They Pledge Aid, Nations Express Surprise at the Ineffective U.S. Response to the Crisis 2005," *Los Angeles Times*, September 3, 2005, A1.

72. "'It's Insane.'"

73. Arjun Appadurai, "Putting Hierarchy in Its Place," *Cultural Anthropology*, 3 (1988): 36–49; see also Raka Shome, "Race and Popular Cinema: The Rhetorical Strategies of Whiteness in the City of Joy," *Communication Quarterly* 44 (1996): 507.

74. Sam Coates and Dan Eggen, "A City of Despair and Lawlessness; Thousands Stranded in New Orleans; Troops Pour In," *Washington Post*, September 2, 2005, A1.

75. Brummett, *Rhetoric in Popular Culture*, 167–74; See also Coates and Dan Eggen, "A City of Despair."

76. The frozen metonymy of blacks desperately living in chaotic urban inner cities has been exploited by neoconservative and black realism discourses. See Lacy, "White Innocence Heroes," 215–216; "White Innocence Myths," 33–34.

77. Martin Kasindorf, "Waves of Evacuees Swamp Host Cities; Many of 500,000 May Never Return to What Was 'Home,'" *USA Today*, September 6, 2005, A1. Notably, hyperbolic quantitative expressions such as this one (e.g., 500,000 evacuees) exceeds the population of New Orleans. We argue such discourse reflects the media emphasis on describing scenic motivations of epic human proportions, which enabled government officials and rescue workers to absolve themselves of blame and responsibility for the delays.

78. James Dao and N. R. Kleinfield, "More Troops and Aid Reach New Orleans; Bush Visits Area; Chaotic Exodus Continues," *New York Times*, September 3, 2005, A1.

79. David R. Roediger, *Towards the Abolition of Whiteness: Essays on Race, Politics, and Working Class History* (New York: Routledge, 1994); see also Matthew Frye Jacobson, *Whiteness of a Different Color: European Immigrants and the Alchemy of Race* (Cambridge, MA: Harvard University Press, 1998).

80. Ibid.

81. Martin Kasindorf, "Waves."

82. Lee Feinswog, Tom Van den Brook, and Mark Memmott, "Influx of Refugees Swells Baton Rouge; Shelters, Schools Packed, and People Keep Coming," *USA Today*, September 2, 2005, A3.

83. Coates and Eggen, "A City of Despair."

84. Kasindorf, "Waves."

85. Wil Haygood, "In Baton Rouge, A Cool Welcome; Class Divisions Among Blacks Greet New Orleans Evacuees," *Washington Post*, September 6, 2005, A19.

86. James Janega and Howard Witt, "City's Cries Heeded; Troops, Supplies Finally Arrive in Beleaguered Region," *Chicago Tribune*, September 3, 2005, 1.1

87. Haygood, "In Baton Rouge."

88. Ibid. Stories, such as this one, featured caricatured language of Louisiana residents, offering an anthropological or folk quality to the discourse, while reinforcing the subjects' intellectual inferiority to and distance from the newspaper readers.

89. Kevin Cullen and Stephen Smith, "A Grim Search for Bodies; Victims Are Retrieved, Control Slowly Taken," *Boston Globe*, September 5, 2005, A1.

90. Sarah DeBacher, "Readers Write: Hurricane Katrina," *Atlanta Journal-Constitution*, September 5, 2005, A14.

91. Haygood, "In Baton Rouge."

92. Early news reports of the catastrophe in Haiti in 2010 following a severe earthquake threaten to taint Haitian victims in similar terms, calling them "refugees in their own country" and predicting "a lot of looting in the coming days and a lot of people who deliberately take advantage of the situation." *Nightline*, January 13, 2010. http://abcnews.go.com/nightline; *Newshour*, January 14, 2010, BBC World Service. http://www.bbc.co.uk/programmes/p005rcox#-.

93. Joseph Campbell, *The Hero with a Thousand Faces*, 2nd ed. (Princeton, NJ: Princeton University Press, 1968). See also William G. Doty, *Myth: A Handbook* (Tuscaloosa: Alabama Press, 2004), 109, 146.

94. Scott Gold, Allen Zarembo, and Stephen Braun, "Katrina's Aftermath: Guardsmen Arrive in New Orleans; Pace of Evacuations Is Stepped Up; The Mayor Hopes the Last Stranded Residents Will Be Out of the Sodden City in Five Days. Bush Tours the Devastated Area, and Supplies Are Trucked In," *Los Angeles Times*, September 3, 2005, A1.

95. Thomas Farragher and Brian MacQuarrie, "Wounded City Buoyed by Troops' Response; Order Restored; Mass. Offers Space for 2,000," *Boston Globe*, September 4, 2005, A1.

96. Michael Martinez and James Janega, "Guard Troops Move In, Work to Restore Order; Critics Blast Pace of Relief Effort; Hospitals Evacuated," *Chicago Tribune*, September 4, 2005, 6.

97. "From Bad to Worse" [Editorial], *Washington Post*, September 2, 2005, A28.

98. Nichole Gaouette and Richard Serrano, "In Katrina's Aftermath: Chaos and Survival; Survivors Wait as Disaster Builds; Officials Say They're Doing All They Can. Experts Had Foretold Numerous Problems," *Los Angeles Times*, September 2, 2005, A1.

99. Gold, Zarembo, and Braun, "Katrina's Aftermath."

100. Gaouette and Serrano, "In Katrina's Aftermath."

101. Ibid.

102. Charlie Savage, "Slow Response Exposes Holes in Planning," *Boston Globe*, September 4, 2005, A26.

103. Scott Gold, David Zucchino, and Stephen Braun, "Hundreds Refuse to Evacuate; 'We're Trying to Convince Them There's Nothing for Them Here,' Official Says," *Los Angeles Times*, September 6, 2005, A1.

104. Ibid.

105. Ibid.

106. Ibid.

107. McFadden, "Bush Pledges."

108. Lynn Duke and Teresa Wiltz, "A Nation's Castaways; Katrina Blew in, and Tossed up Reminders of a Tattered Racial Legacy," *Washington Post*, September 4, 2005, D1.

109. Ibid.

110. Duke and Wiltz, "A Nation's Castaways"; William Neikirk and Mike Hughlett, "Critics Say Bias Delayed Relief to Disaster Area," *Chicago Tribune*, September 3, 2005, 1.1.

111. Tomas Alex Tizon, "Katrina's Aftermath: Images of the Victims Spark a Racial Debate; Some Say Authorities' Response Time Is Affected by the Victims' Skin Color. Others Say Such Accusations Are a Distraction Right Now," *Los Angeles Times*, September 3, 2005, A11.

112. Ibid.

113. Neikirk and Hughlett, "Critics Say."

114. Tribune, AP News Services, "Racism Charged in Slow Flow of Relief Supplies," *Chicago Tribune*, September 6, 2005, 9.

115. Angela Rozas and Howard Witt, "The Dreadful Toll; 'It is Going to be About as Ugly of a Scene as . . . You Can Imagine,' Warns Homeland Security Chief on New Orleans' Dead; Area Nursing Homes Begin Own Grim Tally," *Chicago Tribune*, September 5, 2005, 1.1.

116. Neikirk and Hughlett, "Critics Say."

117. Ibid.

118. Tizon, "Katrina's Aftermath."

119. Ibid.

120. Burke, *A Grammar*, 121–70.

121. Waymer and Heath report that government officials named the hurricane "an act of God" to minimize their liability. See Damion Waymer and Robert L. Heath, "Emergent Agents:

The Forgotten Publics in Crisis Communication and Issues Management Research," *Journal of Applied Communication Research* 35 (2007): 88–108.

122. Duke and Wiltz, "A Nation's Castaways."

123. Rozas and Witt, "The Dreadful Toll."

124. McFadden, "Bush Pledges"; Robert D. McFadden and others, "New Orleans Begins a Search for Its Dead," *New York Times*, September, 5, 2005, A1.

125. McFadden, "New Orleans Begins." Bob Dart, "Braced for an 'Ugly Scene,'" *Atlanta Journal-Constitution*, September 5, 2005, A 1.

126. The rescue workers included: generic rescue workers, hospital helicopter rescue workers, hospital rescue boat workers, medical workers, local police officers, firefighters, FEMA workers, evacuation bus drivers, and ambulance and supply vehicle drivers.

127. Brian MacQuarrie, "LA Governor Calls for More Troops as Violence Rises in New Orleans; Rescue Work Hampered; Flood Abating," *Boston Globe*, September 2, 2005, A1. See also Scott Allen, "Specialists Warn of Health Disaster," *Boston Globe*, September 2, 2005, A1. Steve Sternberg, "For City's Historic Hospital, Help Is Needed 'in a Hurry'; Charity Fights for Survival," *USA TODAY*, September 2, 2005, A1.

128. Coates and Eggen, "A City of Despair." See also Peter Slevin, "Obstacles on the Way to Drier Ground," *Washington Post*, September, 1, 2005, A1.

129. McFadden, "Bush Pledges"; Kevin Cullen, "Chief Defends Officers' Efforts," *Boston Globe*, September 6, 2005, p. A11.

130. Dart, "Braced"; Peter Slevin and Peter Whoriskey, "New Orleans Steps up Evacuations; As Rescues Continue, HHS Chief Warns of High Death Toll," *Washington Post*, September 5, 2005, A1. The Danziger Bridge incident involves police officers who shot six civilians, killing two of them. Five former officers have pleaded guilty to federal charges in connection with the Danziger case. See "Law & Disorder," *Frontline*.Television program. Produced and Directed by Thomas Jennings. Written by Thomas Jennings and Seth Bomse. Boston: WGBH, August 25, 2010.

131. Peter Grier and Patrik Jonsson, "US Disaster with Few Rivals: Katrina Displaced at least 500,000 and Cut Power to 2.3 Million," *Christian Science Monitor* September 2, 2005, 1.

132. Coates and Eggen, "A City of Despair."

133. Gold, Zucchino, and Braun, "Hundreds Refuse to Evacuate."

134. Gold, Zarembo, and Braun, "Katrina's Aftermath."

135. Ellen Barry, "In Katrina's Aftermath: Chaos and Survival; A Rescue Team Reaches Only Despair," *Los Angeles Times*, September 2, 2005, A23.

136. "The Great Flood of '05," Editorial, *Washington Post*, September 1, 2005, A28.

137. Madigan, "Bearing Witness," 2005, 2.1.

138. Gold, Zarembo, and Braun, "Katrina's Aftermath."

139. Ibid.

140. Ibid.

141. Ibid.

142. Ibid.

143. McFadden, "Bush Pledges."

144. Many of the media stories featuring dangerous black looters, criminals, and rapists cited reports by public officials and law enforcement officers, many of whom were black (e.g., Compass, Nagin, and Holden).

145. Laura Maggi and Brendan McCarty, "Judge in Danziger cases sickened by 'raw brutality of the shooting and the craven lawlessness of the coverup,'" *Times-Picayune* [National Web Edition], April 7, 2010. http://www.nola.com.

146. Aaron David Gresson III, *Racial Pain, Recovery Rhetoric, and the Pedagogy of Healing* (New York: Peter Lang, 2004).

147. Susan Faludi, *The Terror Dream: Myth and Misogyny in an Insecure America* (New York: Picador, 2007), 379.

148. Ibid., 387.

149. Carol A. Stabile, *White Victims, Black Villains: Gender, Race, and Crime News in U.S. Culture* (New York: Routledge, 2006), 184.

150. Lacy, "White Innocence Heroes."

2 Tales of Tragedy

Strategic Rhetoric in News Coverage of the Columbine and Virginia Tech Massacres

Cynthia Willis-Chun

School shootings have become an all-too-familiar part of the U.S. mediascape. The news breaks slowly at first, with tense reports of violence on campus and assurances that more information will be forthcoming. As details emerge, the number of victims is released, the perpetrators are identified, and media then grapple with the complex task of making sense of what seem to be senseless acts of violence. The discourse that follows such incidents is also fairly predictable: age-old debates around gun control are revived, concerns about young men in crisis are aired, and questions about prevention, mental health, and media influence come to the fore. Such was the case with both of the shootings I consider in this chapter: the 1999 Columbine High School and 2007 Virginia Tech massacres. Both set records for the number of people killed, with Virginia Tech's total of 33 victims (including the shooter, Cho, himself) displacing Columbine's earlier 15 (also including the gunmen) to become first on the list.

The exact number of school shootings that have occurred in the United States is not available, as statistics regarding violence on campuses do not differentiate gun violence from other forms of homicide. The *Indicators of School Crime and Safety* report, produced by the U.S. Department of Education and U.S. Department of Justice, notes that during the 2007–2008 school year alone, there were 43 "school-associated violent deaths," a number that included "homicide, suicide, legal intervention (involving a law enforcement officer) or unintentional firearm-related death in which the fatal injury occurred on the campus of a functioning elementary or secondary school in the United States" or while the victim was on the way to or from school or a school activity.[1] Statistics gathered from the 1992–1993 school year through the 2007–2008 school year indicate that there were a total of 742 school-associated violent deaths, including 396 homicides of youths ages 5–18.[2] Data about post-secondary schools indicate that, between 1997 and 2007, a total of 238 homicides occurred on college campuses,[3] though again there's no indication as to how many of these deaths are the result of gun violence or the kind of large-scale aggression that the media tend to associate with the term "school shooting."

Though more than a decade has passed, the killings at Columbine High School have become "the paradigmatic model for such stories," referenced by other school shooters and used as a kind of benchmark by the media.[4] The Columbine shootings were shocking both for their brutality and for their chilling premeditation. Diaries found in Dylan Klebold and Eric Harris's bedrooms revealed that they had been planning the assault for a year and that the pair had done reconnaissance to determine what time of day the cafeteria would be the most crowded with students.[5] Eight years later, Klebold and Harris's legacy took center stage again, as Cho Seung-Hui, a 23-year-old English major, gunned down 32 people on the Virginia Tech campus before taking his own life.[6] Cho had legally purchased two handguns prior to the attacks, the first from an online site at the beginning of February and the second in mid-March from a Virginia gun shop.[7] Although Cho's planning was not as extensive as Klebold and Harris's, his calculated decision to leave campus after killing his first victim so that he could mail a package of his writings and digitally recorded monologues to NBC suggests that he had given some forethought to his actions.[8]

In many ways the media portrayed the killers similarly, as troubled loners bent on destroying the individuals who contributed to their alienation.[9] Despite these parallels, however, there are significant differences between the shootings, in particular the fact that, whereas Columbine's Klebold and Harris were both white, U.S. citizens, and middle class, Cho was a permanent resident of the United States, having moved as a child from South Korea in hopes of finding greater economic opportunity in the States, though his family's economic situation remained modest. In this chapter, I examine newspaper portrayals of Cho, Klebold, and Harris as a means of determining how press accounts make sense of the young men and their actions and, in particular, how the media navigate the problematic of these "outsiders within" whose rebellion resulted in tragedy.[10] Considering these two instances of school shooting in conjunction is appropriate not only because of Cho's professed admiration for Klebold and Harris, but also because it provides a means for determining how the presumed sameness of school shooters prevailed in both cases, despite differences in their settings, race/ethnicity, and nationality, and because it helps us understand how each case required careful negotiation by the press in order to preserve the innocence of the dominant culture. In this chapter, I argue that race/ethnicity, class, gender, sexuality, and nationality function strategically within the press's rhetoric about the school shootings, situating the killers as aberrant outsiders and allowing the public to distance itself from them. I conclude with the contention that more consideration should be given to the killers' tactical rhetorics, as their self-representation offers a unique opportunity for scholars to understand how the men viewed themselves within systems of power rendered visible through their bloodshed.

Media Discourses and Sense Making: Strategic Rhetoric and Intersectionality in Press Accounts

Although it is tempting to dismiss media descriptions of criminality as necessary, invariable, and even inconsequential, doing so ignores the strategic dimensions of such rhetoric. The press does more than report the news; it shapes the public's understanding of events by drawing upon (and contributing to) common cultural values.[11] Thus, we can understand descriptions of school shooters and explanations of their actions as working within dominant discourses. By marking various aspects of the identities of Klebold, Harris, and Cho (such as their gender, race/ethnicity, nationality, class, and sexuality), the press situates them in relationship to dominant society, ultimately positioning them as deviant monsters. Because these men were cast as inadequate with regard to multiple aspects of their identities, I argue that they can be fruitfully read through the concept of intersectionality. As Kimberle Crenshaw explains, intersectionality "argues that racial and sexual subordination are mutually reinforcing."[12] Following Crenshaw's early work with the concept, intersectionality has been expanded to include any number of subjectivities that make up an individual's identity, including sexuality, class, and citizenship. Patricia Hill Collins notes, "Intersectional paradigms remind us that oppression cannot be reduced to one fundamental type, and that oppressions work together in producing injustice."[13] Using this "both/and" approach to understanding how axes of domination come together allows rhetorical scholars to make sense of the complexities of discourse, which regularly engages with multiple aspects of identity simultaneously. In the case of the Columbine and Virginia Tech killers, I consider how descriptions of Klebold, Harris, and Cho explain their crimes in terms of different facets of their identities, and what that reveals about the media's attempts to create or negate distance and difference among the gunmen, their victims, and the public.

In this study of media coverage, the press's management of the Columbine and Virginia Tech killers reveals discursive moves that distance the killers from readers and society at large. Such moves, defined as strategic rhetoric by Thomas Nakayama and Robert Krizek, are employed by members of dominant groups such that they reinforce and defend hegemonic power relations.[14] These rhetorics emanate from and reify dominant social structures, contributing to the naturalization of power. Understanding rhetoric as strategic is transformative, in that this perspective allows rhetoric to be denaturalized, as race, ethnicity, gender, sexuality, class, and the like are acknowledged as social constructions and are therefore open to redefinition and dehierarchization.

My study of the shootings focuses on mainstream U.S. newspaper and wire coverage. Although an examination of alternative and international press accounts would certainly be revealing, such an approach would likely offer a rather different perspective on the killers. My goal is to identify the mainstream representation of these cases. To that end, I examined a week's worth of coverage from each event in order to gain a sense of the killers' portrayals, beginning with articles that had little to no detail about the perpetrators and by the end of the week included the perspectives of their families. I used broad search terms ("Columbine" and "Virginia Tech," respectively) in the LexisNexis database, an approach which yielded a total of 13,083 articles (4,859 on Columbine and 8,224 on Virginia Tech). Although these search terms were necessarily over-broad, they allowed for a comprehensive sense of the coverage that more focused searches might lack.

Once gathered, I first discarded irrelevant and duplicate articles, and then analyzed the resulting 414 articles' portrayals of the killers.[15] Rather than establishing specific analytical categories and attempting to impose them upon the articles, I instead worked inductively to draw recurring themes from the news coverage as well as comparisons between the two incidents. Of particular interest were descriptions of the killers and their motivations for the violence, especially when tied to identity categories such as race/ethnicity, nationality, sexuality, gender, and class.

The Scene of the Crimes: Setting and Class as Controlling Factors

In his epic poem *The Waste Land*, T. S. Eliot wrote that "April is the cruelest month," and both the Columbine and Virginia Tech tragedies bear that out.[16] Klebold and Harris opened fire on their classmates on April 20, 1999—only a few weeks before graduation and just two days after attending Columbine High's senior prom. Cho's strike took place just four days short of the Columbine massacre's eighth anniversary on April 16, 2007.

In both the Virginia Tech and Columbine massacres, a refrain that echoed from those at the scene and those writing about the shootings was "It can't happen here."[17] While this sentiment is understandable in that many Americans rarely see themselves as potential targets of violence, when paired with descriptions of the shootings' settings the meaning becomes more fraught. In regard to Columbine, several news reports noted that the violence was particularly out of place given the setting—a middle-class suburban high school. The class status of the killers themselves was discussed at length, with several papers reporting the cost of Klebold's and Harris's houses ($328,000 and $184,000 respectively).[18] Implicit here is the idea that while violence is imaginable and even expected in urban areas, violence is nearly inconceivable in the suburbs and from suburban kids. Mia Consalvo argues that, in stories about Columbine, "The discussion of race (or its non-discussion) was … submerged within a classist argument—the belief that violence can be escaped through white flight to the suburbs."[19] An editorial in the *San Jose Mercury News* notes, "People have become accustomed to, even hardened to, violence in urban schools. It's dismissed as a product of drugs and gangs."[20] In this quotation and others like it, "urban" functions as a code for racialized and financially unstable, suggesting that the violence at Columbine High was all the more shocking because it defied American assumptions about both whiteness and middle class-ness. Furthermore, descriptions of Columbine High as a "normal" school naturalize not just the physical space itself as free from violence,[21] but the whiteness and middle class-ness as well. Such a move strategically overlooks the symbolic and material violence inherent in racial and class privilege, suggesting that it is abnormal in this setting, and by implication, in other settings.

Coverage of the Virginia Tech shootings included similar sentiments about the unlikelihood of such violence, but the reasons for this were somewhat different. Whereas much of the outrage about the Columbine killings had to do with the incongruity of mass murder in a comfortable suburban setting, much of the discourse around the Virginia Tech shootings revealed upset over the breach of the supposedly inviolable ivory tower of academia. An editorial in the *Charlotte Observer* laments, "You could not imagine it anywhere. But especially not here, among these gorgeous stone buildings, across the flat green lawn of the Drillfield in the middle of campus."[22] Similarly, an article in the New York *Daily News* noted that school shootings are "cruelest for their innocent settings,"[23] and an editorial called the Virginia Tech campus "idyllic."[24] Such descriptions position college campuses as sacrosanct, removed from the real world of (race and class) conflict and therefore as particularly shocking sites of violence. In their work on the Columbine shootings, Audrey Kobayashi and Linda Peake found that "One theme that emerges from the commentary over the events is a sense that the shootings were an extremist act, completely out of the ordinary run of events, an *aberration*."[25] Despite the fact that Cho's grades and test scores won him admission to Virginia Tech, his presence there was called into question through the implicit comparison of the tranquil setting and his disruptive actions, as well as through more overt interviews with students and professors, one of whom stated that she was willing to resign rather than have him in class. She proclaimed, "I've taught troubled youngsters. I've taught crazy people. It was the meanness that bothered me."[26] The theme of deviance pervades the Virginia Tech coverage, positioning Cho as a contaminating force within the edenic surroundings of the classroom (so much so that he was tutored one-on-one in creative writing instead of attending class) and the campus more broadly.[27]

Young (Heterosexual) Men in Crisis: Masculinity and Sexuality in Columbine and Virginia Tech

The theme of young men in crisis is one that commonly emerges in coverage of school shootings, and it certainly arose following these attacks. In the wake of the Columbine killings, an editorial notes that "all of the perpetrators have been boys,"[28] and an article in the Newark *Star-Ledger* describes Klebold and Harris as having "evolved from typical high school outsiders into angry young men desperate for revenge."[29] Following the Virginia Tech shooting, an editorial in the *Pittsburgh Post-Gazette* reminded its readers that "95 percent of all mass murderers are men."[30] Another editorial in Florida's *Bradenton Herald* reminds readers that "Colleges, high schools, middle schools, even an Amish one-room school with elementary-age students—all have been settings for angry males settling grievances with guns."[31] The reasons for this malaise are much debated, with some reports indicating that the advances of young women have disempowered their male counterparts,[32] while others blame a world that offers instant gratification as a means of problem solving,[33] and still others contend that men simply are not taught how to manage their emotions productively.[34] While statements such as these reflect the reality that most (though not all) school shooters have been men, they also pathologize masculinity by suggesting that it necessarily begets violence. Although news reports bemoaning a (seemingly ever-present) crisis of masculinity stop just short of excusing male perpetrators for their crimes, they nevertheless assist in naturalizing masculine violence.

Along with expressing concern about the waning of hegemonic masculinity, some press reports indicate that failed or deviant sexuality may have contributed to the killers' aberrant behavior. As the media intensified their investigation into the Trenchcoat Mafia and the bullying that Klebold and Harris endured from their peers, reports surfaced that the gunmen were "taunted and chastised" for being gay, presumably because of their close relationship.[35] Although Klebold's prom date vehemently denied he was gay, such allegations nevertheless call the pair's sexuality into question, suggesting that their failure or inability to comply with dominant standards of heterosexism led to censure from their peers and may have at least partly inspired their attack.

Similarly, an article in the *Boston Herald* suggests that the deaths of 32 people may have been due simply to Cho's jealousy over a "relationship gone bad."[36] This explanation implies not only that Cho was incapable of sustaining a relationship with a member of the opposite sex, but that he was so enraged because of it that he lost (masculine) control over his emotions and lashed out with spectacular violence. Also at play in Cho's portrayal was the notion of the "yellow peril," a term that articulates the sexual drive of Asian and Asian American men to their foreignness.[37] Much was made of the fact that Cho's first victims were a young woman student and her resident advisor, whose deaths were labeled a "domestic incident" by the press and the university. Interviews with Cho's suitemates verified his awkwardness with women, as they recalled that Cho claimed to have "an imaginary girlfriend" named Jelly who was a supermodel and "traveled through space."[38] Stories of this kind situated Cho within stereotypes about Asian American masculinity, which is often cast as "passive, impotent, and simultaneously lascivious," such that "heteromasculinity is not so much a failure as unavailable or a lack."[39] Thus, Cho's thwarted sexuality was understood as leading to violence, an unfortunate but not unexpected result of his ethnicity.

The media suggest that the killings at both Columbine and Virginia Tech were a result of the failed masculinity and sexuality of the gunmen, as it contributed to their status as outsiders, providing grounds for mocking from their peers and an explanation for their violence. Although this notion may have some merit, it nevertheless ought to give readers pause, as such discourse functions to cast attention onto *deviant* sexuality and gendering rather than considering the possibility that such violence could be related to the *normative* demands of heterosexuality and masculinity. This brand of strategic rhetoric thus allows readers to avoid self or societal critique, as they are reassured that the problem lies not with the dominant culture, but with those who fail to comply with it.

Good Boys Gone Wrong: White American Rebellion at Columbine

Although press accounts of the Columbine killers did not explicitly question their nationality, their participation in the "Trenchcoat Mafia"—a neo-Nazi organization that openly expressed its disgust for athletes, African Americans, and Hispanics[40]—allowed the press implicitly to challenge the men's Americanness. Much was made of the fact that the shootings were planned for April 20, 1999, a date presumably chosen to coincide with what would have been Hitler's 110th birthday.[41] Klebold and Harris were marked as doubly deviant: incapable of assimilating into conventional high school cliques and fascinated not with trends or prom dates but with Hitler.[42] Todd Ramlow explains that the killers' veneration of Hitler "was the most common motif establishing their disavowal of American normality. This characterization was (and continues to be) the most difficult to resist, since Nazi Germany has been cast as the antithesis of everything America presumably stands for."[43] In this sense, the Columbine killers occupy a liminal state: simultaneously all-American boys gone wrong and un-American miscreants bent on destruction. This liminality should not be dismissed, however, as an inherent by-product of their rampage or social scene. As Kristen Hoerl notes in her study of the Columbine killings and suburbia, "the shooters created an ideological as well as a physical threat to the hierarchical social order."[44] In this sense, the press's construction of the killers' deviance can be read as an attempt to contain the ideological danger they posed.

Confounding the press still further was the discovery a few days after the killings that Klebold's mother was Jewish and his family at least somewhat observant, as the young man was reported to have griped about participating in Passover seders.[45] Unable to account for this incongruity in Klebold's behavior, the press did little more than lament how difficult it must have been for the killer's parents to cope with this facet of his life. Although casting Klebold as white may be reflective of the American acceptance of Jewishness as "almost white,"[46] I contend that to note Klebold's ethnicity and then cast it aside is meaningful, creating a present absence around the killer, who became just another angry kid in suburbia—a space inherently associated with whiteness,[47] and allowing the scene to subsume the agent. The elision of this aspect of Klebold's identity resulted in a rejection of his Jewishness in favor of whiteness, so much so that Klebold was not—and still has not been—considered an exception among the other young white men who are the most common perpetrators of school shootings.

While the parallels between the Virginia Tech and Columbine massacres are many, the shooters' choice of victims is a major point of divergence. For the most part, Cho is thought to have killed indiscriminately, choosing only his first target and killing the others based on their location rather than their identities.[48] In contrast, witnesses claimed that Klebold and Harris specifically targeted jocks and minorities in their rampage. However, instead of considering the racial ramifications of this revelation, the press focused on the killers as disenfranchised teens retaliating against the athletes who persecuted them.[49] The public was repeatedly and overtly assured by both the press and official investigators that the Columbine shootings were not racially motivated. Out of the 13 individuals killed, only one was African American, a statistic that District Attorney Dave Thomas invoked when denying that the killers targeted minorities, despite the claims of student eyewitnesses.[50] However, when one considers that Columbine High's student body of 2,000 included only approximately two dozen African Americans, the death of a single one is striking,[51] as are eyewitness statements regarding the shooters' distaste for African Americans and their delight at seeing a "black kid's brain."[52]

Despite evidence that the shootings were, in fact, at least partly about race, many publications contributed to the whitewashing of this violence, such as the *Philadelphia Inquirer*, which ran a headline proclaiming, "Victims Were Cross-Section of School's Student Body."[53] Similarly, an Associated Press piece bore the title "Families Mourn Innocent Victims Caught in Wrong Place at Wrong Time," even as the story's lead contradicted the coincidental nature of the attacks: "Isaiah Shoels was shot in the head because he was *the wrong color* and in the wrong place at the wrong time."[54] The repetition of happenstance in both titles and the lead allows it to overshadow the brief acknowledgment of race as a factor in the killings, and permits journalists and the public to avoid a complicated discussion of the racial history of public schools, Littleton, or the United States more generally, and to instead "suggest that the boys' deviancy was to blame for their racism."[55] Though contradictory, the press's dismissal of the killers' supposed racist motivations and its simultaneous suggestion that Klebold and Harris were white supremacists is hardly surprising. As Audrey Kobayashi and Linda Peake explain, "For most people, including those reporting on the Columbine massacre, racism is naturalized out of existence, and therefore it evades definition in most normative analyses, including those of the popular press. They literally cannot see it."[56] To probe further into the racial motivation of the killings might force a consideration of whiteness, bringing to light a construct that fights to remain unnoticed. Thus, the violence wrought by whiteness hid in plain sight, as the press invoked its own brand of white privilege in sidestepping the issue. In so doing, the press reified the (white/dominant) public's tendency to do likewise, allowing issues of race to remain unexamined and the victims to be rendered fungible.

Cho as Cipher: Confounding Asian/Americanness and Virginia Tech

Whereas whiteness and Americanness were central components in the construction of the Columbine killers, Cho Seung-Hui was immediately marked because of his conflicted nationality and shortcomings as a "model minority." Cho's legal status in the United States—permanent resident alien—became a common refrain, functioning simultaneously as a description of the man and an explanation of his rage. The continual questioning of Cho's nationality by the mainstream media—which marked him as Asian and Korean rather than American—situated him as always-already other.[57] Interviews confirmed this othering, as classmates reported that Cho faced taunts from other students including "Get out of this country," epithets such as "chink or Chinatown,"[58] and was told to "go back to China" after a teacher forced him to read aloud in class.[59] Min Hyoung Song notes that the nationality of Korean Americans seems to remain "patently suspect" despite their naturalization, an argument that resonates with coverage of Cho.[60] His status as an "alien" is pregnant with meaning: Cho was cast as an alien by the press, was alienated from his peers in class, and—perhaps most damning—maintained his legal alien status through his decision not to pursue U.S. citizenship.[61] The importance of this final aspect of his alienation should not be downplayed; his refusal to become a citizen, despite the fact that he qualified for naturalization, can be read as an intentional rejection of the United States and of Americanness as part of his identity. Thus, whereas Klebold and Harris were seen as threats to the mythic American Dream,[62] Cho stands outside it. That someone would choose to live in the United States and yet remain estranged from its citizenry fits easily into the mediated vision of Cho as a mumbling outcast, a cipher whose death guaranteed his literal and symbolic incomprehensibility.

This characterization of Cho stands in contrast to the rest of his family, who were portrayed as "model minorities," with his parents' success in the workplace paving the way for his sister's achievement in college. The "model minority myth" is paradoxical in its affirmation of color-neutral ideology, which suggests that Asian Americans presumably succeed because of their self-sacrifice, hard work, and education, and the concomitant assumption that at least some of these predilections are derived from Asian cultural values.[63] In Cho's case, reports of his struggles in the classroom were offered as evidence of his deviance,[64] leaving readers to wonder how he gained admission to Virginia Tech. Cho's aberrant Asianness is made particularly evident in an article that compares the killer to one of his victims, Henry Lee, whose family fled from communist China to Vietnam and then to the United States. In contrast to reports of Cho as introverted and awkward, Lee is described as well liked among his U.S. teachers, classmates, and co-workers, so much so that his family nicknamed him "White Boy" and questioned why he had no Asian friends.[65] Pensri Ho explains that the model minority myth functions hegemonically "at the expense of Asian Americans, whose celebrated efforts and achievements will never enable them to achieve 'Whiteness' because they can never truly shed their 'Non-Whiteness.'"[66] Lee and Cho's parallel trajectories make this balancing act clear, in that the former is praised for his assimilation into whiteness, whereas the latter is castigated for his failure to be adequate in either Asianness or Americanness. In this sense, Cho not only failed in regard to his citizenship; he also failed in his ethnicity, becoming an outsider within his own family, his classes, and the nation.

Technology and the Discursivity of Identity

Although school shootings have captivated the national consciousness at least since Charles Whitman killed 14 and wounded 31 from his perch on the University of Texas Tower in 1966, new technology has changed the stakes considerably for both the press and the perpetrators. In the case of the 1999 shootings at Columbine High School—dubbed "the nation's first interactive siege" by CNN's Judy Woodruff—news outlets were chastised for encouraging students trapped in the building to use their cell phones to call in and for airing live coverage that could have revealed the location of students hiding from the shooters.[67] In the case of the 2007 shootings at Virginia Tech, a student used his cell phone to capture video of gunfire exchanged between police and the killer and became so wrapped up in his role as "citizen journalist" that he ran toward the shots rather than away from them.[68]

Beyond victims' and bystanders' use of technology to get information or report on events, over the past decade the perpetrators have also taken advantage of the Internet and video recording to obtain information on incendiary devices, to purchase supplies, and to create web pages, online profiles, and videos that hint at, explain, and even celebrate their acts. In Cho Seung-Hui's case, a man who was described as silent and even ghostlike gained a voice through the multimedia materials he sent to NBC, dominating news broadcasts with his vitriol.[69] Rather than remaining ciphers whose motivations and plans were mysterious, the Virginia Tech and (to a lesser degree) Columbine killers in fact assisted in establishing the lenses through which their actions would be viewed. This use of videos and web pages is of particular interest to rhetorical scholars, because they constitute what Aristotle would call atechnic or inartistic proof, proof that the rhetor does not invent, but that exists prior to the process of discourse creation.[70] In the case of school shootings, documentation left by the killers complicates media attempts at sense making, as the narratives constructed by the press must incorporate these texts into their coverage while maintaining appropriate distance from the killers.

Self-mediation on the part of the killers constitutes a form of tactical rhetoric, shaping and potentially countering press discourse.[71] These materials function as postmortem interviews when shooters commit suicide or are killed by police. The absence of the killers themselves lends greater weight to self-made productions that reveal their plans and motivations and contribute to the shooters' depiction within the media. Press accounts quote liberally from these materials, teasing out as much meaning as possible from them, and in some cases using them to make sense—or underscore the senselessness—of violence. The advent of easily accessed digital technologies complicates traditional understandings of producer/consumer power relations. Power dynamics are not simply reversed through the participation of the public in media production, however. While Klebold, Harris, and Cho all contributed to their own portrayals through their use of technology, the media ultimately framed and contained the gunmen's depictions. For example, for a brief period individuals were able to visit Klebold and Harris's personal websites and examine their profiles, thereby gaining a sense of how the killers envisioned themselves and their role in the shootings at Columbine. However, AOL's control over these sites limited the opportunity for the public to access this tactical rhetoric, as the sites were taken down by the company following the shootings.[72] Although mirror sites were created that displayed the material elsewhere on the web, those sites were also shut down once they were discovered.[73] Along similar lines, parts of Cho's monologues were distributed (first by NBC and later via a number of media outlets), but the commentary that accompanied their airing no doubt modified and perhaps even undercut his message, allowing viewers to peer into the mind of a murderer while still containing him. This ability for Cho to speak from the grave is nevertheless significant, as changing systems of distribution and production shift both the stakes and the possibilities of identity formation through digital discursivity.

One avenue for further research into these tragedies is what Cho, Klebold, and Harris's self-produced rhetoric contends about their crimes. The gunmen's discourse offers at least some sense of what drove them to kill, and in both cases this information was largely rejected by the mainstream media, which categorized the productions as "rants," "diatribes," and "lunacy."[74] While scholars must take care not to glorify violence and its trappings, simply dismissing such rhetoric is a missed opportunity. On one hand, these materials might be understood as jeremiads, apocalyptic demands for repentance lest viewers meet a fateful end, delivered too late for those killed, but imbued with warnings about the social structures that prompt violence. On the other, they may offer insight into the killers' own understanding of their place within systems of power.[75] Overlooking the rhetoric of these killers and its handling by the press is dangerous, as it enables the public to see itself as apart from the gunmen, rather than as necessarily implicated in the social structures that made such violence possible.

Implications

A comparative view of press accounts about Klebold, Harris, and Cho makes clear that these killers are not simply portrayed as individuals gone awry. Rather, these killers are necessarily entangled in a web of identity categories that the media reference to explain their reasons for committing violent acts. Far from justifying the gunmen's criminality, such accounts distance readers—and the press itself—from them, focusing on the aberrant nature of these men, rather than on systemic ills that might have contributed to their rampages and, in fact, still exist. This rhetorical maneuvering assures readers that they are not like the killers, relieving the public of the responsibility of interrogating intersections of power that may have contributed to their violence. Thus, readers are left secure in the knowledge that *they* are not monsters, that they did not help to create the killers, but they are also left vulnerable to further attack through their own willful ignorance abetted by the media. Coverage that focuses on deviancy from this mainstream perspective establishes the killers' otherness by marking them as capable of participating in dominant society but failing to do so. The implication of such accounts is that the killers were given every chance at participating properly in the mainstream but either would not or could not manage to do so and therefore lashed out against it.

Perhaps more intriguing is the fact that in both cases, press reports restored hierarchies that had been, at least in part, upended by the killers, and, still more compelling, returned to obscurity the intersections of power dominant in U.S. society. Foucault notes that studies of criminals have attempted "to constitute a new objectivity in which the criminal belongs to a typology that is both natural and deviant."[76] It is this understanding of criminality that explains the apparent contradictions in the portrayals of Cho, Klebold, and Harris; they were said to be attempting to destroy the very systems in which they so desired to partake. Both Klebold and Cho were cast simultaneously as ethnic others (Jewish and Korean, respectively) and as Americans, but media discourses suggest that it was their failure to succeed at either that turned them into killers. Similarly, Klebold, Harris, and Cho were described as loners and as would-be paramours, and press accounts suggest that it was their inability to secure heterosexual relationships that pushed them to murder. Dismissing such contradictions as poor logic or media sensationalism misses the point of what we might learn from the portrayals of these men: they were caught in interlocking webs of power, incapable of fulfilling any and all of the demands that their identities placed upon them. An examination of these killers does not simply suggest the power of the press to create public understandings of deviance, but also makes evident the material consequences of intersectionality for both bystanders and those caught in its web.

Finally, where Klebold, Harris, and Cho demanded and won momentary control over their portrayals through the use of violence and their production of identity in the form of multimedia documents found after their deaths, the media did likewise via their rhetorical constructions. In this manner, the press avoided a critique of the social world that created and empowered these individuals, instead opting to maintain the status quo through a valorization of the victims and an attendant marginalizing of the killers from the mainstream. This is perhaps the most chilling implication of this study, in that this tendency on the part of the media allows power structures to continue unexamined, subsuming even vernacular attempts at thwarting them. In this sense, the question remains as to how many times this chilling script of deviance, violence, and containment has to be repeated before consideration is shifted from the killers as problems in themselves to the killers as symptomatic of pervasive social ills.

NOTES

The author would like to express her gratitude toward Daniela Baroffio-Bota, Ph.D., whose input was essential in the formative and draft stages of this chapter, and to Jade S. Anthony, MPA, in the U.S. Department of Education's Office of Safe and Drug-Free Schools, for her invaluable assistance in compiling the data on school violence.

1. National Center for Education Statistics, "Indicators of School Crime and Safety: 2007," http://nces.ed.gov/programs/crimeindicators/crimeindicators2007/tables/table_01_2.asp?referrer=report: 80.

2. Along with these homicides, there were also 92 suicides of youths ages 5–18. The remaining 254 school-associated violent deaths may include individuals falling outside this age range and/or individuals who died of causes other than homicide or suicide. National Center for Education Statistics, 80. See also U.S. Department of Education, "Criminal Offenses: Murder/Non-negligent Manslaughter," http://www.ed.gov/admins/lead/safety/crime/criminaloffenses/edlite-murder.html; U.S. Department of Education and U.S. Department of Justice Office of Justice Programs. "Indicators of School Crime and Safety, 2009." Washington, DC: GPO, 2009. http://www.securityoncampus.org/images/pdf/doe2001.pdf; U.S. Department of Education Office of Postsecondary Education, "The Incidence of Crime on the Campuses of U.S. Postsecondary Education Institutions: A Report to Congress." Washington, DC: GPO, 2001. http://www.securityoncampus.org/images/pdf/doe2001.pdf.

3. Security on Campus, Inc., "College & University Campus Crime Statistics," http://www.securityoncampus.org/images/pdf/99/co_murder.pdf; Security on Campus, Inc., "College & University Campus Crime Statistics, 1998–2000," http://www.securityoncampus.org/images/pdf/98/1998_2000.pdf.

4. Amy Brandzel and Jigna Desai, "Race, Violence, and Terror: The Cultural Defensibility of Heteromasculine Citizenship in the Virginia Tech Massacre and the Don Imus Affair," *Journal of Asian American Studies* 11, no. 1 (2008): 67.

5. John Hendren, "Detailed Diary Discloses Plans, Motives of Gunmen in Massacre," Associated Press, April 24, 1999, AM cycle, http://www.lexis-nexis.com/.

6. Cho's parents indicated that the family adopted the western convention of listing the surname last. Allen G. Breed and Aaron Beard, "AP Exclusive: Cho Family is 'Hopeless,'" Associated Press Online, April 20, 2007, http://www.lexis-nexis.com/. However, some news reports state that Cho preferred the Korean standard of placing the surname first. David Cho and Amy Gardner, "An Isolated Boy in a World of Strangers: Cho's Behavior Alarmed Some Who Knew Him; Family Humbled by 'This Darkness,'" *Washington Post*, April 21, 2007, Met. 2 edition, http://www.lexis-nexis.com/. I have opted to abide by Cho's inclination, though I acknowledge that this decision may be contentious.

7. Raja Mishra and Marcella Bombardieri, "Closer Look Reveals Cho's Isolation: Hard Working Student Let Few Inside His World," *Boston Globe*, April 22, 2007, http://www.lexis-nexis.com/.

8. *Boston Globe*, "Something Wrong, Nothing Done," April 20, 2007, http://www.lexis-nexis.com/; Dave Goldiner, "If Only We Could See 'Our' Tapes, Say Littleton Kin," *Daily News* (New York), April 20, 2007, city final edition, http://www.lexis-nexis.com/.

9. Jules Crittenden, "High School Horror: Reign of Terror Inside Colo. High School," *Boston Herald*, April 21, 1999, third edition, http://www.lexis-nexis.com/; Neva Chonin, "Permanent Resident, Alienated," *San Francisco Chronicle*, April 22, 2007, final edition, http://www.lexis-nexis.com/.

10. I will use the term "men" throughout, though Klebold and Harris were 17 and therefore legally minors.

11. Carolyn Kitch, "Twentieth-Century Tales: Newsmagazines and American Memory," *Journalism and Communication Monographs* 1, no. 2 (1999).

12. Kimberle Crenshaw, "Mapping the Margins: Intersectionality, Identity Politics, and Violence Against Women of Color," *Stanford Law Review* 43, no. 6 (1991): 1283.

13. Patricia Hill Collins, *Black Feminist Thought: Knowledge, Consciousness, and the Politics of Empowerment* (New York: Routledge, 2000), 18.

14. Thomas K. Nakayama and Robert L. Krizek, "Whiteness: A Strategic Rhetoric," *Quarterly Journal of Speech* 81, no. 3 (1995): 291–309.

15. Examples of "irrelevant" articles include announcements regarding the cancellation of various sporting events following the Columbine killings. Many of the duplicate articles were drawn from wire reports.

16. T. S. Eliot, *The Waste Land* (New York: W.W. Norton, 1922/2000), 5.

17. See Don Aucoin and Drew Jubera, "Colorado School Massacre: Children Killing Children; Television: An 'Interactive Siege' Unfolds," *Atlanta Journal and Constitution*, April 21, 1999, home edition, http://www.lexis-nexis.com/; Jim Carney, "Portage Student Recounts Day at Virginia Tech," *Akron (OH) Beacon Journal*, April 16, 2007, http://www.lexis-nexis.com/; Rachel Sauer, "Shootings Bring Up Memories of Past School Horrors," Cox News Service, April 20, 1999, http://www.lexis-nexis.com/; Tommy Tomlinson, "Shattered by a Chilling Blow," *Charlotte Observer*, April 16, 2007, http://www.lexis-nexis.com/; Dave Wedge and Jessica Heslam, "Campus Massacre: 'No One Deserved to Die'; Police Probe for Motive as University Mourns," *Boston Herald*, April 18, 2007, http://www.lexis-nexis.com/.

18. Susan Greene and Bill Briggs, "World of Darkness: Comfortable Suburbs Harbor Troubled Teens," *Denver Post*, April 22, 1999, http://www.lexis-nexis.com/.

19. Mia Consalvo, "The Monsters Next Door: Media Constructions of Boys and Masculinity," *Feminist Media Studies* 3, no. 1 (2003): 37.

20. *San Jose Mercury News*, "Unfathomable Violence," April 21, 1999, http://www.lexis-nexis.com/.

21. Christine Evans and Douglas Kalajian, "How Can You Tell When Your Kid Is Headed for Real Trouble?" Cox News Service, April 22, 1999, http://www.lexis-nexis.com/.

22. Tomlinson, "Shattered by a Chilling Blow."

23. Jordan Lite, "Some Mass Murderers Aim to Be 'More Sensational Than the Last,'" *New York Daily News*, April 16, 2007, http://www.lexis-nexis.com/.

24. Tomlinson, "Shattered by a Chilling Blow."

25. Audrey Kobayashi and Linda Peake, "Racism Out of Place: Thoughts on Whiteness and an Antiracist Geography in the New Millennium," *Annals of the Association of American Geographers* 90, no. 2 (2000): 394.

26. *Capital* (Anapolis, MD), "Gunman Mailed Manifesto Between Attacks," April 19, 2007, http://www.lexis-nexis.com/.

27. Manny Fernandez and Marc Santora, "In Words and Silence, Hints of Anger and Isolation," *New York Times*, April 18, 2007, late edition-final, http://www.lexis-nexis.com/.

28. *Lancaster (PA) New Era*, "What Can We Do to Prevent More Horrors Like Littleton?" April 21, 1999, http://www.lexis-nexis.com/.

29. John Hassell, "Pair Were Bright But Odd, and Teasing Never Stopped," *Star Ledger* (Newark, NJ), April 22, 1999, final edition, http://www.lexis-nexis.com/.

30. James Alan Fox, "Why They Kill: Mass Shooters Tend to Be Alienated Loners with Access to High-Powered Weapons," *Pittsburgh Post-Gazette*, April 18, 2007, Sooner edition, http://www.lexis-nexis.com/.

31. *Bradenton (FL) Herald*, "Black Monday: A Senseless Massacre—and No Easy Answers," April 18, 2007, http://www.lexis-nexis.com/.

32. Ross MacKenzie, "Littleton Puts Needed Light on the Abject Condition of Our Boys," *Richmond (VA) Times Dispatch*, April 25, 1999, city edition, http://www.lexis-nexis.com/.

33. Jerry Schwartz, "Looking for Explanations for Schoolhouse Massacres," Associated Press, April 21, 1999, http://www.lexis-nexis.com/.

34. Joan Ryan, "Requiem for Lost Boys—and Their Victims," *San Francisco Chronicle*, April 21, 1999, final edition, http://www.lexis-nexis.com/.

35. Douglas Montero, "What Pushed Outcasts Over the Edge?" *New York Post*, April 26, 1999, http://www.lexis-nexis.com/.

36. Peter Gelzinis, "Campus Massacre: Random Violence Reminds Us Evil Lurks Everywhere," *Boston Herald*, April 17, 2007, http://www.lexis-nexis.com/.

37. Yuko Kawai, "Stereotyping Asian Americans: The Dialectic of the Model Minority and the Yellow Peril," *Howard Journal of Communication* 16, no. 2 (2005): 115.

38. Michael E. Ruane, "A List of 'Little Incidents': Former Roommate of Cho Recalls Odd Behavior; 'Who Does This?' He Thought," *Richmond (VA) Times Dispatch*, April 22, 2007, final edition http://www.lexis-nexis.com/.

39. Brandzel and Desai, "Race, Violence, and Terror," 72.

40. Greene and Briggs, "World of Darkness."

41. *Austin American Statesman*, "Puzzling Search for Answers," April 21, 1999, home edition, http://www.lexis-nexis.com/; Mark Kizla, "Sons of Columbine as Different as Good and Evil," *Denver Post*, April 22, 1999, http://www.lexis-nexis.com/; *Lancaster New Era*, "What Can We Do."

42. Floyd Flake, "The Road to Columbine High," *New York Post*, April 23, 1999, http://www.lexis-nexis.com/.

43. Todd Ramlow, "Bad Boys: Abstractions of Difference and the Politics of Youth 'Deviance,'" *GLQ: A Journal of Lesbian and Gay Studies* 9, no. 1–2 (2003): 120.

44. Kristen Hoerl, "Monstrous Youth in Suburbia: Disruption and Recovery of the American Dream," *Southern Communication Journal* 67, no. 3 (2002): 273.

45. Andrea Peyser, "Blaming Parents a Shameless Cop-Out," *New York Post*, April 27, 1999, http://www.lexis-nexis.com/.

46. See Michael Rogin, *Blackface, White Noise: Jewish Immigrants in the Hollywood Melting Pot* (Berkeley: University of California Press, 1998).

47. Consalvo, "Monsters Next Door"; Hoerl, "Monstrous Youth"; George Lipsitz, *The Possessive Investment in Whiteness: How White People Profit from Identity Politics* (Philadelphia: Temple University Press, 1998).

48. Mishra and Bombardieri, "Closer Look Reveals."

49. See Hoerl, "Monstrous Youth."

50. Mike Williams, "Harsh Reality Hits Shocked Littleton, Colo.," Cox News Service, April 22, 1999, http://www.lexis-nexis.com/. Michael Shoels, the father of a victim, repeatedly asserted that his son Isaiah had been killed at least partly because of his race. Several press accounts include this claim, however relatively few of the stories actually engage with this contention. Mark Davis, "Victims Were Cross-Section of School's Student Body," *Philadelphia Inquirer*, April 23, 1999, http://www.lexis-nexis.com/; Mike McPhee, "Remembering the Slain: Isaiah Shoels

Son Killed by 'Hatred,' Father Says," *Denver Post*, April 23, 1999, 2nd edition, http://www.lexis-nexis.com/.

51. Mike Williams, "Father's Agony: African-American Son Slain for Race," Cox News Service, April 22, 1999, http://www.lexis-nexis.com/.

52. Joseph B. Verrengia, "Families Mourn Innocent Victims Caught in Wrong Place at Wrong Time," Associated Press, April 21, 1999, http://www.lexis-nexis.com/.

53. Davis, "Victims Were Cross-Section."

54. Verrengia, "Families Mourn Innocent Victims"; emphasis mine.

55. Mia Consalvo, "Monsters Next Door," 37.

56. Kobayashi and Peake, "Racism Out of Place," 395.

57. Chonin, "Permanent Resident, Alienated."

58. Mishra and Bombardieri, "Closer Look Reveals."

59. Simone Weichselbaum, "He Knew Cho 8 Yrs., But Killer Never Said a Word to Him," *Philadelphia Daily News*, April 21, 2007, http://www.lexis-nexis.com/.

60. Min Hyoung Song, "Communities of Remembrance: Reflections on the Virginia Tech Shootings and Race," *Journal of Asian American Studies* 11, no. 1 (2008): 6–7.

61. Cho's family moved to the United States when he was a boy, and his sister became a citizen.

62. Hoerl, "Monstrous Youth."

63. Kawai, "Stereotyping Asian Americans," 110.

64. Cho and Gardner, "An Isolated Boy."

65. E. A. Torreiro and James Janega, "Parallel Paths of Victim, Killer," *Chicago Tribune*, April 23, 2007, http://www.lexis-nexis.com/.

66. Pensri Ho, "Performing the 'Oriental': Professionals and the Asian Model Minority Myth," *Journal of Asian American Studies* 6, no. 2 (2003): 150.

67. Quoted in Aucoin and Jubera, "Colorado School Massacre."

68. Mike Cassidy, "Cassidy: Digital Tools Were Potential Life Savers During Virginia Tech Massacre," *San Jose Mercury News*, April 16, 2007, http://www.lexis-nexis.com/.

69. Weichselbaum, "He Knew Cho."

70. Aristotle, *On Rhetoric: A Theory of Civic Discourse*, ed. George A. Kennedy (New York: Oxford University Press, 1991), 1.2.1–2.

71. The distinction between strategic and tactical rhetoric is an important one introduced by de Certeau and elaborated by Phillips. Further study of killers' rhetorical maneuvering would benefit from a consideration of this concept. Michel de Certeau, *The Practice of Everyday Life* (Berkeley: University of California Press, 1984); Kendall R. Phillips, "Rhetorical Maneuvers: Subjectivity, Power and Resistance," *Philosophy and Rhetoric* 39, no. 4 (2006).

72. Patti Hartigan, "To Stop the Violence, the Play's the Thing: Cyberlinks," *Boston Globe*, April 23, 1999, city edition, http://www.lexis-nexis.com/.

73. Klebold and Harris also created "basement tapes," which the police did not release to the media. A federal judge later sealed them from public view. Jim Spencer, "Horrifying Deeds Can Inspire Twisted Kindred," *Denver Post*, April 20, 2007, final edition, http://www.lexis-nexis.com/.

74. Howard Kurtz, "For Virginia Tech Killer's Twisted Video, Pause But No Rewind," *Washington Post*, April 23, 2007, http://www.lexis-nexis.com/; *News & Observer* (NC), "Testimony to Evil: Tapes and Writings Make Clear the Breadth and Depth of Violence within Young Cho Seung-Hui," April 20, 2007, final edition, http://www.lexis-nexis.com/; Kevin Simpson and David Blevins, "Germany Lured Harris But Pal Klebold Not as Fascinated with the Culture," *Denver Post*, April 24, 1999, 2d edition, http://www.lexis-nexis.com/; Neil Steinberg, "Media

Can't Look Away: Sharing Gunman's Rants with World Was the Right Thing to Do," *Chicago Sun Times*, April 22, 2007, final edition, http://www.lexis-nexis.com/.

75. One example of this type of rhetoric is Cho's condemnation of "rich kids" obsessed with materialism and hedonism, as quoted in one of his self-produced videos that suggests he was aware and resentful of his contingent social status. *Capital*, "Gunman Mailed Manifesto."

76. Michel Foucault, *Discipline and Punish: The Birth of the Prison*, trans. Alan Sheridan (New York: Random House, 1977/1995), 259.

3 N-word vs. F-word, Black vs. Gay

Uncovering *Pendejo* Games to Recover Intersections

Catherine R. Squireso

A continuing concern for scholars is whether dominant news media provide adequate frameworks to understand marginalized groups' lived experiences and political interests. Dominant news frames typically reduce marginalized groups' political interests to a zero-sum game, often pitting groups against each other.[1] For example, following the 2008 passage of California Proposition 8 (an anti–gay marriage ballot initiative), mainstream media headlines declared that Blacks and gays[2] were at war. Some exit polls showed that 70 percent of Black voters backed the ballot measure.[3] Further investigations debunked these reports,[4] but the initial news reports framed marginalized groups in antagonistic terms, obscuring the intersections among racial, ethnic, gender, and sexual identities. To make sense of this media practice, Stuart Hall contends that news frames articulate relationships between racial and sexual groups, while privileging particular understandings of social identity and political interests. The newspaper headlines about Prop 8 obscured intersections between black and gay identities, erasing Black gays and lesbians from view.

This chapter examines the media framing of divergent black and gay identities in media stories alleging that Black actor Isaiah Washington called his white co-star (T. R. Knight) a faggot. In doing so, the media framed Black and gay communities as distinctive, essentially *de-intersecting* Black and gay identities. Moreover, media discourse encouraged audiences to rank black and gay epithets, while condemning African Americans as hypocrites for using them. The narrow focus on Washington's hateful speech act and framing Washington as representative of all blacks obscured the role institutional power and dominant social hierarchies play in reinforcing discriminatory policies and practices.

My media analysis is inspired in part by Hasian and Delgado's theory, which integrates critical rhetorical studies and critical race theory to "assess the ways in which public . . . notions of race influence the ways in which we create histories, cultural memories, narratives, myths, and other discursive units."[5] I also incorporate black feminist approaches into my media analysis to recognize the intersectionality of cultural identities,[6] in hopes of revealing "the ways that social categories mutually construct each other."[7] I also show moments within the news coverage when Black and white LGBTs (lesbian, gay, bisexual, and transgender) work as allies to resist dominant media frames, and I recognize shared political interests across identity groups that dominant media usually depict as divergent.

News Frames and Black "Pathologies"

Qualitative and quantitative studies of race and news have shown the media's negative recirculation of images of Black individuals, culture, and communities. These "modern racist" discourses do not adhere to the tenets of biological racism from the nineteenth and early twentieth centuries, but rather suggest that *cultural* pathologies keep Black Americans from experiencing and reaping the benefits of the American Dream. From the Moynihan Report's condemnation of "black matriarchy" to the "welfare queen" and "black-on-black crime," news media have normalized discourses that blame African Americans for continued disparities in income, education, and health.[8]

Media spectacles routinely erupt after a famous African American celebrity makes a bigoted remark about other marginalized group members (usually gays). By doing so, the media expose African Americans to be hypocrites, while releasing white Americans from any moral responsibility or reparations.[9] In fact, allegations about black homophobia are a recurring topic in media discourse, such as rappers' homophobic lyrics, black men "on the down low," and black clergy supporting anti-gay ballot initiatives.[10]

These stories are told as "progressive" stories, because they assert that homophobia is wrong, but they also play what Hurtado calls "*pendejo* games";[11] that is, they offer space to discuss difference and oppression, while employing dominant hegemonic frames of reference. Therefore, news reports essentially frame Blackness as heterosexual and gayness as White. To challenge these practices, I employ an intersectional perspective to provide "a powerful tool for identifying potential sites of political common cause"[12] as well as deconstructing "common sense" constructions of race, gender, and sexuality.

Recovering Intersections of Black and Gay Identities

To expose de-intersections of cultural identities, Dreama Moon and Thomas Nakayama analyzed the dominant media coverage of the murder of a gay Black man.[13] They found that news articles suggested that neither racism nor homophobia motivated the white youths charged with the crime, while the press also muted the voices of Black and gay activists who called for hate crime charges.[14] When Black or gay voices were included in the news stories, the press presented each group's identity and interests as divergent.[15]

Similarly, Carbado found that Black gays and lesbians' experiences in the military were not included in the LGBT campaigns against the military's "Don't Ask/ Don't Tell" (DA/DT) policy.[16] Carbado criticized white-led LGBT organizations for comparing racial segregation with anti-gay policies in the Armed Forces to DA/DT, because the analogy implied racism in the military is over at the same time as it erased the experiences of Black gays and lesbians, who are subject to both racism and heterosexism. Some Black heterosexual activists also bristled at the analogy, asserting that gay identity is "chosen," whereas racial identity is not. Carbado concluded that both blacks and white LGBT organizations "reinscribed the black heterosexual *racial* subject and the white gay and lesbian *sexuality* subject as authentic identity positions . . . [T]o be Black is to be heterosexual; to be homosexual is to be white."[17]

Black Male Celebrity and Homophobic Speech

The news media frame racial and sexual "realities" through popular celebrities' speech acts in limited ways. While celebrities do not have legislative or judicial power over the public, news about celebrities shapes and reflects common understandings of moral values, appropriate behavior, and the relevance of social identity to one's station in life.[18] Mainstream media often compel Black celebrities to be "role models" for the entire Black public, or assume their behavior and opinions are reflective of the larger Black population.[19] Dominant media institutions also reward Black celebrities who perform their racial identity in non-threatening ways. Mainstream media celebrate Black stars, such as Michael Jordan or Oprah Winfrey, as allegedly "transcending race," thereby implying that there is no racism in the sports/entertainment industry.[20] By contrast, Black celebrities who question the racial status quo in the United States are excoriated (e.g., Kanye West).[21]

As news media produce and ever-expand "infotainment" stories about African American male celebrities, media feeding frenzies about their offensive or hateful speech have become common. From Louis Farrakhan's anti-Semitic remarks[22] to NBA star Tim Hardaway's declaration that he "hates gay people," mainstream news media highlight and then dissect these famous Black men's intolerant expressions of other marginalized social groups. These incidents bring multiple facets of celebrities' social identities into the spotlight, along with the "facts" of the case. Their own moral character and that of their racial group (black) are implicated in news discourse. This presents an opportunity for media commentators to render judgments not only on the individual celebrity, but also on the group.

A recent case involving a Black male celebrity's homophobic remarks is that of actor Isaiah Washington, who allegedly called his white male (then-closeted) co-star, T. R. Knight, a faggot during an October 2006 rehearsal for the hit ABC television drama, *Grey's Anatomy*. Rumors of the incident did not gain wide circulation until the January 2007 Golden Globe Awards show, where Washington used the term "faggot" on camera, while denying the incident at the rehearsal. Washington made formal apologies for using the term, and then underwent psychological counseling for "rehabilitation." He also made public awareness ads with GLAAD (Gay and Lesbian Alliance Against Defamation) against homophobic language. Washington later claimed that he never directed the epithet toward Knight, but at another actor during a heated argument.[23] Washington's contract with ABC was not renewed.

I conducted a qualitative content analysis of over 100 mainstream print and broadcast news stories about the Washington case, which revealed a troubling pattern of how media report on bigoted speech acts.[24] The media framed political interests and identities of blacks and gays as divergent and incongruous. Specifically, three main themes emerged: (1) hate speech is a matter of *individual* insensitivity; (2) Black Americans are beneficiaries of a double standard for bigoted speech that punishes white Americans; and (3) society believes anti-black epithets deserve sanction more than anti-gay epithets.

Although these three arguments dominated mainstream coverage, there were important moments within a handful of stories in which Black LGBT and white gay activists, writers, and their allies were able to contest this frame by considering the role of institutions, and by making visible the experiences and opinions of Black LGBTs.

Theme 1: Racial Epithets Are Spoken by Insensitive or Ignorant Individuals

The majority of stories emphasized the culpability and rights of *individual speakers*, thereby speculating about the individual's intelligence, sincerity, and temperament. By doing so, the news stories echoed neoconservative claims that racism and homophobia exist primarily as individual behaviors, and that bigoted behaviors are only held by a small (and ever-decreasing) number of people who lack the social capital to do real harm. Such discourse privileges individual rights and experiences over group-based rights and experiences.

Most of the articles about Isaiah Washington compared him with white celebrities who made racist or anti-Semitic remarks, such as Don Imus, Michael Richards, and Mel Gibson.[25] While diagnosing the stars' mental state, many newspapers observed that the stars actually *benefited* from media attention after making the hateful remarks.

It has become a Hollywood cliché: Utter bigoted language in anger. Issue a carefully fashioned apology ... Meet with civil rights leaders for support ...

Mr. Washington adhered to the script for public penance. But while Mr. Gibson went into alcohol treatment ..., Mr. Washington took an extra step to show remorse, mollify detractors and probably save his career. [26]

Thus, celebrity penance includes apologies and rehab, neither of which ultimately will lead to an investigation of racism and heterosexism in the entertainment industry. Moreover, the preoccupation with the damage to a celebrity's image and career usurps concerns about the damage done to people subjected to hate speech and discrimination. This pattern confirms Moon and Nakayama's observation that periodic public punishment of individual offenders deflects attention away from systemic reproduction of racism and homophobia.

Equating Washington with Imus and Gibson was also problematic. Imus had a long history of making racist, sexist, and homophobic remarks on his nationally syndicated talk show. Moreover, Imus and Gibson quickly rebounded from their public shame after making their apologies. Imus was removed from his MSNBC radio show in 2007, only to return to a radio show on WABC in 2008. He signed a contract for a national television show for Fox Business Network in 2009. Gibson starred in 2010's *Edge of Darkness*. After a brief stint on a failed revival of the *Bionic Woman* on NBC, Isaiah Washington's career remains in limbo.

Theme 2: Blacks Enjoy a Double Standard on Bigoted Language

Although Washington's behavior was the main focus of the media stories, his racial or group identity became part of the discourse. News commentators accused African Americans of engaging in a double standard by using offensive speech. For example, the *Chicago Sun-Times* subtitled a blogosphere roundup, "DIFFERENT WORD, SAME HATE": "If some white man had called [Washington] the n-word, he would be suing them from here to the moon and back. If the show keeps him they are as bad as he is."[27] Likewise, a guest commentator on Fox News declared, "there are certain protected classes you cannot insult"[28] and dismissed the furor over Washington's remarks as proof of identity politics excesses.

These stories reflect paradoxes: Blacks (and LGBTs) enjoy a double standard, while heterosexual whites are unable to exercise their "freedom" to use hate speech without sanction. The frustration of losing the ability to intimidate racial Others indiscriminately resonates with Ronald Hall's diagnosis of "entitlement disorder."[29] Hall contends that white heterosexual males' quality-of-life standards were built on the oppression of women, LGBTs, and people of color, with whom they had a "colonial" relationship of dominance. Not surprisingly, this colonial frame of reference may be hard to shake; thus, some white men suffer from entitlement disorder as they experience discomfort and disillusionment in the wake of social and legal reforms, such as affirmative action or anti–sexual harassment laws, that aim to improve the quality of life for subordinate social groups.

A letter writer explicitly stated that Black people were in danger of losing their "moral authority" and claims to racial justice:

> If any group can understand the experience of being overtly discriminated against for an intrinsic characteristic that has nothing to do with their humanity or values, it should be African Americans. They should be natural allies with any oppressed minority. Civil rights must extend to everyone or to no one. To the extent that African Americans reject this simple idea, they abandon any claim they have to the moral superiority—and benefits—of the civil rights era.[30]

The neoconservative logics of white victimhood implicit in the writer's letter allow this argument to shift from condemning Washington's homophobic remarks to rescinding retroactively civil rights gains for all African Americans. Such rhetoric echoes the neoconservative claim that "Blacks have abused and victimized whites by exploiting their guilt for their racist past."[31] Whites who claim racial victimhood on the basis of a lack of freedom to spout bigotry without reprisal effectively are playing a *pendejo* game that equates the power to engage in name-calling with hegemonic sociopolitical dominance.

The power that Blacks have to induce feelings of guilt in whites pales in comparison to the hegemonic power that white-dominated legal and corporate institutions wield to reinforce heterosexism. The *pendejo* game focuses on the hypocrisies of black celebrities who should "know better," or should be more tolerant because of their group history, thereby deflecting attention away from how institutional reforms that might be effectively implemented.[32]

Importantly, the media viewed Washington's homophobic statement as representative of African Americans' sentiments about homosexuality. While many white celebrities and pundits condemned Imus and Gibson, they did not treat Imus's or Gibson's gender/racial and anti-Semitic slurs as representative of *all whites*. Instead, the media viewed these white celebrities as making a personal or career mistake, while framing them as redeemable subjects. In contrast, black commentators were recruited to opine on the alleged homophobia of "black people."

This practice of finding "racial spokespersons" to diagnose and attribute individual behaviors to the pathologies of all blacks is a common practice by conservatives in mainstream media forums.[33] The logic of the discourse suggests that if a Black conservative makes negative statements about black culture, they are valid, which sanctions whites to endorse the black pathologies thesis, consequently reinforcing Black stereotypes. One example of this occurred on Fox News channel's *O'Reilly Factor*. Host Bill O'Reilly asked his guest, a Black author named Touré, to opine upon why the NAACP (National Association for the Advancement of Colored People) awarded Isaiah Washington an acting prize in the wake of the homophobic incident.

> **TOURÉ:** I would say black people in general are really not that concerned with homophobia, don't link that oppression to the oppression of us, don't see any relationship between the two struggles for gay rights, civil rights, black power. So they would excuse him for using this kind of word and being homophobic like this publicly.
>
> **O'REILLY:** Why is that?
>
> **TOURÉ:** I think black people are not really seeing a relationship, Bill. They're like, "they choose to be gay. We didn't choose to come here." So why—you know, even in casual conversation to make that sort of a link, for me to make that link, black people get very offended.[34]

These remarks suggest that Blacks should naturally empathize with any oppressed group, but are silent as to whether heterosexual whites should ally with LGBTs against homophobia.

Theme Three: The N-word Is Worse than the F-word

Another way black and gay identities were dissociated from one another was in debates over whether the "N-word" (nigger) was more hateful than the "F-word" (faggot).[35] Journalists and interviewees asked whether marginalized groups, and society at large, felt more or less outrage at the words. Their comparisons suggested a hierarchy of oppression, where Blacks were more sympathetic and victimized than gays, because "nothing" is as hurtful or controversial as the "n-word."

> Michael Richards goes berserk in a nightclub, hurling the n-word over and over at hecklers. The shock is universal . . . *Grey's Anatomy* star Isaiah Washington, backstage at the Golden Globe Awards, uses a slur against gays—sometimes called the f-word . . . The reaction from the gay community is strong, but not as widespread or deeply felt throughout the culture . . . "If you could assign a cultural value to the unacceptability of words, the n-word is at the top of the list, no question," says Robert Thompson, professor of popular culture at Syracuse University.[36]

On NPR's *Talk of the Nation*, the host asked a civil rights historian to compare the relative sting of the two words.

> **MR. MCWHORTER:** I get the feeling that we are on our way to making [the F-word] as prescribed as the N-word. And the fact that today the F-bomb, the F-word that we're talking about today can be tossed around rather casually I think is because there is still a remnant, even in a respectable discourse, of a sense that there's something vaguely ridiculous or perverted or irregular about homosexuality.[37]

In echoes of the practice of finding spokespersons to represent marginalized groups' (blacks) opinions, journalists included remarks from white gay speakers who legitimized the claim that "nigger" is the most powerful slur in circulation:

> Conservative gay scholar Andrew Sullivan . . . said, "Nothing has the power of the n-word."[38]

Many articles and on-air exchanges included discussion of how gay or black people use slurs among themselves, yet still censure members of out-groups who use the very same words. This practice was viewed as pathological by commentators.

> The situation isn't helped, [Samuel Taylor] says, by groups using the forbidden words among themselves but being upset when outsiders use them . . . [H]e compares blacks using the n-word and gays using the f-word to the Stockholm Syndrome, where powerless hostages start to identify with their captors.[39]

Not only was the practice compared to mental illness, but it also re-engaged the "double standard" argument. During a discussion on ABC's *News Now*, a reporter and Republican strategist bemoaned about the unfairness and strangeness of Jewish people who "use the word JAPS [Jewish American Princesses] when referring to each other" and Blacks who "freely use the [N-word]" when Christians and Whites cannot do the same.[40] NPR host, Neil Conan, read an email message from a gay listener who chastised other gay people for using terms like "queer."

> **NEIL CONAN:** And here's an e-mail from Alex in Minneapolis:
>
> It seems that the Q-word—i.e. queer—has become acceptable in mainstream culture as well as LGBT culture. Personally, I hate this word. It means freak of nature.[41]

The *pendejo* game of "which word is worse" induces audiences to rank marginalized groups' oppression, leaving out the fact that many people are insulted by both words. Moreover, the issue is not whether dominant society finds one word less offensive, or whether blacks/gays are "comfortable" using these words among themselves; rather, we should debate whether hate speech incidents compel institutions to take racism and heterosexism seriously in terms of public policies and cultural practices.

Re-connecting Black and Gay: Interventions against Dominant Frames

Only a handful of stories included viewpoints from LGBT spokespersons or discussions of the institutional aspects of racism and homophobia. These commentators took the opportunity to reject the frame black vs. gay, and to discuss institutional racism and sexism. *Entertainment Weekly* commentator Mark Harris wrote:

I'm sorry that the overall non-reaction to Washington's behavior helped to reinforce a perception that some quarters of the African-American community tolerate homophobia . . . I'm sorry that it took ABC half the TV season to remind itself of its corporate responsibility. I'm sorry that not a single sponsor of *Grey's Anatomy* had the guts to speak up, even last week . . . I'm sorry that so many actors choose . . . to stay in the closet, since the more out actors there are, the less okay homophobia in entertainment becomes. [42]

Similarly, on NPR's *Tell Me More*, two Black gay commentators, Keith Boykin and Jasmyne Cannick, gave their opinions on the network's role in racism and homophobia.

MS. CANNICK: I mean, one, you know, Isaiah is just another in a long list of minority actors that have been let go from the network in the past year and a half, two years . . . I mean, not only have they let go a significant number of African-Americans, but, you know, Rosie O' Donnell, who's a lesbian, George Lopez and *The George Lopez Show*, which was Latino. [43]

Then, the host set up the *pendejo* game of "which word is worse":

MARTIN: Let's say there was a white actor who is part of a diverse ensemble cast who called an African-American actor the N-word under the same circumstances. Do you think that an apology would be considered sufficient?

MR. BOYKIN: I think it's a fair question, Michel. I just think in this case, you have to take into context who this person is and [what is his history]—Don Imus is completely different from Isaiah Washington. Don Imus had a history of racist, anti-Semitic homophobic slurs. Isaiah Washington has a history of being pro-gay, and is very supportive of the community. [44]

Boykin made two key moves here. First, he refused to equate the single act of one Black actor with multiple affronts committed by a white radio star. Second, his description of Isaiah Washington asserts a positive relationship between the black heterosexual actor and gay communities. Boykin ended with concerns about ABC television's track record with diversity.

MR. BOYKIN: *Lost* is one of my favorite shows on television. And one of the reasons why I liked it is because of the diversity of characters on the show, including African-Americans, who's [sic] my people. They are none now. Zero. All of them are gone . . . And for Isaiah Washington to leave in the context of what's going on in *Lost* and *Desperate Housewives* and *The View*, I think it does set a disturbing trend about the importance of black actors and black performers and talent in Hollywood. [45]

The inclusion of Black LGBT commentators lent an embodied presence of people who are both black and gay, contradicting the bifurcation Black/Gay that dominated most reporting on the story.

Discussion

Challenging *pendejo* games that de-intersect identities by generalizing individual statements made by celebrities deserves scholarly attention and critique. Detine Bowers calls for members of oppressed groups to resist falling into the rhetorical scripts set up by dominant media makers.[46] By indicting the television industry's racist and homophobic casting practices, these participants refused to become part of a narrative that would pit blackness against gayness. Their interventions invited audiences to see black and gay identities as overlapping and called for solidarity against discrimination by institutions.

These *pendejo* games obscure institutional power in their focus on individual acts. For example, the fact that some public figures are punished to a lesser degree for their transgressions based on their social location is lost in comparisons between Washington and other celebrities. As mentioned earlier, Don Imus retained his radio show and recently regained a position on television with Fox Business Network. Likewise, Rush Limbaugh was not even put on leave without pay for playing racist songs about Barack Obama; and, neither he nor his television counterpart, Glenn Beck, has lost his position for continually using racist-homophobic scare language comparing the president's policies to the "anal rape" of the nation.[47] Beck was off the air for a week, but Fox never told Beck to apologize for these or other remarks, including his on-camera statement that President Obama has a "deep-seated hatred for white people."[48] The implication is that discourse by badly behaving blacks (and other people of color) meant the forfeiture of their group's moral superiority, which gave white celebrities, entertainers, and media figures the "right" to use hate speech (about blacks, gays, and women) without penalty or sanction.

These *pendejo* games encourage publics to flatten identities and consider them as existing along a single axis. Media narratives that de-intersect identities and focus on individual acts distract us from the ways in which institutions and social practices act on bodies and groups in ways that reflect the complexity of identities. When the discourse separated Black from gay and presented Washington's racial identity as more important than his heterosexual male identity in making a slur, the problem of heterosexism faded into the background in favor of a discussion of intergroup conflict. Reinforcing the black-heterosexual/white-homosexual binary erased the bodies and experiences of African American LGBT communities, and the ways in which gay Blacks are affected by both racism and heterosexism in media and other socioeconomic spheres.

Likewise, discussions of whether "faggot" was as offensive as "nigger," and why some gays and blacks use the terms among themselves, displaced the origins of these terms. Racial and sexual slurs emanate from social hierarchies and norms, not merely individual whims and subaltern practices. Rather than encourage a "crab-in-the-barrel" fight for who's got it the worst, discourses that acknowledge intersectionality can reveal common ground during moments of intergroup controversy. This can provide more space for participants and audiences to imagine coalitions across seemingly solid lines of identification. When Boykin reminded NPR listeners of the shrinking roster of actors of color as well as insensitivity to LGBT people in network television, he directed them to the locus of media production and decision-making power. It is this power-identity matrix behind the scenes that set the stage for Washington's remarks.

While the re-intersecting of identities does not guarantee marginalized groups will assemble on common ground, elevating evidence for the needs for coalitions to challenge dominant narratives that privilege competition is an important move. Recognizing that race is sexualized reveals how we need to look within and across identity groups to find axes of shared experience and shared interests. Critical rhetorical analysis and critical race theories help us to recognize when we are being played by *pendejo* games and direct us to resuscitate intersectional renderings and understandings of social identities.

NOTES

An earlier version of this chapter was presented as part of the 2009 Midwest Winter Workshop at the University of Minnesota. The author thanks Kirt Wilson and other participants for their thoughtful comments. Many thanks also to Daniel Brouwer for invigorating conversations on the topic, and to the editors and anonymous reviewers who provided clear, concise direction for revision.

    1. Hemant Shah and Michael C. Thornton, *Newspaer Coverage of Interethnic Conflict: Competing Visions of America* (Thousand Oaks, CA: Sage, 2004).

    2. In this chapter, I use the terms Black, black, African American, and Black American interchangeably to reflect the recurrent discussions of nomination within communities of African descent. In quotations, I use the forms used by the speakers/writers in their original. I also use a variety of terms, including gay, homosexual, lesbian, and LGBT, to refer to individuals and social groups that are legally and socially discriminated against on the basis of sexuality and/or gender display.

    3. Examples include the *Washington Times* front page headline, "Blacks, Hispanics nixed gay marriage" (November 8, 2008, p. A01), and the *Los Angeles Times'* editorial "Gay/black tension" (November 15, 2008, p. A22).

    4. See analysis and commentary by pollsters, statisticians, and others on *Daily Kos* at http://www.dailykos.com/storyonly/2008/11/7/34645/1235/704/656272, on *Five Thirty Eight.com* at http://www.fivethirtyeight.com/2008/11/prop-8-myths.html, and commentary from the Social Science Research Council at http://www.ssrc.org/blogs/immanent_frame/2008/11/09/pointing-fingers-after-prop-8/.

    5. Marouf Hasian, Jr. and Fernando Delgado, "The trials and tribulations of racialized critical rhetorical theory: Understanding the rhetorical ambiguities of Proposition 187," *Communication Theory* 8 (1998): 245–70.

6. Over the past two decades, Black feminist scholars have examined the ways in which dominant legal and media discourses refuse to acknowledge the lived realities of both hetero- and homosexual women of color. For example, Patricia Williams' *Alchemy of Race and Rights* (Cambridge: Harvard University Press, 1991) dissects how liberal discourses within law ignore the experiences and struggles of Black women in the United States. Cathy Cohen's *The Boundaries of Blackness* (Chicago: University of Chicago Press, 1999) analyzes how both Black and white newspaper coverage of the HIV/AIDS crisis overlooked African American LGBT communities and reinforced the prevailing stereotype that gay and lesbian people with AIDS (PWAs) are white. Patricia Hill Collins' recent work, *Black Sexual Politics: African Americans, Gender, and the New Racism* (New York: Routledge, 2004), concentrates on how Black leaders who ignore sexism and homophobia not only damage prospects for coalition across oppressed collectives, but also obscure the scope and depth of gender and sexual oppression that damage African American community and individual psyches.

7. Elizabeth Cole and Nesha Haniff, "Building a home for Black Women's Studies," *Black Women, Gender, and Families* 1 (2007): 27.

8. See Michael K. Brown et al., *Whitewashing Race: The Myth of a Color-Blind Society* (Berkeley: University of California Press, 2004); Martin Gilens, *Why Americans Hate Welfare: Race, Media and the Politics Of Anti-Poverty Policy* (Chicago: University of Chicago Press, 1999); Wahneema Lubiano, "Like being mugged by a metaphor: Multiculturalism and state narratives," in *Mapping Multiculturalism*, ed. Avery F. Gordon and Christopher Newfield, 64–75 (Minneapolis: University of Minnesota Press, 1996).

9. See discussions in Angela Dillard, *Guess Who's Coming to Dinner Now? Multicultural Conservatism in America* (New York: New York University Press, 2004); Aaron D. Gresson, *The Recovery of Race in America* (Minneapolis: University of Minnesota Press, 1995); Catherine Squires, *Dispatches from the Color Line: The Press and Multiracial Identity* (Albany: SUNY Press, 2007).

10. Robin R. Means Coleman and Jasmine Cobb, "No way of seeing: Mainstreaming and selling the gaze of homo-thug hip hop," *Popular Communication* 5 (2007): 89–108; Patricia Hill Collins, *Black Sexual Politics* (New York: Routledge, 2004); Ronald L. Jackson, *Scripting the Black Masculine Body: Identity, Discourse, and Racial Politics in Popular Media* (Albany: SUNY Press, 2006); J. L. King and Karen Hunter, *On the Down Low: A Journey into the Lives of Black Men Who Sleep with Men* (New York: Random House, 2004); Jonathan Landrum Jr., "Black gays ask clergy for tolerance," *Washington Post*, January 22, 2006, A17.

11. Aida Hurtado, *The Color of Privilege: Three Blasphemies on Race and Feminism* (Ann Arbor: University of Michigan Press, 1996).

12. Cole and Haniff, "Building a home," 36–37.

13. Dreama Moon and Thomas Nakayama, "Strategic social identities and judgments: A murder in Appalachia," *Howard Journal of Communications* 16 (2005): 87–107.

14. Ibid., 99.

15. Ibid., 101–2.

16. Devon W. Carbado, "Black rights, gay rights, civil rights: The deployment of race/sexual orientation analogies in the debates about the "Don't Ask, Don't Tell" policy," in *Black Men on Race, Gender and Sexuality*, ed. D. W. Carbado, 283–302 (New York: New York University Press, 1999).

17. Ibid., 291.

18. Neal Gabler, *Life: The Movie: How Entertainment Conquered Reality* (New York: Vintage, 2000); Neil Postman, *Amusing Ourselves to Death: Public Discourse in the Age of Show Business*

(New York: Penguin, 1985, 2005); Graeme Turner, *Understanding Celebrity* (Thousand Oaks, CA: Sage Publications, 2004).

. **19.** Todd Boyd, ed., *Out of Bounds: Sports, Media and the Politics of Identity* (Bloomington: Indiana University Press, 1997).

20. David L. Andrews, "The Fact(s) of Michael Jordan's Blackness: Excavating a floating signifier," *Sociology of Sport Journal* 12 (1996): 125–58; Lauren Berlant, "National brands/national body: Imitation of Life," in *The Phantom Public Sphere*, ed. Bruce Robbins, 173–208 (Minneapolis: University of Minnesota Press, 1993); Dana Cloud, "Hegemony or concordance? The rhetoric of tokenism in "Oprah" Winfrey's rags-t-riches biography," *Critical Studies in Mass Communication* 13 (1996): 115–37.

21. Jackson, *Scripting the Black Masculine Body*, 2007.

22. See S. Craig Watkins' analysis in his piece "Framing protest: News media frames of the Million Man March," *Critical Studies in Media Communication* 18 (2001): 83–102.

23. Scott Collins, "Kiss & make up? Isaiah Washington's return to the hit 'Grey's Anatomy' after his gay-slur flap may make for one touchy set," *Los Angeles Times*, February 5, 2007. Accessed from Lexis/Nexis on July 20, 2007. *Larry King Live*, "Encore Presentation— Interview with Isaiah Washington." Broadcast on CNN July 8, 2007. Transcript accessed from Lexis/Nexis on July 20, 2007.

24. David L. Altheide, *Qualitative Media Analysis* (Thousand Oaks, CA: Sage, 1996). Transcripts from major news television broadcasts, major U.S. newspapers, and radio broadcasts were gathered using the Lexis-Nexis database. All stories that were more than 500 words and focused on Isaiah Washington's remarks and conduct were gathered from the first reports of the remarks until after he made a public service announcement for GLAAD, totaling 108. I read through the stories multiple times, taking margin notes and categorizing themes. Parts of the analysis were presented in a colloquium with graduate students at the University of Minnesota. I thank the participants for their insights and comments.

25. To briefly recap the deeds of (in)famous men: Imus ranted about the physiques of the Rutgers University women's basketball team, calling them "nappy headed hos"; Richards repeatedly called Black patrons at a comedy club "nigger" in an improvisational moment; and Mel Gibson spouted anti-Semitic epithets at a police officer after being arrested for DUI.

26. Mireya Navarro, "My big bad mouth," *New York Times*, February 8, 2007. Accessed from Lexis/Nexis on July 20, 2007.

27. "The new F-word: Actors and real people spin the language of hate," *Chicago Sun-Times*, January 28, 2007. Accessed from Lexis/Nexis on July 20, 2007.

28. Fox News Watch, "'Quick Takes on the media.'" January 27, 2007, 6:50 EST. Accessed from Lexis/Nexis on July 20, 2007.

29. Ronald E. Hall, "Entitlement disorder: The colonial traditions of power as white male resistance," *Journal of Black Studies* 34 (2004): 562–79.

30. Don Howe, "Letter to the Editor: African Americans and homophobia," *Los Angeles Times*, February 21, 2007. Accessed from Lexis/Nexis on July 20, 2007.

31. Gresson, *Recovery of Race in America*, 8.

32. This trend of looking at people of color as culprits continues. The *New York Times* November 10, 2009 edition ran a front-page, lengthy feature story about a Puerto Rican state senator (who is of African descent) who opposed gay marriage, despite the fact that all ten of the African American state senators in New York voted in favor of gay marriage, and 30 Republican senators (all White) voted against it. Likewise, the *Washington Post* framed former Mayor Marion Barry's opposition to Washington, DC's legalization of gay marriage as indicative of the

Black community's stance, despite the fact that the city council—which is populated by many Black members—passed the measure with ease. Since the stories ran, Black and gay bloggers have roundly criticized the coverage for stereotyping Blacks as homophobes.

33. See discussions of the strategic use of conservatives of color in public debates over race in: Dillard, *Guess Who's Coming to Dinner Now?* (2004); Earl Sheridan, "The new accommodationists," *Journal of Black Studies* 27 (1996): 152–71; and Detine L. Bowers, "When outsiders encounter insiders in speaking: Oppressed collectives on the defensive," *Journal of Black Studies* 26 (1996): 490–503.

34. *The O'Reilly Factor*, March 5, 2007. Transcript accessed from Lexis/Nexis on July 20, 2007.

35. In this chapter, I use N-word and F-word in text to refer to the ways in which commentators used these substitute terms for "nigger" and "faggot." Unless otherwise specified, the usage in the quotations is original to the media texts.

36. Phil Kloer, "War of words: And what terms of abuse are most provocative?" *Atlanta Journal-Constitution*, January 25, 2007. Accessed from Lexis/Nexis on July 20, 2007.

37. *Talk of the Nation*, "Are all slurs created equal?" Broadcast on National Public Radio February 8. 2007. Transcript accessed from Lexis/Nexis on July 20, 2007.

38. Wyatt Buchanan, "Reaction to Coulter's slur hints at shift in view of gays," *San Francisco Chronicle*, 2007, March 9. Accessed from Lexis/Nexis on July 20, 2007.

39. Kloer, "War of words," 2007.

40. ABC *News Now*. "Perspectives: Don't call the N-word." Broadcast on February 16, 2007. Accessed from Lexis/Nexis on July 20, 2007.

41. *Talk of the Nation*, "Are all slurs created equal?"

42. Mark Harris, "Sorry situation," *Entertainment Weekly*, February 2, 2007. Accessed from Lexis/Nexis on July 20, 2007.

43. *Tell Me More*, "The *Grey's Anatomy* shake-up." Broadcast on National Public Radio June 14, 2007. Accessed from Lexis/Nexis on July 20, 2007.

44. Ibid.

45. Ibid.

46. Bowers, "When outsiders encounter insiders," 1996.

47. Limbaugh aired a song called "Barack the Magic Negro" on his nationally syndicated show. Media Matters has catalogued a plethora of on-air comments from Beck, Limbaugh, and other conservative shock jocks likening Obama's policymaking to vaginal and anal rape. For example, Limbaugh conjured a fantasy of Obama directing his minions in the Federal Reserve to "get up there and you rape them"; Neal Boortz told his audience that Obama's administration was "gonna rape us. They're gonna bend us over and nail us"; and Dan Savage told listeners in April 2009 that "Obama is raping America. Obama is raping our values. Obama is raping our democracy." Media Matters, "Conservative media frequently accuse progressives of 'raping' Americans." Accessed at http://mediamatters.org/research/ on November 19, 2009.

48. Beck made these remarks during a roundtable discussion on *Fox & Friends* on July 28, 2009: "This president, I think, has exposed himself as a guy—over and over again—who has a deep-seated hatred for white people, or the white culture." Video and transcript of the segment available at http://www.dailykostv.com/w/001989/.

II Whiteness

4   Quentin Tarantino in Black and White

Sean Tierney

Director Quentin Tarantino's first film, *Reservoir Dogs*, was released by Miramax in 1992. His 1994 film *Pulp Fiction* brought Tarantino mainstream success. In 1997, he released *Jackie Brown*, starring former Blaxploitation actress Pam Grier. *Kill Bill Vols. 1* and *2* were released in 2003 and 2004. *Death Proof* was Tarantino's half of 2007's *Grindhouse*, a double-feature he shared with Robert Rodriguez. Collectively, his films have earned US $859 million worldwide.[1]

Tarantino's visibility in the pop culture pantheon, combined with his outspokenness, make him a public figure of note; his films, his boundless energy in promoting himself and his works, his views about his work and other subjects, his frequently erratic and/or eccentric public behavior, and even his mannerisms (e.g., a rapid-fire speech pattern, often interspersed with florid hand gestures) make him a natural focal point for media attention. By extension, his films and his frequent presence in the public eye make him a significant subject for study, because he is both a *producer* and a *product* of the culture industries. Of particular interest in this chapter is his public rhetoric about and with African Americans and the concept of Blackness.[2]

Seeing the White Elephant

Research has previously shown how whiteness is operationalized or deployed, either consciously or unconsciously.[3] Whiteness scholarship frequently seeks to re-particularize or "make strange" certain behaviors that whiteness normalizes both actively and passively.[4] Through this process, whiteness "gains particularity while losing universality."[5] Richard Dyer's work in both whiteness and star studies is an obvious starting point for the present study. Dyer's *Stars* elucidates the construction of stardom as a conglomeration not just of the actor and media text, but also of publicity, criticism, and discourse about and surrounding the star. In *Heavenly Bodies*, he also notes that a star is partially composed of, and immutably tied to, all publicly available information of, by, or about that performer. Dyer's (1997) work on whiteness is seminal, making him one of the founding voices in the field. Dyer's *White* illustrates the ways in which the invisibility of whiteness functions in cinema, encouraging research that makes whiteness *re-visible*, especially in media.[6] Whiteness studies frequently focus on the deployment of power

81

in language as well as media, and have specifically examined language appropriation of African Americans.[7] In addition, whiteness research has addressed Tarantino and/or his films.[8]

Tarantino's unique status as both a culture industry *producer* (film director)
and a culture industry *product* (as a celebrity) makes the study of him more significant than were he a subject who was only one of the two. In a parallel fashion,
the present study is an examination of a star who is a *product of whiteness* and a
producer of it. As much as he might characterize himself as a maverick director,
Tarantino works for and within the structure of the U.S. film industry. Similarly,
he benefits greatly from systemic whiteness, while simultaneously contributing to
its structure and maintenance.

Quentin Tarantino's public rhetoric about issues of Blackness as well as the
racial realities both of and between Black and White are illustrative of whiteness
in many ways. An examination of his public statements on these topics demonstrates how Tarantino both benefits from, as well as contributes to, the maintenance of whiteness and white privilege. This study will demonstrate, that Tarantino and his rhetoric are (in direct contradiction to his own stated views) neither
progressive nor beneficial and are in fact signifiers of the very racism he claims
they help dismantle. It is important to recognize this contradiction, because
doing so allows us to see how, in this instance, whiteness maintains its power,
even as it claims to be dismantling it. This is the central deceit at work in Tarantino's rhetoric, and it is critical that such phenomena are brought under scrutiny,
so that they can be recognized for what they are, in hopes that they will no longer
function problematically in the service of whiteness.

This chapter examines readily available public statements made by Tarantino in interviews and his public rhetoric about African Americans and 'Blackness' found online. The data were limited to mediated statements and behaviors
directly attributed to Tarantino from verifiable sources; anecdotal evidence was
not used, while direct quotations or statements made by Tarantino or about Tarantino from reputable sources (i.e., noted film critics) were included. The data
were gathered by searching for paired terms or phrases, including Tarantino's
name and terms likely to provide pertinent results.[9] Hundreds of results were
examined, and those containing statements by or about Tarantino and pertaining
to issues of race (representation, racism, his own views) were analyzed. The data
gathered and presented are representative of Tarantino's public rhetoric about the
issue of race in terms of Black and White as it pertains to his own history, films,
and views.

This study focuses on Tarantino as a media manifestation in terms of his public image, as constituted and represented by his public rhetoric. As a person, however, he is nevertheless inexorably connected to this public persona.[10] Tarantino's

public rhetoric on race illustrates Frankenberg's three-part definition of whiteness: first, as "a location of structural advantage, of race privilege." Second, "as a 'standpoint,' a place from which White people look at ourselves, at others, and at society." Third, "as a set of cultural practices that are usually unmarked and unnamed."[11]

For the present study, *race privilege* is the ability to say and do things that are offensive, even racist, without threat or fear of social reprisal. The *standpoint* from which Tarantino sees himself, as well as others and society, is another hallmark of whiteness. His belief in his ethnic variability based on a non-ethnic central humanity, combined with an exceedingly narrow definition of what "Black" means, are well-established markers of whiteness. His *cultural practices*, including appropriation, an insistence on the veracity of his position and views, as well as his blithe dismissal of criticism and/or vociferous counter-accusations are not *marked* or *named* as being racist, socially inappropriate, or illustrative of whiteness. A critical examination of these phenomena advances whiteness scholarship by situating a public figure squarely within the frame of whiteness and re-characterizing his words and actions as being problematic.

A common rhetorical tactic of whiteness is the assertion that race and color are meaningless, at least (or especially) for the white person making the claim.[12] Such assertions are based on an appeal to "innate humanness" around which race or culture is placed and/or replaced.[13] The "hyperconscious white subject" operates as an empty or blank slate upon which the subject may "fill" or decorate itself with what the subject feels to be representative, or even authentic, signifiers of race and ethnicity.[14] In essence, the "transparency of whiteness allows one to view the taking on of other cultural practices as an extension of one's own universal humanness."[15]

This concept informs the first of Frankenberg's tripartite definition of whiteness: "a location of structural advantage, of race privilege."[16] Race privilege is at the core of this assumed lack of race: "There is no more powerful position than that of being 'just' human . . . those who occupy positions of cultural hegemony blithely carry on as if what they say is neutral and unsituated—human not raced."[17] The privileged, or un-raced, may speak and act in ways that the unprivileged, or raced, may not. To have race is to go without privilege. The words, thoughts, and ideas of the un-raced privileged will carry further and have more weight than those of the unprivileged *raced*. It is this privilege that both enables and informs the standpoint "from which White people look at ourselves, at others, and at society."[18] The privilege also helps to explain, conceal, and protect the "cultural practices that are usually unmarked and unnamed."[19]

Many times, this deracinated, non-cultured (white) self is contrasted with or defined through a distinct assignment of attributes or roles to culture or ethnicity specifically of non-whites often based in the perception that other cultures somehow have a clearer or richer definition and/or sense of culture.[20] The construction of whiteness as emptiness, and African American culture as a contrasting and definitive entity, informs a key aspect of his public rhetoric.[21]

"Black" On the Inside

Tarantino claims to have grown up "surrounded by black culture. I went to an all black school. It is the culture that I identify with . . . we all have a lot of people inside of us, and one of the ones inside of me is black. Don't let the pigmentation fool you; it is a state of mind."[22] This kind of ethnic detachment, wherein the subject feels empowered to deny the reality of his/her ethnicity, is "one significant aspect of the construction of white identity . . . an interpretive framework that privileges individualism and racial neutrality."[23] According to Tarantino, he "grew up around a lot of black guys . . . One of the closer father figures I had in my life was not too dissimilar from [*Jackie Brown's*] Ordell . . . He wasn't a gunrunner and he wasn't killing people, but he was doing shady stuff."[24] He also asserts that he "grew up among black losers, con-men, you know, those shifty loser asshole guys. I have more of a connection and feel an inner personality with black culture than I do with Italian culture."[25] Tarantino has stated that "Whenever I get violent I turn into a black male," noting that "When I get mad or when I get in a fight I talk with a black dialect."[26] While relating a story about a confrontation he was involved in, he asks, "How much do I want to whip this guy's ass? He was a big black guy, and they're used to white guys backing down. I don't back down, especially to big black guys. That gives me a psychological advantage."[27]

Tarantino has stated that "some of the people in my life I have admired the most were older black women. I have a lot of respect for them."[28] According to actress Tilda Swinton, a member of the 2004 Cannes film festival jury, Tarantino spent three days speaking in the voice of Irma P. Hall, the African American actress in *The Ladykillers*.[29] Tarantino's intent may have been to make an *homage* to Hall, but it is a very telling example of how ethnicity, public behavior, and acceptance are structured: Tarantino's behavior was characterized as eccentric rather than insensitive or inappropriate. It is also an example of how white privilege allows one to carry out an impersonation that goes unmarked or unnamed as tasteless, offensive, racist, or insulting publicly. How might the media (and their audiences) react to Spike Lee spending three days publicly speaking in the voice of Zsa Zsa Gabor? The fact that we immediately see a different scenario shows how differentially power is distributed.

White appropriations of a *perceived* cultural essence and/or entry into that culture (while in fact remaining impervious to the negative aspects of that cultural reality and its consequences) both derive and benefit from a position of privilege: Whites' "departures from their own racial positions and identities [are] symbolic or temporary: they [are] not permanently 'unwhitened.'"[30] The ability to deny the sociopolitical ramifications of one's physical appearance, and the knowledge, as well as power, to ensure that assertion will go unchallenged, is a uniquely white privilege in America. Contrary to Tarantino's assertion, it is clear that a simple disavowal of ethnicity is insubstantial and useless, especially for non-whites claiming anti-racist intent or orientation.[31] Tarantino may indeed believe he has a black person inside him, but his outside persona, which is seen by police officers, real estate agents, and African Americans, remains white. He will not be arbitrarily stopped by law enforcement for Driving While Black *On the Inside*.

For many in America, their inescapable racial or ethnic exterior conveys upon them a set of potential restrictions or negative possibilities regardless of education, financial status, or personal bearing. Some people's ethnicities are forced upon them with even more dire consequences. James Byrd, horribly murdered *because he was black*, did not have the life-saving luxury of being able to deny or minimize an ethnicity he may have felt was unrepresentative of his inner self. The same perceptions correlating black with negative dynamics that motivated the murder of an innocent black man also contribute to Quentin Tarantino's status as a popular director and a multimillionaire.

In a 2007 interview with the British edition of GQ magazine, Tarantino claimed that he had, in a previous life, been "a black slave in America. I think maybe even like three lives. Yeah, I know that . . . I've got nothing I could say that would not make me sound like a horse's ass. It's just a feeling. A knowing."[32] If Tarantino made this claim as an attempt at humor, it would likely be considered tasteless at best and amusing at worst. Yet for him to do so seriously, and to expect to be believed, is a significantly troublesome, insensitive, and to many outrageous act that implicates both the speaker and those who accept such statements.

Compounding the negative impact of the issue, his only proof is his "sense of knowing," an assertion that is simultaneously as smug as it is empirically beyond proof. Tarantino both defends and essentially seals off the basis of his claim from critique or explanation by stating an immutable, incontrovertible truth based solely on *his knowledge of it*. Tarantino's belief that he is, or should be, somehow associated not just with a specific ethnicity but with one of America's most significant and serious cultural and historical phenomena subordinates the history and experience of the people who suffered the consequences. It reduces American slavery to something a white person may appropriate freely (until they choose not to) and without consequence. Tarantino appropriates the meaning and import of what it means not only to have been an African American and a slave in the nineteenth century, but by extension what it means to be an African American presently living with the consequences of slavery. While an exact, sweeping definition of what it means to be an African American today or in the nineteenth century may not be possible, it is certain that "multimillionaire white film director" falls outside of the scope of such a definition.

Tarantino perhaps wishes to begin laying the publicity groundwork for his "Southern gothic" film genre, which he has expressed both interest and intent in making. These films are Tarantino's contribution to the discussion of "America's horrible past with slavery and stuff . . . they deal with everything that America has never dealt with because it's ashamed of it."[33] The director has no doubt in his ability or qualifications to direct such films: "I can deal with it all right, and I'm the guy to do it. So maybe that's the next mountain waiting for me."[34] Given Tarantino's stated film tastes, his "Southern gothic" would likely re-make *Mandingo*, with dialogue much more evocative of *Amos & Andy* than *Guess Who's Coming to Dinner*. It should also be reiterated that Tarantino's appropriation of the American slavery experience is very likely a means of garnering publicity for the director's proposed film, as opposed to any deep-seated concern about race relations in America. It is an example of how the "display of affiliation enables white people to insist on being the center of attention."[35]

"Black" on Film

Tarantino believes he possesses an ability to transcend his own ethnicity and to take on those of his characters in what he believes is a valid way: "In the case of *Jackie Brown*, it really enabled me to be able to write truthfully, heartfeltedly [sic] and realistically, and to become the characters of Jackie Brown and Ordell . . . I become the characters as I am writing them . . . It was a spell I was under and I could not break it because I did not want the work to suffer from it."[36] Tarantino's vision of race in his films is diametrically different from those who take notice of their "white maleness": "More or less every single thing I've ever done in film is about the division between black and white in this country. And how this division actually is a sham."[37] Denial (and transgression) of this division is crucial to Tarantino's access to those parts of African American culture he wishes to utilize or appropriate for his films. Tarantino believes that he is creating accurate representations of African Americans that lessen the "division between black and white," a premise based "on the self-flattering presumption of initial benevolence and the assumed luxury of a possible disengagement."[38]

Tarantino's explanation of his casting of Pam Grier in *Jackie Brown* is worthy of examination for the ways in which it reveals some of his conceptions of African Americans:

The fact that she is black ended up giving the piece even more depth; not in a cheesy way or a cheap way . . . She has worked her way down the ladder. She is hanging on by her fingernails with this shitty ass job; she has got nowhere to go . . . At 44 she is probably going to have to go to jail for a year and start all over again. The cops are fucking with her. It made the dilemma more crystal clear, having to be a black woman in that situation. It just gave it more depth.[39]

In his view, this particular set of circumstances is best embodied by an African American. In casting a black woman as a desperate, downtrodden criminal, he willfully accedes to common stereotypes about certain behaviors and the ethnic associations they entail. Yet, Tarantino claims that in doing so he is actually improving the narrative; we might usefully ask for whom it is improved.

In the same interview, Tarantino explains his use of "black" dialect as part of the broader social issue of code-switching:

Blacks in America in particular have two voices. It is called "getting a job." The way they are with their friends or their family is not the way they present themselves in the work place. I am not talking about everybody. I am not making sweeping generalisations here, but by and large people can move in and out of dialects. If we are going to talk specifically about blacks, that is a specific thing about blacks. We all do that. We all have different voices. We all have completely different voices. I definitely have a different voice when I am angry. If I am going to fuck you up, I am going to have a completely different voice than I am having standing here right now. We all have that, and that is highlighted by a different dialect going on inside of a white community.[40]

Tarantino claims not to be making sweeping generalizations, yet that is precisely what he is doing. By speaking of "blacks" as a unified, undifferentiated group, with no qualifier such as "some," he totalizes a diverse group. This conundrum is compounded by his subsequent statement that "we all" engage in precisely the same activity he has just marked as "black." He also implies that the white community has a "different dialect." Such a statement serves to highlight once again Tarantino's assumed ethnic multiplicity: where whites have a different dialect than blacks, Tarantino has *both*.

In another interview, his characterization of black audiences implicitly makes value judgments about their viewing behavior and intellect compared to other (i.e., white) audiences: "I'm used to making ass-kickers. And [*Jackie Brown*] is not an ass-kicker. It's an ass-kicker when you watch it with a black audience. But for other audiences—and we're trying to get all audiences in there—it's much more of a resonant work."[41] According to Tarantino, black audiences will respond to *Jackie Brown* in a visceral, emotional, and presumably vocal (in the theater) manner, while "other" audiences will, by virtue of their higher capacities, respond to the film's mature and reflective resonances with a higher degree of sophistication.

When asked if *Jackie Brown* was, in his mind, a black film, he responded:

> No, I don't subconsciously think it is a black film; it is a black film . . . It was made for black audiences actually. It was made for everybody, but that was the audience. If I had any of them in mind, I was thinking of that because I was always thinking of watching it in a black theatre. I didn't have audiences ridiculously in mind because I am the audience, but that works well for that too because I go to black theatres.[42]

Tarantino's logic appears to be that the film's intended audience is black, though not its sole viewers. Additionally, and perhaps *because* Tarantino views films in "black" theaters (a term he does not clarify), he is also somehow the (black) audience. The same person who would insist that we not allow his pigmentation to fool us also explains *Kill Bill* to a Japanese interviewer as "made for black theaters . . . A black audience is like, 'Ha ha ha ha!' You Japanese are a little more subdued when you watch a movie."[43] In another interview about *Kill Bill*, he claims it "doesn't have the pretentiousness of a big movie epic. This is made for black theaters, for exploitation cinema that covers the whole globe."[44] The equation of black theaters with exploitation films and a lack of pretension speaks more to *Tarantino's* experiences in *certain* theaters showing *certain* films than it does about what does or does not constitute a "black theater."

The privileged, un-raced standpoint from which Tarantino speaks about the un-privileged/raced "differentially distributes general epistemic authority to make judgments and determinations, such that, for example, whites often assume the right to decide the true or accurate racial identity of everyone . . . this is an extension of an essentially white privilege."[45] Tarantino's justifications for his black identification seem to be a rhetorical reversal, a common whiteness strategy used to disguise white hegemonic power, control, and privilege.[46] By claiming a black background, narrow as it is in sociocultural terms, he seeks both to explain and validate his characterizations. In essence, he would have us believe that the "truth" of his characters is grounded in the "truth" of his own past.

"Black" Public Language

Tarantino's frequent use of the word *nigger* in dialogue had become an issue after the release of *Pulp Fiction* (1994) and remained an issue when *Jackie Brown* (1997) was released. For Tarantino, "the word nigger is probably the most volatile word in the English language. The minute any word has that much power, as far as I'm concerned, everyone on the planet should scream it. No word deserves that much power. I'm not afraid of it. That's the only way I know how to explain it."[47] He asserted a lack of both repentance and fear when queried about his use of the word: "that's the way my characters talk in the movies I've made so far . . . I grew up around blacks and have no fear of it, I grew up saying it as an expression."[48] Tarantino, by then a world-renowned director of Hollywood films and far removed from the lives of the (predominantly criminal) black characters he creates, is contributing to "maintaining the illusion that individual whites can appropriate aspects of African American experience for their own benefit without having to acknowledge the factors that give African Americans and European Americans widely divergent opportunities and life chances."[49]

Many African Americans felt that such appropriative use of the word constituted a misunderstanding and misinterpretation of the films Tarantino claims to have been influenced and inspired by: "Tarantino took the swagger of Blaxploitation without the political context. *Nigger* is used a little bit too blithely in [his] pictures, and it becomes sort of un-morphed from the political context, and I think there's a danger in that, people think that you can just say it and it doesn't mean anything."[50] Tarantino's dialogue is also suspected of being distinctly *unrepresentative* of the Blaxploitation genre; Tarantino's "overuse of the word, and I quote, 'nigger,' is, uh . . . interesting. I mean, even when you look at the Blaxploitation films of that period, the word wasn't really that overused or popular."[51] Tarantino's words and actions involving his film dialogue are an unfortunate example of how whites not only "impose misinformation, we also often refuse to accept people of color as they know themselves."[52]

During a televised interview in Britain, Tarantino was told that his own in-character use of *nigger* was unrealistic, that there was no way a white man could get away with saying that to a black man. Tarantino's response, "I do," elicited applause from the studio audience.[53] It is likely the audience was applauding Tarantino's claim of cultural fluidity, such that he can say things seemingly forbidden to whites. But, it is also likely that they were applauding his defiance of not only the taboo but the power (and the people who wield it) that would prohibit white use of the word. The audience venerates Tarantino's willingness to cross, and capability of crossing, cultural lines as well as his refusal to be prohibited from doing so. The audience's response shows that they share some of the same thoughts and ideas, and perhaps the same arrogance and resentment, about race as Tarantino does.

One of the most vocal critics of Tarantino's use of *nigger* was Spike Lee; their public feuding was both heated and protracted. During the disagreement, Lee was waiting to watch a film with his wife in the Angelica Theatre when Tarantino "came up to me and told me that he knows black people better than me. So I just laughed at him."[54] According to Tarantino, Lee was engaged in the argument strictly for publicity and political reasons:

> My biggest problem with Spike was the completely self-serving aspect of his argument. He attacked me to keep his "Jesse Jackson of cinema" status . . . before I came along, you had to get Spike Lee's benediction and approval if you were white and

dealing with black stuff in a movie. Fuck that. This destroyed that, and he's never had that position again. I wasn't looking for his approval, and so he was taking me on to keep his status. I hated it, because a celebrity feud is one of the most tasteless, trite, trivial things somebody in my position can engage in, to be drawn into something so beneath you.[55]

This situation is emblematic of how race configures discourse, such that a white high-school dropout can have credibility in a disagreement with an African American who graduated both Morehouse College and NYU film school, a film director noted for his continued efforts to grapple with America's racial realities in an intelligent and thought-provoking manner, and an acknowledged figure in the culture *whose language use is being discussed*. Tarantino's comments show how whiteness "has been predominantly self-protective; any challenge to its authority must be systematically made invalid in order to maintain its position."[56] If the ethnicities were reversed, would the discussion have even take place? Tarantino, who frequently asserts his lack of fear of African Americans, claims to have "destroyed" Lee's status; he "never had that position again." The implicit addendum here is that Tarantino could fill the now-vacant position of representing blackness and black issues in film. One might say that Spike Lee was stripped of his "Jesse Jackson of cinema" status by the "D.W. Griffith of race relations."

For Tarantino, the use of racist language does not constitute racism, especially when the intent of racism is absent. White people "tend to view intent as an essential element of racial harm; nonwhites do not."[57] In a 1997 interview, he refutes those who would critique his writing:

Is somebody saying that they actually think, in their heart of hearts, I'm a racist? . . . But I don't think anyone can actually, truly say that. But if you're not calling me a racist, then you're simply talking about, do I have the right to write black characters? And do I have the right, as a writer, to tell the truth as I see it, as far as the characters talk? To me, if the answer to that is no, that's racist.[58]

Writing dialogue using racist language is not racist, Tarantino suggests. Questioning him or his presumed right to create and speak through these characters, however, *is* racist. Tarantino defends his use of racist language and stereotypes through a denial of personal racism. This trope, which often revolves around qualifiers like "I'm not racist, but Black people are/do/say . . ." has been previously noted.[59] It is most often used to deflect accusations of racism while in fact maintaining and/or re-inscribing racist assumptions, which implicitly suggest that there are rational reasons for said racism.

Tarantino asserts that he is not racist, because that is not his intent. He also asserts that he is not racist, *because he says he isn't*. Yet, such a position is not only a form of rejection, but inherently an assertion of power and privilege.[60] In its most unflattering guise, "I'm not racist because I say I'm not" becomes an arrogant device of white privilege: An opinion has no truth and means nothing unless the (white) individual deigns to validate it by adopting it as his/her own. The social privilege endowed by whiteness bestows the unimpeachable disavowal of personal racism in discussions *about* racism, rendering them inherently unequal, because one side may simply dismiss the other out of hand, claiming their opponents' ignorance or refusal of the truth as they "know" it. His rhetoric illustrates how the "proclaiming of our alliance in a visible, emphatic manner has a performative quality that demands instant recognition and approval . . . to the extent that it functions as a demand, this display constitutes an endeavor to extend and underline the authority of the white person."[61]

Tarantino was unrepentant about his dialogue: "Sneeringly, Tarantino once referred to white liberals as 'the most sensitive human beings on the planet,' and he loved nothing more than to thumb his nose at their bleeding hearts."[62] His characters' use of racial slurs does not constitute a positive contribution to the American dialogue on race as much as it provides a *prurient environment*, in which whites say "something really nasty and really evil, and let's share this secret thrill."[63] Hoon calls this *hooliganism*, after Sartre's description of anti-Semites as "filled with self-reflexive doubleness and distance, an enigmatic, nervous energy as though they are always already answering an invisible accusation."[64] Tarantino's dialogue and his defense of it seem to ring with a gleeful, willfully adolescent revelry in negative behavior for nothing more than the sake of shocking others, self-amusement, and a vain display of the privilege of engaging in such behavior.

That is perhaps the most potentially harmful aspect of Tarantino's use of the word *nigger*. While he might claim to be disempowering a word he feels is too powerful (though he is unafraid of it), this does little or nothing to advance substantive dialogue on race and racist language. Instead, it sanctions and may even encourage use of the term for strictly prurient reasons. Tarantino's use of the word may be an attempt to conceal his own whiteness, or to disempower it, but his use of it, and the uses he likely engenders, differ little if at all from its use as a racist epithet uttered by avowed racists in the not-too-distant past.

Tarantino's defense of his writing and his views is a claim to artistic liberty or immunity; the freedom of art must be absolute. For Tarantino, artistic liberties allow him to place himself and his work beyond (or above) recrimination; doing otherwise would inherently impinge on artistic freedom of expression. Thus, Tarantino implicitly seems to invoke a constitutional right to his position and his work, and to imply that any limitation is therefore almost criminal in ideological terms. In addition, because constitutional freedoms are ostensibly a right of citizenship, he is not asking for, or taking, any more freedom than every American is entitled to. Thus, he supposedly defends freedom for all Americans. But, as we have seen, freedom in America is neither equally distributed nor equally available. Unsurprisingly, that distribution is affected, if not dictated, by race.

As provocative as Tarantino and his dialogue may be, there is a significant exception in his catalog of slurs that prevents him from achieving what might be termed "equal offensivity." Peppered as it is with derogatory references to women, homosexuals, Asians, and African Americans, his dialogue contains no anti-Semitic terms. Tarantino's characters have certainly uttered remarks that can be considered insulting to Jewish people, or evocative of Jewish stereotypes. In *Reservoir Dogs*, a character excoriates a colleague's refusal to tip a waitress by saying "I don't even know a fucking Jew who'd have the balls to say that." A character in *Pulp Fiction* refers to "old fucking Jews." Another character explains his aversion to pork by saying "I ain't Jewish, I just don't dig on swine." In *Kill Bill Vol. 2*, a character asserts that "I don't Jew out of my comeuppance." Yet these lines, while certainly offensive, avoid using anti-Semitic racial or ethnic terms. It is noteworthy that the same characters who use words like *jungle bunny, nigger, slope, gook, bitch, faggot, cooze, whore, fuck machine,* and *cunt* somehow do not use words like *jewboy, hebe, Yid, sheeny,* or *kike*. Even *Inglorious Basterds'* Nazi Colonel Landa, "The Jew Hunter," does not use anti-Semitic slurs. Tarantino's racist, homophobic, misogynistic characters seem to have an empty space in their palette of slurs, an absence much less prevalent in their real-life counterparts.

When Spike Lee asked Tarantino why he believed he could use *nigger* so freely, while Michael Jackson was widely criticized for using the term *kike* in a song, Tarantino asserted:

> The words *nigger* and *kike* are not the same word. *Kike* is not common parlance among Jews. The other word has maybe 12 different meanings, depending on the context it's spoken in, who is saying it and the way he's saying it. So to equate *nigger* with *kike* does not take into account the way the English language works today. And I am working with the English language.[65]

By defining what constitutes "common parlance" among Jews and comparing it to that of the black community, Tarantino claims to know what constitutes common parlance among blacks. Certainly, the word *nigger* is used more often than *kike* in *pop* culture discourse, and by *some* blacks, but Tarantino's claim is much more totalizing and therefore that much more egregious and erroneous. It also assumes a homogeneity that, unsurprisingly, follows his narrow, stereotypical conception of what, or whom, is "black."

Tarantino's free use of language and Michael Jackson's forced modification of his lyrics illustrate the reality that it is acceptable to use some racial slurs in American media, but not others. Why are people any less shocked by the word *nigger* than *kike*? We might ask ourselves, why is the use of *nigger* openly debated as a free speech issue, yet to do the same with *kike* seems outrageous? Why have we accepted *nigger* and its utterance to such an extent? Why is it that you as a reader may feel an instinctive negative response to my repeated use of the word *kike*? I assert that it is because we have been socialized and acculturated to know that some words are acceptable and some are not, and that there is no debate or discussion about their inappropriateness. The conflict between Tarantino and Spike Lee, or more accurately the disparate racial reality of Tarantino and Michael Jackson, illustrates that fact implicitly and explicitly.

Tarantino's offensive dialogue is not normal, natural, "human," or all-encompassing. It assaults only those who do not have the power to stop it. Conversely, his racist language is not aimed at those he knows not to offend, people who could potentially stop his dialogue from being heard altogether. It may be no coincidence that, while Tarantino "knows" he has lived previously as an African American slave, he does not claim to have been a Holocaust victim. If an artist of Michael Jackson's stature could be pressured into changing his art, Tarantino could be pressured as well.

The acceptability of offensive terms referring to specific groups is inversely proportional to the social power held and wielded by those groups. There is little or no debate over the use of *kike*, because any such discussion is inherently "off the table." We can use and discuss *nigger* in public *because we know that there will be little or no social power exercised against us for doing so.* There is no debate on the public use of insults like *cracker*, because it is irrelevant; the social power and status of recipients render the point moot. The recipients often find it humorous, which only reinforces its inherently powerless nature. If the social power to curtail public anti-Semitism exists, it therefore *could* similarly exist for others. The fact that such social power *does not* exist speaks loudly about power distribution in American society. When African Americans wield adequate social power, the public, mediated use of *nigger*, as well as the debate about its use, will change significantly. The new reality of President Barack Obama will accelerate that change; to use the word *nigger* is, for at least four years, to implicitly insult and degrade the Commander-in-Chief.

Who has freedom and who bears the consequences of that freedom? Given the differential deployments of social power aimed at Quentin Tarantino and Michael Jackson, we must ask if it is really freedom, or if some are freer than others. Some people have the freedom to insult others who do not have the social power to curtail, prevent, or disallow it. Nor can those insulted disseminate a response, insulting or not, as loudly and widely as their insulter can. When we factor race into that construct, "freedom" can suddenly appear much the same as privilege, grounded as it is in social power. Yet, the freedom to insult is not absolute. In American media and society, some people are "free" to bear the burden of, and *for*, others' freedom of speech.

Implications and Recommendations

Quentin Tarantino's appropriation of a perceived blackness can be seen as a hallmark of the "postmodern" condition, where everyone is everything and history is dead. Such a standpoint, however, inevitably benefits some more than others. Unsurprisingly, it also tends to reify rather than challenge power structures. Thus, postmodernism is still intractably modern, and in the same vein Tarantino's anti-racism is intractably racist. Such re-characterizations are crucial in a society where race and power are so strongly interrelated.

Although not addressed in this chapter, Tarantino's blatant Orientalism, much of which operates from the same core whiteness that informs his appropriations of "blackness," deserves and indeed demands critique.

Tarantino's status as a pop culture figure lends his words and actions greater visibility than that of ordinary individuals, and his films' global distribution guarantees the dissemination of not only the images and stories they contain, but also the ideas and ideology of their director. Those are perhaps the most salient reasons why critique and re-characterizations of the director and his films is crucial. By denying Tarantino the luxury of being non-racially "human" (a luxury he himself denies via his construction of "blackness") and by situating him within a specific critical framework, we can therefore reevaluate his views, his actions, and his films. While Tarantino's public persona is seen as eccentric or perhaps controversial, he is not soundly derided as racist, inflammatory, or exploitative.

Whiteness serves power by preserving its structures. In the Land of the Free, some are freer than Others, and that freedom, or privilege, is couched in terms of seemingly unimpeachable ideas such as an essential humanity. Thus, to deny Tarantino (or others) the "right" to flit between cultures, taking what he likes, while remaining immune from the rest, would seem, at first, a terrible denial of humanity. But in this guise, an essential humanity that enables ethnic variability is not a liberation from racism but a perpetuation of it. The *interior* "human's" movement toward (or away from) ethnicities is usually based on *exterior* attributes. This construct implicitly ignores or devalues the Other's interior attributes, and by extension their humanity. The "humanity" of whiteness is a contradiction in more ways than one.

Interaction between ethnicities is not inherently exploitative, negative, or indefensible. However, the ways in which the interaction is conducted, the conditions in which the interaction takes place, and the relative costs and benefits to both sides would ideally factor into the experience. Truly progressive interethnic communication would not engender racism, degradation, and exploitation.

1. The domestic and foreign (where available) grosses for Tarantino's five films in U.S. dollars are as follows:

1992 *Reservoir Dogs*	Domestic: $ 2,832,029	
1994 *Pulp Fiction*	Domestic: $107,928,762	Worldwide: $213,928,762
1997 *Jackie Brown*	Domestic: $ 39,673,162	
2003 *Kill Bill Vol. 1*	Domestic: $ 70,099,045	Worldwide: $180,949,045
2004 *Kill Bill Vol. 2*	Domestic: $ 66,208,183	Worldwide: $152,159,461
2007 *Grindhouse*	Domestic: $ 25,037,897	Worldwide: $ 25,422,088

(www.boxofficemojo.com)

2. For the present study, it is my intention to focus on some of Quentin Tarantino's problematic words and actions pertaining to African Americans. Yet this study barely scratches the surface of an unfortunately deep reservoir of similar issues with other racial groups. One of the most salient has to do with Tarantino's portrayals of Asians onscreen as well as his and his employers' interaction with Asian cinemas in business and creative terms. Their Orientalism is a subject rife for examination, but it is driven by distinctly different characteristics from the issue of blackness, and therefore goes unexamined here.

3. Ruth Frankenberg, *White Women, Race Matters: The Social Construction of Whiteness* (Minneapolis: University of Minnesota Press, 1992); Ruth Frankenberg, ed., *Displacing Whiteness: Essays in Social and Cultural Criticism* (Durham: Duke University Press, 1997); Richard Dyer, *White* (New York: Routledge, 1997). Ronald L. Jackson II, "White Space, White Privilege: Mapping Discursive Inquiry into the Self," *Quarterly Journal of Speech* 85.1 (1999): 38–54. Thomas Nakayama and Robert L. Krizek, "Whiteness as a Strategic Rhetoric," in *Whiteness: The Communication of Social Identity*, ed. Tom Nakayama and Judith N. Martin (Thousand Oaks, CA: Sage, 1999), 87–106.

4. Dyer, *White*.

5. Nakayama and Krizek, 92.

6. Frankenberg, *White Women, Race Matters*; Allen Kwan, "Seeking New Civilizations: Race Normativity in the *Star Trek* Franchise," *Bulletin of Science, Technology and Society* 27.1 (2007): 59–70.

7. Dreama Moon and Thomas K. Nakayama, "Strategic Social Identities and judgments: A murder in Appalachia," *Howard Journal of Communications* 16.2 (2005): 87–107. Michael A. Chaney, "Coloring Whiteness and Black Voice Minstrelsy: Representations of Race and Place in *Static Shock*, *King of the Hill*, and *South Park*," *Journal of Popular Film and Television* 31.4 (2004): 167–75.

8. Henry Giroux, "Racism and the Aesthetic of Hyperreal Violence: *Pulp Fiction* and Other Visual Tragedies, in *Quentin Tarantino: Interviews*, ed. Garry Peary (Jackson: University Press of Mississippi, 1998); Paul Gormley, "Trashing Whiteness: *Pulp Fiction*, *Se7en*, *Strange Days*, and Articulating Affect," *Angelaki: Journal of the Theoretical Humanities* 6.1 (2000): 155–71; Sean Tierney, "Themes of Whiteness in *Bulletproof Monk*, *Kill Bill*, and *The Last Samurai*," *Journal of Communication* 56.3 (2006): 607–24.

9. Terms paired with the director's name included words designed to produce the most pertinent results, i.e., *race, racist, racism, Black, Blackness, African American*, and *nigger*. It should be noted that there were no results found in which Tarantino expressed a reversal of or remorse or regret for any of the views/statements examined here.

10. Dyer, *Heavenly Bodies.*

11. Frankenberg, *White Women, Race Matters,* 1.

12. Tierney, "Themes of Whiteness."

13. Frankenberg, ed., *Displacing Whiteness.* Charles Gallagher, "White Racial Formation: Into the Twenty-First Century," in *Critical White Studies: Looking Behind the Mirror,* ed. Richard Delgado and Jean Stefancic (Philadelphia: Temple University Press, 1997).

14. Robyn Wiegman, "Whiteness Studies and the Paradox of Particularity," *Boundary 2,* 26.3 (1999): 115–51. Frankenberg, ed., *Displacing Whiteness.*

15. Jolanta Drzewiecka and Kay Wong, "The Dynamic Construction of White Ethnicity in the Context of Transnational Cultural Formations," in *Whiteness: The Communication of Social Identity,* ed. Tom Nakayama and Judith N. Martin (Thousand Oaks, CA: Sage, 1999).

16. Frankenberg, *White Women, Race Matters,* 1.

17. Dyer, *White,* 2.

18. Frankenberg, *White Women, Race Matters,* 1.

19. Ibid.

20. Ibid. Tierney, "Themes of Whiteness."

21. Gormley, "Trashing Whiteness."

22. Adrian Wootton, "Quentin Tarantino interview (I) with Pam Grier, Robert Forster and Lawrence Bender," *guardian.co.uk* (1998).

23. France Widdance Twine, "Brown Skinned White Girls: Class, Culture, and the Construction of White Identity in Suburban Communities, in *Displacing Whiteness: Essays in Social and Cultural Criticism,* ed. Ruth Frankenberg, 238 (Durham: Duke University Press, 1997).

24. Bob Strauss, Five Questions with the King of Pulp. *E! Online* (1997).

25. Quentin Tarantino, Interview, in John L. Jackson Jr., *Harlemworld: Doing Race and Class in Contemporary Black America* (Chicago: University of Chicago Press 2001), 203–4.

26. Peter Biskind, *Down and Dirty Pictures: Miramax, Sundance and the Rise of Independent Film* (London: Bloomsbury, 2004), 316. Quentin Tarantino, Interview, in John L. Jackson Jr., *Harlemworld,* 203–4.

27. Quentin Tarantino, Interview, *Playboy Magazine,* 2003.

28. Wootton, "Quentin Tarantino interview (I)."

29. Roger Ebert, *Roger Ebert's Movie Yearbook 2005* (Kansas City: Andrews McMeel Publishing, 2004), 814.

30. Frankenberg, *White Women, Race Matters,* 113.

31. Linda Alcoff, "What Should White People Do?" *Hypatia* 13.3 (1996).

32. Quentin Tarantino, "Tarantino Embraces Past Lives," *Contactmusic.com* (2008).

33. Quentin Tarantino, "I'm Proud of My Flop," *Telegraph.co.uk,* 4/27/2007.

34. Ibid.

35. Deborah Root, *Cannibal Culture: Art, Appropriation and the Commodification of Difference* (Boulder, CO: Westview, 1996), 231.

36. Wootton, "Quentin Tarantino interview (I)."

37. Biskind, *Down and dirty pictures,* 119, 318.

38. Ella Shohat and Robert Stam, *Eurocentrism: Multiculturalism and the Media* (New York: Routledge, 2000), 344.

39. Wootton, "Quentin Tarantino interview (I)."

40. Ibid.

41. Peter Keough, "Independents' Daze: Quentin Tarantino and Gus Van Sant on Playing Hollywood's Game," *The Worcester Phoenix*, 01/02/1998.

42. Wootton, "Quentin Tarantino interview (I)."

43. Tomohiro Machiyama, "Tarantino Interview," *Japattack.com* (2003).

44. Tarantino, Interview, *Playboy Magazine*, 2003.

45. Alcoff, "What Should White People Do?"

46. Barry Brummett, *The World and How We Describe It: Rhetorics of Reality, Representation, Simulation* (Westport, CT: Praeger, 2004).

47. Manohla Dargis, "West Looks East: *City on Fire* and *Reservoir Dogs*," *L.A. Weekly*, March 17–23, 1995.

48. Joshua Mooney, "Interview with Quentin Tarantino, *Movieline* (August 1994), 54.

49. George Lipsitz, *The Possessive Investment in Whiteness: How White People Profit from Identity Politics* (Philadelphia: Temple University Press, 1998), 120.

50. Elvis Mitchell, Interview, in Isaac Julian (dir.): *BaadAsssss Cinema: A bold look at 70s Blaxploitation films*, IFC Entertainment (2002).

51. Edward Guerrero, Interview, in Isaac Julian (dir.): *BaadAsssss Cinema: A Bold Look at 70s Blaxploitation Films*, IFC Entertainment (2002).

52. Debian Marty, "White Antiracist Rhetoric as Apologia," in *Whiteness: The Communication of Social Identity*, ed. Tom Nakayama and Judith N. Martin (Thousand Oaks, CA: Sage, 1999), 55.

53. Wootton, "Quentin Tarantino interview (I)."

54. Spike Lee, "Interview: Getting Spikey: *The Context* interviews Spike Lee, director of *Bamboozled*," www.thecontext.com (2001).

55. Biskind, *Down and dirty pictures*; Tarantino, Interview, *Playboy Magazine*, 2003.

56. Sarah Projansky and Kent Ono, "Strategic Whiteness as Cinematic Racial Politics," in *Whiteness: The Communication of Social Identity*, ed. Tom Nakayama and Judith N. Martin (Thousand Oaks, CA: Sage, 1999), 152.

57. Barbara Flagg, "'Was Blind, But Now I See': White Race Consciousness and the Requirement of Discriminatory Intent," in *Critical White Studies: Looking Behind the Mirror*, ed. Richard Delgado and Jean Stefancic (Philadelphia: Temple University Press, 1997), 630.

58. Strauss, "Five Questions with the King of Pulp."

59. Philomena Essed, *Understanding Everyday Racism: An Interdisciplinary Theory* (Thousand Oaks, CA: Sage, 1991); Cornel West, *Race Matters* (Boston: Beacon Press, 1993).

60. Widdance Twine, "Brown Skinned White Girls."

61. Root, *Cannibal Culture*, 231.

62. Biskind, *Down and dirty pictures*, 119.

63. Amy Taubin, quoted in Henry Giroux, "Racism and the Aesthetic of Hyper-real Violence: *Pulp Fiction* and Other Visual Tragedies," *Social Identities* 1.2 (1995): 333–54.

64. Hoon Song, "Seeing Oneself Seeing Oneself: White Nihilism in Ethnography and Theory," *Ethnos* 71.4 (2006): 476.

65. Tarantino, Interview, *Playboy Magazine*, 2003.

5 Patrolling National Identity, Masking White Supremacy

The Minuteman Project

Michelle A. Holling

Efforts at both presidential and congressional levels to strengthen national security by mending "broken" borders and passing immigration reform legislation
have advanced with varying degrees of success following the September 11 tragedy.
Efforts at the federal level have included President Bush's failed "guest worker"
program, a proposed but defeated House Bill 4437 (the Border Protection,
Anti-terrorism, and Illegal Immigration Control Act of 2005), and the passage
of House Bill 418 (the Real ID Act of 2005).[1] At the state level, in 2004 Arizona
voters passed Proposition 200, requiring proof of citizenship when registering to
vote or applying for public benefits. Proposition 200 led *Newsweek* reporter Scott
Johnson to characterize Arizona as "the cradle of the anti-immigration movement
[making] the state a magnet for vigilantes."[2] At the center of this movement, in
response to perceived government disinterest and irresponsibility, is the vigilante
group, the Minuteman Project, which is the focus of this chapter.

Portraying itself as a citizen's group monitoring the border for "invading illegal
aliens," the Minuteman Project (hereafter MMP) was founded in 2005 by James
Gilchrist and Chris Simcox.[3] Initiated by a month-long encampment in April
2005 along the Arizona-Mexico border, the MMP is now notorious as a border
policing organization, with leaders who carefully craft an ideologically infused
message and identity. This identity helps to advance the cause of securing adherents and challenging the government in an attempt to hold it accountable. The
argument made by the MMP is that the government is responsible for the nation's
safety and therefore should be responsive to the needs of those who experience
the immigration problem near the border. The MMP gets its message across by
accessing media, which include both institutionally sanctioned networks and self-
produced sites. There, the MMP conveys its message of disaffection and frustration in hopes of inspiring individuals to action.[4] This chapter addresses the various ways the website www.minutemanproject.com constructs the organization's
identity, while simultaneously framing undocumented immigrants.

Although people might be tempted to ignore or dismiss the MMP without first subjecting it to critical scrutiny, such an approach would achieve little
in terms of understanding the development of this seemingly innocuous group
that seeks ordinary citizens' support in protecting the nation. Four years after

September 11, 2001, the MMP came on the scene by appealing to the "average Joe," who could ostensibly demonstrate his commitment, dedication, and love for country by joining the group. Identifying the ways by which the MMP maintains its identity and seeks to recruit new members is an important endeavor, particularly when considering the organization's appeal to prospective members and its growth. The MMP received considerable media publicity in 2005, in part after developing local chapters and experiencing the breaking off of other off-shoot extremist organizations. Now, the MMP is "one of the country's largest, richest and most influential nativist extremist groups,"[5] a group worthy of scholarly attention. Central to appealing to "Joe" citizen was the MMP's website, which became an important means by which to disseminate its cause. My examination of the website addresses the symbols used to "address publics" and to rally them to action.[6] Recent scholarship suggests a continued need to study a movement's use of symbols addressed to publics via the Internet (websites in particular). Such sites serve as a venue for understanding the establishment of collective identities and the ideological frames supporting them.[7]

My interest in examining the MMP[8] focuses on the suasory nature of their self-constructed identity, as opposed to institutional "media framings"[9] of them. In the name of protecting the nation and "doing what Congress won't do" (as the MMP proclaim), MMP rhetoric serves to legitimate an "American"[10] identity shaped by resonant and recurrent themes of patriotism, masculinity, militarism, and multiculturalism. I argue that such an identity subtly masks the white supremacist values undergirding the MMP's stated purpose, while also enabling it to air a public grievance that claims the U.S. government post–9/11 has fallen short of its responsibility to protect its citizenry from invaders crossing the nation's border.

Equally integral to its identity are the ways the MMP frames immigrants as colonizers, and as dehumanized, externalized, and criminalized subjects. This framing adds a sense of efficacy to their stated actions of organizing a "neighborhood border watch." In this chapter, I offer additional comments about the importance of studying the MMP website, coupled with a discussion of the theoretical approach informing my analysis. Following this are two analytical sections regarding the MMP's self-constructed identity and its framing of undocumented immigrants. I end the chapter by discussing the MMP as a recovery project responsive to discourses of a gendered "white pain."[11]

Studying the MMP

Scholars note that the relative accessibility and utility of the Internet by movement and hate groups helps lend groups legitimacy, serves as a tool for recruitment, facilitates their ability to acquire resources, and affirms group identity and promotes solidarity, while also offering a space for emergent cyber-movements.[12] In particular, websites "can act as an introduction to a particular group."[13] The MMP's website introduces the group by addressing the "who, what and why" of its existence. In fact, supporters posting comments on the MMP website (www. minutemanproject.com) explicitly say the website enabled them to increase their knowledge of the MMP and/or gave them "hope in a day and age when thing's [sic] look as bleak as they sometimes do," hence playing a key role in facilitating the public's comprehension of them. Yet, in what ways is the content on the website used to construct an identity that allows visitors of the site ultimately to become supporters or members?

Analysis of the original MMP website, which went live in April and continued through to June 2005, contains several hundred pages of content. Over the years the website homepage and content have changed, as websites often do, making much of what is analyzed in this chapter no longer publicly available. At the time I studied the original website, however, individuals interested in learning about the MMP, along with events during and following the MMP encampment, would have found content housed under several links, including: "Home," "Photos," "About," "LEO" [law enforcement officer], "Articles" [random news articles reprinted by the MMP], "FAQs," "SOP" [standard operating procedures], "Events," "Links," and "Feedback," which the MMP divides into "positive" and "negative" posts.[14] The last link totals 337 posts, which includes both supportive and unsupportive posts (265 and 72, respectively). Also included in my analysis are an MMP recruitment poster and a 36-second MMP recruitment video.

During the three-month period noted, I downloaded and examined all available content from the website using a critical-rhetorical post-structuralist perspective. Such an approach means I discerned themes and symbols, noting in particular the historical dimension of such symbols, their recombined and therefore hybrid forms, diverse visual images, and culturally specific "ideographs" and "frames" characteristic of immigration rhetoric.[15] In my analysis, I am particularly conscious of the identity framing among groups or movements, because paying attention to strategies of configuring identity assists me in explaining how movement rhetoric functions and how it helps to convey grievances and produce calls to action.[16] When taken together, the means by which the MMP constructs its identity and frames the Other as "illegal aliens" reflects traces of "white absolutism" that scapegoats others in an effort to ameliorate white masculine pain.[17]

"Americans Doing the Jobs Our Government Won't Do!"

This phrase or "frame" serves as a counter-argument by the MMP to the U.S. government. "Frames" refer to the selection and emphasis of particular ways of understanding social issues, making salient particular problems, causes, and solutions in the process.[18] The use of frames is evident in MMP rhetoric, particularly on the homepage of its website, but also in news media of Gilchrist and Simcox. Adapting the frame from what has become an adage (i.e., "immigrants do the jobs Americans won't do") already "resonates" with the public at large, thereby requiring minimal, if any, interpretation by the MMP. Entman opines that frames are powerful, because of their ability to call attention to specific dimensions of reality simultaneously, directing attention away from other aspects of reality that carry implications for action taken by individuals or groups.[19]

MMP framing of immigration drew upon a period of nativist retreat following 9/11, when heightened concerns over "national security" conveyed most notably in "terror threat level alerts," anxieties about "terrorists" crossing a porous U.S.-Mexico border, and (un)successful legislative policies, such as those noted at the outset of this chapter, were evident. News media articles about the MMP reinforced these political threads. Additionally, they called attention to the need for immigration reform and border control to control the border crossings of drugs and gun runners, smugglers, and terrorists, and the increase in day laborers in cities across the nation.[20] Presented in tandem, then, the frame used by the MMP calls attention to an exigence they are willing to remedy. Deflected from recognition in the frame "Americans doing the job . . ." are the multinational policies such as NAFTA and CAFTA and the related economic implications for "Americans"; however, news media programs tended to fill that gap by referencing the "high cost of free trade" or the "cheap labor" of immigrants when discussing the MMP.[21]

By implication, the MMP emerged during a period of political and economic turmoil when nativists confidently asserted their claims of "xenophobic belongingness."[22] Hence, the MMP rallied support for its objective during a period when dominant discourse paralleled that of the MMP's emphasis on "threats." Even with the support of dominant discourse, however, the MMP still needed to assert an identity that positioned it and its members on the side of the nation in order to appeal to prospective members and supporters. Thus, the MMP constructed an "American" identity that had the potential to tap into a democratic multicultural impulse. By strategically referring to U.S. heterogeneity and the ideals of anti-discrimination, the MMP could safeguard itself against potential accusations of racism.

Patriotic Nationalists

The MMP constructs a rhetorically compelling identity that solicits not only potential supporters, but also media attention itself through its "revolutionary patriotism," which is nominally linked to the American Revolution. The most obvious and logical resources the group draws on (given their name) are images of the revolutionary Minutemen of Massachusetts. The MMP uses these images to connect its project to a historically compelling narrative of anti-colonial, revolutionary struggle. The recruitment poster is an apt illustration featuring an American flag shield with 13 stars and a town crier ringing a bell, while in the background a Paul Revere-like figure rides atop a horse. Wrapped around these symbols is a border centering an American eagle with 13 stars symbolizing the colonies. Another image on the website depicts an American revolutionary patriot with binoculars and a cell phone positioned strategically as a visual substitution for a musket.[23] The parallels between the MMP and the revolutionary Minutemen go beyond obvious analogies: Paul Revere rides through Massachusetts warning of a British Invasion in April 1775; he is the ultimate patriot who, out of immense love for country, supports and defends it. Then, there are the MMP minutemen in April 2005, dutifully keeping watch over the border between Arizona and Mexico, alerting the Border Patrol of any signs of a possible "illegal alien" invasion. Whereas the Minutemen forced British troops back to Britain, their contemporary brethren work to keep the "illegals" from leaving Mexico. By implication, the United States is a colony whose "sovereign border" is threatened by "illegal aliens," along with "drug dealers and potential terrorists," and hence is in need of the MMP's protection. Appropriating visual images from the American Revolutionary era and drawing an analogy between the MMP and the original Minutemen enables, if not hastens, the establishment of an "American" identity, thus providing justification for the MMP's motivations and actions.

The appeal of the analogy is not lost on MMP supporters, two of whom shared the following: "If I lived there [AZ] I would be by the side of the other PATRIOTS volunteering their time" and "It really does a man's heart good to see a citizens group like yours echo the spirit of the founding fathers." Other examples implicitly condone violence through their *revolutionary* references to the Boston Tea Party: "God Bless and let it [no stated referent] work as well as the Boston tea party" and "The time has come for another 'Boston Tea Party' and it will take place in Arizona." Finally, one other posting bears citation, as it underscores the righteousness with which the MMP act:

> Dear Minutemen and Minutewomen Volunteers, You all need to realize you have adophted [sic] and tooken [sic] the legacy and title of the "Minuteman" from back when our wonderful nation started. Even though there were some woes about the organization our founding fathers and I belong to we need to realize something.
> Your efforts and goals are just. Your ambitions and intentions are good.

Supporters' acceptance of the analogy likening the MMP to the original Minutemen betrays complicity with its faulty logic. In short, the MMP strives to maintain its identity as resisting an imperial power, a strategy that figures the United

States (and themselves) as victim. But, accepting that premise requires viewing "illegal immigrants" as possessing similar imperial powers to their analogous historical counterpart (i.e., Britain) and neglecting the political and/or economic non-imperial exigencies that compel immigrants to migrate.

Another way in which the website connects the present-day struggle to the colonial era is through the MMP's characterization of itself as "a citizen's neighborhood watch along our border" group that depends on the MMP members' status as lawful citizens. Neighborhood watch programs date back to the colonial period when "night watchmen" patrolled the streets.[24] In much the same way, the MMP works to "induce people to exercise some degree of social control in the environments where they live . . . to enforce standards of behavior in their own neighborhoods," thus positioning citizens as surveillors, who act as the "eyes and ears for law enforcement."[25] The swiftness with which the MMP adopted a familiar colonial approach to surveillance in turn legitimizes its existence and: (1) broadens its appeal to common citizens who may have anxieties about national security or be disaffected by national politics; and (2) offers citizens a façile way of involving themselves in the national politics on a local level, thus demonstrating themselves to be "good citizens" acting as enforcers of a crime-free and orderly society.

At heart, the MMP constructs itself as a "maligned and misunderstood group of truly patriotic nationalists."[26] The MMP characterizes members as misunderstood and suggests their actions have been critiqued by those who prefer the status quo (e.g., those content with the continued "violation of U.S. sovereignty" and with the "unenforcement of U.S. immigration laws," or those who "whine," "naysay," "moan," or do nothing). By locating themselves within a patriotic narrative, one in which they are active and their opponents are passive, the MMP members attempt to steel themselves from critique: to critique the MMP metonymically serves as a critique of the whole history of patriotism and even of being an "American." Such a move, however, relies upon an ahistorical understanding of patriotism that has a raced dimension when considering, for example, service in the armed forces and the denial, recognition, and/or conferral of citizenship rights.[27] Moreover, the "racial dictatorship" that defined "'American' identity as white'" belies the white supremacy informing the patriotism of the MMP.[28]

Righteousness, Masculinity, and Militarism

Integral to instantiating their identity as "patriotic nationalists" is the sense of righteousness with which they act. This righteousness gains strength from a legal absolutist and a masculine militaristic ethos. Consistently, the MMP emphasizes undocumented immigrants who violate the "rule of law" in contrast to MMP members who act within or on the side of the law, such as when Gilchrist replied to a negative posting, "there is nothing 'hateful' about operating within the *rule of law* to *support* the *rule of law*."[29] Repeatedly reiterating the "rule of law" functions to support legalistic "absolutism" that masks white supremacy. Lacy explains that "Rhetors who offer explicit appeals for white supremacy constitute 'absolutists' who operate from a 'positivistic or classic world view,' which is 'populated with essences, realities, intrinsic good and evils. . . . White absolutists exploit religion and science to explain and justify white supremacy."[30] In the case of the MMP, members' appeals to white supremacy are masked by their use of the "revolutionary" Minutemen analogy; yet, their constant emphasis on and appeal to being within their rights to carry out their actions follows from a commitment to valuing juridical power. Instead of religion or science as justification, they rely upon the rule of law and First Amendment rights to do what they advocate. Replying to "negative feedback," Gilchrist repeatedly reminds his detractors of his First Amendment rights: "The MMProject volunteers will assemble peaceably, and stoically, under the First Amendment."

The masculine-militaristic ethos of their rhetoric anchors the MMP volunteers' sense of righteousness and assertion of a right to assemble. Delineated in the "SOP" is a "code of ethics and behavior," which includes no contact with immigrants, "spotting and reporting," and no drawing of firearms or any safety item. In addition, the MMP encourages its volunteers to exercise "self-restraint, discipline, responsibility, character, accountability, and temperament." Such masculine attributes strongly parallel the "code of conduct" guiding military service. There exists a militaristic dimension to individuals' actions, which surfaces in their use of weapons, literal and metaphorical. Although the MMP explicitly claim not to condone carrying firearms by volunteers, and do not prohibit a volunteer from having one for "the purpose of self-defense," the fact remains that approximately two-thirds of its personnel are armed.[31] Perhaps comfort is to be derived from the "distinction between long arms, that is, rifles, which he [Simcox] considered to be offensive, and sidearms, which he categorized as defensive," henceforth acceptable, "but not to be removed from holster."[32] A "video camera" functions as a metaphorical weapon that "is your insurance policy . . . It is as much a tool for self-defense as is your sidearm," along with "night vision devices" that are also "part of the fun."

Combining the forms of weapons, the implied hunting metaphors (e.g., "spotting and reporting" or that their media policy is one of "open season"), and military language (e.g., "force-multipliers," "intruders," "mission," "battle," "invasion by enemies foreign and domestic," "volunteers will be defending," "communication center," "intelligence reports") that is ever-present in the MMP's rhetoric further instantiates the "absolutist" nature of their rhetoric. The righteousness with which the MMP describes its members and its organization operating gains force from its grievance against Congress, which supposedly places the safety of its citizenry in harm's way and thereby enables the MMP to promote a "sense of efficacy" in actions it encourages among its adherents.[33]

Multicultural, Assimilationist, and Responsive

The MMP's façade of multiculturalism is the final dimension of the organization's identity construction, a construction that discursively combines its willing compliance with the tenets of U.S. liberty with a mythical construction of the United States. As discussed earlier, qualities of self-restraint and discipline that the MMP seeks in its volunteers are those that anyone could embody. Any volunteer, no matter his/her "vocation, race, color, creed, age, gender, physical disability, etc.," is welcome. Indeed, the MMP positions itself as non-discriminatory and heterogeneous by reflecting a membership derived from different professions (e.g., "law enforcement, lawyers, truckers, physicians, CPAs, heavy equipment operators, engineers, aircraft pilots, decorated war veterans, journalists, a Ph.D. in Chemistry, and educators/teachers, etc."). Furthermore, the MMP is comprised of "more than 1,000 patriotic Americans of *diverse racial* and *ethnic* backgrounds . . . we are *multi-racial* and *multi-ethnic*. Eight of our participants are married to immigrants, and 16 are . . . immigrants."[34] Upon closer investigation, however, the MMP is implicitly slanted in two ways: toward white males and, additionally, "more than half of participants were prior military, with many of those being Vietnam veterans."[35] Important to bear in mind is the climate in which the MMP comes into being—that is, workers experiencing the consequences of economic policies that allow for exporting labor abroad, coupled with resurgent patriotism, xenophobia, and nativism. Citing their member demographics creates an *illusion* of a U.S. multicultural community banding together against a foreign Other. Professing its "diversity" across social class, racial, and ethnic lines enables the MMP to deflect accusations that they are "vigilantes," racists, or supremacists. The limits of their multicultural project, however, become apparent in their emphasis on assimilation; subsequently, the MMP's "diversity" is merely cosmetic.

Communicated in the MMP discourse is a fear that an assimilated nation is disappearing specifically because of "illegal immigrants' refusal to assimilate," which results in a fractured nation.

> The men and women volunteering for this mission are those who are willing to sacrifice their time . . . [and] cozy home to muster for something much more important than acquiring more "toys" to play with while their nation is devoured and plundered by the menace of tens of millions of invading illegal aliens. Future generations will inherit a tangle of rancorous, unassimilated, squabbling cultures with no

common bond to hold them together, and a certain guarantee of the death of this nation as a harmonious "melting pot."

What is desired, then, is a charitable, forgiving, assimilated, and harmonious culture. Becoming assimilated would include acquiring "legal" status, learning English, becoming culturally assimilated, not seeking accommodations, and identifying with the nation, thus subordinating any and all ethnic affiliations. As stated by one supporter, "I'm not a Mexican-American, but an *American* of Mexican heritage. I served four years in the U.S. Army." That supporter continues:

> My one parent who is a LEGAL immigrant was NEVER accommodated like illegal immigrants are of today (my other parent is American who did military service for the US). I was brought up to speak ONLY English (I am glad too) . . . forbidden to learn the language of my parent who became a LEGAL immigrant . . . other cultures or nationalities seem to have no problem speaking English when coming here legally to the US and I have worked around a lot of different nationalities since I moved to southern California years ago . . . Mexicans want to be coddled and accommodated but what about other immigrants here legally [?]

Ideologically, the presence of multiculturalism and assimilation offer a productive illusion to help mask the "racial pain" felt from innumerable sources, while at the same time reasserting power and dominance over the process of and grounds for inclusion of extant cultural groups.[36]

At play in the MMP discourse is "color-blind rhetoric."[37] Delineating membership composition, advocating assimilation, distancing themselves from "separatists, racists or supremacy groups or individuals" per their homepage, and engaging in "denial" reflects an embrace of color-blind ideology that seeks to undercut charges of the MMP being "racist." Strategically, "denial," as Doane explains, is "an integral component of the 'color-blind' paradigm . . . the claim that racism is a historical phenomenon that is no longer a significant problem in the American society."[38] Denying the force of history is made most explicit in a reply Gilchrist posted to negative "feedback" received:

> Invasions were not created by Americans, as you claim. Whatever territorial conquests occured [sic] hundreds, or thousands, of years ago are not the fault of people alive today. Present civilizations should not be punished for the perceived unfairness of some historical event. That is like punishing a child for a transgression the child's great-great-great grandfather is perceived to have committed 250 years ago.

The MMP's comment discursively denies the ramifications that followed from territorial conquests in the past which produced inequities that are carried forth to today. Instead, what is conveyed is that whatever aspersions are to be cast should not be toward the beneficiaries of "territorial conquests," but instead toward those who have failed to assimilate and embrace the nation; subsequently, the MMP upholds white supremacy.

Finally, the MMP's inclusion of both "positive" and "negative" "feedback" on their website conveys a sense of belonging and a pretense of responsiveness. Posting adherents' opinions and viewpoints facilitates "emotional investments" in a group by having them feel a sense of cohesion that is heightened through the "negative" feedback posted.[39] "Negative" postings contain verbal taunts, characterizations of the MMP as "racists," "vigilantes," "thugs," or "stupid rednecks" among other profane names, threats of violence (e.g., physical, sodomy, rape, and death), while also offering arguments about immigrants' role in founding the country and making economic contributions.[40] Some of Gilchrist's responses occasionally reflect an antagonistic tone, evidenced in comments such as this one: "I invite you to confront me for a public debate in Tombstone in April, which will be televised, to put forth your reasons why U.S. immigration laws should be ignored," and "Finally, as far as your intimidating warning (invitation) to stay out of Texas . . . I have but one compelling revelation for you: Arizona is only our first gig. Texas is next." More often heard are Gilchrist's efforts to advance developed responses in which his own personal experiences and motivations informing the MMP are shared with opponents. Offering a space for negative commentaries on the MMP's website invites individuals to exercise their right to voice their opinions and, hence, becomes yet another way to proffer an "American" identity by gesturing toward a democratic project while also providing a platform for Gilchrist to clarify and extend his project.

Supplementing the MMP's identity is their performance of it and framing of the Other, which lends purpose to their existence. Briefly stated, the MMP enact their identity by monitoring the border and "assisting" the U.S. Border Patrol (U.S.B.P.). The U.S.B.P. did not "officially" support the MMP and, in fact, declined offers by the MMP to act as auxiliaries, yet "privately field agents say they welcome the effort."[41] Some agents made known their occupation as U.S.B.P. agents explicitly, as in an email message to Gilchrist expressing their appreciation of assistance by the MMP. A desired relationship with the U.S.B.P. is important, because it is a reminder of the legal "absolutism" informing the MMP's discourse. Emblematic of goodness, the U.S.B.P. are "defenders of our border . . . patriotic men and women" and backed by the rule of law, yet under-supported in their effort to patrol the border. As such, the MMP lent its assistance during the April 2005 "neighborhood patrol."

"They Are a Menace to a Safe, Orderly, and Prosperous Society"

In a post–cold war era, Kent Ono and John Sloop argue that the nature of the "enemy" has shifted from "an integrated, coherent enemy to a disintegrated, incoherent enemy," resulting not only in a lack of clarity about who "we" are as a nation but also in the construction of an enemy that is multiplied, racialized, and femininized.[42] With respect to the MMP, the quotation opening this section implies a victimhood mentality reliant upon the MMP's understanding of undocumented immigrants or the "enemy" whose stealthy nature will necessitate using "night vision devices."[43] "Framing" the enemy occurs in two ways: the enemy appears either as a colonizer or as a dehumanized and racially criminalized figure who puts the United States at risk.

"Illegal Aliens" as Colonizers

The MMP constructs its own identity in the name of protecting a nation that is being "devoured and plundered" by "illegal aliens," who are able to cross a "porous" border, an act directly attributable to government inattention. Even though the MMP does not explicitly label "illegal aliens" as "colonizers," this connection is intimated through the MMP's harkening back to colonial-revolutionary era discourse and replies made by Gilchrist posted under the "feedback" link. In response to a self-identified "Arizona resident/teacher/single mom," who argued against the country being "invaded," Gilchrist replies:

> While illegal aliens are not necessarily evil, they are a menace to a safe, orderly and prosperous society when they swarm into a nation by the tens of millions, namely, what has occurred [sic] to the United States during the past 40 years. The result of a massive illegal alien invasion into a nation is colonization and ultimate domination, not assimilation into the existing culture of the nation invaded.

Gilchrist suggests undocumented immigrants are unsafe, disorderly, and poor, and these factors disrupt "the existing culture of the nation" founded upon white supremacy. Where "White imperialists and colonizers frequently described their adventures as patriarchal conquests, penetrations, or invasions,"[44] Gilchrist's reply suggests a reversal of imperialism. That is, "illegal aliens" are the ones who penetrate and invade, consequently placing the United States at risk, which requires action by the MMP, who then can assert their masculinity and be justified in their actions.

Imagining undocumented immigrants as colonizers bent on undermining a seemingly unified and historically compelling "American" identity is a rationale for the militaristic language invoked by the MMP as part of its discursive identity. Specific "ideographs," namely invaders, intruders, and enemies, illustrate this point. Because of their cultural nature, ideographs, as McGee notes, are a powerful means of conveying motives. "Invasion, intruders, and enemies" are particularly persuasive because of the recency of 9/11. In this context, the three ideographs are motivators for action to protect the nation and serve to cement the connection between the MMP and its audiences. For instance, the MMP claims that there is an *"invasion* by *enemies* foreign and domestic." The MMP's job is to "spot the *intruders"* so as to stop the "illegal alien *invasion"* of the United States.[45] The ideographs require no elaboration by the MMP because of their ubiquity in cultural discourses; more importantly, the use of a "heterosexual metaphor,"[46] such as "invasion," suggests emasculation felt by the MMP that must be attended to. Given the "mobs of illegal aliens" crossing the border, who have been vilified in states such as California and Arizona, the MMP needs only to appeal to a public's insecurities and a resurgent xenophobic patriotism and to tap into masculine concerns of being dominated in order to rally a collective against the racial colonizer.

Discursively framing immigrants as colonizers assists in diagnosing "illegal" immigration as the cause of societal problems, including feelings of MMP members of being displaced within their own nation. In so doing, the MMP instills a sense of fear and alienation in order to generate support among a polity, thus underscoring the need for buildup along the border. Aiding the fear is the MMP recruitment video, an important framing device to represent visually migrants' colonization of the United States. Punctuating the video's opening are the words "The," "Minuteman," "Project" that fade in and orient viewers to identify with the MMP's cause, as "Civil Homeland Defense" moves across the screen. Becoming visible to viewers is a male figure with binoculars who surveys the mountainous region where cadres of individuals walk. The image is so familiar that viewers ought to be able to identify "them." U.S.-based material practices that consequently e/race Mexican bodies within the politics of the border space have shaped characterizations of Mexican immigrants as "on the move."[47] Following that, the action-oriented statement "Regaining our borders" moves across the bottom of the screen, followed by the question "Will the battle be won?? [sic]" The 36-second video interpellates viewers into assuming an "American" identity. They are invited to identify with the MMP, which constitutes a "civil homeland defense," and to oppose the colonizing "devouring and plundering" immigrants who cross a porous border. There is a sense that protecting the nation vis-à-vis the southern border is also about lessening "white pain" and protecting white supremacy against an insatiable immigrant appetite.

According to the MMP, the power of the colonizer is so great that immigrants threaten to "cheapen" American citizenship, inflict chaos on the United States and its citizenry, and overturn centuries of progress. Paradoxically, suggesting that undocumented immigrants may "cheapen" citizenship implies an inferior and lower civilization that places the nation at risk of becoming "rancorous, unassimilated, squabbling cultures." The MMP romanticizes the nation as a "harmonious 'melting pot.'" The images of a quiescent melting pot contrasted against the plundering and menacing hoards invites volunteers to the struggle against the colonizers. Within MMP discourse, undocumented immigrants are a presence that opens up the opportunity to enact their identity and reclaim a sense of entitlement presumably usurped by "illegal immigrants."

"Illegal Aliens" as Dehumanized, Externalized, and Criminalized

Supporters' and/or members' comments and anecdotes about "illegal aliens," posted to the "feedback" link, provide additional insight into the MMP's framing of the Other. Supporters reveal their financial support (e.g., "Can I donate to your cause with a check?"; "Please accept my $50 Paypal payment, sent a few minutes ago"), moral support (e.g., "my thoughts and prayers are with you in this most urgent issue"; "I wish you all success and Godspeed"; and "God bless you, and every one of those blessed people who are joining you"), as well as ideological support by referencing registration for the April 2005 encampment, expressing words of appreciation (e.g., "you are not vigilantes . . . but men and women of honor and of the highest integrity deserving, if any ever were, of bearing the title of American Patriot"; "Your efforts should be applauded and supported by The [sic] American people, congress [sic] and the President"). Combined supporters' posts function synecdochically to characterize the MMP's view of the Other, which is through dehumanization, externalization, and racial criminalization.

Language used throughout the MMP website casts immigrants as "illegals" or "illegal aliens." Such an identity emanates not only from discursive practices, as Ono and Sloop note, but also from the movement of bodies across a national line, the border. Following suit is the MMP recruitment video, which depicts bodies moving across an open desert-like mountainous region. The legislative nomenclature conveyed by "illegal aliens" circumscribes any articulation or consideration of what immigrant identities might look like apart from such understandings. Because the state-based, juridical identity of "illegal" is always already racialized, it should be clear that the (national) border is one site for the struggle over and the creation of a national-racial space. MMP supporters' use of the terms "illegals" and "illegal aliens" dehumanizes immigrants, although it is a bit tamer in comparison to characterizations of the Other as nonhuman, subhuman, and primitive as identified by Michael Lacy.[48]

Visible among MMP supporters is their "scapegoating" of immigrants, who offer a target on which to "externalize blame." To one supporter, "illegals are ruining our country. Around here [GA] . . . hispanics [sic] are the majority." Certainly a number of reasons exist to explain why the country is in dire straits, but no others are considered, because, to the supporter, "illegals" is sufficient explanation in itself. Lacy suggests that "absolutists blame an external racial scapegoat for real or perceived loss, competition, economic catastrophe, or social upheaval. In doing so, they resist blaming themselves [or] challenging their absolutist worldview."[49] The perceived threat of "illegals" and fear of their "invasion" is locatable in whole communities across the nation whom supporters indict, such as "the illegal Latin, Hispanic and Haitian-Creole populations in Southern Florida" or the "illegal alien Hispanic community" in Bend, Oregon, that dramatize the need to patrol the border(s). The His-panic dimension in supporters' comments glosses over the ways that Latina/os' presence and self-articulations point to the ways they have already contributed to redefinitions of what being an "American" means.[50]

Perhaps in spite of such contributions, MMP supporters criminalize immigrants discursively with an emphasis on il/legal migration, thus casting issues "within an 'us'/'them' framework."[51] Among MMP supporters, criminalizing immigrants is about the *act* of breaking the law, emphasized by several supporters who call attention to their own migration to the United States through *legal* means. But, criminalizing immigrants is also about their *resentment*—resenting "illegal aliens" who do not follow the "rule of law." Extending the us/them antagonism are supporters' characterizations of immigrants as "destroyers" who engage in an "invasion" of, or a "mass exodus" to, the United States, subsequently underscoring immigrants as a force of nature to be reckoned with. The "invasion" of "illegal aliens" creates a feeling of being imprisoned. One supporter shares that he is unable to leave his home in California, which is along the southern border area, because he is "being invaded by these criminals from Mexico." The criminalizing tone is illustrated by other supporters who reference "Mexican's [sic] who cross the border" or who cite an "illegal alien from Guatemala" charged with murdering a young girl that could have been prevented were "proper safeguards" in place. Such populations, but "Mexicans" in particular, have the potential to take over the country, as expressed by one supporter: "I hate to think that our forefathers secured the country through many wars, only for us to loose [sic] it because the mexicans [sic] breed at such a higher rate . . . They are uneducated, and have nothing to offer the US except some cheap manual labor." The "feminization"[52] of immigrants evident through the "breeding" reference is familiar and, in the case of the MMP, underscores the perceived importance of their work.

Many ways in which the MMP views the Other are intertwined—to dehumanize an Other facilitates externalizing blame onto them, or to criminalize an Other implies they lack qualities, virtues, or characteristics valued by humanity. Yet, each perception of "illegal aliens" may also stand as an independent argument allowing for a tiered level of buy-in by potential supporters of the MMP and what they represent. Finally, the MMP's framing of immigrants begs the question of what is distressful about "illegal aliens" supposedly "colonizing" the United States. And, what or whom will be "destroyed" in such a process? White supremacy? An "American" identity?

Discussion

The implicit fear conveyed by the MMP about the loss of an "American" identity intimates "white pain." Aaron Gresson explains it as "a form of racial pain," which is "caused by voluntary or forced identification with a 'spoiled racial identity.'"[53] Recognizing that "American" is not the "spoiled racial identity" to which Gresson refers, there is something to be said for the ways "American" has carried historical traces of whiteness and existed as a spoiled identity, reaping the benefits of white supremacy based on the oppression and domination of various racial and ethnic groups. In this regard, Gresson continues explaining that white pain is about a loss of a sense of self due to a "loss of the axis around which so much of white identity has been constructed in the United States."[54] For "Americans" unaccustomed to being victimized as a nation, 9/11 shook and unsettled what it was to be "American." The United States' entrance into war then is about "America's recovery of 'something' lost."[55] The MMP taps into the fragility of being an "American" and participates in a "recovery of 'something' lost"—a recovery project of past idea(l)s by patrolling the border, thus acquiring symbolic social power that responds to white *masculine* pain.

The nuances of white masculine pain derive from a national sense of victimhood stemming from acts of terror and from fear of Other's colonization of the United States. Even though the MMP members express concern about terrorists, their attention primarily focuses on the enemy they recognize as undocumented immigrants. The challenges to their right to be here evince the fear about, and permeability of, "American" identity. Ironically, current and historical legal migration and changing demographics facilitate these fears and the fluidity of American identity. Regardless, the MMP members express fears of becoming a numerical minority, being displaced from one's employment, home, geographic locale and nation, and being a potential victim of crimes committed by immigrants. To overcome victim status and to respond to the pain that emasculates the nation and its inhabitants is a desire to "fight back" both abroad and at "home" and facilitates the reassertion of white masculinity. Thus, the "Minuteman Project" is a recovery project to ameliorate the sense of pain from displacement. Implicated in their project is a recovery of old idea(l)s, including men (with big guns) as saviors, colonies founded by white fathers, and "American" as white, assimilated, and "melted," all of which help maintain white supremacy.

The project of recovering what is perceived to be lost ideals continues today through the work of the Minuteman Project, the chapters it maintains across the United States, and the Minuteman Civil Defense Corps. Yet, such a project confronts attacks on its legitimacy and contends with resistance. Beginning in 2005, political leaders characterized the actions of the MMP as "vigilantism"; later that year, the Congressional Immigration Reform Caucus concluded that MMP organizations "are potentially dangerous and legally problematic."[56] In subsequent years, the MMP would split[57] and its original leaders Gilchrist and Simcox have since been ousted from the very organizations they created, contending with charges of fraud and embezzlement.[58] And, most recently, the Southern Poverty Law Center has identified splinter MMPs and the Minuteman Civil Defense Corps as "nativist extremist groups"[59] and as spawning more extreme paramilitary elements.[60] These issues have certainly dampened the MMP's ability to claim that its goal is simply to patrol the border. They have also significantly complicated their ability to stay disassociated from explicitly white supremacist groups. Finally, there are the resistance efforts against the MMP, which are outside the focus of this chapter. Opposition to the MMP during its first border encampment in Arizona was portrayed on television news programs and continues to be carried out by various groups (e.g., National Alliance for Human Rights and Gente Unida). Studying oppositional rhetoric is important to critique "discourses of freedom" in part to counterbalance "critiques of domination"[61] reflected here in this study of the MMP.

NOTES

The author extends thanks to Kent Ono and Michael Lacy for their support of and thoughtful suggestions on this chapter. An early version of this manuscript entitled "The Minuteman Project and Migrant Narratives: Producing and Productions of the Border, Its Beneficiaries, and National-Racial Space" (Greg Dickinson, co-author) was presented at the National Communication Association Convention, San Antonio, Texas (November 2006).

1. HB 4437 which would have mandated, among other things, building a 700-mile long fence along the U.S.-Mexico border, was passed by the House but not the Senate; HB 418, which was passed by both houses of Congress, calls upon every state to overhaul its driver's license laws and procedures such that all license applicants will have to provide proof of citizenship to obtain a driver's license.

2. Scott Johnson, "The Border War," Newsweek, April 4, 2005, 29. http://www.lexisnexis.com (accessed July 3, 2008).

3. The MMP acts as "internal vigilance operations" situated under the "Minuteman Headquarters," a national organization that also includes Minuteman Civil Defense Corps (MCDC), functioning as "U.S. civil border operations," led by Simcox. Jim Gilchrist is "a retired California accountant" who was defeated in his bid for a congressional seat in Orange County, California: http://www.jmgilchrist.com (accessed January 3, 2006). Chris Simcox is "a former grammar school teacher and publisher of a local newspaper in Tombstone, Arizona" (Frederick A. Peterson and John E. Stone, "Results and Implications of the Minuteman Project," A Field Report Submitted to the Congressional Immigration Reform Caucus (2005): 1–30).

4. Focusing exclusively on the "Border Fence Project" initiative by the Minuteman Civil Defense Corps, Robert DeChaine similarly characterizes the MCDC as a movement. He notes their reliance on "hypermedia" to "mobilize popular attitudes," to communicate its agenda, and

to remain in the public eye and in conversations relative to immigration reform (D. Robert DeChaine "Bordering the Civic Imaginary: Alienization, Fence Logic, and the Minuteman Civil Defense Corps," *Quarterly Journal of Speech* 95 (2009): 43–65.

5. David Holthouse, "Minute Mess: Minuteman Leader Ousted, Forms New Group," *Intelligence Report*, Summer 2007. http://www.splcenter.org/intel/intelreport (accessed January 3, 2010).

6. Raymie McKerrow, "Critical Rhetoric: Theory and Praxis," *Communication Monographs* 56 (1989): 91–111.

7. Josh Adams and Vincent J. Roscigno, "White Supremacists, Oppositional Culture and the World Wide Web," *Social Forces* 84 (2005): 759–73; Melissa A. Wall, "Social Movements and Email: Expressions of Online Identity in the Globalization Protests," *New Media and Society* 9 (2007): 258–77.

8. I focus exclusively on the first "Minuteman Project" as led by Gilchrist and Simcox rather than offshoot groups such as the "San Diego [CA] Minuteman" or the "Herndon [VA] Minuteman" that formed several months after the MMP.

9. Todd Gitlin, *The Whole World Is Watching: Mass Media in the Making and Unmaking of the New Left* (Berkeley: University of California Press, 2003).

10. I purposely place quote marks around "America" and "American" as a way to delimit Eurocentric understandings of the Americas. References to "America" in MMP discourse operate from an assumption that it is *the one and only* "America."

11. Aaron David Gresson III, *America's Atonement: Racial Pain, Recovery Rhetoric, and the Pedagogy of Healing* (New York: Peter Lang, 2004).

12. Wall, "Social Movements"; Adams and Roscigno, "White Supremacists"; Gitlin, *The Whole World Is Watching*; Catherine Helen Palczewski, "Cyber-movements, New Social Movements, and Counterpublics," in *Counterpublics and the State*, ed. Robert Asen and Daniel C. Brouwer (Albany: SUNY, 2001), 161–86.

13. Adams and Roscigno, "White Supremacists," 762–63.

14. Unless otherwise noted, all quoted material by the MMP comes from their website links and the URL from which I downloaded and printed available discourse.

15. Robert M. Entman, "Framing: Toward Clarification of a Fractured Paradigm," *Journal of Communication* 43 (1993): 51–58; Michael Calvin McGee, "The 'Ideograph': A Link Between Rhetoric and Ideology," *Quarterly Journal of Speech* 66 (1980): 1–16; Kent A. Ono and John M. Sloop, *Shifting Borders: Rhetoric, Immigration, and California's Proposition 187* (Philadelphia: Temple University Press, 2002).

16. Richard B. Gregg, A. Jackson McCormack, and Douglas J. Pederson, "The Rhetoric of Black Power: A Street-Level Interpretation," *Quarterly Journal of Speech* 55 (1969): 151–60; Hank Johnston and John A. Noakes, ed., *Frames of Protest: Social Movements and The Framing Perspective* (Lanham, MD: Rowman and Littlefield, 2005); Adams and Roscigno, "White Supremacists"; Wall, "Social Movements."

17. Michael G. Lacy, "Exposing the Spectrum of Whiteness: Rhetorical Conceptions of White Absolutism," *Communication Yearbook* 32 (2008): 277–311.

18. Entman, "Framing"; Gitlin, *The Whole World Is Watching*; Johnston and Noakes, *Frames of Protest*.

19. Entman, "Framing," 52.

20. Based on a cursory review of news-related articles published in the *New York Times*, *USA Today*, and the *Washington Post* from March to December 2005, I found that newspapers would lead, intertwine, or follow up stories about the MMP with the political threads noted in the text

(e.g., Amy Argetsinger, "In Ariz., 'Minutemen' Start Border Patrols," *Washington Post*, April 5, 2005; Timothy Egan, "Wanted: Border Hoppers. And Some Excitement, Too," *New York Times*, April 1, 2005; Andrew Pollack, "2 Illegal Immigrants Win Arizona Ranch in Court Fight," *New York Times*, August 19, 2005. http://lexisnexis.com (accessed July 3, 2008).

21. Iterated on CNN during episodes of *Lou Dobbs Tonight* (i.e., "Activist Bay Buchanan Supports Minuteman Project," April 1, 2005; "Minuteman Project Highlights Problems with U.S. Border Policy," April 4, 2005; and "Project Minuteman Continues in Southwest," April 11, 2005. http://www.lexisnexis.com (accessed April 24, 2005)).

22. Raka Shome, "Space Matters: The Power and Practice of Space," *Communication Theory* 13 (2003): 39–56, 47.

23. This particular image was located on the national organization for the original Minuteman Project. http://www.minutemanhq.com (accessed June 19, 2005). However, as of January 3, 2010, a different image is in place that continues to reflect a patriot, but absent the binoculars and cell phone.

24. Information retrieved from the National Crime Prevention Council. http://www.ncpc.org (accessed July 7, 2008).

25. Respectively, James Garofalo and Maureen McLeod, "The Structure and Operations of Neighborhood Watch Programs in the United States," *Crime and Delinquency* 35 (1989): 326–44; Glen Custred, "Where Are My Juice and Crackers?: Citizens along America's Southwestern Border Have Organized a Neighborhood Watch," *American Spectator* (July–August 2005): 20–25.

26. Peterson and Stone, "Results and Implications," 7.

27. Recently, Amaya has argued that legislative bills of 2003, which grant citizenship posthumously to soldiers killed in battle, is an "illiberal practice" because consent from those for whom citizenship was granted was absent and because it masks the classed and raced aspects inhering in the armed forces (Hector Amaya, "Dying American or the Violence of Citizenship: Latinos in Iraq," *Latino Studies* 5 (2007): 3–24). As for the racialization of citizenship, see Ian F. Haney López, *White by Law: the Legal Construction of Race* (New York: New York University Press, 1996).

28. Michael Omi and Howard Winant, *Racial Formation in the United States: From the 1960s to the 1990s*, 2nd ed. (New York: Routledge, 1994), 66.

29. My emphasis.

30. 280.

31. Peterson and Stone, "Results and Implications," 6.

32. Iterated by Lou Dobbs, obtained from transcript of *Lou Dobbs Tonight*, air date April 4, 2005. http://www.lexisnexis.com (accessed April 24, 2005).

33. Wall, "Social Movements," 270, 272.

34. My emphasis.

35. Peterson and Stone, "Results and Implications," 6.

36. Gresson, *Racial Pain*, 13.

37. See also Carrie Crenshaw, "Colorblind Rhetoric," *Southern Communication Journal* 63 (1998): 244–56.

38. Ashley Woody Doane, "What Is Racism? Racial Discourse and Racial Politics," *Critical Sociology* 32 (2006): 255–74.

39. Wall, "Social Movements," 270, 272.

40. This last point is not surprising. Recent scholarship reveals that when the issue of immigration arises, supporters for humane treatment of immigrants invoke their contributions (Ono and Sloop, *Shifting Borders*; Marouf Hasian, Jr. and Fernando Delgado, "The Trials and Tribula-

tions of Racialized Critical Rhetorical Theory: Understanding the Rhetorical Ambiguities of Proposition 187," *Communication Theory* 83 (1998): 245–70.

41. Reported by Casey Wian for the *Lou Dobbs Tonight* show, air date April 11, 2005. http://www.lexisnexis.com (accessed April 24, 2005).

42. Ono and Sloop, *Shifting Borders*, 37.

43. Extending extant literature about rhetorics of immigration, Cisneros deftly accounts for its visual dimensions by examining television news discourse and the uncharted metaphor of immigrants as "pollutants." His analysis brings to light the ways news media portray immigrants by accounting for visual content (e.g., camera angles and placement, video directionality, subjects behind and in front of the camera) that augments verbal arguments advanced about immigration (J. David Cisneros, "Contaminated Communities: The Metaphor of 'Immigrant as Pollutant' in Media Representations of Immigration," *Rhetoric and Public Affairs* 11 (2008): 569–601).

44. Lacy, "Exposing the Spectrum," 290.

45. My emphasis. The ideographs are identified in the "SOP," "Events," the MMP recruitment poster, and a transcript from Fox News, air date April 18, 2005.

46. Lacy, "Exposing the Spectrum," 290.

47. Shome, "Space Matters," 45, 47.

48. Lacy, "Exposing the Spectrum," 294–95.

49. Ibid., 292.

50. On this point, refer to Bernadette M. Calafell and Fernando P. Delgado, "Reading Latina/o Images: Interrogating *Americanos*," *Critical Studies in Media Communication* 21 (2004): 1–21.

51. Ono and Sloop, *Shifting Borders*, 56.

52. Ibid., 39–40.

53. Gresson, *Racial Pain*, 16–17.

54. Ibid., 22.

55. Ibid., 31.

56. Both former Presidents Bush and Vicente Fox of Mexico labeled the MMP's efforts as "vigilantism" (Billy House, "Hayworth says Bush insulted Minutemen," (28 April 2005). http://www.azcentral.com/arizonarepublic/news/articles/0428minuteman-dc28.html (accessed July 6, 2008); Peterson and Stone 27).

57. Reportedly the MMP "splintered as a result of ego-driven battles between Gilchrist and Simcox" (Zvika Krieger, "Time's Up: The Minutemen Turn on Each Other," *New Republic*, November 19, 2008. http://www.tnr.com (accessed December 1, 2008).

58. Holthouse, "Minute Mess"; Anonymous, "Anti-Immigration Groups: Second Minuteman Group in Bitter Split," *Intelligence Report*, Fall 2007. http://www.splcenter.org/intel/intelreport (accessed January 3, 2010).

59. Casey Sanchez, "Blunt Force: San Diego Nativist Group Faces Troubles," *Intelligence Report*, Summer 2007. http://www.splcenter.org (accessed January 28, 2009).

60. David Holthouse, "Nativists to 'Patriots': Nativist Vigilantes Adopt 'Patriot' Movement Ideas," *Intelligence Report*, Fall 2009. http://www.splcenter.org/intel/intelreport (accessed January 3, 2010).

61. McKerrow, "Critical Rhetoric."

6 Control, Discipline, and Punish

Black Masculinity and (In)visible Whiteness in the NBA

Rachel Alicia Griffin and Bernadette Marie Calafell

In the United States, numerous media headlines have been dedicated to high-profile cases about race and racism in sport.[1] The most notorious incidents include Al Campanis of the Dodgers, Jimmy (the Greek) Snyder of CBS, Air Force football coach Fisher DeBerry, Don Imus and the Rutgers's University women's basketball team, head coaches Lovie Smith and Tony Dungy going to Super Bowl 41, and most recently, Golf Channel anchor Kelly Tilghman's comments on Tiger Woods. While these cases dominated the headlines, they gave visibility to issues of race, power, privilege, and voice in sport.[2] Sport is inextricably linked with contemporary struggles surrounding racial identity, racism, and politics in U.S. American society,[3] so much so that sports as popular culture "are part of the everyday experience of most people."[4]

Communication scholars have focused on issues concerning race, politics, and sports.[5] For example, Michael Butterworth[6] highlighted how George W. Bush utilized sports to fuel his political agenda. Fernando Delgado mapped the political and ideological tensions present in the U.S. print media coverage of the 1998 World Cup game.[7] Other works have examined Chicano-Latino masculinities in boxing,[8] or the framings and representations of black masculinities and bodies in the National Basketball Association (NBA)[9] and the National Football League,[10] as well as the taken-for-granted nature of whiteness in sports.[11] Barry Brummett argues that, as we experience popular culture, we participate in rhetorical struggles surrounding dominant ideologies, power, privilege, and the social hierarchies in which we operate.[12] As a popular culture site, we position sport (such as NBA basketball) as a pedagogical space that is instructive of how racial hierarchies in the United States reflect larger systems of domination. Margaret Duncan and Brummett write that the presentation of sports relies on narrative strategies such as storytelling, the sharing of history, and the creation of stock characters.[13] As such, the critiques of sports and athletes "offer unique points of access to the constitutive meanings and power relations of the larger worlds we inhabit."[14] In this chapter, we turn a critical eye toward the NBA and position the league as a site of struggle over meanings of race.

Since sports are part of the everyday lives of people, NBA discourses influence the social fabric of human relations via the media. David Leonard contends that professional basketball is a cultural site at which dialogues about race, class, American values, and national identity occur.[15] Likewise, corporate discourses also constitute popular culture and are nationally and internationally consumed by people via a global media. For example, Todd Boyd and Kenneth Shropshire recount the cultural significance of the infamous rivalry between Magic Johnson of the Lakers and Larry Bird of the Celtics: "To side with the Lakers or the Celtics was to embrace a racial position and a specific set of cultural politics. . . . The battles between Magic and Bird, L.A. and Boston, black and white, could be described as the late twentieth century's version of an acceptable race war."[16] Furthermore, Ben Carrington notes the "racial signification of sport," indicating that "Sports contests . . . act as a key signifier for wider questions about identity within racially demarcated societies in which racial narratives about self and society are read both into and from sporting contests that are imbued with racial meanings."[17]

Thus, in this chapter, we critique the "allegorical power of sport" in relation to historical and contemporary manifestations of white supremacy.[18] In doing so, we seek to show how sport as a form of popular culture reifies whiteness within and beyond the social institution of sport. In particular, we focus on NBA Commissioner David Stern. We situate his embodiment of white hegemonic masculinity as a political performance that is rife with racialized messages concerning power, privilege, and control.[19] In our examination of strategic uses of whiteness in professional basketball, we build upon previous rhetorical work. For instance, Michael Butterworth and Nick Trujillo have examined figures centrally connected to sports, whiteness, and masculinity as a way to locate and problematize commonsense meanings surrounding race, sports, and politics.[20]

Recently, the NBA has been the focus of numerous controversial media headlines, propelling issues of race and racism to the front pages of newspapers. Of specific interest in this chapter is the League's 2005 dress code policy, which followed the much discussed 2004 Detroit Piston's brawl. By examining Stern's reactions to racist accusations, we expose his whiteness, and make visible his political position and power. To do so, we highlight the contradictions embedded within Stern's claims that race is insignificant and position his rhetorical embodiment of white masculinity within U.S. histories in order to reveal white paternalistic ideologies. Stern's symbolic representation of whiteness (i.e., power, authority, control, etc.) often masks the reproduction of stereotypical notions of blackness (i.e., deviance, immaturity, danger, etc.).[21] We first contextualize sport and the historical relationships between black and white men. Then, we map and deconstruct the discursive space of whiteness in media discourses dedicated to the 2004 Detroit Piston's brawl and the 2005 dress code Stern oversaw.[22] Finally, we discuss the social implications of Commissioner David Stern's embodiment of white, hegemonic masculinity contextually.

Sport and the Politics of Race and History

The history between blacks and whites in U.S. sports is replete with notions of white supremacy and inequality. In the realm of sport, white men have historically been situated in positions of ownership and control over black male athletic bodies that were ideologically fixed as hypersexual, violent, and suspicious.[23] Ironically, black males also became representative of desired mystique and wonderment. Subsequently, the black male body became a site for spectacular white consumption and enticement, but this only worked so long as black men could be controlled. In this context, black males were expected and forced to perform for white audiences. For example, during slavery, white masters would enter their slaves in foot-racing competitions and jockey races to compete against other plantation owners' slaves. The owners received both the public praise and financial rewards for the athletic abilities and performances of their slaves.[24] In addition to voyeuristic consumption and forced competition, arguably the most devastating and sickening consequence and display of the white custodial gaze upon black bodies was that of lynching for white pleasure. The sport was to hunt for the black man whose body at the climax of spectatorship was tormented as a form of entertainment.[25] After slavery and the illegalization of lynching, the voyeuristic white gaze and white control over black male bodies remained steadfast; hence, the exploitation and appropriation of blacks by whites for pleasure and profit continued. For instance, in spite of their success, legendary black athletes, such as Jack Johnson, Jesse Owens, and Joe Louis, were criminalized, broke, and/or discarded as useless at the end of their athletic careers.[26]

The historical relationships between black men and white men in sports are directly relevant to understanding how the industry of professional basketball represents, reflects, and reifies historical constructions of blackness and whiteness. Extending our contextual understanding of history, race, and sport into the present day, several high-profile athletes have documented the presence of race and racism in the NBA, including Bill Russell, Kareem Abdul-Jabbar, Dennis Rodman, and Charles Barkley.[27] While it may be tempting to dismiss their perspectives based on the common extreme financial success (albeit often short-lived) of NBA players, Harry Edwards observed that black men who are extremely financially successful in the realm of professional sport learn to conceal the oppressive nature of whiteness.[28] Similarly, Derrick Bell reminds us that, "Despite undeniable progress for many, no African Americans are insulated from incidents of racial discrimination. Our careers, even our lives, are threatened because of our color."[29] In the section that follows, we will briefly recount the history of integration in the NBA to contextualize how the contemporary white power structure embodied by Stern continues to struggle to control black male bodies hegemonically.

The NBA as a Racialized Space

October 31, 1950, marked the day the color barrier in the NBA fell.[30] The honor, or perhaps burden, of initially breaking the color barrier in the NBA is attributed to Chuck Cooper, Nat "Sweetwater" Clifton, and Earl "Moon Fixer" Loyd.[31] Blacks and whites alike claimed the initial integration of sports as progressive, yet integration has also been critiqued as a vehicle of white supremacist persistence.[32] According to William Rhoden, not only did integration allow whites to have control over and gain profit from black male bodies, but they did so while claiming that racism did not exist, thereby elevating themselves to being democratic humanitarians. Therefore, while blacks were slowly "allowed" into the league, they were also limited to the playing court.[33] Since 1950, the overall demographic representation of blacks in the NBA has increased slightly. Although this process was slow at first, a major demographic shift occurred in the late 1970s and early 1980s, during which time the playing force became predominantly black. Nevertheless, the NBA's current "front office hiring practices do not nearly reflect the number of players of color competing."[34] Thus, whites remain the dominant ethnic majority at every level of ownership and administration. The only exception to the white majority is among the black players who, during the 2006–2007 season, represented 75 percent (330/522) of the players, in comparison to white players who represented 21 percent (91/522).[35]

While the NBA may present itself as an organization that has transcended race and racism, its history of integration, current ethnic demographics, and the discursive embrace of racist ideologies under the direction of Commissioner Stern indicate that this is not actually true.

Rhetorics of Whiteness

We examined Stern through his strategic performances of whiteness in media coverage of the 2004 Detroit brawl and the 2005 dress code.[36] Susan Birrell and Mary McDonald assert, "Reading sport critically can be used as a methodology for uncovering, foregrounding, and producing counter-narratives, that is, alternative accounts of particular events and celebrities that have been decentered, obscured, and dismissed by hegemonic forces."[37] We undertook a critical examination of Stern's discourses through the lens of strategic rhetoric to explicate how his embodiment of white hegemonic masculinity masks systems of domination. Our study follows critical rhetorical projects that are concerned not only with uncovering oppressive discourses, but also with highlighting how discourse can espouse freedom.[38] To do so, we operate from a critical perspective guided by theories of whiteness as a way to unearth the oppressive nature of Stern's rhetoric (or lack thereof) surrounding race and racism. Similarly, in his analysis of the media coverage of baseball players Sammy Sosa and Mark McGwire, Butterworth states: "Analysis of this coverage reveals the extent to which whiteness is a taken-for-granted norm in discussions about race and how sports media produce and perpetuate a discourse that privileges whiteness."[39] Inspired by Butterworth's work, we seek to make visible Stern's white privilege and the way it extends the normalization of whiteness in the NBA and beyond. We also seek to highlight players' voices, which are most often overshadowed and/or dismissed via Stern's performance of whiteness.

Thomas Nakayama and Robert Krizek note that whiteness is normalized through discourses that position it as everything and nothing simultaneously. Whiteness as a subject position is unmarked, and in its lack of recognition maintains its dominance, or normalizing position, along with being defined, and centered, contra the Other.[40] Nakayama and Krizek further argue that whiteness is constructed as natural; therefore, whiteness eludes a critique of the systems of power that determine its positioning. Eduardo Bonilla-Silva refers to the invisibility of whiteness as "colorblindness," which becomes manifest as "racism without 'racists.'"[41] Furthermore, Sarah Projansky and Kent Ono write, "in response to various social changes and social movements, the history of whiteness in the United States entails a history of modifications to renegotiate the centrality of white power and authority—this is what we call *strategic whiteness*."[42] Strategic whiteness can be tied to a new form of racism, which Patricia Hill Collins argues is "characterized by a changing political structure that disenfranchises people, even if they appear to be included."[43] Collins argues that the new racism relies on mass media more than ever to disseminate and justify racist beliefs and norms often represented as colorblind, anti-racist, and/or racially transcendent. Illuminating filmic representations that appear to be liberatory, while actually reinforcing hegemonic structures, Projansky and Ono ask, "But what kind of racial politics and politics of representation allow these films to claim an anti-racist edge while nevertheless subtly recentering whiteness in the process?"[44] A similar question can be raised with regard to Stern and the perception of the NBA as a racial equalizer. In response to the work of communication scholars who call for examinations of strategic performances of whiteness within the media,[45] we examine the NBA as a site where the new racism is articulated most keenly through Stern's rhetoric, which, we argue, works to mask or normalize racism and hegemonic beliefs.

Stern's performances of white privilege and hegemonic masculinity are further read against other bodies of literature that have explored the nexus of white masculinity and sports. Butterworth persuasively argues for understanding whiteness as tied to civilization and American exceptionalism in baseball discourses, especially as it relates to Otherness.[46] Trujillo's work on Nolan Ryan and hegemonic masculinity addresses physical force and control, occupational achievement, familial patriarchy, frontiersmanship, and heterosexuality. Motivated by these works, we are attentive to the relationship between whiteness and hegemonic masculinity in order to locate frames for understanding NBA Commissioner Stern's rhetoric. Specifically, we address his history in the league, mediated responses, and actions as they relate to whiteness and masculinity. Taken together, these fragments offer lenses through which to examine Stern's rhetoric, while being mindful of the performative, textual, and contextual factors surrounding him.[47]

The Arrival of David Stern

David Stern began his career with the NBA in 1978 as legal counsel. He became the league's executive vice president in 1980 and commissioner in 1984.[48] Prior to his appointment, in the NBA's so-called darkest hour, major news articles reported that three out of four NBA players were on drugs.[49] When Stern was appointed, the league was in severe turmoil.[50] League controversies in 1984 included franchise failure, a lack of corporate sponsorship, labor issues, drug use, and accusations of racism. Stern described the situation this way: "This is the first sport where it became fashionable and allowable to talk about race. Our problem was that sponsors were flocking out of the N.B.A. because it was perceived as a bunch of high-salaried, drug-sniffing black guys."[51] Hence, from the onset of his career as commissioner, Stern normalized whiteness as a nonracialized space by repeating discourse that marked the racialized "other" as criminal. He echoed white middle-class sensibilities, while maintaining the invisibility of whiteness as a normative position of structural advantage. In many ways, Stern embodied hegemonic civility (a tactic he draws upon frequently): "normalized or naturalized behavior—appropriate behavior—even as the action can be incivil or even silencing in order to uphold the hegemonic order . . . Hegemonic civility is an organized process which results in suppressing or silencing any opposition, in favor of the status quo."[52] Stern also affirmed Collins's argument that, "The combination of physicality over intellectual ability, a lack of restraint associated with incomplete socialization, and a predilection for violence has long been associated with African American men."[53] Reading further into Stern's comments regarding the perception of the league "as a bunch of high-salaried, drug-sniffing black guys,"[54] Maharaj contends that, from Stern's perspective, an economic solution was necessary to address the NBA's issues; economic in that league profits could be improved by managing perceptions of NBA players (namely black men) in the media spotlight. In this sense, Stern's role as the white patriarch who could restore order to an out-of-control organization brimming with uncivilized players becomes visible.

As a leader in the professional sports industry, Stern is widely credited with having saved the league from bankruptcy, expanding the franchise, capitalizing on star power, marketing, engaging international initiatives, and serving the public. He has secured his reputation as the most successful commissioner in professional sports.[55] In doing so, he has been described as "a thinker," "an innovator," "brilliant," and "progressive."[56] Speaking to his financial skills, a mere ten years after his appointment as commissioner, the league had increased its annual revenues by 1,600 percent.[57]

In addition to that success, Stern has been positioned as a cultural icon through his management of meaning. To anyone remotely familiar with professional basketball, he has become symbolic of power, discipline, and rescue. More specifically, when members of the NBA (owners, teams, referees, players, etc.) become a media spectacle, it is Stern who comes to the forefront of the organization as a white patriarchal figure to soothe the public rhetorically and thereby repair any damage to the NBA's image. Yet, despite his most concerted efforts to do so and simultaneously declare the NBA a space in which race does not matter, he falls subject to suspicion. We argue that Stern has become a complex symbol of racism, paternalism and, indirectly, slavery itself. In the following section, we highlight Stern's reactions to the 2004 Pistons brawl and the 2005 dress code as a means of further understanding his performance of whiteness and its strategic reification of dominant power structures.

2004 Detroit Brawl

On November 19, 2004, during a game between the Detroit Pistons and the Indiana Pacers, a brawl ensued that included both players and fans engaging in physical altercations at the Palace of Auburn Hills in Michigan. The contact between players and fans began after a Detroit fan threw a cup of liquid on Pacer Ron Artest, who had just been engaged in an on-court conflict with Piston player, Ben Wallace. Reacting immediately, Artest climbed into the stands after the fan who had thrown the cup of liquid on him, and mayhem ensued. In a visual sense the racial composition of NBA players and fans was striking: all of the players involved were black, while most of the fans were white.[58] Although no one was seriously injured, the incident played repeatedly on media channels for weeks. The media described the brawl as a great disaster in American sports history, and the event became a source of humiliation and embarrassment for the NBA.[59]

To understand the cultural and political impact of the brawl, we must remember that the white voyeuristic gaze is deeply rooted in U.S. American sport. The intent of the gaze is to commodify blackness so that it appeals to consumers willing to spend the most money consuming the sport, which tend to be white middle and upper-class people. According to Jack McCallum, the image of the black players fighting with mostly white fans "will not sit well with those white fans who see some African American players—lavishly paid, richly tattooed and supremely confident—as the embodiment of all that is wrong with sports."[60] In this light, the brawl takes on a new meaning as a moment in which issues of race, class, and gender became of public significance. In essence, the "innocence" of sport and the ability of it to function as a racial equalizer was brought into question.

Soon after the brawl, Stern held a public press conference, in which his task was to repair the NBA's tarnished image, apologize, and publicize the punishments being handed down. He said, "The actions of the players involved wildly exceeded the professionalism and self-control that should fairly be expected from NBA players."[61] As a result of the brawl, the following disciplinary actions were taken: Pacer Ron Artest was suspended for the remainder of the 2004–2005 season, Pacer Stephen Jackson was suspended for 30 games, Pacer Jermaine O'Neal was suspended for 25 games, Pacer Anthony Johnson was suspended for five games, Pacer Reggie Miller was suspended for one game, Piston Ben Wallace was suspended for six games, and Pistons Elden Campbell, Derrick Coleman, and Chauncey Billups were suspended for one game.[62] When asked if the heaviest penalty leveraged against Ron Artest (suspended for the remainder of the season) was a unanimous decision, Stern replied, "It was unanimous 1-0," asserting his absolute power to enforce this decision.[63] He followed by saying, "I don't mean to make light of it, it was my decision. And I decided it . . . it is my responsibility to decide on penalties for player conduct and this is the one I decided on."[64] Stern made it very clear that the boundary had been set for player behavior as a result of the brawl. Stern said: "I am less concerned in the future, because whatever doubt our players may have about the unacceptability of breaching this boundary, they now know the line is drawn and my guess is it won't happen again; certainly not by anyone who wants to be associated with our league."[65] In essence, if another player were ever to dare to enter the stands again, he would face serious and deliberate consequences.

Despite Stern's explanations, noticeably absent was any acknowledgment of players' perspectives. Following the incident, several players called attention to the fans who were also responsible. For example, Quentin Richardson said, "Man there are going to be some lawsuits. You don't think some of those fans aren't going to want some NBA money?"[66] David Harrison offered, "Nobody gets paid to have stuff thrown at them unless they're circus clowns in a little booth."[67] Similarly, when asked if Artest was at fault, Alonzo Mourning responded, "Hell no, it's not Artest's fault. What has this come to, when a fan feels he has the right to throw something at a player on the court?"[68] In a similar vein, Sam Cassell said, "If the fans throw something, we've got to protect our honor."[69] According to the players, their astronomical salaries do not justify or mitigate the racialized mistreatment they experience as black professional athletes.[70] It is important to note that, officially, both players and fans violated the social contract of sport: the players by entering the stands and the fans by coming onto the court.[71] However, Stern's decisive punishments implied that the black players were largely at fault. According to Linda Tucker, "Such dismissals of the players' perspectives entirely overlook the players' experiences and knowledge of what it means to be Black men in the United States."[72]

Stern's embodiment of white patriarchal control as the commissioner is located in the hypermasculine space of sport, which embraces performances of toughness and dominance.[73] Stern's actions and discourse can be read critically as bringing order and civility to the brute force of black masculinity. Collins argues that the myth of upward social mobility through sports is governed by the rule that one must "submit to White male authority in order to learn how to become a man."[74] This mythology and rule is apparent in Stern's role as patriarch, falling under what Collins calls the father-figure thesis that "assumes that young Black men need tough coaches who will instill much-needed discipline in the lives of fatherless and therefore unruly Black boys."[75] Clearly, the brawl is emblematic of white (male) voyeuristic consumption, the fear of blackness, and the dominant need for black, male bodies to be safely contained. Thus, in the moments when the black players came off the court and went into the stands, blackness became uncontrollable, spilling into the safety of white space, and the arena became a savage space where the black bodies of the players climbing into the stands were represented as "violent beasts" going after "innocent" white fans. Having a "black" threat in "white" space was especially problematic from the League's standpoint because of the corporate bottom line. A significant proportion of league revenue is generated based on the NBA's ability to provide and guarantee a safe space for whites to consume blackness. This explains why the penalties handed down were racialized and lopsided against the black male athletes, since the league itself failed to take any major responsibility.

Despite the harsh punishments the players received, Stern did describe the fans' behavior at the Palace in particular but also at large as inappropriate. Explicitly, he expressed his "shock" at and "revulsion" for the incident in its entirety, rather than focusing solely on players. In addition, he said, "We patronize our athletes and our fans by accepting the fact that they should be allowed to engage in something less than civilized conduct." Stern continued:

> Over the years, at all sporting events, there's developed a combination of things. First, the professional heckler, who feels empowered to spend the entire game directing his attention to disturbing the other team at any decibel level, at any vocabulary. Then, an ongoing permissiveness that runs the gamut from college kids who don't wear shirts and paint their faces and think that liberates them to say anything, to NBA fans that use language that is not suitable to any family occasions.[76]

Despite his addressing the problematic behavior of sports fans, what Stern did not directly admit to was how the league creates franchise environments that are likely to spark racialized violence and aggression. By stating that the brawl was an isolated incident, Stern framed it as a disastrous fluke, overlooking the roles of capitalism, racism, and sexism as they work together to form the environment in which sport is consumed. More pointedly, the NBA's capitalistic desire for profit created an entertainment atmosphere that included alcohol, obnoxious noise-makers, freebees, cheerleaders, and music to hype up the crowd and keep fans coming back. While none of these decisions on behalf of the league are directly responsible for the brawl or other instances of violence in franchise arenas, they heighten tensions that reinforce hegemonic masculinity. Hence, sporting arenas are designed to appeal to white patriarchal culture in which violence, aggression, and alcohol consumption are encouraged as expressions of manhood. These sports arenas include predominantly white fans and black players, which inevitably produces cultural clashes in a society organized in part by racial hierarchies.[77]

2005 Dress Code

In the aftermath of the brawl and the collective bargaining process, the NBA adopted a new dress code for players (not applicable to the predominantly white coaches or owners), to be enforced on opening day of the 2005–2006 basketball season.[78] The dress policy restricted players from wearing shorts, T-shirts, throwback jerseys, trainers, sneakers, work boots, do-rags, chains, pendants, and medallions. The players were required to wear collared dress shirts or turtlenecks, dress slacks or dress jeans, sport coats, and presentable shoes with socks when attending league events and not in uniform.[79] According to Stern, "we decided that the reputation of our players was not as good as our players are, and we could do small things to improve that."[80] Further justifying the new policy, Stern explained:

> There are different uniforms for different occasions. There's the uniform you wear on
> the court, there's the uniform you wear when you are on business, there's a uniform
> you might wear on your casual downtime with your friends and there's the uniform
> you might wear when you go back home. We're just changing the definition of the
> uniform that you wear when you are on NBA business.[81]

Stern's executive decision to change the image of the NBA via dress elicited protest and accusations of racism.

Contesting the dress code, Stephen Jackson was quoted as saying that the "NBA's new dress code is racially motivated."[82] Jackson was also quoted as saying, "as far as the chains, I definitely feel that's a racial statement. Almost 100 percent of the guys in the league who are young and black wear big chains. So I definitely don't agree with that at all."[83] Paul Pierce of the Boston Celtics said, "When I saw the part about chains, hip-hop and throwback jerseys, I think that's part of our [black] culture. The NBA is young, black males."[84] Allan Iverson, believed to be a strong motivation for the new dress code after wearing military fatigues, a do-rag, and a baseball hat on an ESPN television broadcast, said, "They're targeting my generation—the hip hop generation."[85] Vowing to protest, Iverson also said, "I dress to make myself comfortable. I really do have a problem with this. It's just not right. It's something I'll fight for."[86] He was also quoted saying, "just because you put a guy in a tuxedo, it doesn't mean he's a good guy,"[87] and "You can put a murderer in a suit, and he's still a murderer."[88]

In a dismissive response to the players' protest and public accusations of racism, Stern responded, "If the dress code affects black players more than others it is more because of circumstance than design."[89] Furthermore, regardless of the resistance from Black players who felt racially targeted by the new dress policy, Stern indicated with certainty that the dress code would be complied with since, from his perspective, the new dress code is in the best interest of the NBA image.[90] The possible consequences for violating the new policy included fines, game suspensions, and being fired. In response to players' opposition to the policy, Stern took an authoritative stance: "If players are really going to have a problem, they will have to make a decision about how they want to spend their adult life in terms of playing in the NBA or not."[91] Stern's veiled threat of unemployment for the players reinforced the weight of his comments. Allan Iverson, who initially strongly opposed the dress code, was later quoted as saying, "I don't have a problem with it. I'll do it for the rest of the season."[92]

Although Stern's justification of the new policy rendered the hip-hop style of dress closely associated with professional basketball a "raceless" uniform, it is vital to recognize that hip-hop is far more than a mere uniform; rather, it is a cultural performance that represents a generation, a lifestyle, and a personae.[93] From a position always already mindful of whiteness, one can see how the dress code—by banning throwback jerseys, work boots, do-rags, chains, pendants, and medallions—also limits expressions of blackness that are associated with hip-hop style. Reflecting upon the stance of the NBA against hip-hop styles of dress, Jeffrey Lane asserts that the league made a defiant decision to redefine its relationship to hip-hop.[94] Taking further note of the NBA's interests espoused via Stern, the dress code is a clear indication of the leagues' move to separate distinctly from hip-hop culture, regardless of some player's identification with the hip-hop generation. Even more indicative of the labor of whiteness in the NBA is the explicit ban of jerseys and sneakers, two items associated with hip-hop that also contributed significantly to the league's $3 billion in league merchandise sales in 2004.[95] Therefore, the implementation of the policy denotes a desire to control "blackness" for profit. In essence, cultural artifacts of hip-hop ("blackness") are acceptable for sales, but not for image. To replace the banned items, the code called for collared dress shirts or turtlenecks, dress slacks or dress jeans, sport coats, and presentable shoes with socks—all of which are aligned with a white, upper-class style of fashion. The dress code policy positioned Stern as superior, which affirms the historical ideology of white paternalism rooted in chattel slavery. Therefore, the dress code in and of itself becomes symbolic of the desire to control and dilute the expression of blackness according to white norms.

Implications

Since 1989, the Center for the Study of Sport and Society and the Institute for Diversity and Ethics in Sport have released a Racial and Gender Report Card, grading the NBA on racial and gender representation. For the 2006–2007 season, the NBA remained an industry leader, earning an "A" for racial diversity, which supports the image of the NBA as a progressive organization. In addition, David Stern is one of the most highly acclaimed commissioners in sports history. The NBA's reputation as progressive league and cultural symbol, as well as Stern as symbolic representation of what a business leader should be, coupled with imagery of "good" and "bad" black men in the NBA, is important. Given U.S. American history, the cultural significance of Stern positioned as a white man overseeing a predominantly black playing workforce becomes exceptionally problematic. Our study suggests that Stern utilized his white male identity to assert power, maintain control, and reinforce the status quo of whites as the brain trust of the organization, while blacks were confined to their bodies and positioned at the mercy of whites. Therefore, while Stern embodies a strategic position to protect organizational profit, the players are situated in tactical positions always in reaction to the [white] powers that be.[96] We are not arguing that white men cannot be positioned as superior to black men in organizational hierarchies, but rather we are offering a framework to critique the cultural implications of Stern's performance. We illuminate one facet of the representation of the new racism, which is defined by the idea that race is insignificant and is no longer as prominent as it used to be. Our inquiry also offers a means for scholars to continue the close examination of the strategic performance of whiteness in sport at the intersections of multiple identities, such as race, sexual orientation, nationality, and gender.

Randy Martin and Toby Miller comment, "If we are to think the world of sport, but also to imagine the world through sport, we begin to see that sport has more to teach us than can be learned from any single game."[97] We build on this perspective by asking scholars to consider what else we might find if we examine the performance of marginalized and/or privileged identities in the context of sport? We ask what additional lessons are being taught to multiple audiences through the NBA and in particular Stern? Commenting on the implications of race, Stern said, "That's both fact of life and a cop-out, I deal with that as a marketing problem, as a challenge. It was our conviction that if everything else went right, race would not be an abiding issue to the N.B.A. fans, at least not as long as we handled it correctly."[98] Stern articulated and normalized the dominant belief that race is insignificant, while privileging a white supremacist capitalist patriarchal viewpoint.[99] In fairness, it is also important to recognize that, like Stern, many black players are in pursuit of capitalistic profit and often publicly comply with (or at least do not publicly resist) dominant ideologies of whiteness. While their complicity in the context of history is both frightening and problematic, it is different from Stern's efforts to appease, strengthen, and reproduce whiteness. Thus, although both are likely driven by desire for profit, black male athletes are functioning on a "field of power" in which the rules, interests, and desires of whites are rooted at the foundation.[100] The predominantly white owners, managers, coaches, advertising executives, media outlets, and consumers define the parameters in which black male professional athletes operate. While complicit, black athletes are packaged, sold, disciplined, and dehumanized under the gaze of whiteness as objects for voyeuristic consumption. They are situated as "inferior" regardless of the price tag. Perhaps this reflects the mind-set of the fan who felt justified to throw a cup at Artest which sparked the 2004 Detroit brawl.

Shome reminds us that whiteness is maintained not necessarily by overt displays of whiteness, but rather by its everyday "unquestioned racialized social relations that have acquired a seeming normativity and through that normativity function to make invisible the ways in which whites participate in, and derive protection from, a system whose rules and organizational relations work to their advantage."[101] Given this, it is vital that we continue to unpack Stern's discourse to reveal its insidious contributions to the normalization of whiteness. When Stern situates himself, or is situated, as white, he inhabits a cultural "position that is secured, maintained, and enjoyed through a structural deprivation of advantages, opportunities, and benefits to people of color."[102] Given Stern's implicit loyalty to corporate interests, there are political, social, and economic implications for the NBA's success as an organization that has "transcended" issues of race and racism, including but not limited to the negative representations of black masculinity, affirmation of whiteness as superior, and the often forgotten yet appalling circumstances that surround most black males in contemporary U.S. American society. In this chapter, we have sought to address how a white man in a position of extreme power, managing the black face of the NBA, begs our attention as critical scholars to be mindful of the importance of seemingly liberating "post-race" projects. In essence, we believe that there is a larger set of discursive principles being embedded in our beliefs and practices through sport that lends itself to the perpetuation of white superiority and black inferiority. In this vein, our analysis of Stern necessitates ongoing dialogue that critically reflects upon not only the workings of whiteness in sports but also the ways in which critical understandings of race and racism in sport can aid in positive social transformation. Thus, without critical and ongoing critiques of whiteness, people of all ethnic backgrounds will continue to ingest messages of indifference, dismissal, and disregard, which will subsequently stymie the movement for racial equality.

NOTES

This chapter is derived from a larger dissertation project entitled *White Eyes on Black Bodies: History, Performance, and Resistance in the NBA* that was written by Rachel Griffin and advised by Bernadette Calafell. Both authors would like to thank the editors and the anonymous reviewers for their challenging questions and thoughtful remarks. Without their patient support, carving this chapter out of the larger project would have been far more difficult.

1. Given the lack of agreement within the literature relied upon, the terms race and ethnicity will be used interchangeably throughout this chapter.

2. From a critical standpoint, all of these events have rendered issues of race and racism in sport highly visible. In 1987, when asked if racial prejudice might explain the lack of blacks in Major League Baseball in managerial and ownership positions, Campanis responded, "No, I don't believe it's prejudice. I truly believe that they may not have some of the necessities to be, let's say, a field manager, or perhaps a general manager. So it just might be— why are black men, or black people not good swimmers? They just don't have the buoyancy." In 1988, Jimmy (the Greek) Snyder was fired by CBS Sports after commenting on air that blacks were "bred" to be athletes. In 2005, Air Force Coach Fisher DeBerry was reprimanded for insinuating that his black players were faster than his white players. In 2007, Don Imus was suspended and then fired after referring to the women on Rutger's basketball team as "nappy-headed hos" on his radio show. Also in 2007, NFL coaches Lovie Smith and Tony Dungy were celebrated as the first two African American coaches to compete at the Super Bowl. Lastly, Kelly Tilghman was suspended for two weeks after suggesting that those who want to challenge Tiger Woods should "lynch him in a back

alley." For reported accounts see Associated Press, "Golf Channel Anchor Suspended for Tiger Woods 'Lynch' Comment," http://www.foxnews.com; John Clayton, "Smith, Dungy Will Make This a Classy Super Bowl," http://sports.espn.go.com/espn; Michael Goodwin, "CBS Dismisses Snyder," *New York Times*, in Penrose Library Nexus Lexus, http://0-www/lexisnexis.combianca.penlib.du.edu (accessed 17 February 2008); News Services, "Campanis Apologizes for His Racial Remarks," *Washington Post*, 1987 pp. B2; James Poniewozik, "Who Can Say What?" *Time Magazine*, 23 April 2007, pp. 32–38; Michael Wilbon, "Misplaced Fury Over Racism," *Washington Post*, 29 October 2005, http://www.lexisnexis.com/us/Inacademic/delivery (accessed 10 March 2008).

3. Michael Butterworth, "Race in 'the Race': Mark McGuirre, Sammy Sosa, and the Heroic Construction of Whiteness," *Critical Studies in Media Communication* 24 (2007): 228–44; Butterworth, "The Politics of the Pitch: Claiming and Contesting Democracy through the Iraqi National Soccer Team," *Communication and Critical/Cultural Studies* 4 (2007): 184–203.

4. Barry Brummett, *Rhetoric in Popular Culture* (New York: St. Martin's Press, 1994), 21.

5. For examples, see Timothy J. Brown, "Allan Iverson as America's Most Wanted: Black Masculinity as a Cultural Site of Struggle," *Journal of Intercultural Communication Research* 34 (2005): 65–87; Butterworth "Race in 'the Race'"; Butterworth "The Politics of the Pitch"; Michael L. Butterworth, "Ritual in the 'Church of Baseball': Suppressing the Discourse of Democracy After 9/11," *Communication and Critical/Cultural Studies* 2 (2005): 107–29; Fernando Pedro Delgado, "Major League Soccer: The Return of the Foreign Sport," *Journal of Sport and Social Issues* 21 (1997): 287–99; Delgado, "The Fusing of Sport and Politics: Media Constructions of U.S. Versus Iran at France 98," *Journal of Sport and Social Issues* 27 (2003): 293–307; Delgado, "Golden But Not Brown: Oscar De La Hoya and the Complications of Culture, Manhood, and Boxing," *International Journal of the History of Sport* 22 (2005): 194–210; Margaret Carlisle Duncan and Barry Brummett, "The Mediation of Spectator Sport," *Research Quarterly for Exercise and Sport* 58 (1987): 168–77; Duncan and Brummett, "Types and Sources of Spectating Pleasure in Televised Sports," *Sociology of Sport Journal* 6 (1989): 195–211; Duncan and Brummett, "Liberal and Radical Sources of Female Empowerment in Sport Media," *Sociology of Sport Journal* 10 (1993): 57–72; Thomas P. Oates, "The Erotic Gaze in the NFL Draft," *Communication and Critical/Cultural Studies* 4 (2007): 74–90; Nick Trujillo, "Hegemonic Masculinity at the Mound: Media Representations of Nolan Ryan and American Sports Culture," *Critical Studies in Mass Communication* 8 (1991): 290–308; Nick Trujillo and Leah Vande Berg, "Sportswriting and American Cultural Values: The 1984 Chicago Cubs," *Critical Studies in Mass Communication* 2 (1985): 262–82.

6. Butterworth, "The Politics of the Pitch."

7. Delgado, "The Fusing of Sport and Politics."

8. Delgado, "Golden Not Brown."

9. Brown, "Allen Iverson."

10. Oates, "The Erotic Gaze."

11. Butterworth, "The Race in 'the Race'"; Caroline Fusco, "Cultural Landscapes of Purification: Sports Spaces and Discourses of Whiteness," *Sociology of Sports Journal* 22 (2005): 283–310; Daniel A. Grano, "Ritual Disorder and the Contractual Morality of Sports: A Case Study in Race, Class, and Agreement," *Rhetoric and Public Affairs* 10, 3 (2007): 445–74; Richard C. King, "Cautionary Notes on Whiteness and Sports Studies," *Sociology of Sports Journal* 22 (2005): 397–408; Mary G. McDonald, "Mapping Whiteness and Sport: An Introduction." *Sociology of Sports Journal* 22 (2005): 245–55.

12. Brummett, *Rhetoric in Popular Culture*.

13. Duncan and Brummett, "The Mediation."

14. Susan Birrell and Mary G. McDonald, *Reading Sport: Critical Essays on Power and Representation* (Boston: Northeastern University Press, 2000), 3.

15. David J. Leonard, "The Real Color of Money: Controlling Black Bodies in the NBA," *Journal of Sport and Social Issues* 30, 2 (2006): 158.

16. Todd Boyd and Kenneth L. Shropshire, "Basketball Jones: A New World Order?" in *America Above the Rim: Basketball Jones*, ed. Todd Boyd and K. L. Shropshire (New York: New York University Press, 2001), 7.

17. Ben Carrington, "Sport, Masculinity, and Black Cultural Resistance," *Journal of Sport and Social Issues* 22 (1998): 280.

18. Randy Martin and Toby Miller, *Sportcult* (Minneapolis: University of Minnesota Press, 1999), 6.

19. For the purpose of this chapter, we focus on Stern's body being read as white and male. We are aware that Stern identifies as Jewish as well (Joseph Siegman, *Jewish Sports Legends: The International Jewish Sports Hall of Fame*, 2nd ed. (Washington, DC: Brassey's, 1997), and has been honored by the International Jewish Sports Hall of Fame. However, in the media he is very rarely identified or explicitly read as Jewish. Although not addressed within the foci of this chapter, the historical relationships between black and Jewish groups offer rich potential for the continued analysis of Stern's embodied performance as the NBA commissioner. For discussion of black and Jewish histories, see, for example, Cornel West, "On Black-Jewish Relations," in *Readings for Diversity and Social Justice: An Anthology on Racism, Antisemitism, Sexism, Heterosexism, Ableism, and Classism*, ed. Maurianne Adams, Warren J. Blumenfield, Rosie Castaneda, et al. (New York: Routledge, 2000), 177–81.

20. Butterworth, "The Politics of the Pitch"; Butterworth, "Race in 'the Race.'"

21. As critical scholars, it is important for us to acknowledge that Stern has sparingly been identified as Jewish. Although we do not aim to dismiss this aspect of his ethnic and/or religious identity, it is not a focus of our analysis based upon the lack of media coverage that positions him as Jewish. In essence, Stern is largely visible and positioned in the media as a white male rather than as a white, Jewish male. Despite our focus on his white male identity, we are greatly supportive of future research projects that incorporate his Jewish identity at the intersections as well.

22. These particular NBA events and policies were selected based upon the extensive media coverage they received via magazines, newspapers, television, etc.

23. Ronald L. Jackson and Celnisha Dangerfield, "Defining Black Masculinity as Cultural Property: Toward an Identity Negotiation Paradigm," in *Intercultural Communication: A Reader*, 10th ed., ed. Larry Samovar and Richard Porter (Belmont, CA: Wadsworth, 2002), 120–30; Gitaniali Maharaj, "Talking Trash: Late Capitalism, Black (Re)Productivity, and Professional Basketball," in *Sportcult*, ed. Randy Martin and Toby Miller (Minneapolis: University of Minnesota Press, 1999), 227–40.

24. William C. Rhoden, *Forty Million Dollar Slaves: The Rise, Fall, and Redemption of the Black Athlete* (New York: Crown Publishers, 2006).

25. It is also important to recognize that black women and whites were lynched as well. However, the majority of those lynched were black men (Robert Gibson, "The Negro Holocaust: Lynching and Race Riots in the United States, 1880–1950," Yale-New Haven Teachers Institute. http://www.yale.edu/ynhti/curriculum/units/1979/2/79.02.04.x.html).

26. Ernest Cashmore, *Black Sportsmen* (London: Routledge, 1982); Harry Edwards, *The Revolt of the Black Athlete* (New York: Free Press, 1969); Douglass Hartmann, "The Politics of Race and Sport: Resistance and Domination in the 1968 African American Olympic Protest

Movement," *Ethnic and Racial Studies* 19, 3 (1996): 548–66; Mike Marqusee, "Sport and Stereotype: From Role Model to Muhammad Ali," *Race & Class* 36, 4 (1995): 1–29.

27. See, for example, Kareem Abdul-Jabbar and Peter Knobler, *The Autobiography of Kareem Abdul-Jabbar* (New York: Bantam, 1983); Charles Barkley and Michael Wilbon, *I May be Wrong: But I Doubt It* (New York: Random House, 2003); Bill Russell and William McSweeny, *Go Up for Glory* (New York: Coward McCann, 1996).

28. Edwards, *Revolt of the Black Athlete*.

29. Derrick Bell, *Faces at the Bottom of the Well: The Permanence of Racism* (New York: Basic Books, 1992).

30. Richard Lapchick, *Smashing Barriers: Race and Sport in the New Millennium* (Lanham, MD: Madison Books, 2001).

31. Cooper (1926–1984) was the first black player to be drafted into the NBA by the Boston Celtics on April 25, 1950 (Arthur Ashe, *A Hard Road to Glory: A History of African American Athletes since 1946* [New York: Warner Books, 1988]). Clifton (1922–1990) was the first black player to sign an NBA contract: he signed with New York Knicks on May 3, 1950 (Ashe, *Hard Road to Glory*; Ron Thomas, *They Cleared the Lane: The NBA's Black Pioneers* [Lincoln: University of Nebraska Press, 2002]). Lloyd (1928–) became the first black player to play in a regular season game for the Washington Capitols on October 31, 1950 (Marc J. Spears, "First Black Player Recalls NBA Days," *Boston Globe*, January 24, 2008).

32. See Edwards, *Revolt of the Black Athlete*; Richard C. King, David J. Leonard, and Kyle W. Kusz, "White Power and Sport: An Introduction," *Journal of Sport and Social Issues* 31, 1 (2007): 3–10; Rhoden, *Forty Million Dollar Slaves*.

33. Beyond the integration of African Americans into professional basketball as players, Bill Russell was hired as the first black coach in 1966 by the Boston Celtics (Thomas, *They Cleared the Lane*). Next, Ken Hudson was the first black referee in the NBA in 1968 (Roscoe Nance, "Hudson Helped Pave the Way for Other Referees," *USA Today*, February 18, 2003). In 1972, Wayne Embry was named the first black general manager in the league appointed by the Baltimore Bullets (Wayne Embry and Mary S. Boyer, *The Inside Game: Race, Power, and Politics in the NBA* [Akron: University of Akron Press, 2004]). Most recently, Robert Johnson became the first African American majority team owner of the Charlotte Bobcats during the 2000–2001 season (Brett Pulley, "He's Got Game," *Forbes Magazine* 171, no. 4, 46).

34. Lapchick, *Smashing Barriers*.

35. For a numeric breakdown of ethnic representation in the league, see "The 2006–2007 Season Racial and Gender Report Card: National Basketball Association" (Lapchick, Bustamante, and Ruiz).

36. The media coverage utilized as data for this chapter was drawn from a larger dissertation project that utilized critical race theory as a theoretical and methodological means to situate the National Basketball Association as a professional sports league in which both race and racism matter. As such, the 2004 brawl and 2005 dress code were selected based on the extensive media coverage that each received, and comments made by both Stern and black players in reaction to these events are positioned as focal points to map, interrogate, and reveal the oppressive workings of whiteness.

37. Birrell and McDonald, *Reading Sport*, 11.

38. Raymie McKerrow, "Critical Rhetoric: Theory and Praxis," Communication Monographs 56 (1989): 91–111; Kent A. Ono and John M. Sloop, "Commitment to Telos— A Sustained Critical Rhetoric," *Communication Monographs* 59 (1992): 48–60.

39. Butterworth, "Race in 'the Race,'" 229.

40. Thomas K. Nakayama, "Show/Down Time: 'Race,' Gender, Sexuality, and Popular Culture," *Critical Studies in Mass Communication* 11 (1994): 162–79; Nakayama and Krizek, "Whiteness."

41. Eduardo Bonilla-Silva, *Racism Without Racists: Color-Blind Racism and the Persistence of Racial Inequality in the United States* (Lanham, MD: Rowman and Littlefield, 2003), 1.

42. Projansky and Ono, "Strategic Whiteness," 152.

43. Patricia Hill Collins, *Black Sexual Politics: African Americans, Gender, and the New Racism* (New York: Routledge, 2004), 34.

44. Projansky and Ono, "Strategic Whiteness," 151.

45. Ibid.; Moon and Nakayama.

46. Butterworth, "Race in the 'the Race.'"

47. Dwight Conquergood, "Performance Studies: Interventions and Radical Research," *Drama Review* 46 (2002): 145–56; Michael Calvin McGee, "Text, Context, and the Fragmentation of Contemporary Culture," *Western Journal of Speech Communication* 54 (1990): 274–89.

48. NBA Media Ventures, "David J. Stern," 7 November 2007. http://www.nba.com/nba101/david_j_stern_bio.html.

49. David DuPree, "NBA Drug Use: High-Risk Recreation," *Washington Post,* 21 March 1982, M1; E. M. Swift,"From Corned Beef to Caviar; NBA Commissioner David Stern," *Sports Illustrated* 74, 21 (1991): 74–87; Jim Walker, "NBA Drug Use Up, Says Study," *The Chicago Tribune,* 20 August 1980, D3.

50. Maharaj, "Talking Trash."

51. Jane Gross, "N.B.A.'s Rebuilding Program Is Showing Results," *New York Times,* 23 December 1984, 3.

52. Tracey Owens Patton,"In the Guise of Civility: The Complicitous Maintenance of Inferential Forms of Sexism and Racism in Higher Education," *Women's Studies in Communication* 27 (2004): 65.

53. Collins, *Black Sexual Politics,* 152.

54. Gross, "N.B.A.'s Rebuilding Program."

55. NBA Media Ventures; Swift, "From Corned Beef to Caviar."

56. Swift, "From Corned Beef to Caviar."

57. Maharaj, "Talking Trash."

58. Bill Saporito, "Why Fans and Players Playing So Rough: The Worst Brawl in NBA History Highlights the Combustible Mix of Rabid Spectators and Strutting Athletes. Is the Game Itself Losing Out?" 6 December 2004, *Time Magazine.* Accessed 22 February 2008 from http://0-find.galegroup.com.bianca.penlib.du.edu.

59. Grano, "Ritual Disorder."

60. Jack McCallum, "The Ugliest Game: An NBA Brawl Exposes the Worst Player and Fan Behavior and Serves as a Frightening Wake-Up Call," *Sports Illustrated,* 29 November 2004. Accessed 3 March 2005 from http://0-find.galegroup.com.bianca.penlib.du.edu.

61. NBA Press Conference, "David Stern NBA Press Conference," 22 November 2004. Accessed 21 December 2007 from http://www.insidehoops.com/conferene-transcript.shtml.

62. Ibid.

63. Ibid.

64. Ibid.

65. Ibid.

66. L. Lage, "Indiana 97, Detroit 82," *Associated Press,* 2004, November 20. Accessed February 13, 2008 from http://sports.yahoo.com/nba/recap

67. McCallum, "The Ugliest Game."

68. Ibid.

69. Ibid.

70. We differentiate between the overt racism that past players endured, arguing that current players endure more covert forms of racism that speak to Collins's articulation of the new racism. For example, following integration, it was not uncommon for black players to be refused services on the road (hotel, restaurants, etc.) based on their skin color; and, while such explicitly racist practices would not likely occur in contemporary society, it is not uncommon for black players to be represented and/or perceived as animalistic, biologically superior, and unfit for managerial and ownership positions. See Rhoden, *Forty Million Dollar Slaves*, for further discussion.

71. Grano, "Ritual Disorder."

72. Linda Tucker, "Blackballed: Basketball and Representations of the Black Male Athlete," *American Behavioral Scientist* 47 (2003): 317.

73. R. W. Connell, *Gender and Power: Society, the Person and Sexual Politics*, (Palo Alto: Stanford University Press, 1987); Toby Miller, *Sportsex* (Philadelphia: Temple University Press, 2001).

74. Collins, *Black Sexual Politics*, 154.

75. Ibid., 157.

76. Saporito, "Why Fans."

77. Mark Starr, "Starr Gazing: NBA Brawl Shouldn't Surprise Anyone," *Newsweek* (Web Exclusive), November 26, 2004.

78. Charles Gardner, "NBA's Dress Code; Clothes Call; Dress Code Doesn't Suit All Players," *Milwaukee Journal Sentinel*, 19 October 2005. Accessed 11 February 2007 from http: www.findarticles.com/p/articles/mi_qn4196.

79. John Eligon, "Dressing Up Basketball? Been There, Done That," *New York Times*, 27 October 2005. Accessed 26 December 2005 from http://select.nytimes.com/search/restricted/article; Mike Wise, "Opinions on NBA's Dress Code Are Far from Uniform," *Washington Post*, 23 October 2005. Accessed 29 January 2008 from http://www.washingtonpost.com/wp-dyn/content/article/2005.

80. Eligon, "Dressing Up Basketball?"

81. Darren Rovell, "Stern Sure Players Will Comply with New Dress Code," 18 October 2005. Accessed 21 December 2007 from http://sports.espn.go.com/espn/print

82. Sports Briefing, "Pro Basketball: Dress Code Called Racist," *New York Times*, 20 October 2005. Accessed 26 December 2005 from http://select. Nytimes.com/search/restricted/article.

83. ESPN, "One-Size-Fits-All Dress Code Draws Divergent Views," 18 October 2005. Accessed 11 February 2007 from http://sports.espn.go.com/espn/print.

84. Sports Briefing, "Pro Basketball."

85. Chris McCosky, "Some Pistons Are Unhappy About Talk of a Dress Code," *Detroit News*, 9 October 2005. Accessed 11 February 2007 from http:www.detnews.com/2005/pistons.

86. Ibid.

87. Rovell, "Stern Sure Players Will Comply."

88. Wise, "Opinions."

89. Michael Cunningham, "NBA's New Rules on Apparel Are a Good Fit for Most Players," *Collegian Online*, 14 November 2005. Accessed 11 February 2007 from http://blue.utb.edu/collegian/2005/fall.

90. Rovell, "Stern Sure Players Will Comply."

91. Richard Carter, "NBA's New Dress Code: Racist or Just Smart Business?" *New York Amsterdam News*, 17–23 November 2005: 41.

92. Cunningham, "NBA's New Rules."

93. For discussions on how appearance (i.e., styles of dress, hairstyle, etc.) can serve as articulations of identity that demonstrate resistance and/or complicity, see Murray Forman and Mark A. Neal, eds., *That's the Joint: The Hip Hop Studies Reader* (New York: Routledge, 2004); Dick Hebdige, *Subculture: The Meaning of Style* (London: Routledge, 1979); Noliwe M. Rooks, *Hair Raising: Beauty, Culture, and African American Women* (New Brunswick, NJ: Rutgers University Press, 1996).

94. Jeffrey Lane, *Under the Boards: The Cultural Revolution in Basketball* (Lincoln: University of Nebraska Press, 2007).

95. Ian Thomsen, "Why Fans Are Tuning Out the NBA" *Sports Illustrated*, February 2005, 70.

96. James C. Scott, *Domination and the Arts of Resistance: Hidden Transcripts* (New Haven: Yale University Press, 1990); Michel de Certeau, *The Practice of Everyday Life* (Berkeley: University of California Press, 1984).

97. Martin and Miller, *Sportcult*, 13.

98. Gross, "N.B.A.'s Rebuilding Program," 3.

99. bell hooks, *Teaching Community: A Pedagogy of Hope* (New York: Routledge, 2003).

100. Pierre Bourdieu, *Practical Reason: On Theory of Action* (Cambridge, UK: Polity, 1998).

101. Raka Shome, "Outing Whiteness," *Critical Studies in Mass Communication* 17, 3 (2000): 366.

102. Ibid., 368.

III Vernacular Resistances

7 Declarations of Independence

African American Abolitionists and the Struggle for Racial and Rhetorical Self-Determination

Jacqueline Bacon

By the late 1830s, many African American abolitionists began publicly expressing a desire for independence from white antislavery leaders with whom they had previously collaborated. In powerful statements declaring their desire for self-determination, they argued that their white colleagues' attempts to control and restrict their rhetoric and activism were offensive and oppressive. In doing so, they critiqued white abolitionist leaders' racism, affirmed African Americans' right to create arguments on their own terms, and uncovered the history of black rhetorical activism that gave them empowering precedent for their efforts. These declarations challenged the established power relationships within the abolition movement, enabled new voices to emerge, and brought unique arguments into the public debate.[1]

The black abolitionists' declarations of independence during the 1840s and 1850s constitute important statements about freedom within the context of oppression, explorations of the role rhetoric plays in seeking such liberation, and examples of discursive resistance to control. As scholars interested in the intersections of race and rhetoric, it is vital that we engage historical as well as contemporary texts and adopt fresh perspectives for analyzing discourse of the past. Just as discussions of racial conditions in the United States apart from their historical contexts are incomplete, when we consider racial rhetoric apart from its historical roots, we overlook the groundbreaking discursive work done by historical figures, such as black abolitionists whose voices have frequently been ignored, yet upon whose foundations subsequent efforts are built. This recovery effort expands the rhetorical canon and requires scholars to reconsider the historical record itself about the intersections of race and rhetoric. As we explore the discursive functions of these significant, yet frequently ignored, rhetorical texts, we expand the extant record of accounts of autonomous liberation practices used by African Americans. We also reframe the ways we understand the linkages among race, agency, and discourse, both in the past and in the present.

While studies of the rhetoric of black abolitionists frequently focus on the tactics African Americans used to establish their credibility and argue against slavery, their declarations of independence are relatively unexplored. This discourse protests oppression as well as creates and affirms community.[2] In particular, it represents examples of vernacular rhetoric, defined by Kent A. Ono and John M. Sloop as "discourse that resonates within and from historically oppressed communities"; that emanates from a "critical framework" toward the dominant culture; and "that does not exist only as counter-hegemonic, but also as affirmative, articulating a sense of community that does not function solely as oppositional to dominant ideologies." Such discourse is often ignored, Ono and Sloop indicate, in favor of "the discourse of the empowered," yet vernacular texts demand our critical attention, because they "gird and influence local cultures first and then affect . . . cultures at large" as well as "render power relations among subjects visible."[3] With societal hierarchies exposed and challenged, black rhetors use vernacular discourse to call into question the very bases for white supremacy and, as Dexter B. Gordon asserts, to create "collective black practices" which "functioned to re-structure the social relations between whites and blacks." African American abolitionists' declarations of independence that appeared in black newspapers, autobiographical writings, and speeches may be overlooked by scholars who place more emphasis on well-known and more-publicized texts. Yet, these texts are crucial to our understanding of black abolitionist discourse and its influence on rhetoric and race in the United States.[4]

Such critical attention to the arguments for independence of black abolitionists affords us the opportunity to explore three neglected areas that have important implications for scholars of race and rhetoric. First, although various historical studies consider the tactics employed by African Americans in order to take agency within discursive spheres,[5] we do not often encounter texts by black rhetors that explicitly address the implications of controlling their own rhetoric. In addition, as scholars have argued, the racialized assumptions and standards that empower white participants in the public sphere and disenfranchise African Americans (as well as others) are profoundly influential, yet are frequently unstated and unchallenged, due to the power of what Michael Lacy calls a discourse of "white absolutism" that "centers white masculinity" and "negat[es] black, nonwhite, and feminine archetypes."[6] Although studies have analyzed examples of rhetoric in which whiteness is implicit and normative,[7] we need further explorations both of the alternatives created by African Americans to conventional discursive rules and of the historical context for these standards as well as the resistance to them. Finally, scholars have explored the significance of antebellum African Americans' control over their history as key to the creation of empowering identities.[8] Yet, attention has not generally been given to a less common, but similarly critical, discursive act: the writing of the history of African American rhetoric by antebellum black intellectuals themselves, in which they explicitly relate and assess the rhetorical efforts of their precursors.[9]

These three areas of inquiry guide my analysis of African American abolitionists' declarations of their independence. I examine the rhetoric generated by three men who responded in various texts created between 1840 and 1860 to white abolitionists' presumptions and attempted domination: James McCune Smith, Samuel Ringgold Ward, and William J. Watkins. I consider first the ways these rhetors equated speaking for themselves and control of their discourse with autonomy, freedom, and self-determination. I then turn to their critiques of the rules of rhetorical engagement created and promoted by white abolitionists, and to their articulation of alternative standards for judging the effectiveness of discourse. Finally, I explore these rhetors' constructions of histories of abolitionist persuasion that give African American abolitionists central and formative roles, thereby reversing the power relationships between white and black abolitionists and creating an inclusive history of African American discursive practices.

Historical and Biographical Background

Roughly 18 percent of the U.S. population in 1830 was black (2,328,642 people, according to the 1830 census), yet only about 14 percent of these more than two million African Americans were free (319,599 people). By 1840, the black population was approximately 17 percent (2,873,648 by the 1840 census), with roughly 13 percent of those free (386,293).[10] Those free African Americans faced severe restrictions on their legal and political participation and educational opportunities; across the North, they were threatened with assaults from white mobs and were at risk of being kidnapped, labeled as fugitives, and sold into slavery, with indifference and complicity by public officials enabling such violations.

In spite of these formidable obstacles, African Americans emerged as both the primary creators of and innovators in the abolition movement in the United States. Black antislavery agitation and persuasion began as early as the Revolutionary period and was particularly strong by the late 1820s. Many white reformers were persuaded to join the abolition movement because of the groundwork laid by their African American colleagues. During the 1830s, white and black abolitionists worked together in organizations such as the American Anti-Slavery Society and on projects such as the promotion of the *Liberator*, William Lloyd Garrison's antislavery newspaper.

However, by the late 1830s, African American abolitionists began publicly expressing a desire for rhetorical independence from their white colleagues. White abolitionists frequently harbored prejudices against African Americans and consequently restricted their participation in striking ways. Black abolitionists were offered less prestigious roles than their white counterparts by white leaders, were paid less, and frequently were told how and where they should write and speak. Clearly, such treatment was offensive to African American abolitionists and put them in a trying and ultimately untenable situation. There were also concrete disagreements between white and African American abolitionists. While many white abolitionists favored moral suasion and opposed physical resistance, African Americans became increasingly disillusioned with the limitations of these approaches. In their emphasis on Southern bondage, white abolitionists frequently overlooked the improvement of conditions for free African Americans, goals which black abolitionists saw as intrinsically related to ending literal slavery. As a result, African American abolitionists from the 1840s onward sought independent outlets through which to express their rhetoric and activism. They used media and organizations that were led and controlled by African Americans, such as black newspapers and literary, religious, and fraternal societies, and wished to advocate antislavery tactics that various influential white colleagues rejected, such as political action and physical resistance. In many cases, African American abolitionists both worked within these autonomous organizations and continued to participate with white colleagues in organizations such as the American Anti-Slavery Society.[11]

James McCune Smith, Samuel Ringgold Ward, and William J. Watkins became involved in the movement during the late 1830s and 1840s. Smith, born in New York City in 1813 to a slave woman and a white father, was freed in 1827 by New York's Emancipation Act. A community leader, physician, and proprietor of the first black-owned pharmacy, Smith was an active member of African American organizations and wrote for and edited various black newspapers. Ward was born a slave in 1817. His parents escaped when he was young, settling first in New Jersey and then in New York. Ward served as an educator, Congregational pastor, and antislavery lecturer. He established and edited various reform newspapers as well as worked to aid runaway slaves. Facing indictment after his involvement with the rescue of a fugitive apprehended in Syracuse in 1851, he emigrated to Canada, where he founded the newspaper the *Provincial Freeman* for Canada's black community. William J. Watkins was born around 1826 to free black parents in Baltimore. His father, William Watkins, was an educator and abolitionist. The younger Watkins moved to Boston in the late 1840s, where he was an activist, spokesman, and writer against slavery; and, for a time, an associate editor of *Frederick Douglass' Paper*.[12]

"Entire Freemen": Liberty and Rhetorical Self-Determination
Free but Not Equal: Black Rhetors Challenge White Control

The racism of white abolitionists and their desire to control African Americans' participation in the movement was manifested in whites' attempts to limit and manage the persuasion of their black colleagues. White antislavery leaders advised African American abolitionists to narrate facts, while whites offered explicit arguments. Former slaves were counseled that in order to be credible, they should not appear too educated or erudite. These directives were grounded in appeals to natural law that, as Lacy indicates, are marshaled by white absolutists to make "white supremacy seem objective, essential, and natural" and to disenfranchise nonwhites.[13] This advice also indicates that white abolitionists accepted and perpetuated assumptions about race, discernment, and eloquence that threatened to limit blacks' rhetorical agency severely. Like their white contemporaries, who adopted white supremacist beliefs, white abolitionists assumed that blacks were childlike, emotional rather than logical, and unable to attain rhetorical expertise. This required a level of intelligence whites assumed unavailable to those of African descent. Therefore, most white abolitionists believed that black liberation depended upon whites for protection and salvation (either through slavery, in the view of proslavery advocates, or liberation by white saviors, in the views of white abolitionists). These bedrocks of American racial thought became canonical through influential texts, such as Thomas Jefferson's *Notes on the State of Virginia*, and then were used to cast doubts on the authenticity of Phillis Wheatley's poetry and Frederick Douglass's own writings, for example. Because white abolitionists controlled various venues in which their African American colleagues wrote and spoke, such as Garrison's *Liberator* and the American Anti-Slavery Society lecture circuit, their attempts to impose restrictions on their black colleagues based on these racist presumptions were continual obstacles.[14]

Yet, African American abolitionists rejected whites' attempts to limit them and created forceful, empowered arguments that expressed their particular concerns, experiences, and perspectives. They also directly addressed the implications of white control of their discourse and of independence from these constraints. Consider, for example, James McCune Smith's comments about the treatment of Frederick Douglass by white abolitionist leaders in his introduction to Douglass's 1855 *My Bondage and My Freedom*: "[T]hese gentlemen . . . did not delve into the mind of a colored man for capacities which the pride of race led them to believe to be restricted to their own Saxon blood. Bitter and vindictive sarcasm, irresistible mimicry, and a pathetic narrative of his own experiences of slavery, were the intellectual manifestations which they encouraged him to exhibit on the platform or in the lecture desk." White abolitionists may have sought the oratorical talents of their black colleagues, but they restricted them to narrating their personal experiences, rather than logically addressing whites' arguments. Douglass, though, Smith related, realized that, in the words of Lord Byron, "Who would be free, themselves must strike the blow" by controlling his own discourse and activism.[15]

African American abolitionists highlighted the racist assumptions underlying white abolitionists' "guidance" for their black colleagues. Writing from Canada in his newspaper the *Provincial Freeman*, Samuel Ringgold Ward laments, "Some [white abolitionists] . . . desire that we should be free; but as to our being regarded and treated as equals, *that* is another thing. . . . They assume the right to dictate to us about all matters; they dislike to see us assume or maintain manly and independent positions." William J. Watkins chastises whites who would direct and control African American reformers, as well as blacks who did not resist these constraints: "We apparently think, more can be accomplished without than with us. . . . We must not consent to be ignored, in the Anti-Slavery warfare."[16]

"The History of Their Native Country": Racial and Revolutionary Precedents

The presumption that African Americans needed white direction was condescending and demonstrably false, so indicates Ward's 1855 account of his life and antislavery career. To support his case, Ward used examples of his own counsel to black associates, the leadership Douglass displayed through his oratory, and the efforts of unnamed leaders of African American state and national conventions. It is "altogether out of the question," Ward asserts, to try to "keep a people rooted to the soil" who have such "gifted leaders" among them. Ward issues an implicit warning to those who would aim to keep them "rooted" by attempting to control their discourse: "[L]ook at the materials which the blacks have at command. . . . They are *Americans*; they are well taught in the history of their native country. . . . They know what to say, to whom to say it, and at what time." The fundamental American impulse to be free and determine one's own future that Ward invoked for African Americans is manifested in words as well as in political action.[17]

African American abolitionists resisted whites' attempts to control their discourse as the only way to gain true liberty. The reconstitution of the nation's history served as a powerful precedent for black abolitionists' rhetorical self-determination. In a report to the 1847 National Convention of Colored People and Their Friends in Troy, James McCune Smith and his colleagues George B. Wilson and William H. Topp affirm the importance of a national African American press: "The first step which will mark our certain advancement as a people, will be our Declaration of Independence from all aid except from God and our own souls." Connecting the foundational text of the United States and its Revolution with the establishment of an institution—a national black press—that will allow African Americans to control their own discourse, Smith and his associates link rhetorical and literal freedom. Conversely, they describe their confined position when whites managed their rhetoric: "Our friends sorrow with us, because they say we are unfortunate! We must . . . command something manlier than sympathies. We must command the respect and admiration due men, who, against fearful odds, are struggling steadfastly for their rights."[18]

Speaking in 1853 to African Americans in New Bedford, Watkins similarly rejects whites' condescending attitudes and invokes the spirit of the American Revolution, particularly the Declaration of Independence, as illustrative of the proactive stance black abolitionists took to speak for themselves: "We ask no favors. . . . We ask not for sympathy. We demand our rights as men, as freemen, as citizens of the United States. . . . Ah! we cling to the principles of your Declaration of Independence . . . with inflexible tenacity. . . . [W]e do not present ourselves before the usurpers of our rights as obsequious suppliants for favor, but as men conscious of our rights, and resolved at all hazards to obtain them."[19]

Rhetoric, Independence, and Manhood

The repetition of the word "men" in these statements suggests another dimension of African American male abolitionists' control of their rhetoric. Masculinity is linked to the control of their own discourse that enables them to become, as Smith and Watkins assert, subjects worthy of "respect," rather than the objects of "sympathies." Manhood—a key element both of American Revolutionary rhetoric and of African Americans' views of freedom—depends upon self-determination. Ideals of masculinity for antebellum African Americans (which were not, as scholars indicate, merely derived from white conceptions, but constructed in light of racial and community traditions and influences) depended upon their assertiveness, self-reliance, resistance to oppression, and service to the community. Expressing one's manhood could take the form of physical as well as economic, intellectual, and rhetorical resistance to oppression.[20] In rhetorical terms, manhood enabled men to articulate their own positions boldly and to define their own terms.

For African American abolitionists declaring their independence, the connections among manhood, freedom, and rhetorical self-determination called for affirmative rhetorical stances, rather than reactive positions based on whites' presumptions. In an 1854 editorial in *Frederick Douglass' Paper*, Watkins counsels African Americans to adopt this bold, authoritative ethos: "We are men, conscious of the dignity of manhood, and as MEN, so we speak to the noble advocates of Freedom. . . . We would have no one suppose that we are suppliants for favor; what we DEMAND is our unrestricted rights as freemen." In a contribution published in the newspaper the following year, Watkins supplies even more detail about how African American men should aim not to be "objects of sympathy" but subjects of their own discourse and destiny. "We must not, if we would be *respected*, and have our manhood *recognized*," he asserts, "assume the position of mere suppliants for favor, feeding upon the innutritious husks of the white man's sympathy. . . . [W]e must not be content . . . with bowing with obsequious deference to the dicta of assumed superiority. . . . We must give orders as well as execute; command as well as obey."[21]

Racial and Rhetorical Rules of the Abolitionist Public Sphere
"The Deeper Relation of Things": Narrative and Logic

To "command as well as obey," African American abolitionists had to challenge norms for public rhetoric that inherently disenfranchised and infantilized them. As scholars have demonstrated, in civic debate in the United States, powerful yet unwritten rules work to favor white participants while disempowering African Americans.[22] Yet, as black abolitionists sought autonomy in their antislavery efforts, they challenged these standards, laying bare the usually invisible presumptions that served to diminish their discourse, destabilizing power relationships and allowing for the emergence of new norms and models of public discourse that gave them discursive authority.

White leaders frequently discouraged African American abolitionists from offering anything but narratives about their experiences and told them to leave the "logical" arguments to their white colleagues. As Smith's aforementioned comments in his introduction to Douglass's *My Bondage and My Freedom* indicate, Douglass resisted this control. In addition, Smith's framing of Douglass's text also overturned the discursive rules, which were employed to reify a false bifurcation between logic and testimony to restrict African Americans' rhetoric. "It has been said of Mr. Douglass," Smith asserts, "that his descriptive and declamatory powers, admitted to be of the very highest order, take precedence of his logical force." Yet, Smith rejects the characterization of logical reasoning as a more valid form of persuasion than description or narration. "To such a mind [as Douglass's]," Smith remarks, "the ordinary processes of logical deduction are like proving that two and two make four." By contrast, Douglass's persuasion "goes down to the deeper relation of things, and brings out what may seem, to some, mere statements, but which are new and brilliant generalizations, each resting on a broad and stable basis." The ability to make logical arguments is a skill conventionally valued as a marker of rhetorical competence. In the antebellum period as well as others, logical skills were assumed to be unavailable to rhetors of color (or women), who were conceived to be rhetorically ineffective. For Smith, though, logic displayed by "ordinary" rhetors is, on its own, just a "showy display." Black abolitionists held that logic was to be combined with the experiences of African Americans, enabling "brilliant generalizations" to emerge. This offered an alternative rhetorical model, enabling black abolitionists to assume a unique and superior basis of authority from white abolitionists.[23]

Righteous Anger

Rhetoric that is based on both experience and logic clearly resonates emotionally as well as intellectually. Yet, emotional displays of anger are frequently viewed by the advocates of conventional rhetorical rules as detracting from or undermining persuasion. This formulation is frequently used against black speakers and writers, who are dismissed because they are ostensibly "too angry" or inappropriately sensitive on racial topics.[24] But, African American rhetors, both past and present, have challenged this view and demonstrated, as Eddie S. Glaude, Jr. indicates, that "radical rage" is a powerful alternative to an attitude of "servility" that can enable them to "speak events unspoken regardless of the feelings of whites" and to bring into sharp focus the evils of white supremacy. I have argued elsewhere that rage "inform(s) an empowered, assertive black voice" that is both vehement and rational. In an 1855 editorial in *Frederick Douglass' Paper*, recounting his treatment by a professed abolitionist who would not give him a job on account of his race, Watkins embraces righteous anger: "His face reddened, *and so did mine*; his with shame, mine with indignation." From this forceful position, he makes a powerful charge: "[T]he accusation we make, in candor and sincerity, against the Abolitionists, as a class, is that they lack the moral courage to actualize their ideas."[25] The anger Watkins has felt in response to racism and slavery provides him the moral authority to strongly indict his white colleagues.

In contrast to those who would cast emotional antagonism in the public sphere as inappropriate, Watkins demonstrates that anger is a necessary response to pervasive racial discrimination. After avowing in his 1853 speech in New Bedford that African Americans intend to "agitate, and *agitate*, and AGITATE" for their rights, he defends this vehement position: "I will not submit to a quiet excommunication from the pale of American citizenship. I have the right, and I shall exercise it fearlessly and boldly, and above-board, to call in question the validity of the process by which . . . I am made an alien in the land of my birth." Watkins also avers in an 1855 editorial that rage is a fitting response to the treatment of African American abolitionists by their white colleagues. Watkins responds particularly to the offensive charge that black abolitionists should be "grateful" to whites for their participation in the public sphere and that those who want independence are "ungrateful." Watkins responds forthrightly, "The first man who dares whisper the word, 'ingratitude,' to us in this connection, will be treated as he deserves. Despite our alleged innate inferiority, we can discern the black side, as well as the white side of the Abolition picture."[26]

Exposing Interests

Watkins called attention to the fact that abolitionists ground their arguments about race in their own perspective; that is, there is "a black side" and "a white side of the Abolition picture." Frequently in debates about race in the public sphere, white rhetors are assumed to be "objective" and "neutral," while African Americans are cast as inherently biased. All participants in the public sphere have an inherent stake in the outcome of racial debates, of course, but because whites' interests are unspoken and taken for granted, they are frequently cast as "impartial" participants in debates about race.[27] As a result, Carrie Crenshaw maintains, the "submerged or silent rhetoric of whiteness" reinforces white privilege and the inherent authority attributed to whites' arguments.[28]

African American abolitionists, though, challenged the privileging of white abolitionists' discursive locations as objective or more credible than blacks'. Watkins demonstrates that whites' claims to neutrality are offensive and false, laying bare whites' interests in the abolition debate: "A white man, a professed Abolitionist, remarked to the writer a few weeks since, 'Your people will never, sir be done paying us for our efforts in your behalf' . . . [to] which a consciousness of our manhood impelled us to rebuke: 'in our behalf?' we responded: 'Why sir, you are laboring for yourself and posterity.'" Watkins explicitly argues that all Americans have an investment in the outcome of the antislavery debate, while implicitly suggesting that white abolitionists' arguments are inherently based on their own interests. In his 1853 speech in New Bedford, Watkins makes this charge directly, noting of white abolitionists, "If they are our real friends, we want them near unto us, and round about us, when their proximity will be advantageous to *us*, as well as to themselves."[29]

Ward also called attention to white abolitionists' (concealed) interests in the outcome of antislavery debates and the ways these biases influenced their advocacy. In an 1840 letter to the *National Anti-Slavery Standard* defending independent black activism, Ward notes that white reformers' arguments were based on their own welfare as much as on those of African Americans: "Abolitionists have not so much regard for the rights of colored men as they think they have. When press, speech, and others of their own rights were jeopardized by the spirit of slavocracy, they raised their united voice, as men should, in self-defence. But now, when their own rights are somewhat secure, they appear to cease feeling identified with us."[30] By showing that white as well as black abolitionists argue based on their own interests, Ward undermines arguments that whites occupied a higher moral ground because of an ostensible objectivity. In doing so, Ward names the usually unspoken biases that motivate white rhetors.

"Our Platform": Histories of African American Rhetoric
African Americans and the History of Antislavery Rhetoric

As African American abolitionists challenged the rhetorical rules that their white colleagues used to restrict them, they also confronted and altered the rhetorical histories favored by white abolitionists. In general, the writing of history is a rhetorical act of constructing group identities. As nineteenth-century African Americans wrote their own histories, they resisted collective narratives about themselves and created alternative identities that give agency to blacks as subjects rather than objects.[31] As they sought independence from whites, black abolitionists wrote a very specific type of historical account of the development of African American rhetoric. African American abolitionists well knew that the assertion that white abolitionists established the antislavery movement was false; they were also aware that black antislavery rhetoric had a long history that predated whites' efforts.[32] Writing their history challenged whites' claims to authority over their African American colleagues' discourse and offered blacks a powerful alternative narrative that gave weight to their independent rhetorical efforts.

In an 1855 letter to *Frederick Douglass' Paper*, Smith establishes that African American antislavery rhetoric not only predated, but also influenced, whites' later efforts: "The colored people . . . almost began the present movement; they certainly antedated many of its principles. . . . William Lloyd Garrison and the *Liberator* owe their evangel to the free colored people. . . . Mr. Garrison came on one platform, and remains on it, in this matter, in which the eloquence of words belongs to him, of action to us: our action antedating his words, and giving force to them. " In a letter published the following week, Smith notes that the previous correspondence contained "an important misprint": instead of "'Mr. Garrison came on one platform,' &c., it should read, 'Mr. Garrison came on *our* platform.'" This was a significant change: the platform belonged first to African American abolitionists.[33]

Smith adds to his history in subsequent articles published in *Frederick Douglass' Paper*, celebrating the accomplishments of African American orators who commemorated the abolition of the international slave trade in 1808; the editors and writers of the first African American newspaper *Freedom's Journal*; and Philadelphia activists John Bowers and John Gloucester, who presided over an 1827 meeting "for the purpose of erecting a high school for colored youth." As a result, "when, in 1830–31, Mr. Garrison came among them, he found the Colored People already a power on the earth." African American abolitionists were not in debt to white abolitionists, who, Smith asserts, had "nothing to *teach* us in the matters of Anti-Slavery." The influence went in the opposite direction; the rhetorical foundation was laid by black activists who shaped white reformers' subsequent work. "[T]he free colored people," Smith asserts, "are now, in 1855, on the same platform laid down by John Bowers and John Gloucester, in April, 1827 our platform, on which the anti-slavery host came in 1833."[34] Smith's history describes and corrects the historical record. It also creates a confident black masculine identity. Smith's assertive declarations encourage his African American colleagues to see themselves as leaders who control their own discourse.

The African Roots of African American Abolitionist Rhetoric

Notably, African American abolitionists looked back for the historical roots of their rhetoric, not just to their prior efforts in the United States, but also to Africa. In an 1853 speech given to the Cheltenham Literary and Philosophical Institution in England, published in the *Cheltenham Free Press* and reprinted in the *Pennsylvania Freeman*, Ward traces—as did many nineteenth-century black historians—African Americans' history back to Egypt,[35] demonstrating that Egypt is the source for the Greek and Roman philosophy that is the foundation of the so-called Western tradition: "We had it from our European ancestors; they had it from the Greeks and Romans, who had it from the Jews—the Jews from the Egyptians and Ethiopians—in other words from Africa.—Moses graduated in a college of Egypt—a black college." Ward then refers to "Tertullian, Cyprian, St. Augustine"; all of them were, he notes, "black bishops" and "among the most shining lights of the Church of God."[36] Notably, they all figure in the rhetorical tradition that, as Ward asserts, extends from Africa to the United States.

Ward's observation resonates with what has been established by later scholars of African American rhetoric, namely that its roots lie in African as well as American traditions and philosophy.[37] Ward invokes this history, which authorizes African American abolitionists' rhetoric as part of a tradition that honors their African heritage. White abolitionists cannot claim control over this discourse, which predates not only the antislavery movement but also the United States. The platform, as Smith asserts, belongs to African Americans by their own right—indeed, it has belonged to them since ancient times.

Conclusion: "Talking Back," Going Forward

Black abolitionists' "Declarations of Independence" explored in this chapter enhance our understanding of the intersections of race and rhetoric both past and present and of the ways in which discourses about race function to empower as well as to disempower, and to create new paradigms as well as to dismantle conventional ones. When we examine vernacular discourse that bolsters the community and articulates identity while protesting slavery, we expand the canon and our understanding of the scope of abolitionist rhetoric and even perhaps notions of American rhetoric in general. Black abolitionist rhetors used vernacular discourse (in black forums) to challenge the very basis of societal inequality, to reshape the struggle for freedom, and to claim the central role African Americans would play in it.

Susan M. Ryan notes that antebellum African American rhetoric reveals the ways in which black rhetors "quite energetically talk[ed] back" to those who would limit them, "exceeding the categories . . . set up to contain them."[38] The rhetoric of African American abolitionists reveals that they "talked back;" they explicitly named and challenged the racial standards that gave white abolitionists power in the public sphere. They also highlighted what their resistance to racialized discursive norms meant for their own agency. Such rhetoric exemplifies how racial norms in the public sphere influence discourse and encourages scholars to consider how these criteria should be scrutinized, reconsidered, or overturned.

In addition, this analysis features rhetorical debates with profound racial implications in contemporary America, providing possible insights into such issues as reparations, affirmative action, and political leadership. All of these issues require an appreciation of how African Americans and people of color "talked back" to powerful whites' attempts at restricting rhetorical expressions. They lay the groundwork for understanding later generations of vernacular rhetoric. Vernacular rhetoric, as black abolitionists' "Declarations of Independence" demonstrate, emanates from a uniquely empowered space of critical resistance to dominant norms and enables African Americans to recreate the very foundations for judgments of eloquence, authenticity, and efficacy.

From the antebellum period to today, black vernacular rhetors not only challenge whites' views of race, racial issues, and racial rhetoric but also suggest that African Americans' perspectives on the intersections of race and rhetoric are based on broader attention to the ways race impinges on rhetorical context, identity, and power. In doing so, they create subjectivities that are based on their own definitions, rather than exclusively whites' definitions. These definitions include masculinity (and, although not explored in this chapter, femininity), American and African identities and histories, "authentic" blackness, and intelligence. For African American abolitionists, these redefinitions of self were positions from which they could challenge the conventional white assumptions that they had to "prove" their intelligence or their worth, articulate an American identity that encompassed dissent and anger, and look back to African history and traditions for the foundations of their eloquence. Contemporary black rhetors choosing vernacular forms similarly refashion the very foundations of debate about race and reinforce and extend the definitions of eloquence of their abolitionist forebears, empowering African Americans as the subjects and leaders of discussions about racial issues.

Finally, black abolitionists' narratives remind us that there is precedent for contemporary efforts to seek alternative accounts of the foundations of African American discourse. Indeed, African American abolitionists both rewrote the conventional history of American protest rhetoric and reached back beyond their history in the United States to African traditions. They challenged their white colleagues—who would write them out of accounts of antislavery protest—and proudly affirmed African Americans' profound influence on the development of abolitionist discourse and American rhetoric in general. In doing so, they anticipated the efforts by researchers of early black American rhetoric and later, Afrocentric theorists, who have greatly expanded our comprehension of the history of African American discourse. They also remind us of the explicitly political implications of writing histories of rhetoric. The "Declarations of Independence" of African American abolitionists—texts both African and American, hopeful and defiant, forward-thinking and attentive to the past—powerfully illustrate how the public sphere, its rules, and its history have been and will continue to be transformed by black rhetors committed to controlling their own rhetorical pasts, presents, and futures.

NOTES

The author would like to thank the editors of this volume as well as Glen McClish for helpful comments throughout the writing and revision process.

1. In keeping with current scholarly conventions, I use the terms *African American* and *black* interchangeably. The rhetors featured in this chapter generally preferred the (no longer appropriate) term *colored*—as well as, in some cases, *black*—as readers can see from various quotes.

2. Historians and some scholars in communication have explored African American abolitionists' pursuit of autonomy and have in some cases explored how this goal influenced their rhetoric; see Jacqueline Bacon, *The Humblest May Stand Forth: Rhetoric, Empowerment, and Abolition* (Columbia: University of South Carolina Press, 2002); Evan Carton, *Patriotic Treason: John Brown and the Soul of America* (New York: Free Press, 2006), 94–97; Stanley Harrold, *American Abolitionists* (Harlow, UK: Pearson Education Limited, 2001), 19–28, 51–60; James Oliver Horton and Lois E. Horton, *In Hope of Liberty: Culture, Community, and Protest Among Northern Free Blacks, 1700–1860* (New York: Oxford University Press, 1997), 240–68; James Jasinski, "Constituting Antebellum *African American* Identity: Resistance, Violence, and Masculinity in Henry Highland Garnet's (1843) 'Address to the Slaves,'" *Quarterly Journal of Speech* 93 (2007): 27–57; Benjamin Quarles, *Black Abolitionists* (New York: Oxford University Press, 1969), 42–56; C. Peter Ripley et al., eds., *Black Abolitionist Papers*, 5 vols. (Chapel Hill: University of North Carolina Press, 1985–92), 3:20–26 (in subsequent notes, *Black Abolitionist Papers* will be abbreviated *BAP*). In addition, Gary S. Selby ("The Limits of Accommodation: Frederick Douglass and the Garrisonian Abolitionists," *Southern Communication Journal* 66 [2000]: 52–66) and John Sekora ("Black Message / White Envelope: Genre, Authenticity, and Authority in the Antebel-

lum Slave Narrative," *Callaloo* 10 [1987]: 482–515; "'Mr. Editor, If You Please': Frederick Douglass, *My Bondage and My Freedom*, and the End of the Abolitionist Imprint," *Callaloo* 17 [1994]: 608–26) consider the rhetorical tensions and strategies in the abolitionist arguments of Frederick Douglass as he aimed to establish independence from white leaders, particularly William Lloyd Garrison. However, there has not been a full exploration of black abolitionists' explicit articulation of the effect of the limits placed on their rhetoric by white leaders, assertion of their right to determine their own rhetorical efforts, and creation of discourse that challenged and defied white abolitionists' attempts to control them. Nor have the specific texts that I consider been examined by communication scholars or historians of rhetoric for their significance as discourse that resists domination and opposes the rules governing public discourse that disenfranchise African Americans.

3. Kent A. Ono and John M. Sloop, "The Critique of Vernacular Discourse," *Communication Monographs* 62 (1995): 20–22; Dexter B. Gordon, *Black Identity: Rhetoric, Ideology, and Nineteenth-Century Black Nationalism* (Carbondale: Southern Illinois University Press, 2003), 39. See also Bernadette Marie Calafell and Fernando P. Delgado, "Reading Latina/o Images: Interrogating *Americanos*," *Critical Studies in Media Communication* 21 (2004): 6–7; Gerard A. Hauser, *Vernacular Voices: The Rhetoric of Publics and Public Spheres* (Columbia: University of South Carolina Press, 1999) 82–110; Kent A. Ono and John M. Sloop, *Shifting Borders: Rhetoric, Immigration, and California's Proposition 187* (Philadelphia: Temple University Press, 2002), 113–17.

4. My work is part of the growing attention among scholars of African American abolitionist rhetoric to vernacular texts. This work is relatively recent in the history of the study of the rhetoric of abolition. Historically, much scholarship on abolitionist rhetoric focused on traditional white male figures such as Garrison and his followers. By the 1990s, however, emphasis was being placed on African American rhetors. Although in many cases the focus has continued to be on more well-known figures such as Frederick Douglass and white-dominated settings such as the American Anti-Slavery Society, there is a large and growing body of work that considers vernacular discourse as well. See, for example, Lena Ampadu, "Maria W. Stewart and the Rhetoric of Black Preaching: Perspectives on Womanism and Black Nationalism," in *Black Women's Intellectual Traditions: Speaking Their Minds*, ed. Kristin Waters and Carol B. Conaway (Burlington: University of Vermont Press, 2007), 38–54; Jacqueline Bacon, *Freedom's Journal: The First African American Newspaper* (Lanham, MD: Lexington Books, 2007); Bacon, *Humblest*; Ella Forbes, "Every Man Fights for His Freedom: The Rhetoric of African American Resistance in the Mid-Nineteenth Century," in *Understanding African American Rhetoric: Classical Origins to Contemporary Innovations*, ed. Ronald L. Jackson II and Elaine B. Richardson (New York: Routledge, 2003), 155–70; Jasinski, "Constituting"; Drema R. Lipscomb, "Sojourner Truth: A Practical Public Discourse," in *Reclaiming Rhetorica: Women in the Rhetorical Tradition*, ed. Andrea A. Lunsford (Pittsburgh: University of Pittsburgh Press, 1995), 227–45; Shirley Wilson Logan, "*We Are Coming*": The Persuasive Discourse of Nineteenth-Century Black Women (Carbondale: Southern Illinois University Press, 1999); Charles I. Nero, "'Oh, What I Think I Must Tell This World!' Oratory and Public Address of African American Women," in *Black Women in America*, ed. Kim Marie Vaz (Thousand Oaks, CA: Sage Publications, 1995), 261–75; Carla L. Peterson, "*Doers of the Word*": African American Women Speakers and Writers in the North, 1830–1880 (New York: Oxford University Press, 1995); Ebony A. Utley, "A Woman Made of Words: The Rhetorical Invention of Maria W. Stewart," in *Black Women's Intellectual Traditions: Speaking Their Minds*, ed. Kristin Waters and Carol B. Conaway (Burlington: University of Vermont Press, 2007), 55–71. There have also been important studies that consider the less familiar vernacular texts of well-known figures; see, for example, Valerie Babb, "'The Joyous Circle': The Vernacular Presence

in Frederick Douglass's Narratives," *College English* 67 (2005): 365–77; Gregory P. Lampe, *Frederick Douglass: Freedom's Voice, 1818–1845* (East Lansing: Michigan State University Press, 1998); Glen McClish, "'The Spirit of Human Brotherhood,' 'The Sisterhood of Nations,' and 'Perfect Manhood': Frederick Douglass and the Rhetorical Significance of the Haitian Revolution," in *African Americans and the Haitian Revolution: Selected Essays and Historical Documents*, ed. Maurice Jackson and Jacqueline Bacon (New York: Routledge, 2010), 123–39; Sekora, "Mr. Editor."

5. See, for example, Bacon, *Humblest*; Jacqueline Bacon and Glen McClish, "Descendents of Africa, Sons of '76: Exploring Early African American Rhetoric," *Rhetoric Society Quarterly* 36 (2006): 1–29; Celeste Michelle Condit and John Louis Lucaites, *Crafting Equality: America's Anglo-African Word* (Chicago: University of Chicago Press, 1993); Mitch Kachun, *Festivals of Freedom: Memory and Meaning in African American Emancipation Celebrations, 1808–1915* (Amherst: University of Massachusetts Press, 2003); Logan, *"We Are Coming"*; Glen McClish, "'New Terms for the Vindication of Our Rights': William Whipper's Activist Rhetoric," *Advances in the History of Rhetoric* 9 (2006): 97–127; Peterson, *"Doers"*; Kirt H. Wilson, "The Racial Politics of Imitation in the Nineteenth Century," *Quarterly Journal of Speech* 89 (2003): 89–108.

6. Michael G. Lacy, "Exposing the Spectrum of Whiteness: Rhetorical Conceptions of White Absolutism," *Communication Yearbook* 32 (2008): 279.

7. Jacqueline Bacon, "Reading the Reparations Debate," *Quarterly Journal of Speech* 89 (2003): 185–89; Lisa A. Flores, Dreama G. Moon, and Thomas K. Nakayama, "Dynamic *Rhetorics of Race*: California's Racial Privacy Initiative and the Shifting Grounds of Racial Politics," *Communication and Critical/Cultural Studies* 3 (2006): 182–88; Steven R. Goldzwig and Patricia A. Sullivan, "Narrative and Counternarrative in Print-Mediated Coverage of Milwaukee Alderman Michael McGee," *Quarterly Journal of Speech* 86 (2000): 218–25; Patricia A. Sullivan, "Signification and African American Rhetoric: A Case Study of Jesse Jackson's 'Common Ground and Common Sense' Speech," *Communication Quarterly* 41 (1993): 2–14.

8. Stephen Howard Browne, "Counter-Science: African American Historians and The Critique of Ethnology in Nineteenth-Century America," *Western Journal of Communication* 64 (2000): 268–84; John Ernest, *Liberation Historiography: African American Writers and the Challenge of History, 1794–1861* (Chapel Hill: University of North Carolina Press, 2004); Benjamin Quarles, *Black Mosaic: Essays in Afro-American History and Historiography* (Amherst: University of Massachusetts Press, 1988), 109–34; Ahati N. N. Toure, "Nineteenth Century African Historians in the United States: Explorations of Cultural Location and National Destiny," in *Black Cultures and Race Relations*, ed. James L. Conyers, Jr. (Chicago: Burnham Inc., 2002), 16–50.

9. An exception is Glen McClish's examination of the efforts of William G. Allen, the first African American professor of rhetoric, to establish a history of black oratory ("William G. Allen's 'Orators and Oratory': Inventional Amalgamation, Pathos, and the Characterization of Violence in African American Abolitionist Rhetoric," *Rhetoric Society Quarterly* 35 [2005]: 55–57).

10. The exact census percentages are as follows: in 1830, the black population was 18.1 percent, with 13.7 percent of those free; in 1840, the percentages were 16.8 percent and 13.4 percent, respectively (Campbell Gibson and Kay Jung, "Historical Census Statistics on Population Totals By Race, 1790 to 1990, and By Hispanic Origin, 1970 to 1990, For The United States, Regions, Divisions, and States," U.S. Census Bureau, September 2002, < http://www.census.gov/population/www/documentation/twps0056.html >, Table 1).

11. This brief historical outline is based on the more extensive accounts in the following studies: Bacon, Freedom's Journal, 13–30; Bacon, *Humblest*, 15–50; Carton, *Patriotic*, 94–97; Harrold, *American Abolitionists*, 19–28, 51–60; Horton and Horton, *In Hope*, 240–68; Phillip Lapsansky, "Graphic Discord: Abolitionist and Antiabolitionist Images," in *The Abolitionist Sisterhood: Wom-*

en's *Political Culture in Antebellum America*, ed. Jean Fagan Yellin and John C. Van Horne (Ithaca: Cornell University Press, 1994), 216; Joanne Pope Melish, *Disowning Slavery: Gradual Emancipation and "Race" in New England, 1780–1860* (Ithaca: Cornell University Press, 1998), 165–71; Quarles, *Black Abolitionists*, 42–56; Ripley et al., *BAP*, 3:20–26; William G. Shade, "'Though We Are Not Slaves, We Are Not Free': Quasi-Free Blacks in Antebellum America," in *Upon These Shores: Themes in the African American Experience, 1600 to the Present*, ed. William R. Scott and William G. Shade (New York: Routledge, 2000), 118–38; Carol Wilson, *Freedom at Risk: The Kidnapping of Free Blacks in America, 1780–1865* (Lexington: University Press of Kentucky, 1994).

12. These brief biographical sketches draw from various sources: Ronald K. Burke, *Samuel Ringgold Ward: Christian Abolitionist* (New York: Garland, 1995); Louis A. DeCaro, *"Fire from the Midst of You": A Religious Life of John Brown* (New York: New York University Press, 2002), 200; Mason I. Lowance, ed., *Against Slavery: An Abolitionist Reader* (New York: Penguin Books, 2000), 235–36; Ripley et al., *BAP*, 3:343–44, 3:350–51, 4:155–56; John Stauffer, ed., *The Works of James McCune Smith: Black Intellectual and Abolitionist* (Oxford: Oxford University Press, 2006), xix–xxxiii; Albert J. Von Frank, *The Trials of Anthony Burns: Freedom and Slavery in Emerson's Boston* (Cambridge: Harvard University Press, 1998), 21–23; Samuel Ringgold Ward, *Autobiography of a Fugitive Negro: His Anti-Slavery Labours in the United States, Canada, & England* (London, 1855).

13. Lacy, "Exposing," 283.

14. Thomas Jefferson's opinion was infamously put forth in his *Notes on the State of Virginia*, in which he declared that people of African descent were "in reason much inferior" to whites; he mused, "I think one could scarcely be found capable of tracing and comprehending the investigations of Euclid"; and observed, "never yet could I find that a black had uttered a thought above the level of plain narration" (1787; reprint, ed. David Waldstreicher [New York: Bedford/St. Martin's, 2002], 177). Jefferson dismissed Wheatley's poetry in particular as "below the dignity of criticism" (178). On doubts about Douglass's authorship of his autobiographical works and Wheatley's writing of the poetry published under her name, as well as related questions about other African American writers, see Jared Gardner, *Master Plots: Race and the Founding of an American Literature, 1787–1845* (Baltimore: Johns Hopkins University Press, 1998), 160–62; Shirley Wilson Logan, *Liberating Language: Sites of Rhetorical Education in Nineteenth-Century Black America* (Carbondale: Southern Illinois University Press, 2008), 1–2; John Hope Franklin, *Mirror to America* (New York: Farrar, Straus, and Giroux, 2005), 273; Frances Smith Foster, *Written by Herself: Literary Production by African American Women, 1746–1892* (Bloomington: Indiana University Press, 1993), 30–43. In some cases, contemporary observers suggested that Douglass's eloquence was the result of his "white blood"; see comments in an untitled 1895 editorial in the *New York Times* (27 February 1895); Robert S. Levine, *Martin Delany, Frederick Douglass, and the Politics of Representative Identity* (Chapel Hill: University of North Carolina Press, 1997), 55; William S. McFeely, *Frederick Douglass* (New York: W. W. Norton, 1991), 132. For further discussion of white abolitionists' perpetuation of these presumptions, their manifestation in white depictions of such figures as Sojourner Truth, and the effect it had on their black colleagues, see Bacon, *Freedom's Journal*, 268–73; Bacon, *Humblest*, 29–33; Sekora, "Black Message," 496–509; Sekora, "Mr. Editor," 609–12; Ripley et al., *BAP*, 3:20–22; Roseann M. Mandziuk, "Commemorating Sojourner Truth: Negotiating the Politics of Race and Gender in the Spaces of Public Memory," *Western Journal of Communication* 67 (2003): 276–77.

15. James M'Cune [McCune] Smith, introduction to *My Bondage and My Freedom*, by Frederick Douglass (New York, 1857), xxii–xxiii. The very fact that Douglass's 1855 autobiography was introduced by one of his African American colleagues—in contrast to his 1845 *Narrative of the*

Life of Frederick Douglass, An American Slave, introduced by Garrison—is significant, a particular manifestation of the desire for independence and self-determination this chapter examines. For further discussion, see Sekora, "Mr. Editor," 614–16.

16. Samuel Ringgold Ward, "Editorial Correspondence," *Provincial Freeman*, 10 June 1854; William J. Watkins, "What Are We Doing?" *Frederick Douglass' Paper*, 2 February 1855.

17. Ward, *Autobiography*, 95–97.

18. James McCune Smith, George B. Wilson, and William H. Topp, "Report by the Committee on a National Press of the National Convention of Colored People and Their Friends, Presented at the Liberty Street Presbyterian Church, Troy, New York, 6 October 1847," in *BAP*, 4:7–8. Ripley et al. note that this report "was largely Smith's work" (*BAP*, 4:7). There were, of course, black newspapers before this time, including the first, the ground-breaking *Freedom's Journal*; Smith and his colleagues' report mentions these publications but notes that their financial difficulties demonstrate that a national, cooperative effort—as opposed to one which places responsibility upon "one man"—is needed ("Report," 9).

19. William J. Watkins, "Extracts from a Speech, Delivered at the Celebration of West India Emancipation by the Colored Citizens of New Bedford, by Wm. J. Watkins, of Boston," *Frederick Douglass' Paper*, 26 August 1853.

20. On antebellum African Americans' conceptions of manhood, its relationship to freedom, and its communal implications, see Bacon, *Freedom's Journal*, 123–30; Christopher B. Booker, *"I Will Wear No Chain!" A Social History of African American Males* (Westport: Praeger, 2000), 57–58; Darlene Clark Hine and Ernestine Jenkins, "Introduction: Black Men's History: Toward a Gendered Perspective," in *A Question of Manhood. Vol. 1: "Manhood of Rights": The Construction of Black Male History and Manhood, 1750–1870*, ed. Darlene Clark Hine and Ernestine Jenkins (Bloomington: Indiana University Press, 1999), 2–3, 30–31; James Oliver Horton and Lois E. Horton, "Violence, Protest, and Identity: Black Manhood in Antebellum America," in *Free People of Color: Inside the African American Community*, by James Oliver Horton (Washington, DC: Smithsonian Institution Press, 1993). 387, 391; McClish, "Spirit," 135; Craig Steven Wilder, *In the Company of Black Men: The African Influence on African American Culture in New York City* (New York: New York University Press, 2001), 123–41; R. J. Young, *Antebellum Black Activists: Race, Gender, and Self* (New York: Garland Publishing, 1996), 67–81.

21. William J. Watkins, "One Thing Thou Lackest," *Frederick Douglass' Paper*, 10 February 1854; William J. Watkins, "Are We Ready for the Conflict?" *Frederick Douglass' Paper*, 9 February 1855.

22. Jacqueline Bacon, "'Acting as Freemen': Rhetoric, Race, and Reform in the Debate over Colonization in *Freedom's Journal*, 1827–1828," *Quarterly Journal of Speech* 93 (2007): 62–67; Bacon, "Reading," 185–89; Jamie Owen Daniel, "Rituals of Disqualification: Competing Publics and Public Housing in Contemporary Chicago," in *Masses, Classes, and the Public Sphere*, ed. Mike Hill and Warren Montag (New York: Verso Books, 2000), 72–74; Flores, Moon, and Nakayama, "Dynamic," 182–88; Goldzwig and Sullivan, "Narrative," 218–25; Sullivan, "Signification," 2–14; Thomas R. West, *Signs of Struggle: The Rhetorical Politics of Cultural Difference* (Albany: State University of New York Press, 2002), 14–15.

23. Smith, Introduction, xxvii. Jeannine Marie DeLombard discusses how Smith's introduction to Douglass's *My Bondage and My Freedom* calls attention to Douglass's ability to meld testimony with personal accounts from which he claims "the ability and right to construct meaning" (*Slavery on Trial: Law, Abolitionism, and Print Culture* [Chapel Hill: University of North Carolina Press, 2007], 137–42).

24. Bacon, "Acting," 62–64; Bacon, "Reading," 186–89; Goldzwig and Sullivan, "Narrative," 222–24; Sullivan, "Signification," 3–4, 7; West, *Signs*, 97–102. Indeed, to cite a striking recent example, the continuing presence of public discomfort with black anger was made painfully clear during the historic 2008 election season when then candidate Barack Obama was maligned because of his association with the Reverend Jeremiah Wright, whom public commentators deemed "inappropriate" and even "un-American" because of his harshly critical rhetoric. Obama was pressured to distance himself from his pastor and eventually induced to resign his membership in Wright's church. The problematic dimensions of the public reaction to Wright and Obama's (arguably necessary, in political terms) rejection of him demonstrate the continuing denigration of African American rhetors who are deemed "emotional" and "too angry" as well as the ongoing resonance of the prophetic black voice in challenging white supremacy and American hegemony.

25. Eddie S. Glaude, Jr., *Exodus! Religion, Race, and Nation in Early Nineteenth-Century Black America* (Chicago: University of Chicago Press, 2000), 358; Bacon, "Acting," 66; Watkins, "One Thing."

26. Watkins, "Extracts"; Watkins, "Are We Ready."

27. Bacon, "Acting," 62–64; Bacon, "Reading," 186–89; Carrie Crenshaw, "Resisting Whiteness' Rhetorical Silence," *Western Journal of Communication* 61 (1997): 253–57; Daniel, "Rituals," 73; Goldzwig and Sullivan, "Narrative," 222, 224; Thomas K. Nakayama and Robert L. Krizek, "Whiteness: A Strategic Rhetoric," *Quarterly Journal of Speech* 81 (1995): 299.

28. Crenshaw, "Resisting," 256.

29. Watkins, "Are We Ready"; Watkins, "Extract."

30. Samuel Ringgold Ward, letter to editor, *National Anti-Slavery Standard*, 2 July 1840. Ward's critique reflects the progression of white abolitionist argument during the 1830s, which, as DeLombard demonstrates, began by positioning slavery as a threat to free speech and due process for white Americans (*Slavery*, 41–58).

31. Ernest, *Liberation*; Wilson Jeremiah Moses, *Afrotopia: The Roots of African American Popular History* (Cambridge: Cambridge University Press, 1998); Quarles, *Black Mosaic*, 109–34; Toure, "Nineteenth Century"; Joe W. Trotter, Jr., "Introduction: Pennsylvania's African American History: A Review of the Literature," in *African Americans in Pennsylvania: Shifting Historical Perspectives*, ed. Joe William Trotter Jr., and Eric Ledell Smith (University Park: Pennsylvania Historical and Museum Commission and the Pennsylvania State University Press, 1997), 2–5.

32. Although, unfortunately, the inaccurate view that whites created antislavery protest has long been perpetuated in scholarly as well as popular accounts, historians have demonstrated that African Americans were the primary innovators of both the movement and its rhetoric; see Bacon, *Humblest*, 15–17; Bacon, *Freedom's Journal*, 259–64; John Hope Franklin and Alfred A. Moss, Jr., *From Slavery to Freedom: A History of African Americans*, 8th ed. (New York: Alfred A. Knopf, 2000), 199–200; James Oliver Horton and Lois E. Horton, *Black Bostonians: Family Life and Community Struggle in the Antebellum North*, 20th Anniversary Edition (New York: Holmes & Meier, 1999), 88–90; Horton and Horton, *In Hope*, 203–14; Quarles, *Black Abolitionists*, 3–18; Ripley et al., *BAP*, 3:3–12.

33. Communipaw [James McCune Smith], "From Our New York Correspondent," *Frederick Douglass' Paper*, 26 January 1855; Communipaw [James McCune Smith], "Frederick Douglass in New York," *Frederick Douglass' Paper*, 2 February 1855. (Smith often signed his pieces for *Frederick Douglass' Paper* with the pseudonym Communipaw; see Frederick Douglass, "Fifth Volume," *Frederick Douglass' Paper*, 17 December 1852).

34. Communipaw [James McCune Smith], "From Our New York Correspondent," *Frederick Douglass' Paper*, 16 February 1855; Communipaw [James McCune Smith], "From Our New York Correspondent," *Frederick Douglass' Paper*, 11 May 1855. Scholarship has provided ample evidence to back up Smith's claims about how African American abolitionists' early antislavery activism influenced white reformers, established the foundational principles of abolitionism, and continually shaped the abolitionist efforts of both white and black abolitionists; see sources cited in note 32, above.

35. Bacon, Freedom's Journal, 149–56; St. Clair Drake, *Black Folk Here and There: An Essay in History and Anthropology*, 2 vols. (Los Angeles: Center for Afro-American Studies, University of California, Los Angeles, 1987), 1:1–4,130–34; Kachun, *Festivals*, 31–33; Moses, *Afrotopia*, 23–25; Quarles, *Black Mosaic*, 118–20; Toure, "Nineteenth Century," 26–28.

36. Ward, "Origin."

37. Molefi Kete Asante, *The Afrocentric Idea*, revised and expanded edition (Philadelphia: Temple University Press, 1998); Molefi Kete Asante, *Race, Rhetoric, and Identity: The Architecton of Soul* (Amherst, NY: Humanity Books, 2005), 151–58; Kermit E. Campbell, "We Is Who We Was: The African/American Rhetoric of *Amistad*," in *African American Rhetoric(s): Interdisciplinary Perspectives*, ed. Elaine B. Richardson and Ronald L. Jackson II (Carbondale: Southern Illinois University Press, 2004), 204–20; Clinton Crawford, "The Multiple Dimensions of Nubian/Egyptian Rhetoric and Its Implications for Contemporary Classroom Instructions," in *African American Rhetoric(s): Interdisciplinary Perspectives*, ed. Elaine B. Richardson and Ronald L. Jackson II (Carbondale: Southern Illinois University Press, 2004), 111–35; Venita Kelley, "'Good Speech': An Interpretive Essay Investigating an African Philosophy of Communication," *Western Journal of Black Studies* 26 (2002): 44–54; Logan, *We Are Coming*, 23–43.

38. Susan M. Ryan, *The Grammar of Good Intentions: Race and the Antebellum Culture of Benevolence* (Ithaca: Cornell University Press, 2003), 186.

Transgressive Rhetoric in Deliberative Democracy

The Black Press

Michael Huspek

Central to deliberative democracy is the ideal of communicative equality, whereby all prospective participants, including historically marginalized people, are guaranteed a level playing field to exercise their rights to propose, question, and critique courses of collective action and to have their expressed ideas recognized and engaged by others, including dominant group members.[1] This ideal improves the quality of political life for all: it enables historically marginalized groups to exert influence within the political order, as their arguments are heard and assessed on their own merits; and it broadens opportunities for genuine dialogue and informed collective action among all sectors of an increasingly enlightened public.[2]

At the same time, a basic assumption of deliberative democracy is that participants act in a rational manner, marked by adherence to shared norms of public discourse. Following Jurgen Habermas,[3] this process ensures the right to express, question, and challenge validity claims, and stipulates that interlocutors conduct themselves rationally, that is, make claims that accord with expectations that they be sincere, truthful, and appropriate (just). In turn, interlocutors are expected to support their claims with reasons, exhibit an openness to others' claims, and show a willingness to compromise when warranted. These are base-level expectations of rational discourse that are indispensable to deliberative democracy and make it possible for shared understandings and consensus-based courses of action. Such results are arrived at within an atmosphere of mutual trust;[4] and, where they are absent, discourses are likely to collapse under the weight of actors' self-doubt, delusion, mistrust of others, or other pathologies that germinate within atmospheres of sheer power or demagoguery.[5]

The equal opportunity to participate and use rational discourse appears relatively unproblematic when deliberative democracy stands as an already achieved way of life. Indeed, it is difficult to imagine how the ideal of equality *could* set itself up against the ideal of rational discourse or, conversely, how discourse that upholds rational standards such as openness to criticism *could* co-exist with exclusionary practices without either tendency succumbing to self-contradiction. Imperfect democracies that fall short of being fully deliberative are another matter, however. For example, faced with systematic political exclusions, marginalized groups may resort to transgressive rhetorical forms and strategies that, in an attempt to gain recognition and engagement, violate discursive norms by shocking or offending publics. Privileged groups may in turn view such rhetorical activities and infractions as unacceptable. They may charge marginalized rhetors with irrationality and use the charge as basis for continued exclusion of "transgressors" from significant zones of deliberative participation.

The history of the ethnic press in the United States is a case in point.[6] Where minority groups have appealed for inclusion in the public sphere, they have been ignored, rejected, or at times subject to violent attack.[7] As such, their rhetoric takes on a greater urgency when conveyed by hyperbole, irony, and insult that appear to transgress truthfulness, sincerity, appropriateness, and other base-level norms of rational discourse. For instance, Hemant Shah and Michael Thornton observe that majority audiences in the United States have tended to perceive the ethnic minority press "as professionally unaccomplished, self-serving, gossipy, vulgar, corrupt, and a danger to the more accomplished traditional journalism of the general circulation press."[8]

The historical experiences of the ethnic press in the United States are emblematic of the dilemma faced by imperfect democracies that aim to be more deliberative. Although we know that the rhetoric of excluded groups conveys much that can positively contribute to an increasingly enlightened populace, as John Dryzek notes it also can bring with it coercion, emotional manipulation, and a host of other dangers that accompany anger, frustration, and moral outrage directed toward continued oppressive institutional practices.[9] Iris Young, after making a compelling case for rhetoric as a supplement to rational argument, then cautions that such rhetoric may at times be "strategically manipulated to win the assent of others simply by flattery or fantasy and not by reason."[10] As both Dryzek and Young are well aware, the continued exclusion of marginalized groups from deliberative arenas poses its own dangers. This poses a dilemma as to how actually existing democracies that aspire to become more deliberative are to reconcile, on the one hand, standards of rational discourse, and, on the other hand, transgressive rhetoric that in its tendency to disarm, shock, or offend, invites charges of irrationality.

What should be expected from historically excluded groups by way of discursive efforts to gain recognition and engagement in the face of closed off channels of rational discourse? And what should be the response of audiences whose moral sensibilities undergo attack when excluded groups resort to transgressive rhetorical forms and strategies? In this chapter, I address both concerns. Before doing so, I think normative judgment and recommendation need first to defer to efforts to clarify the nature of transgressive rhetoric, its motivations, why it persists, and the ways in which it is irrational, if in fact it is so.

I begin this chapter with a brief empirical case study of contemporary black rhetoric in the United States, with special attention directed toward its transgressive elements of irony, hyperbole, and insult. I then analyze a limited range of transgressions in light of standards of rational discourse. The analysis shows that transgressive rhetoric is often an expression of frustration in the face of systematic inequalities, voiced in protest against ongoing practices of exclusion, and meant as an appeal for recognition and engagement as prerequisite to democratic discourse which purports to be genuinely egalitarian and rational. From this I argue that although transgressive rhetoric may appear to violate the expectations of rational discourse, it by no means follows that the rhetoric should be considered irrational. Indeed, I think it can be convincingly claimed that transgressive rhetoric often is rational. But in any event, it appears clear enough that charges of irrationality can have no validity unless and until genuine recognition and engagement reveals that the transgressive rhetoric is irrational, if indeed it is. I argue that, short of the condition of genuine dialogic engagement being satisfied, any rationales for exclusion of historically marginalized groups from significant spheres of public dialogue on grounds that their rhetoric is irrational are unfounded. Following the same reasoning, privileged audiences, which previously have withheld recognition and engagement, are faced with the moral obligation to drop walled defenses against excluded groups, despite the transgressive nature of their rhetoric and the shock value or offensiveness it may deliver; for again, as the overall analysis demonstrates, rhetorical transgression, as shocking and offensive as it may appear to be, by no means necessarily translates into irrational discourse. I conclude the chapter by arguing that the divide between transgressive rhetoric and the often erroneous perception of its irrationality can be bridged, and I suggest what that bridge might look like.

The Case of Black Press Rhetoric

Since publication in 1827 of the first African American newspaper in the United States, *Freedom's Journal*, the black press has taken on a leadership role within the black community. This has involved collecting and disseminating information otherwise absent from the white mainstream press, providing a sounding board for minority opinions not otherwise aired, and laying the semantic groundwork for critique of and active engagement with ideas not otherwise made available by its white mainstream counterpart. In this regard, the black press has met with a good deal of success, indicated by at least 278 black-owned and -operated newspapers printed across the United States, with a combined circulation of more than 13 million.[11]

The black press has also sought to reach out to white majority audiences in an attempt to inject African American points of view into public discourse that might give cause for non–African American readers to reflect upon and reevaluate their assumptions regarding race-related beliefs and practices. This strategy, however, has met with limited success. Although most readers of black newspapers also read white mainstream newspapers, the same is not true of a large majority of readers who do not read black newspapers or read them to supplement white newspapers.[12] Since many issues covered in black newspapers are not covered by white mainstream newspapers, most (white) Americans are poorly informed about what is relevant to the black experience in the United States, and thus are poorly situated to respond to grievances rooted in that experience. This reality has been frustrating for many African Americans. Research shows a high degree of black reader dissatisfaction with white mainstream news coverage,[13] and with black newspapers going largely unread by white majority audiences, African Americans view themselves as having few conventional channels through which their appeals might elicit recognition and uptake beyond African-American communities.

The black press has attempted to alleviate this frustration in two ways. First, in order to mobilize black political protest the press has positioned itself as an outspoken critic of institutional structures and practices within the United States.[14] Second, in order to further open up possibilities for reconciliation, the black press has continued to voice appeals for recognition and understanding from the majority populace.[15] In advancing both strategies, black press rhetoric has often been transgressive, challenging dominant social and political practices, as well as the very discursive structures used by majority groups to legitimate these practices.[16] In this regard, the black press employs hyperbole, irony, insult, and other transgressive modes of rhetoric to shock readers in order to elicit attention from otherwise unheeding audiences. Although employing transgressive rhetoric is an understandable strategy in light of the African American experience in the United States, its effectiveness has been viewed by unsympathetic audiences as violating standards of truth, civility, and moral sensibility as rationale for continued nonengagement. How this plays out in empirical arenas can be illustrated by a brief contrastive analysis of the rhetoric of two newspapers, the *New York Times*, and its oppositional counterpart, the black-owned and -operated *New York Amsterdam News*, with special focus on both newspapers' coverage and analysis of a tragic event that had great relevance for African Americans, namely, New York City police officers' shooting of Amadou Diallo and its aftermath.

The Shooting of Amadou Diallo and Its Aftermath

On a February evening in 1999, four New York City plainclothes police officers approached Amadou Diallo, a 22-year-old Guinean immigrant, who was standing inside the vestibule of his Bronx apartment building. Moments after ordering Diallo to raise his hands in the air, the police officers fired 41 shots and killed Diallo, who was unarmed. The shooting was described by one commentator as "a major symbolic event in the history of the city."[17] It received a good deal of public attention and was covered expansively by news media. But, in part because there were no witnesses to the crime, and the police officers who killed Diallo withheld commentary until they were summoned to testify at a criminal trial almost a year later, the public became frustrated, and the city's population became divided over how to interpret the shooting. One side argued that there could have been no conceivable justification for the police to fire 41 shots at an unarmed man. These criticisms were directed at Police Commissioner Howard Safir and Mayor Rudolph Giuliani, who presided over NYC's controversial policy of "stop and frisk" by nonuniformed police, which targeted primarily people of color in New York's low-income neighborhoods. Protesters claimed that extreme police policies, such as this one, were responsible for the killing of Diallo, no less so than were the officers who fired the shots. Daily nonviolent protests were staged for several months until the police officers were tried and acquitted in Albany, New York, some 140 miles from the scene of Diallo's death. City officials, most visibly Mayor Giuliani, urged citizens to withhold judgment about the case. Giuliani assured the public that a fair investigation was under way. And after criminal charges were filed, Giuliani insisted that the officers should be tried in a court of law, not by public opinion.

The *New York Times* and *Amsterdam News* aligned themselves with the opposing sides of the controversy. The *New York Times* avowed to present proper balance in the case, and sought to position itself above the fray. Nevertheless, the highly respected newspaper, with nearly 1.1 million subscribers, almost always supported the views of the city's officials. The *Times* reported expressions of shock and horror at the shooting that were intermixed with a good deal of empathy for the officers who had pulled the trigger. The *Times's* acknowledgement of the highly controversial tactics used by the city's police force was offset by praise for the force's effective work against crime. Additionally, calls for justice to be served meant the city's criminal justice system would be selected as the desired arbiter of the crime. In the course of choosing sides in this manner, the newspaper tended also to delegitimize the opinions aired and courses of action taken "out on the street," beyond official institutional boundaries.

[T]hings are not always what they seem at first, a truism that can be forgotten in times of passion. But it seems worth bearing in mind in the stomach-wrenching death of Amadou Diallo, the unarmed African immigrant gunned down in the Bronx by four police officers who fired an almost inconceivable 41 bullets at him . . . No one is suggesting that Mr. Diallo did anything to warrant such a response, and it is obvious that something went terribly wrong. But charged words like "murderers," "massacre," and "execution" have been casually tossed around in street protests . . . While the anger is understandable, it is unclear how anyone can reach such damning conclusions based upon available evidence.[18]

The *New York Times* drew attention to "charged words" that have been "casually tossed around on the street," but failed to engage seriously the context in which those words were spoken. In so doing, the *Times* raised the specter of public outcry, but then dismissed its significance. The newspaper left the impression with its readers that use of such "charged words" (e.g., "murderers," "massacre," or "execution") was a condemnable act that warranted no further serious consideration or engagement. The rationale for this type of practice can be located in the *New York Times Manual of Style and Usage* (1999), which sets forth institutional guidelines for the newspaper's writers.[19] Consider three standards that are promoted in the *Manual*. First, in keeping with "the *Times*'s impression of its educated and sophisticated readership—traditional but not tradition-bound," the *Manual* recommends for its writers a "fluid style, easygoing but not slangy and only occasionally colloquial."[20] Slang, for example, is associated with flippancy, and the *Manual* cautions against its use, for "it can create the embarrassing spectacle of a grown-up who tries to pass for an adolescent."[21] Second, in keeping with the avowed aim to print "all the news that is fit to print," the *Manual* upholds the *Times*'s credo: "To give the news impartially, without fear or favor, regardless of any party, sect or interest involved."[22] This entails favoring "constructions that keep language neutral, a crystalline medium through which journalists report ideas without proclaiming stances."[23] Third, the *Manual* claims to "differentiate itself by taking a stand for civility in public discourse" and does so by counseling respect for group sensibilities.[24] The *Manual* cautions against offensive or coy hints,[25] for example, as well as slurs: "The epithets of bigotry ordinarily have no place in the newspaper. Even in ironic or self-mocking quotations about a speaker's own group—their use erodes the worthy inhibition against brutality in public discourse."[26]

Attending to these standards gives the appearance that a newspaper is committed to truth seeking, conducts itself in an impartial manner, and delivers its contents in a sophisticated style that places the newspaper above the fray of social conflict. Yet, there is good reason to believe that adherence to these kinds of standards may stifle public debate.[27] Specifically, the *Times*'s standards seem to exclude overtly biased truth claims that are delivered in "slangy" or "coarse" terms. This places those groups that *do* advance overtly biased truth claims in a "slangy" or "coarse" manner at a serious disadvantage. The *Manual's* prescribed practices effectively ensure that some vernacular discourse and views do not get printed. This effectively renders the transgressors dependent on reporters who may either dismiss their opinions and viewpoints outright or translate them into terms that may not do justice to their originally expressed views. The latter possibility seems more likely, as indicated by the *Times's* coverage of public displays of political activism and its frequent allusions to undercurrents of danger associated with the nonviolent protests. One of the *Times's* journalists, for example, fretted that public protest of the police shooting "could inflame racial tension,"[28] while other *Times* reporters described the nonviolent protests as "angry demonstration[s]" that had become "nearly a daily rite,"[29] as "fractious crowds," "sometimes unruly," and "tumultuous"[30] were said to be "yelling," "chanting," "demanding," "denouncing," "shouting obscenities at police," and "pumping their fists into the air."[31] One reporter stressed how a Muslim guard "swatted and screamed at those caught up in the crush,"[32] and another noted how "those who came to wave angry banners were penned behind police barricades on Seventh Avenue."[33]

An undercurrent of danger as implied above was often complemented with an inordinate fixation upon protesters' racial composition, nationality, or other characteristics of otherness:[34] "though the crowd was mostly black and mostly female, there was a smattering of yarmulkes and Asian faces in the crowd."[35] Such descriptions were rarely accompanied with serious reportage of the communicative contents of the protest gatherings, but rather pointed to the protesters' visible markings—e.g., "swathed in cream-colored African robes," at times wearing "turbans and sweeping white robes" and at others "gold robes and white African skullcaps."[36] The imagery is unmistakable. On one occasion, protesters were said to have "danced around a drummer," and on another stress in the written description was placed upon "drumbeats of a Japanese Buddhist nun as a bus from Harlem unloaded about 40 protesters who waved anti-police placards while tramping through the mud."[37]

The elite newspaper's exclusion of vernacular statements and expressions, its own use of metaphors of foreign or racial Others, and its tendency to stress threats of violence produced reportage and analysis that was at best superficial, at worst misleading. The *New York Times* did not expose alternative coverage to informed and uninformed readers about how activist groups may experience the world and thereby left its readers confused about the case. No doubt this further contributed to frustration from activist groups and their supporters.

With a subscription rate of approximately 50,000, the New York City–based *Amsterdam News* is self-described as "an intrepid African-American voice on controversial issues." The newspaper covered the police shooting of Amadou Diallo and its aftermath in distinctly different ways from that of its prestigious mainstream counterpart, the *New York Times*. Most indicative of its coverage was the black newspaper's willingness to tap into the vernacular discourse and give it non-redacted expression in its news stories. Drawing upon the "street" perspective, the shooting was presented not as an isolated event, but rather as part of an uninterrupted history of police lawlessness and brutality on blacks, which invoked images of lynching and other acts of violence. The shooting was described not as an accidental tragedy, but rather as a logical outcome of a culture of racism that had been allowed to grow in New York's law enforcement apparatus. The *Amsterdam News* reported that the event should not have been left to smolder beneath layers of legal and administrative procedure, but in fact demanded an immediate, open-aired hearing by way of public protest and debate. These views in the *Amsterdam News* were presented in an emotionally charged manner, a way conspicuously absent in the *New York Times* coverage of the crime:

> If the 4 police officers had shot a horse in front of the Plaza Hotel, the whole city would be outraged. [38]
>
> If four policemen of African ancestry had wantonly executed a European immigrant anywhere in New York City with a hail of 41 bullets, Mayor Rudolph Giuliani would have instinctively snatched the badges from their chests and the lethal weapons from their hips before ordering them held incommunicado without bail at a local lockup. He would then assure all Europeans that punishment would be swift and certain.[39]
>
> [G]o downtown and shoot some cracker 41 times and see what happens.[40]

The newspaper discourse above employed rhetorical tropes used by marginalized (black protest) groups: irony, hyperbole, and insult. *Irony* has long been an effective tool used by black writers[41] to plant an air of incredulity for its readers as prelude to more serious reflection and debate. The hypothetical slain horse referenced above, for example, is likely influenced by the uses of irony in slave narratives, such as Frederick Douglass's. Douglass wrote: "By far the larger part of slaves know as little of their ages as horses know of theirs, and it is the wish of most masters within my knowledge to keep their slaves thus ignorant."[42] Just as Douglass used irony to provoke a view of how slaves were regarded as something less than human, the *Amsterdam News* deploys irony to tap into a wellspring of blacks' collective memory and to appeal to another group, befogged in collective amnesia, to recall an age when slaves were treated on a par with plantation animals and to then use the recollection as basis for critical reflection upon the present.[43]

Hyperbole is vividly displayed in the second of the above citations' functions in ways similar to the way irony functions in black press rhetoric.[44] High-pitched and often cast in a stylistic mode of black street vernacular, hyperbole forgoes rigorous adherence to truth validity claims aimed at empirical accuracy and instead expresses attention-getting moral outrage in response to enduring contradictions and hypocrisies of a white majority that appears blinkered by an ideology of colorblindness.[45] The shooting of Diallo was described as an "assassination," a "slaughter," an "act of brutality,"[46] and an "execution"[47] that was carried out by a "firing squad,"[48] "Giuliani's storm troopers,"[49] the "Mayor's goons,"[50] a "death squad coven of neo-fascist hit men."[51]

The black press routinely deploys *insults*, like the reference "cracker" to describe whites in the third citation above. Typically, insults are aimed at public figures in leadership positions, as Mayor Giuliani is referred to as "a maniac in office," "Fuhrer Giuliani," and "Dictator Giuliani," a "weak, lily-livered monster" who "wants to taste more blood":[52]

> Giuliani is a zero, zero in our book, for he has a license for his 40,000 minions who are called policemen to go out and murder anyone they like. It should not appear strange to you, or anyone else for that matter, that Giuliani's latter-day "storm troopers" have not slaughtered a single person who is white [...] Why is it so? We cannot answer that, but if Giuliani is such an expert at dispatching Black youngsters and Black adults—many who have done absolutely nothing—why, then, is it so difficult for him to demand the holding of white policemen who have been accused of murder by eyewitnesses? [53]

All three rhetorical tropes (irony, hyperbole, insult) constitute an overarching transgressive rhetorical strategy. Insofar as the rhetoric violates stylistics as legitimated in the *New York Times Manual*, so it appears also to violate the norms of rational discourse. Despite its transgressions, however, I believe it is a mistake to conclude either that the discourse is irrational or that it deserves to be excluded from public spheres where rational discourse is accepted currency. This is especially true both where good faith efforts have not been made to understand the motivations for the transgressions and where genuine engagement has not been offered. I shall develop this argument further below as a basis for advancing the additional claim that communicative engagement with transgressors is a moral obligation if imperfect democracies are to approximate deliberative ideals more closely.

Black Press Rhetoric as Prolegomena to Rational Discourse

The rhetorical tropes of irony, hyperbole, and insult can best be analyzed against the norms of rationality they transgress. In order to facilitate the analysis, I employ Habermas's norms of sincerity, truth, and justice as exemplars of rational discourse within deliberative democracy.[54] These norms take the form of presuppositions that are built in to the discourse: speakers are expected to be sincere in terms of what inner states are expressed within their utterances; speakers are expected to be truthful in their efforts to represent the world; speakers' utterances are expected to be appropriate (i.e., not to violate conventional norms of propriety or decorum) in the issuance of moral claims. Transgressive rhetoric used by the black press positions itself against each: irony against the norm of sincerity; hyperbole against the norm of truthfulness; insult against the moral sensibility contained in the norm of appropriateness.

Consider again the above reference: "If the 4 officers had shot a horse in front of the Plaza Hotel, the whole city would be outraged." The use of irony draws readers' attention to the speaker's intended meaning that the city has not been sufficiently moved by the shooting of Diallo and that the deficit of attention is likely a by-product of enduring racial attitudes. The writer's intended meaning is conveyed by means of violating hearers' ordinary expectations within rational discourse—here specifically, the norm of sincerity. Thus, upon having their expectations disrupted, hearers might be provoked to offer a response such as "You don't really mean that, do you?" or "You can't be serious!" Here, drawing upon John Searle's analysis of metaphors, we discern that the writer *intends* for his audience (1) to recognize an egregious violation of an otherwise standard validity claim and (2) to then "figure out what the speaker means."[55] Doing this means that the hearer "has to contribute more to the communication than just passive uptake—and does so by going through another and related semantic content from the one that is communicated."[56] Should the hearer *will* the move from passive uptake to that of active engagement—admittedly a tenuous assumption (see below)—this is accomplished by resort to mutually shared background information, both linguistic and nonlinguistic, as well as powers of rationality and inference.[57]

Hyperbole is no less transgressive. It is meant to invite audiences to step beyond passive uptake and to show a willingness to engage in active dialogue. References to "execution," "firing squad," and "neo-fascist hit men" are not meant as literal truth claims; nor does the writer expect that audiences, black or white, would take them so. Rather, these are meant to challenge the mainstream's conclusions, asserted for example by the *New York Times* without leaving room for debate, that the shooting of Amadou Diallo was simply a "tragedy" that occurred after "something went terribly wrong." Essential to the challenge is that it disrupt readers' ordinary understandings on the hope that it elicits active disagreement in the form of, say, "But that's not true!" or "Surely you're exaggerating, aren't you?" that might then lead writer and audience alike to a more discursively shared, reflective understanding of the event.

A similar interpretation applies to variations of insult. Tropes such as "cussin' out," "abusing," and "reading" all involve "denigrating another to his or her face in an unsubtle and unambiguous manner,"[58] and, by so doing, they violate the built-in expectation of rational discourse that utterances strive to be appropriate. Yet, the tropes are not meant to inflict emotional pain upon their target. Expressed by historically excluded groups, the insult is delivered "uphill" at the dominant or privileged group, and therefore is unlikely to hurt as might insults rolled "downhill" by privileged groups. The intention is to make targeted others and those who speak in their defense "fighting mad"[59]—mad enough perhaps to acknowledge the sources of the "read" and, ideally, fire back an exchange.

A fuller understanding of black press rhetoric can be gained from consideration of Habermas's treatment of the world-disclosing significance of rhetoric, particularly as used in the realm of fiction.[60] Once the rhetorical artist returns from the fictional realm, Habermas stresses, subjective wishes and desires must be pressed into the service of validity claims oriented toward shared, consensus-based understandings. The need for rhetoric therefore *recedes* in the face of other-oriented validity claims that are advanced, clarified, and altered via the intersubjective dimension of dialogue so as to satisfy the general expectations of everyday practice, whether in phatic conversation or something more ambitious, such as collective problem-solving. Habermas's view of rhetoric shares family resemblances with black press rhetoric, which has often functioned historically as a group-specific *subjective* communicative form that calls for intersubjective recognition and engagement from privileged audiences. Black press rhetoric's transgressive traits, on this view, are best regarded as prelude to discursive exchange of a kind that has previously been withheld. Its pitch is meant to entice an otherwise passive and unheeding audience into showing some response that, in turn, might then obligate those who have deployed transgressive irony, hyperbole, and insult to more carefully defend or elaborate validity claims.[61] This, again, would entail that the transgressive aspects of the rhetoric *recede* as subjective claims defer to intersubjective needs for shared understanding, be this through already accepted rational discourse norms or new normative forms that emerge from the dialogue.[62]

In imperfect democracies, there are of course no guarantees that the appeals of black press rhetoric can succeed in eliciting recognition and engagement from audiences that have historically denied excluded groups meaningful access to these prerequisites of communicative equality and discourse-based rationality. However, where black press rhetoric *does* succeed is precisely where it elicits recognition and engagement, and this is also where *its transgressive moves can be expected to recede*. It *does not* succeed, however, when instead of progressive movement toward a reciprocation of discourse claims, the opposite may occur, whereby privileged audiences, either mistakenly or willfully, regard black rhetorical transgressions as violations of rational discourse and so use that view as rationale for continued nonrecognition and nonengagement. In this unhappy case, transgressive rhetoric *does not recede* but rather *escalates within an atmosphere of increased frustration on the part of its users and more steeled resistance from its intended audiences.*

The unsuccessful outcome of transgressive rhetoric constitutes a double loss for deliberative democracy. With continued deployment of transgressive tactics, the rhetoric of excluded groups then continues to exist outside the bounds of discursive engagement with white majorities and so goes unchecked—unlikely to be either effectively questioned or challenged by stakeholders of other points of view—and thus ever susceptible to lapses into collective myth-making that may militate against the possibility for reaching shared understandings that bridge racial divides. For privileged groups, the ongoing exclusion of transgressive rhetoric creates an epistemic stunting, whereby participants are deprived of valuable points of view that carry the potential for a more informed and reflective collective action.

Normative Considerations and Practical Bridgework

The unsuccessful outcome of escalating transgressive rhetoric poses a strategic dilemma for its users, as there appears no obvious means by which to navigate between the poles of withheld communicative equality in the form of continued denials of recognition and engagement, on the one side, and its own transgressive rhetoric that can potentially further alienate privileged audiences, on the other. This dilemma is not itself caused by transgressive rhetoric, however; nor is it evident that transgressive rhetoric needs to be significantly altered or abandoned if the dilemma is to be overcome. As argued above, transgressive rhetoric is an understandable response to the systematic denial of communicative equality. It is eminently rational as an appeal for recognition and engagement along the way to genuinely shared understanding; and it may on some occasions successfully achieve its goal.

This is not to glorify transgressive rhetoric, which always carries the risk of potentially alienating further those who hold up the exclusionary bar to genuine participation. Furthermore, it bears repeating that insofar as transgressive rhetoric—at least initially—takes on something of a subjective life of its own, outside the bounds of genuine intersubjective engagement, its users may lapse into increased frustration and possible self-deception where transgressive validity claims go unchecked along the rails of ritualized, uncontested opposition upon which moral validity claims are neither adequately deciphered nor redeemed. Nevertheless, given the aims of transgressive rhetoric, there is sufficient warrant to argue that de-escalation of the rhetoric is called for *only if recog-*

nition and engagement are offered by privileged others who have historically withheld such. Acknowledgment of this point calls for a moral refocusing of the problem of transgressive rhetoric that shifts the burden from excluded groups to those whose practices and ideological justifications have enforced the exclusion.

Refocusing of the problem, I believe, can best be conducted by means of speech act theory, with special emphasis upon the moral contents of interactions which involve requests, pleas, or appeals that are the underlying aims of so much transgressive rhetoric. Consider, for example, a standard request:

STANDARD REQUEST: Will you kindly pass the sugar?

Should the request be a reasonable one—the sugar being visibly within hearer's reach and outside of the speaker's own reach—we would expect the request to be granted. As users of a natural language, we know that requests that *can* be granted *should* be granted, unless hearer offers sufficient cause for *not* so granting: "So sorry, but my hands really are quite full right now," or "Maybe Dolores can reach it for you more easily?" Indeed, so secure are we in this knowledge that, should the denied request go without explanation, we feel justified in chastising the hearer.

There are of course requests that appear from the hearer's standpoint to be unreasonable. Perhaps the sugar is clearly not within hearer's reach, or hearer knows that speaker's medical condition forbids the ingestion of sugar. In such cases, we'd have insufficient grounds for criticizing the hearer for not granting speaker's request. Nevertheless, a moral presumption built into the request is that *if the request cannot or will not be granted, some stated reason must be provided,* and this irrespective of whether the request appears to be reasonable or not. Thus, where hearer withholds stated reason for not complying with speaker's request, hearer might then earn from the requester a justified moral prompt: "Okay, don't pass the sugar then; but won't you at least give me a reason why?" In sum, whether the request is reasonable or not, pragmatic rules instantiated by the speech act within the communicative relationship between speaker and hearer obligate hearer to respond either by meeting the request or giving reasons for not so doing. (I believe a similar argument holds also for pleas and appeals.)

But what *is* a speaker to do if stonewalled by hearer? There are of course many options, ranging from exiting the situation to wringing hearer's neck. Transgressive rhetoric suggests that an optimal response is communicative. Hence the following:

IRONIC REQUEST: It's interesting that you seem to have no reservations when it comes to giving your horse a sweet treat: Do you not think you might find it within yourself to pass some of that sugar my way?

HYPERBOLIC REQUEST: Can't you see I'm absolutely dying for something sweet? Please pass me the sugar, won't you?

INSULTING REQUEST: Can't you refrain from being such a selfish jerk and pass the sugar my way?

These are the kinds of transgression found in the rhetoric of the *Amsterdam News*, understood as strategic means to elicit uptake where straightforward appeals go unanswered. They violate standard expectations, and may even be found offensive to hearer's moral sensibilities. But, we must bear in mind that the standard, nontransgressive request is likely to have already been issued, perhaps many times, and that these newly issued transgressive forms (1) emanate from a position of some justifiable frustration and (2) are aimed to violate the hearer's expectations only incidentally as a condition for eliciting recognition and response. Thus, although their transgressive nature may likely violate majority audiences' expectations on some level, as a pragmatic matter they deserve engaged uptake. Indeed, the real offense to the incomplete communicative interaction is not the transgressive discourse but rather the hearer's decision to deny recognition and engagement.

On this reasoning, legitimacy should be accorded to the transgressive rhetoric of excluded groups whose appeals have historically fallen short, and a moral call is issued to privileged groups to recognize and respond to the appeals that are at the basis of transgressive rhetoric's seeming infractions. This claim should not be confused with that of the new Hegelians, who argue that truth and justice *necessarily* belong to slaves as part of a heightened consciousness that has developed out of their distinctive relation to masters; that slaves have learned to take masters' interests and dispositions into account, whereas masters have suppressed slaves' own interests and dispositions as a condition of denying slaves' humanity; and that slaves, therefore, are presumed to be better suited to develop understandings that unite masters and slaves in ways that potentially transcend the limits of their relationship. What distinguishes the view being developed here from that of the new Hegelians is the emphasis upon all that is communicative within the relationship between oppressed groups and their oppressors. Although new Hegelians may be correct to state that the slaves' position *may* be conducive to a higher consciousness, I think they may be mistaken in the belief that this is inherently a consequence of the master-slave dialectic. For, without there being genuine communicative engagement between masters and slaves, we cannot know with certainty whether the slaves' consciousness has truly transcended fear, desire for vengeance, or other emotions derived from the experience of slavery. Until, that is, slaves are recognized and engaged as communicative equals—their truth and moral validity claims subject to genuinely critical assessment and challenge—any attributions of a higher consciousness must be considered premature.

My argument is that deliberative democracy needs to ensure that the claims of excluded groups be put to the test, and that without so doing the quality of political life is negatively affected: on the one hand, the transgressive rhetoric of excluded groups, launched within a discursive void where validity claims elicit no uptake and thus go unchecked, may become susceptible to collective myth-making with only the weakest connections to reality. On the other hand, if privileged groups and populations persist in withholding recognition and engagement, they deny themselves valuable prescriptive formulae provided by excluded groups that can point the way to a more genuine democratic order. Responsibility for implementing the conditions for shared dialogue, as I have argued, rests with those who historically have withheld their recognition and engagement. Requests, appeals, and other speech acts conveyed in transgressive rhetoric call out for a response. For privileged audiences to withhold response violates our most fundamental understandings about how such speech acts generate a moral obligation to reciprocate.

Conclusion

In conclusion, we might surmise how the claims conveyed in the transgressive rhetoric of marginalized groups *are* best put to the test of public scrutiny within an open discursive environment. This is a task that has been undertaken by others. In discussing enclaved groups, for example, Cass Sunstein has stated:

> It is not clear what can be done about this situation. But it certainly makes sense to consider communication initiatives that would ensure that people would be exposed to a range of reasonable views, not simply one. [...] An appreciation for group polarization suggests that creative approaches should be designed to ensure that people do not simply read their "Daily Me."[63]

In this regard, James Bohman has recommended that deliberative democracy multiply "non-market avenues of mass public communication" as a means of "building up a vibrant political public sphere";[64] and Michael James has argued for state licensing practices that ensure a greater diversification of media.[65]

More far-reaching recommendations and measures may be needed to bring alternative discourses into closer proximity with extant mainstream sources. Interesting in this regard, the *New York Times* has recently displayed on its Internet site links to news analyses and editorial statements of major foreign newspapers such as the *Guardian* of London, the *Sydney Morning Herald*, and the *Daily Star* of Beirut. Now, the move to include black press rhetoric on its pages would not seem too much of a stretch, albeit the move *would* necessitate that the agenda-setting newspaper relax some of its stylistic restrictions.

In the absence of voluntary inclusion, modest regulatory efforts might be in order. State-enforced dialogue opportunities would seem to offer no substantial intrusion into mainstream newspapers' reportage, analysis, or opinion. It would, however, create a condition whereby more readers are brought into contact with points of view not otherwise readily available to them. And to the extent those viewpoints procure recognition and uptake, so the quality of public discourse would almost certainly be elevated. The mainstream media would find it much more difficult to mask its exclusionary reportage, as it is unlikely, for example, that the newspaper's biased coverage of minority groups' political activism could withstand for long the criticisms of such emanating from its own pages. And, ethnically based alternative media that have shown a penchant for irony, hyperbole, insult, and other rhetorical tropes, finding themselves drawn into dialogue marked by genuine recognition and engagement between equals, might well feel compelled to tailor their rhetorical styles to what has always been the expressed desire of oppressed peoples: real dialogue.

NOTES

The author wishes to express sincerest gratitude to Kent Ono and Michael Lacy for their generous editorial remarks. The author is also grateful to the editor-in-chief of the *Amsterdam News*, Elinor Tatum, for her willingness to take time out of her full schedule in order to talk with me about many of the ideas in this chapter. The final contents of this chapter, however, are strictly my own responsibility.

1. Joshua Cohen, "Deliberation and Democratic Legitimacy," in *The Good Polity: Normative Analyses of the State*, ed. A. Hamlin and P. Pettit (London: Basil Blackwell, 1989); John Dryzek, *Deliberative Democracy and Beyond: Liberals, Critics, Contradictions* (Oxford: Oxford University Press, 2000); Amy Gutmann and Dennis Thompson, *Why Deliberative Democracy?* (Princeton: Princeton University Press, 1996); Jurgen Habermas, "Political Communication in Media Society: Does Democracy Still Enjoy an Epistemic Dimension? The Impact of Normative Theory on Empirical Research," *Communication Theory* 16, no. 4 (2006): 411–26.

2. James Bohman, *Public Deliberation: Pluralism, Complexity, and Democracy* (Cambridge: MIT Press, 1996); Michael Rabinder James, *Deliberative Democracy and the Plural Polity* (Lawrence: University of Kansas Press, 2004): Jurgen Habermas, "Political Communication in Media Society."

3. Jurgen Habermas, *Communication and the Evolution of Society* (Boston: Beacon Press, 1979); "A Reply to My Critics," in *Habermas: Critical Debates*, ed. John Thompson and David Held (Cambridge: MIT Press, 1982); *The Theory of Communicative Action, Vol. 1: Reason and Rationalization of Society* (Boston: Beacon Press, 1984).

4. Richard McKeon, "Dialectic and Political Thought and Action," *Ethics* 65, no.1, 1954, 1–33; Melissa Williams, *Voice, Trust and Memory: Marginalized Groups and the Failings of Liberal Representation* (Princeton: Princeton University Press, 1998).

5. Habermas, "A Reply to My Critics."

6. Frederick Detweiler, *The Negro Press in the United States* (College Park, MD: McGrath, 1922); William Huntzicker, *The Popular Press, 1833–1865* (Westport, CT: Greenwood, 1999); Charlotte O'Kelly, "Black Newspapers and the Black Protest Movement: Their Historical Relationship, 1827–1945," *Phylon* 43, no.1, 1–14, 1982; Charles Simmons, *The African-American Press:*

With Special References to 4 Newspapers, 1827–1965 (Jefferson, NC: McFarland, 1998); Roland Wolseley, *The Black Press, U.S.A.* (Ames: Iowa State University Press, 1971).

7. Catherine Squires, "The Black Press and the State: Attracting Unwanted(?) Attention," in *Counterpublics and the State*, ed. R. Asen and D. Brouwer (Albany: SUNY Press, 2001): 111–36.

8. Hemant Shah and Michael Thornton, *Newspaper Coverage of Interethnic Conflict* (Thousand Oaks, CA: Sage, 2004).

9. Dryzek, *Deliberative Democracy and Beyond*, 52, 67.

10. Iris Marion Young, *Inclusion and Democracy* (Oxford: Oxford University Press, 2000), 77.

11. Reginald Owens, "Entering the 21st Century: Oppression and the African-American Press," in *Mediated Messages and African-American Culture*, ed. V. T. Berry and C. I. Manning-Miller (Thousand Oaks, CA: Sage, 1999), 222–44.

12. Pamela Newkirk, *Within the Veil: Black Journalists, White Media* (New York: NYU Press, 2000).

13. Ibid., 18.

14. Olga Davis, "Vigilance and Solidarity in the Rhetoric of the Black Press: The Tulsa Star," *Journal of Intergroup Relations* 32, no. 3 (2005): 9–31; Michael Huspek, "Black Press, White Press, and Their Opposition: The Case of the Police Shooting of Tyisha Miller," *Social Justice* 31, no.1–2 (2004): 217–41; "'From the Standpoint of the White Man's World': The Black Press and Contemporary White Media Scholarship with Emphasis upon the Work of W. Lance Bennett," *Journal of Intergroup Relations* 32, no. 3 (2005): 67–88.

15. Frankie Hutton, "Democratic Idealism in the Black Press," in *Outsiders in 19th Century Press History: Multicultural Perspectives*, ed. Frankie Hutton and B. S. Reed (Bowling Green, OH: Bowling Green University Popular Press, 1995), 5–20.

16. Michael Huspek, "Habermas and Oppositional Public Spheres: A Stereoscopic Analysis of Black and White Press Practices," *Political Studies* 55, no. 6 (2007): 821–43.

17. Jeffrey Toobin, "The Unasked Question," *New Yorker* 76, no. 2 (2000): 38–44.

18. Charles Haberman, "A Shooting, and Shooting from the Hip," *New York Times*, Feb. 12, 1999.

19. *New York Times Manual of Style and Usage* (New York: Random House, 1999).

20. Ibid., viii.

21. Ibid., 307.

22. Gay Talese, *The Kingdom and the Power* (Cleveland: World Publishing, 1969), 29.

23. *New York Times Manual of Style and Usage*, viii.

24. Ibid., 240.

25. Ibid., 24.

26. Ibid., 308.

27. Carol Conaway, "Crown Heights: Politics and Press Coverage of the Race War that Wasn't," *Polity* 32, no. 1 (1999): 93–118; Douglas Crimp (with A. Rolston), *AIDS Demographics* (Seattle: Bay Press, 1990); Cho Kim, *Bitter Fruit: The Politics of Black-Korean Conflict in New York City* (New Haven: Yale University Press, 2000).

28. Ginger Thompson, "1,000 Rally to Condemn Shooting of Unarmed Man by Police," *New York Times*, Feb. 8, 1999.

29. Kevin Flynn, "8 Arrested Near City hall in Protest of Police Shooting," *New York Times*, Feb. 23, 1999.

30. Susan Sachs, "Anger and Protest at Rite for African Killed by Police," *New York Times*, Feb. 13, 1999.

31. Elizabeth Bumiller (with Ginger Thompson), "Giuliani Cancels Political Trip Amid Protest Over Shooting," *New York Times*, Feb. 10, 1999.

32. Sachs, "Anger and Protest," *New York Times*, Feb. 13, 1999.

33. Eleanor Randolph, "A Long Day of Venting about the City's Police," *New York Times*, May 28, 1999.

34. See, for example, Kent Ono and John Sloop, *Shifting Borders: Rhetoric, Immigration, and California's Proposition 187* (Philadelphia: Temple, 2002).

35. Andy Newman, "Prayer in New York, Protest in Washington," *New York Times*, Feb. 16, 1999.

36. Jodi Wilgoren, "Diallo Rally Focuses on Call for Strong Oversight of Police," *New York Times*, April 16, 1999.

37. Edward Wong, "Parkview: Two Views of Diallo Case," *New York Times*, Feb. 25, 1999.

38. Herb Boyd (quoting Rep. Charles Rangel), "Amadou Diallo's Homecoming: Sharpton and Cochran to lead case against PBA," *New York Amsterdam News*, March 3, 1999. Another conspicuous use of transgressive rhetoric by the black press is its blurring of boundaries between reportage of "objective" facts, on the one hand, and writers' subjective opinions, on the other. This shares a family resemblance with the rhetorical tropes of irony, hyperbole, and insult as analyzed more fully later in the chapter. The point of the reportage is to produce transparently biased truth claims which an informed reader is thought to be capable of deciphering. The transparently biased presentation of facts are meant to stimulate public discussion—this in contrast to the *New York Times*, which is thought to show *no less bias* in its "objective" reportage though without admission of such, thus having the effect of closing off opportunities for expanded public discourse.

39. Alton Maddox Jr., "No Justice! No Peace!" *New York Amsterdam News*, Feb. 24, 1999.

40. Herb Boyd (quoting Alton Maddox), *New York Amsterdam News*, March 24, 1999.

41. Henry Louis Gates Jr., *Figures in Black: Words, Signs and the "Racial" Self* (New York: Oxford University Press, 1987); Shelley Fisher Fishkin and Carla Peterson, "We Hold These Truths to Be Self-evident: The Rhetoric of Frederick Douglass's Journalism," in *The Black Press: New Literary and Historical Essays*, ed. T. Vogel (New Brunswick, NJ: Rutgers University Press, 2001).

42. Frederick Douglass, *Narrative of the Life of Frederick Douglass, an American Slave* (New York: Penguin, 1845 [1986]).

43. Houston Baker Jr., "Critical Memory and the Black Public Sphere," in *Cultural Memory and the Construction of Identity*, ed. D. Ben-Amos and L. Weissberg (Detroit: Wayne State University Press, 1999), 264–96.

44. Henry Louis Gates Jr., *The Signifying Monkey: A Theory of Afro-American Literary Criticism* (New York: Oxford, 1988).

45. Kim, *Bitter Fruit*; Tali Mendelberg, *The Race Card: Campaign Strategy, Implicit Messages, and the Norm of Equality* (Princeton: Princeton University Press, 2001).

46. J. Zambga Browne, "Communities of Color Unite Over Slaughter." *New York Amsterdam News*, Feb. 17, 1999.

47. Gloria Knighton, "Get the Racist Nuts Off the Squad," *New York Amsterdam News*, March 3, 1999.

48. Browne, "Communities of Color."

49. Wilbert Tatum, "Giuliani: A Monster in Our Midst," *New York Amsterdam News*, Feb. 24, 1999.

50. Herb Boyd, "New York's Honor Role," *New York Amsterdam News*, March 24, 1999.

51. Damasco Reyes, "Protests Follow Diallo Funeral," *New York Amsterdam News*, Feb. 24, 1999.

52. Maddox Jr., "No Justice! No Peace!"; Vinette Pryce, "Women's Scorn Lands on City Hall," *New York Amsterdam News*, March 17, 1999; Tatum, "Giuliani: A Monster in Our Midst."

53. Wilbert Tatum, "It's Only a Matter of Time: Giuliani's Political Demise," *New York Amsterdam News*, March 3, 1999.

54. Jurgen Habermas, "The Theory of Communicative Action."

55. John Searle, *Expression and Meaning: Studies in the Theory of Speech Acts* (Cambridge: Cambridge University Press, 1979).

56. Ibid., 115.

57. Ibid., 112.

58. Marcyliena Morgan, "More Than a Mood or an Attitude: Discourse and Verbal Genres in African-American Culture," in *African-American English: Structures, History and Use*, ed. S. Mufwene, J. Rickford, G. Bailey, and J. Baugh (London: Routledge, 1998), p. 263.

59. H. Rap Brown, "Street Talk," in *Rappin' and Stylin' Out: Communication in Urban Black America*, ed. Thomas Kochman (Urbana: University of Illinois Press, 1972).

60. Jurgen Habermas, "On the Distinction Between Poetic and Communicative Uses of Language," in *On the Pragmatics of Communication*, ed. Maeve Cooke (Cambridge: MIT Press, 1988).

61. As Burgess noted: "behind all the sound and fury of this rhetoric may lie the intention merely to force upon the culture a moral decision"; see Parke Burgess, "The Rhetoric of Black Power: A Moral Demand?" *Quarterly Journal of Speech* 54 (April 1968): 124.

62. I develop this idea more fully in a currently unpublished manuscript: Untamed rhetoric in the public sphere: Beyond communicative and strategic action.

63. Cass Sunstein, *Designing Democracy: What Constitutions Do* (Oxford: Oxford University Press, 2001), 36.

64. Bohman, *Public Deliberation*, 141.

65. James, *Deliberative Democracy*, 138.

Commodity Consumption and the Politics of the "Post-Racial"

Roopali Mukherjee

"Post-Racial" Bricolage

We have entered the "post-racial" era, some suggest, a historical moment in which neither cultural practices nor political solidarities cohere predictably along racial lines. The social movements of the 1960s and 1970s, we are told, have bridged historical divides, bringing us closer than ever to a multicultural promised land of equal opportunity and racial equity. The remarkable diversity of civil rights coalitions that radically transformed historical forces of injustice have done their work, these voices insist: it is best we let them wither.

The civil rights struggles have indeed redrawn the American cultural land-scape, and they delivered unprecedented privileges of citizenship and full partici-pation within economic life for vast numbers of African Americans, producing new middle classes. In doing so, they challenged what were stark social and eco-nomic injustices. Although class inequities persist, since the civil right struggles were waged, we can chart a statistically significant rise in the number of blacks and women who have graduated from institutions of higher learning, entered the white-collar work force, moved to the suburbs, and risen to positions of promi-nence at the highest echelons of political and economic power.

These shifts have borne peculiar fruit in terms of their impact on race- and gender-based political solidarities in the current post–civil rights era. As Edu-ardo Bonilla-Silva argues, for example, the racial rhetorics of the current moment point to the rising legitimacy of "colorblind racisms," a combination of white color privilege and workplace tokenisms, racial acknowledgments and erasures that produce the contemporary paradoxes of what he terms "racism without rac-ists."[1] The series of reactionary assaults that took aim at affirmative action and other social justice programs over the course of the 1990s, likewise, would have failed were it not for the formidable rhetorical force of ideological and electoral coalitions—rather than antagonisms—among blacks, whites, and Latinos. These reformulations cemented new constituencies, including a "model majority" of careered white women and members of the black middle- and upper-classes who served to substantiate claims that social justice mandates invented during the civil rights era are themselves racist and unfair, and thus, deserved to be eliminated.[2]

In step with the liberal retreat from racial justice,[3] prominent blacks and women now appear regularly as spokespersons for policy assaults that exact the highest price from blacks and women themselves. Among these voices, Angela Dillard describes newfound alliances that coalesced among "multicultural conservatives," African American and Latino political converts disillusioned by "identity politics" who aligned themselves with the New Right and the Republican Party starting in the 1980s and, abdicating historical solidarities founded on race and ethnic lines, zealously promoted the redemptive possibilities of colorblind individualism, assimilation, and neoliberal standards of entrepreneurial responsibility.[4] Claiming that we now inhabit a post-racial America marked crucially by the declining significance of race, these voices read ongoing disarticulations within racial categories as suggestive of the "end of race" itself.

As racial solidarities that had imbued civil rights demands with so much of their affective and strategic potency endure a series of recalibrations, arguments for the dispensability of social justice programs gain traction within popular consciousness aided by a series of notable cultural shifts. Here, spectacular displays of African American affluence and conspicuous consumption, circulating with the performative repertoires of "bling" hip-hop cultures, add force to claims about "dusky Donald Trumps and brown-skinned Bill Gateses," visible proof of unprecedented gains made by a new entrepreneurial vanguard within black popular culture. As younger generations of African Americans are implicated in shifts heralding the "death of civil rights,"[5] where sentimental nostalgia for civil rights paradigms is seen as traded in for a newer political stance that celebrates entrepreneurial savvy and the virtues of triumphant consumerism, iconic figures like Oprah Winfrey, Magic Johnson, and Colin Powell take shape as rich cultural metonyms for generational transformations within the racial order.

These visible figures complement and substantiate a "new elite," the so-called children of '69, who, having being admitted to prestigious institutions of higher education through the racialized protocols of affirmative action, have ascended, in recent years, to positions of unprecedented prominence and political power. Here, Barack Obama's election to the White House and Sonia Sotomayor's appointment to the Supreme Court serve as proof of just "how far we have come." Their successes drown out evidence of abiding inequities, nudging approval for calls to move past the divisive restraints of affirmative action and redistributive justice, programs seen increasingly as having overstayed their welcome.

As voices from the right and left join in a national introspection marked variously by relief and anxiety about the arrival of a post-racial America, these shifting constituencies and solidarities offer us brief glimpses of the discursive bricolage of the idea of the post-racial.[6] We begin to see the outlines of larger narratives shaping a racial milieu in which neither cultural practices nor political solidarities cohere predictably along racial lines. The historical inequities that delineated access from exclusion, recognition from erasure, and participation from marginality are increasingly assumed to be no longer relevant or "true" in post–civil rights America.[7]

These coalescing racial rhetorics deserve close attention, particularly given their service to neoliberal hegemonies. Within the terms of neoliberalism, these rhetorics serve to shore up the hegemonic credibility of individual entrepreneurialism and market fundamentalisms as universalizing markers of a quintessentially American creed. Neoliberalism defines the latter as "dangerous individuals" who deserve renewed discipline and rigorous rehabilitation so as to produce properly post-racial subjects. As Craig Calhoun argues, these retrenchments are part and parcel of current trends toward the "privatization of risk" that absolves state authorities of their responsibilities for redistribution[8] and care and, as Cheryl Harris points out, they contribute a crucial point of convergence in contemporary racial realism: that ongoing racial inequalities are not the result of racism but of deficiencies in black cultural practices, of black dysfunction.[9]

For scholars seeking to parse these postmodern contingencies of blackness and the limits of political resistance, the task ahead, as Robin Kelley posits, is not to decide *if* race matters anymore but rather to illuminate *how* race matters differently today.[10] Those of us interested in taking stock of the racial order of things within the cultural valences of this moment must begin by acknowledging that we inhabit a discursive terrain marked by equivocation and ambivalence. As wavering standards of what counts as "black" move in step with paradoxes within what it means to organize "black politics" in the neoliberal moment, these ambivalences deserve a careful regard, one that goes beyond mere dismissal or denunciation. Instead, in this chapter I argue that they offer us ground to parse the racial rhetorics of the current moment, illuminating the powerful logics of what is "sayable" and "knowable" about race and, equally, what lurks as "unsayable," and thus, in a sense, is "unknowable" within the so-called post-racial era.

The Case of Black Commodity Consumption

Visible proof of black middle-class transcendence and increased black access to political and cultural privilege have been set in terms of public discourse about how far we have journeyed toward a post-racial America. How racist can we be, after all, if African Americans are among the wealthiest people in the country, if black people have made it all the way to the White House? Within the terms of Lizabeth Cohen's "consumers' Republic,"[11] black advancement within materialist hierarchies stands out as incontrovertible proof of the democratizing power of consumerism, its tenacious capacities to override obdurate inequities. With historically unprecedented levels of visible wealth and buying power, black ascendance toward material privilege emerges as a key indicator within the racial order that serves as a ready shorthand for cultural transformations toward the post-racial. The one stands in for the other, making room for circulating claims about the "end of race" and its tedious fixations. How, the argument goes, could black people persist in their racial claims when they have everything the consumers' Republic can deliver?

I seek to interrogate this equivalence, this hegemonic articulation between material culture and post-racial discourse. In a society fundamentally shaped by race, writes Paul Mullins, "material culture harbors the contradictions over and tensions within racial discourse."[12] Highlighting the work of consumption and acquisitive desire within struggles over race and racial equality, I turn to a comparative reading of two moments in time—one historical, the other contemporary—to reveal how racial ideologies shape discourses of commodity culture, as well as how commodity culture shapes the disciplinary mechanisms of the racial order. The first critical moment returns historically to calls in early black political discourse for a deliberate consumerist politics that promised deliverance into the fantasy of full-fledged democratic citizenship for African Americans. The second outlines contemporary proclamations of the black American Dream epitomized by the hyper-consumerist excesses of ghetto fabulous "bling." These examples offer us the means to interrogate critically equivalences we find circulating between black material ascendance and post-racial hegemonies of the neoliberal moment. They help show how race matters within contemporary culture, and moreover, reveal openings within black commodity cultures themselves that disturb the palliative allure of the idea of the post-racial.

A "Serum for Denegrification"?

While scholars have noted postwar invocations that identified the pursuit of prosperity as a basic component of American citizenship, projecting idealized notions of "consumer citizenship" onto standards of full citizenship,[13] African Americans and most working-class people were often assumed unfit, incapable, and/or undeserving of full integration into the mainstream consumer world of postwar America. While Lizabeth Cohen notes that the most profitable way to operate a free market was to free it from the interference of racial prejudice,[14] business practices of red lining that kept stores from opening in non-white neighborhoods[15] and cultural norms of racial segregation provided for the spatial containment of black consumers, stamping them with a badge of inferiority.[16] As Jason Chambers explains, merchants often operated on a system of credit or barter and thereby enjoyed significant levels of control over black purchasing behavior, denying credit or refusing barters on a whim. They regulated consumerism, not on the basis of an individual's abilities to buy, but instead on grounds of their race; blacks were often offered no choice but items of inferior quality for which there was little white demand.[17] Thus, as Cohen suggests, the policies, priorities, and political culture of the consumers' Republic, while seeking to meet the lofty aspirations of social inclusion and egalitarianism, nevertheless also wove deep inequalities into the fabric of postwar prosperity.[18]

Like other postwar citizens of the consumers' Republic, African Americans sought to enter the vaunted fellowship of American citizenship principally through their pocketbooks. The history of the civil rights movement is peppered with examples of African Americans mobilizing in vast numbers to demand equal access to public sites of consumption—department stores, movie theaters, city buses, and lunch counters. Likewise, the use of labor strikes and boycotts in early demands for black political rights dovetailed with the rise of consumer movements to compel equal treatment from white retailers and businesses.[19] Linking participation in commodity cultures with the privileges of political standing and citizenship, black consumerism emerged from the start as a significant site for struggles over black political subjectivity.

Early African American public discourse such as Booker T. Washington's call to build black wealth and economic self-sufficiency coincided with the rise of the black entrepreneur, and the rituals of luxury consumption and displays of such consumption with "economic emancipation."[20] In his early writings, W. E. B. Du Bois likewise urged black consumerism as a means of social advancement, for "the Negro as consumer could approach economic equality with whites much more nearly than he ever would as a producer."[21]

As Bobby Wilson explains, in the postbellum years, the development of segmented commodity markets enabled "the structural imperatives of capital to expand consumption."[22] These "commodity circuits" also enabled African Americans to substantiate their emancipation from slavery in material terms by "speaking with and through consumption."[23] Proving they possessed leisure time and the freedom to indulge in pleasurable pursuits, black practices of consumerism constituted an "assertiveness," which lent a political dimension to everyday practices like shopping and displaying possessions.[24] Similarly, in his analysis of *Ebony* magazine, Jason Chambers observed that "material goods were a key means of communicating aspirations and showing that blacks were equal to whites."[25]

However, black efforts to acquire and display objects formerly reserved only for whites were consistently interpreted negatively, as a "desire to be white," as little beyond a "serum for denegrification" making it possible, as Frantz Fanon suggested in a different context, for "the miserable Negro to whiten himself and thus to throw off the burden of that corporeal malediction."[26] The question has remained a fraught one, tracing well-worn debates among African Americans over whether black consumption is pathological or subversive. For some, black consumption serves to alleviate "status anxiety,"[27] a crucial means to distance oneself from a "degraded past."[28] For others, the investment in material culture signifies little beyond black attempts at paralleling whites, an exercise in tragic futility and/or proof of abject bamboozlement.

For Chambers, however, black consumption of luxury commodities is best interpreted as "a political action—an emphatically concrete, unambiguous bid for equality."[29] For a group that had been tradable commodities themselves, a status that necessitated being stripped of their humanity, personhood, and identity, material goods were one way in which blacks could make their humanity as visible as possible.[30] Moreover, Michèle Lamont and Virág Molnár contend that black Americans use consumption to express their "collective identity" and ethnic solidarity, and to acquire social membership—that is, to signify their claim to full and equal membership in society.[31] To read such consumption simply as black efforts to be just like white society is to interpret these practices only through the lens of deviance and delusion, and, as Chambers argues, to echo traditional presumptions that locate whiteness as the standard of measure for taste and respectability.

The historical record of white ridicule and racist violence directed at black prosperity, especially when it was greater than their own, is one indication of the ways that black access to material goods destabilized the racial logics of white superiority and black inferiority. Ethnographic and literary accounts alike provide historical instances of white retaliatory violence directed at public displays of black material wealth. For instance, in a 1917 incident, the sight of Henry Watson (a successful black farmer in Georgia) driving his daughter into town in his new car, so incensed a group of white men that they forced Watson and his daughter out of the car at gunpoint, doused the automobile with gasoline, and set it on fire with the warning: "From now on, you niggers walk into town or use that old mule if you want to stay in this town."[32]

In his 1971 autobiography, similarly, novelist Chester Himes recalls his childhood experience of witnessing outraged white neighbors in rural Mississippi at the end of World War I who forced Himes's father's dismissal from his job at the Alcorn A&M University, precipitating the family's subsequent ouster from the state, when they became the first owners of a private automobile in the county.[33] Horrific incidents like the one dramatized in John Singleton's 1997 feature film, *Rosewood*, where poor whites, resentful of black prosperity and economic self-reliance, lynched and chased out residents of an independent black town in 1923 Florida, likewise reveal the kind of visceral rage early displays of black material wealth elicited from whites.

Grace Elizabeth Hale explains that African American acquisition and display of objects blurred distinctions of taste and refinement, producing what she terms a "shock of sameness" as commodities lost their effectiveness as markers of racial hierarchies.[34] To be properly white, these standards insisted, whites had to buy and display ever more elite possessions that unambiguously asserted their superiority over blacks, their racial advantage in economic status, and political standing.

As material culture emerged as a key terrain for struggles over racial rank and difference, standards of taste and cultural capital, rituals of competitive acquisitiveness, and the desire for material possessions served to adjudicate racial regimes of economic access and political standing. Black access to commodities, on the one hand, substantiated the economic bases of full participation in the privileges of democratic citizenship in the United States. To be fully American, blacks bought and displayed material possessions that emphatically and unambiguously asserted their humanity and standing as citizens. On the other hand, such consumption troubled the economic logics of racial difference, muddying standards that had hitherto delineated clear racial categorizations. Commodity consumption emerged as critical ground on which racialized battles over national belonging and political standing played out. And, revealing shopping to be a potentially subversive activity, black commodity practices took shape as potentially political. As barriers to traditional forms of political engagement persisted—racist protocols that unfairly disqualified black voter registrants, white intimidation directed at black voters, and violence against blacks who dared run for political office—cultures of material acquisitiveness were, from the start, imbued with, and troubled by, the rhetorics of race and racial difference.

"Bling" and the Limits of "Post-Racial"

As civil rights struggles ushered unprecedented numbers of black Americans to fuller participation in public life, they also desegregated the African American consumer dollar, delivering its untapped resources to mainstream business interests. Robert Weems, Jr., notes, for example, that by the end of 1960s, corporate marketers including Avon Products, Coca Cola USA, Pepsi Cola Company, Columbia Pictures, Greyhound, R. J. Reynolds Tobacco Company, and others established advertising and outreach practices that extolled black culture and customs; in so doing, they catered to African American investments in racial desegregation and garnered the allegiance of black consumers.[35]

Forty years later, showing steady rates of growth, trends in African American consumer habits are impressive indeed. Nationwide earnings indicators suggest, for example, that African Americans took home an estimated $744 billion in earned income in 2006, their collective buying power rising to $845 billion in

2007, the highest levels in history.[36] Even as the full impact of the 2008 economic upheavals in global finance and credit markets continues to play out, estimates predict that black buying power will surpass the $1 trillion mark by the year 2012.[37]

These patterns of rising consumerism are not unique to African Americans. A recent study by Unity Marketing reported that American households, both black and white, with annual incomes of over $150,000, spend significantly more today than they did a decade ago on status symbols of luxury, including boutique travel and dining, performance automobiles, custom entertainment, spas and beauty services, fashion apparel and accessories, jewelry and watches, wine and spirits, and so on.[38] Thus, black socioeconomic patterns in recent years mirror wider societal trends reflecting late capitalist transformations of workers into consumers, from "civic-citizens" to "consumer-citizens."

Keeping pace with these broader transformations in modes of citizenship, African American cultures of consumption, likewise, reveal a series of adjustments. Displays of affluence encapsulated in cultural vernaculars of the "bling" aesthetic emerged in this context, giving shape to new forms of black consumer-citizenship and as shorthand for the American Dream of the late capitalist moment. As I have argued elsewhere, taking shape over the course of the post–civil rights era, the glitterati of black popular culture (movie stars, pop icons, sports figures) adorned themselves with stylized accoutrements of vertiginous class transcendence (mink coats, Cartier watches, rare automobiles) saturating the iconography of music videos, the red carpet, and the tabloids.[39]

By the end of the 1990s, bling and its vanguard of "hip-hop moguls" had left their mark on a range of media and popular cultural genres, and complicit within claims about an emerging post-racial America, these voices substantiated a new phase in American racial history that broke in important ways from the preceding civil rights era. Celebrations of bling shaped a dossier of visual evidence highlighting the distance that African Americans had traveled since the marches, sit-ins, and boycotts of the 1960s. Shifting the racial rhetorics of the moment, such displays nudged popular consent for neoliberal claims about the declining significance of race.[40] After all, how oppressed could a minority be if its most visible representatives were fixtures on the nation's television screens, idolized as corporate icons in global media flows?

Along with their ideological complicities, however, cultural expressions of bling also offer us clues to how markers of race and racial difference remain embedded within the consumption economies of the late capitalist moment. Black performances of bling emerge as profoundly ambivalent signifiers within contemporary culture, revealing a dappled field of stasis as well as change in how race matters within the cultural valences of the so-called post-racial moment.

As in the past, contemporary trends in black commodity consumption have, for the most part, been interpreted negatively. Thus, for example, Tommy Hilfiger, owner of the luxury apparel brand that bears his name, and which has often been sported by headliners from the hip-hop industry, was quoted in a 1997 interview with *Forbes* magazine dismissing African American consumers of the Hilfiger brand, saying "many of these people would rather have a Rolex than a home."[41] More recently, Frederic Rouzaud, managing director of the Louis Roederer marque that produces and distributes the high-priced Cristal champagne, when asked in an interview with *The Economist* how the product's associations with rap stars affected the brand, replied: "That's a good question, but what can we do? We can't forbid people from buying it. I'm sure Dom Perignon or Krug would be delighted to have their business."[42]

Renewing age-old scripts that black Americans are, at base, ill-equipped to manage wealth and are deserving of racist ridicule for their attempts to buy their way into the privileges of participation in public life, such critiques echo those from other historical moments. These instances of contempt and scorn tend to be veiled and less virulent than those from earlier periods, but as in the past here again we find white businesses attempting to distance their products from black consumers. These attitudes reflect historical anxieties that such associations move brands "downstream," thus losing the cultural and economic capital of white consumer patronage. Common across these episodes, racial associations—and not class alone—emerge as key to uncovering how and what commodity consumption signifies. Shaping norms and interpretations of competitive acquisition within mainstream culture, Hilfiger, Rouzaud, and others articulate new versions of lingering white anxieties about shifts in the economic logics of racial difference. If African Americans are able to buy luxury commodities that had hitherto been the exclusive province of affluent whites, by what standards can whites maintain the material logics of their racial superiority?

Eliding widening disparities in socioeconomic status among Americans of all races, such admonitions isolate black consumerism alone as vulgar and irresponsible. In the post-racial milieu, as cultures of conspicuous consumption shape standards of taste and habits of over-indulgence across racial lines, public dismay and derision focus pointedly on black consumerism as uniquely pathological. Neoliberal, and thus, by definition, "colorblind" exhortations to economic responsibility and self-reliance, we find, are shaped powerfully by the logics of race and racial difference, even as they lurk as "unsayable," and thus, in a sense, "unknowable," within post-racial culture.

The solution to the problem of black engorgement within commodity cultures, these admonitions suggest, is "inconspicuous consumption."[43] Setting up distinctions between rational consumption in contrast with a racial and pathological hyper-consumerism, consumptive desire reemerges as the standard by which the right to political subjectivity is measured. As in episodes from the past, black consumerism is, here again, evaluated and chided by racial standards that locate whiteness as the measure for taste and respectability. As before, black consumers reach symbolically for the privileges of democratic participation by engaging emphatically and unambiguously with commodity culture, and once again it becomes possible to dismiss African American political subjectivity by excoriating such engagements.

Pursuing Néstor García Canclini's suggestion that changes in modes of consumption alter the possibilities and forms of citizenship,[44] we might consider how race is implicated within consumer-citizenship in the contemporary era, that is, how black citizens actualize their political subjectivities from within cultures of bling themselves. Here, in closing, I offer a brief example of black consumer-citizenship emerging from and within the consumerist cultures of bling—a single instance among others that illuminates the promise of a racial politics borne out of the paradoxes of neoliberalism and, equally, the political potency of racial solidarity in the so-called post-racial moment.

During one of many breathtaking media moments in the aftermath of Hurricane Katrina, hip-hop star Kanye West stepped off script during an appearance on "A Concert for Hurricane Relief," NBC's nationally televised benefit for victims of the storm in September 2005, to denounce the president of the United States, saying: "George Bush doesn't care about black people." Deviating from his prepared speech, West exclaimed:

> I hate the way they portray us in the media. You see a black family, it says, "they're looting." You see a white family, it says, "they're looking for food." And, you know, it's been five days [waiting for federal help] because most of the people are black . . . I'm calling my business manager right now to see what's . . . the biggest amount I can give, and just to imagine if . . . I was down there, and those are, those are my people down there. So anybody out there that wants to do anything that . . . can help with the set up, the way America is set up to help, the poor, the black people, the less well-off, as slow as possible.[45]

We might unpack this episode as a case illuminating the ideological tensions of the post-racial era and, specifically, the symbolic and cultural modes of consumer-citizenship that take shape within those tensions. For one, West's critique is specifically antiracist; that is, his tirade against biased news coverage of survivors, the anemic federal response that took days to arrive as he puts it "because most of the people [were] black," each is a pointed recognition of how race and racial inequalities exacerbated the impact of the storm. Each serves as a reminder that the neoliberal state retraces familiar lines of racial neglect and exclusion.

Whites disagreed overwhelmingly with the claim that race had, in any way, impacted the pace and quality of federal disaster relief. In contrast, black Americans registered high levels of familiarity and agreement with West's claims.[46] The ensuing frenzy of racial claims and counterclaims, together with the starkly racialized spectacle of the disaster, served to muddy fantasies of a post-racial America.[47] West's critique highlighted the proximity—rather than distance—of racial logics undergirding contemporary public discourse.

In West's version, Katrina revealed "the way America is set up," a reminder of historical oppressions that endure. Merging in the cultural imaginary with news images of African Americans stranded for days on rooftops, in the Superdome, and outside the New Orleans Convention Center, the star claimed black victims of the storm as his own with the words "those are my people down there." Here, as Clyde Woods notes, the mass suffering of African Americans emerged as a "defining moment," transforming postmodern ambiguities within the category of "black" into a politicized—and specifically racialized—constituency.[48] Making common cause with "[his] people down there," imagining, in front of a national audience, the horror of what it would have felt like "if . . . [he] was down there," West joins in the urgency, not just of action in the face of adversity, but also of black political solidarity in answer to racialized neglect. Recalling modes of political advocacy inherited from the civil rights era, West's voice here disturbs the allure of the idea of the post-racial, signaling an abiding racial order that shapes national standards of inclusion and care.

Second, West's words offer us an example of racial protest that emerged organically—unrehearsed and impassioned—from bling cultures of mainstream hip-hop, a constituency not famous for articulating antiracist critiques of any kind within contemporary culture. Given that West typically positions himself as "an all-American striver,"[49] his oeuvre dedicated to flaunting material possessions and a showy individualism, his post-Katrina outburst is notable because it does not ask, as neoliberal discourses would demand: what is wrong with you that you cannot help yourself? Instead, the star urges action and accountability from the president and from state institutions of relief. Within a discursive context marked by a relentless push to "get the government off our backs," here we have a hip-hop icon demanding that the state step back in.

Indeed, West's exhortation demands nothing less than a new social contract between the state and its citizens, which spells out that which "people have a right to expect from their government in terms of basic human needs which all share in common."[50] Here, West echoes vociferous condemnation that emerged in response to widespread media misuse of the term "refugees" in reference to Katrina evacuees. Reasserting racial lines that mark denials of the privileges and protections of citizenship, the civic exclusion implied here, as Alice Gavin notes, resonated disturbingly with black experiences throughout American history.[51] Although, as Cheryl Harris points out, the claim by blacks in New Orleans that "We are American" served to counter such slights,[52] media impulses to position black victims of the storm as "foreigners" reproduced neoliberal hegemonies that define those in need of public support as "strangers," thus marking the limits of majoritarian identity and hospitality.[53]

Against these currents, West's outburst signifies black opposition to fundamental tenets of neoliberalism, calling attention to the vacuity of calls for "color-blindness," which rely unfailingly on the very logics of race they claim to dispossess. Demanding a new social contract between the state and its citizens, West's voice calls attention to the racial codification and administration of the privileges of citizenship and, as Zenia Kish reminds us, following Foucault's formulation of the racist calculus of biopower, the power over life and death remains the province of a profoundly racial state.[54]

Ironies abound within modes of citizenship that West's outburst signifies. For example, despite the star's forceful articulation of enduring racial dilemmas within the so-called post-racial moment, his call to action privileges private resources as the means to mediate public need. "I'm calling my business manager right now to see what's . . . the biggest amount I can give," West promises, isolating enterprise and philanthropy as favored avenues for action. Eclipsing massive grassroots efforts that emerged as the backbone of the relief and recovery effort across the Gulf states after the storm, and marginalizing daily struggles to hold state authorities to their promise of aid and assistance,[55] West's approach is, at once, racially defined and tactically neoliberal.

As the injury of the storm outlines the racial matrix undergirding neoliberal eviscerations of public assistance and welfare, and even as West's call to action is deliberately racial, the star nevertheless foregrounds modes of civic intervention that remain firmly rooted in neoliberal anthems of enterprise and market solutions. As Wendy Brown cautions, such modes echo structures of opposition favored by Nietzsche's concept of *ressentiment*: "the moralizing revenge of the powerless."[56] Gauging social injury by "universal" standards of liberal subjectivity—wrongs that take shape as individually culpable, and which, in turn, legitimize self-reliant, privatized remedies—West's call "seethes with *ressentiment*." But, consigned to little more than a "moralizing politics," his approach privileges righteous censure above all else, thus precluding a more fundamental attack on capitalism, the structure that is ultimately responsible for the social injuries laid bare by the storm.[57]

Merging civil rights paradigms of inclusionary social justice and neoliberal valences of strident entrepreneurialism, West substantiates the terms and contradictions of new modes of black citizenship. Not reducible to ideological complicity alone, the star articulates the civic potential—at once politically accountable and faltering—that lurks within commercialized black discourses themselves. Within the terms of the consumers' Republic, it becomes impossible to write off such instances of civic intervention as idle posturing. Not unlike the political valences of African American consumer cultures from earlier periods in history, these critiques shape the terms of a racial politics borne precisely out of black consumerism and enterprise.

NOTES

The author would like to thank Madhu Dubey for taking time on the beach to read the chapter and make really useful comments. Thanks also to Kent Ono and Michael Lacy for all their work in bringing this collection together.

1. Eduardo Bonilla-Silva, *Racism Without Racists: Color-Blind Racism and the Persistence of Racial Inequality in America* (New York: Rowman & Littlefield, 2009).

2. Roopali Mukherjee, *The Racial Order of the Things: Cultural Imaginaries of the Post-Soul Era* (Minneapolis: University of Minnesota Press, 2006), 46–52.

3. Stephen Steinberg, *Turning Back: The Retreat from Racial Justice in American Thought and Policy* (Boston: Beacon Press, 1995).

4. Angela D. Dillard, *Guess Who's Coming to Dinner Now? Multicultural Conservatism in America* (New York: New York University Press, 2001), x; Ibid., xv.

5. Todd Boyd, *The New H.N.I.C. (Head Niggas in Charge): The Death of Civil Rights and the Reign of Hip Hop* (New York: New York University Press, 2003).

6. Helene Cooper, "Meet the New Elite, Not Like the Old," *New York Times*, July 26, 2009, Week in Review, 1. Bill Cosby and Alvin F. Poussaint. *Come On People: On the Path from Victims to Victors* (Nashville, TN: Thomas Nelson, 2007). John McWhorter, "Obama and the Black Elite," *Forbes*, January 20, 2009. http://www.forbes.com/2009/01/20/obama-inauguration-race-oped-cx_jm_0120mcwhorter_print.html. John McWhorter, *Winning the Race: Beyond the Crisis in Black America* (New York: Gotham, 2006). Andrew Romano, Aku Ammah-Tagoe, and Brian No, "Black in the Age of Obama," *Newsweek*, April 27, 2009; 42 Ibid., 45. Robert Siegel, "A New, 'Post-Racial' Political Era in America," *All Things Considered*, Washington, DC: National Public Radio, January 28, 2008. Juan Williams, "Obama's Color Line," *New York Times*, November 30, 2007, A23. Robert L. Woodson, Sr., "Obama and a Post-Racial America," *Washington Times*, April 12, 2008, A11.

7. While I do not engage these themes in this chapter, the right-wing impulse to cheer the emergence of a post-racial America should be distinguished from arguments by race theorists like William Julius Wilson, *The Declining Significance of Race: Blacks and Changing American Institutions* (Chicago: University of Chicago Press, 1980); Paul Gilroy, *Against Race: Imagining Political Culture Beyond the Color Line* (Cambridge: Harvard University Press, 2000); and Adolph Reed, Jr., "The Real Divide," in *After the Storm: Black Intellectuals Explore the Meaning of Hurricane Katrina*, ed. David Dante Troutt (New York: New, 2006), 63–70, who urge a broadening of the theoretical purview of race scholarship toward deeper engagements with questions of class and the promise of hetero-ethnic resistances in the era of globalization.

8. Craig Calhoun, "The Privatization of Risk," *Public Culture* 18 (2006): 257–63.

9. Cheryl I. Harris, "Review Essay: Whitewashing Race: Scapegoating Culture," *California Law Review* 94 (2006): 907–43.

10. Robin D. G. Kelley, "Untitled Essay," *Social Text* 42 (Spring 1995): 2.

11. Lizabeth Cohen, *A Consumers' Republic: The Politics of Mass Consumption in Postwar America* (New York: Alfred A. Knopf, 2003).

12. Paul R. Mullins, "Race, Racism and Archaeology," *World Archaeology* 38, 1 (2006): 61.

13. Cohen, *A Consumers' Republic*. Gary Cross, *An All-Consuming Century: Why Commercialism Won in Modern America* (New York: Columbia University Press, 2000). Mary Douglas and Baron Isherwood, *The World of Goods: Towards an Anthropology of Consumption* (New York: Routledge, 1996). John Kenneth Galbraith, *The Affluent Society* (Boston: Houghton Mifflin, 1958/1998).

14. Cohen, *A Consumers' Republic*, 89.

15. Lawrence B. Glickman, "Introduction: Born to Shop? Consumer History and American History," in *Consumer Society in American History: A Reader*, ed. Lawrence B. Glickman (Ithaca: Cornell University Press, 1999), 1–14.

16. Bobby M. Wilson, "Race in Commodity Exchange and Consumption: Separate But Equal," *Annals of the Association of American Geographers* 95, 3 (2005): 600.

17. Jason Chambers, "Equal in Every Way: African Americans, Consumption and Materialism from Reconstruction to the Civil Rights Movement," *Advertising and Society Review* 7, 1 (Spring 2006). Chambers reveals, further, that contemporary preferences among African Americans for brand-name products and chain stores are historically traced to coping strategies that many blacks adopted as a response to these discriminatory practices as a way to assure some measure of quality in the products and customer service they received.

18. Cohen, *A Consumers' Republic*, 403–4.

19. Monroe Friedman, *Consumer Boycotts: Effecting Change Through the Marketplace and the Media* (New York: Routledge, 1999). Meg Jacobs, *Pocketbook Politics: Economic Citizenship in Twentieth-Century America* (Princeton: Princeton University Press, 2005). Kathy M. Newman, *Radio Active: Advertising and Consumer Activism, 1935–1947* (Berkeley: University of California Press, 2004). Cedric J. Robinson, *Black Marxism: The Making of the Black Radical Tradition* (Chapel Hill: University of North Carolina Press, 2000). James B. Stewart, "Civil Rights and Organized Labor: The Case of the United Steelworkers of America, 1948–1970," in *African Americans in the U.S. Economy*, ed. Cecilia A. Conrad et al. (Lanham, MD: Rowman & Littlefield, 2005), 66–80. Robert E. Weems, Jr., *Desegregating the Dollar: African American Consumerism in the Twentieth Century* (New York: New York University Press, 1998). Wilson, "Race in Commodity Exchange and Consumption."

20. Earl Ofari Hutchison, "Black Capitalism: Self-Help or Self-Delusion?" in *African Americans in the U.S. Economy*, ed. Cecilia A. Conrad et al. (Lanham, MD: Rowman & Littlefield, 2005), 271–77. Manning Marable, "History of Black Capitalism," in *African Americans in the U.S. Economy*, ed. Cecilia A. Conrad et al. (Lanham, MD: Rowman & Littlefield, 2005), 231–36. Paul R. Mullins, *Race and Affluence: An Archaeology of African America and Consumer Culture* (New York: Kluwer Academic/Plenum Publishers, 1999). Kathy Peiss, "Making Up, Making Over: Cosmetics, Consumer Culture, and Women's Identity," in *The Sex of Things: Gender and Consumption in Historical Perspective*, ed. Victoria de Grazia (with Ellen Furlough) (Berkeley: University of California Press, 1996), 311–36. Wilson, "Race in Commodity Exchange and Consumption."

21. W. E. B. Du Bois, *Dusks of Dawn: An Essay Toward an Autobiography of a Race Concept* (New York: Harcourt, Brace, 1940), 208.

22. Wilson, "Race in Commodity Exchange and Consumption," 587.

23. Ibid., 593.

24. Ibid.

25. Chambers, "Equal in Every Way."

26. Frantz Fanon, *Black Skin, White Masks* (New York: Grove Press, 1967), 111.

27. Robert E. Weems, Jr., "Bling Bling and Other Recent Trends in African American Consumerism," in *African Americans in the U.S. Economy*, ed. Cecilia A. Conrad et al. (Lanham, MD: Rowman & Littlefield, 2005), 253.

28. Robert E. Weems, Jr., "Consumerism and the Construction of Black Female Identity in Twentieth-Century America," in *The Gender and Consumer Culture Reader*, ed. Jennifer Scanlon (New York: New York University Press, 2000), 166.

29. Chambers, "Equal in Every Way."

30. Ibid.

31. Michèle Lamont and Virág Molnár, "How Blacks Use Consumption to Shape Their Collective Identity: Evidence from Marketing Specialists," *Journal of Consumer Culture* 1, 1 (2001): 31–32.

32. Quoted in Chambers, "Equal in Every Way."

33. Quoted in George Lipsitz, "'Swing Low, Sweet Cadillac': White Supremacy, Antiblack Racism, and the New Historicism," *American Literary History* 7, 4 (Winter 1995): 700.

34. Grace Elizabeth Hale, *Making Whiteness: The Culture of Segregation in the South, 1890–1940* (New York: Vintage, 1999), 125.

35. Robert E. Weems, Jr., *Desegregating the Dollar: African American Consumerism in the Twentieth Century* (New York: New York University Press, 1998), 70–77.

36. Jeffrey M. Humphreys, "The Multicultural Economy," *Georgia Business and Economic Conditions* 67, 3 (Athens, GA: Selig Center for Economic Growth/University of Georgia, 2007). Target Market News, *Annual Report on the Buying Power of Black America* (Chicago: Target Market News Inc., 2007).

37. *African American Market in the U.S.* (New York: Packaged Facts, 2008). Humphreys, "The Multicultural Economy." Magazine Publishers of America, *African American/ Black Market Profile* (New York: Magazine Publishers of America Information Center, 2008). These statistics elide other notable trends, however, eclipsing abiding levels of economic stagnation and heightened levels of financial risk that African Americans uniquely confront in the current economy. For example, although recent years have witnessed unprecedented rates of black homeownership nationwide—from 42.3 percent in 1994 to 49.1 percent in 2004—the subprime mortgage crisis has taken its greatest toll on black and other non-white homeowners. Vikas Bajaj and Ford Fessenden, "The Subprime Landscape, from Detroit to Ithaca," *New York Times*, November 4, 2007, 16. Erin Durkin, "Minorities Hit Hard in Mortgage Crunch," *New York Daily News*, October 28, 2008, 6. Bob Tedeschi, "Subprime Loans' Wide Reach," *New York Times*, August 3, 2008, Real Estate, 10.

38. Pamela Danzinger, *Luxury Report 2006: Who Buys Luxury, What They Buy, Why They Buy* (Stevens, PA: Unity Marketing, 2006).

39. Roopali Mukherjee, "The Ghetto Fabulous Aesthetic in Contemporary Black Culture: Class and Consumption in the *Barbershop* Films," *Cultural Studies* 20, 6 (2006): 599–629.

40. As I have argued elsewhere, the pervasiveness of bling is also a sign of the extent to which what was once dangerous, and hence alluring, about "the street" and "the ghetto" has itself been co-opted into a market commodity. Mukherjee, "The Ghetto Fabulous Aesthetic in Contemporary Black Culture."

41. George E. Curry, "Walking Billboards," *Emerge* 9 (December 1997): 8.

42. Finlo Rohrer, "Taking the Shine Off Cristal," *BBC News Magazine*, June 8, 2006. http://news.bbc.co.uk/2/hi/uk_news/magazine/5056744.stm. Taking a page from historical consumer

rights movements, rapper and hip-hop mogul Jay-Z urged a general boycott of the *Cristal* brand in response to Rouzaud's comment, announcing that he would "no longer support any of [the company's] products through any of my various brands including *The 40/40 Club* nor in my personal life." "Jay-Z Boycotts Cristal Champagne," *BBC News Magazine,* June 19, 2006. http://news.bbc.co.uk/2/hi/entertainment/5086482.stm.

43. Mukherjee, "The Ghetto Fabulous Aesthetic in Contemporary Black Culture."

44. Néstor García Canclini, *Consumers and Citizens: Globalization and Multicultural Conflicts* Trans. George Yúdice (Minneapolis: University of Minnesota Press, 2001), 15.

45. Kanye West, "George Bush Doesn't Care About Black People," September 5, 2005. www.YouTube.com.

46. Kevin Fox Gotham, "Critical Theory and Katrina: Disaster, Spectacle and Immanent Critique," *City* 11, 1 (April 2007): 92. Cheryl I. Harris, "Review Essay," 910–11. Pew Research Center for the People and the Press, "Huge Racial Divide Over Katrina and its Consequences," September 8, 2005. http://people-press.org/reports/pdf/255.pdf.

47. In the wake of West's comments, a number of hip-hop performers joined in offering racial commentaries on the hurricane's underlying impact. The Legendary K.O., a hip-hop group from Houston, Texas, offered a remix of Kanye West's hit single "Gold Digger" that accused Bush of deliberate and racist neglect against African Americans. Rappers Georgia T1, David Banner from Mississippi, and new artists such as Rhymefest, produced songs addressing poverty and other social ills afflicting black communities in the South that were brought to new light in the storm's aftermath. And a number of independent films, likewise, focus on racial inequalities highlighted by the hurricane, including Spike Lee's 2006 *When the Levees Broke,* Jonathan Demme's 2007 *Right to Return: New Home Movies from the Lower 9th Ward,* and Tia Lessin and Carl Deal's 2008 *Trouble the Water.*

48. Clyde Adrian Woods, "Do You Know What It Means to Miss New Orleans? Katrina, Trap Economics, and the Rebirth of the Blues," *American Quarterly* 57, 4 (December 2005): 1005.

49. Jon Pareles, "An All-American Striver Keeps Things in Perspective," *New York Times,* November 4, 2005, E3.

50. Manning Marable, "History and Black Consciousness: The Political Culture of Black America," *Monthly Review* 47, 3 (July/August 1995): 88.

51. Alice Gavin, "Reading Katrina: Race, Space and an Unnatural Disaster," *New Political Science* 30, 3 (September 2008): 335–36.

52. Harris, "Review Essay," 953.

53. Zenia Kish, "'My FEMA People': Hip-Hop as Disaster Recovery in the Katrina Diaspora," *American Quarterly* (2009): 672.

54. Michel Foucault, *The History of Sexuality: Volume I.* Trans. Robert Hurley (New York: Vintage, 1978/1990). David Theo Goldberg, *The Racial State* (Malden, MA: Blackwell, 2002). Zenia Kish, "'My FEMA People,'" 678.

55. Kevin Fox Gotham, "Critical Theory and Katrina," 81–99. Rodney D. Green, Beverly Wright, and Tiffany Hamelin, "Strategies for Recovery from Katrina: Corporate Capitalism, NGOs, Racism, and Class," paper presented at the meetings of the National Economic Association, 2008.

56. Wendy Brown, *States of Injury: Power and Freedom in Late Modernity* (Princeton: Princeton University Press, 1995), 66.

57. Ibid., 26–27, 69.

IV Racialized Complexities and Neocolonialism

10 The Rhythm of Ambition

Power Temporalities and the Production of the Call Center
Agent in Documentary Film and Reality Television

Aimee Carrillo Rowe, Sheena Malhotra, and Kimberlee Pérez

"Welcome to customer care," "Welcome to customer care," Indian call center agents sound out each syllable, carefully articulating their professional U.S.
American accents to greet their phone customers. The PBS WideAngle film,
1-800-INDIA,[1] introduces the Western viewer, perhaps for the first time through
a visual medium, to the Indian worker at the other end of the line. The verbal
"Welcome" (overlayed by a disembodied voice-over) is accompanied by a bar-
rage of disparate images: headphone-wearing Indian agents sitting in sleek office
cubicles nodding while conversing; cycle-rickshaw drivers, pedestrians, scooter
riders, vendors all peopling a crowded, narrow street market; women in brightly
colored saris passing before the camera, their heads covered. "In this dusty suburb of India's capital, New Delhi," a narrator's voice informs us, "old traditions are
colliding with new opportunities."[2]

This chapter orients the Western reader to the politics of recognition through
which the figure of the Indian call center agent is rendered intelligible in the West
through the truth-telling genre of documentary film. We chart the formation of
this highly mediated call center figure through a study of competing discourses
of time and space, nation and globalization, and race, gender, and heterosexuality. We read popular documentaries—which produce and imagine relations of
race, gender, and heterosexuality through power temporalities—through and
against one another: the figure of the Indian woman comes to stand in for "progress." And, heterosexuality is the condition of possibility for imagining a (trans)
national future and a hinge that sutures previous colonial discourses to current
imperial objectives. This occurs while white masculinity serves as a temporal
point of arrival, or a telos of imagined progress. Thus, in this chapter, we demonstrate how documentaries manage U.S. anxieties about globalization and outsourcing evoked by narratives about the call center industry. The figure of the
Indian call center agent is depicted as modernizing (albeit safely at a slower pace
than the U.S. viewer) by learning practices that cultivate identification with a
white U.S. male gaze.

When the Indian outsourcing call center industry (servicing U.S. consumers) began in the late 1990s, the identity of the call center agents was a well-kept

secret. Secrecy masqueraded as operational efficiency: accents were "neutralized," long Indian names gave way to "Johns" and "Janes," and, most importantly, those in the West never *saw* who was doing their work "over there." When *NOW with Bill Moyers* aired the first television news magazine segment on outsourcing in August 2003, the entire industry (and how Western viewers would imagine it) would be radically transformed.[3] The emergence of the call center agent as spectacle marked a shift in the politics of recognition. The body of the call center agent served as a marker of the collapse of time and space produced by globalization, and the anticipated "truth" behind one of global capital's smokescreens was revealed: outsourcing. From this moment forward, the call center agent would become a heavily mediated figure, rendered intelligible in the West through multiple global flows of capital and mediated images, of emerging notions of worker and consumer, and of an unprecedented relationship of time and space, all of which would fall heavily upon their bodies constructed as "global players."

Outsourcing discourse is bound up in the American reliance on, and anxieties about, globalization. Mediated representations about the rising Indian middle-class worker, coupled with stories of India as a global player, come together to construct India as a threat to the United States' global standing and economic security. Additionally, the post–9/11 historical context amplifies anxieties surrounding the Orientalization of the problem the United States faces in the global marketplace. For example, the *NOW* segment framed and produced the politics of outsourcing through semiotic racism (couched in and inextricable from its broadcast on Labor Day), which asserts U.S. nationalism and belonging through its "threatened" labor force.[4]

The topic of Indian call centers saturated public discourse, reaching remarkable levels of attention during the 2004 and 2008 presidential debates. Both Democrats and Republicans appealed to the "American worker" by denouncing the outsourcing of "Americans jobs." This rhetoric centered on the fear that U.S. America would lose jobs, purchasing power, and global standing.[5] These debates marked a particular historical shift between globalizing forces and nation-state politics. Initially, the discussion focused on overseas and cross-border lower-end manufacturing jobs, but this gave way to a concern with the exportation of more sought-after, middle-class, service-sector, and high-tech "white-collar" jobs. These rhetorics betrayed anxieties about downsizing and diminishment resulting from the United States' increasing dependence: a relationship of dependency that would require industries to produce efficiencies of time and space.

In fact, globalization's developments in telecommunications technologies enable an increasingly flexible relationship between multinational corporations and workers by accelerating communications, overcoming distances, and leveling differences. In doing so, American workers could imagine themselves over and against their foreign counterparts through an Orientalist gaze that was revitalized after 9/11. These anxieties, then, may be understood as resulting from newly converging and conflicting temporalities[6] that effectively reorganize space in the service of free market neoliberalism in ways that both threaten and bolster the U.S. nation-state and its attendant imperialisms.[7]

Power geometry, Doreen Massey explains, allows us to conceptualize late capitalism's compression of time and space through its differentiated effects on social groups and individuals, each of whom are "placed in very distinct ways in relation to these flows and interconnections."[8] And, if space must be differentially understood, so too must time be understood, as well as the work of compressing or expanding it. Indeed, we would suggest that temporal disparities, which enable the uneven flow of information services consolidated within the call center industry, constitute disparate *power temporalities*. By this we mean not only the distinct ways in which groups and individuals are placed in relation to emerging spatial relations, but also increasingly disparate global temporalities. What kinds of temporal relations generate sites of affinity and difference within shared geographical space? How does the globalization of the service industry generate time pressures on differently situated global subjects? And, how are those emergent temporalities unevenly distributed, so that some subjects gain time at the expense of others?

To approach these issues of different and uneven temporalities and newly situated global subjectivities, this chapter traces the power temporalities at work in visually mediated discourses produced from both U.S. and Indian perspectives between 2003 and 2007. The mediated discourses contribute to U.S. perceptions of the call center industry, immersing viewers in their complex operations and introducing them to an emerging global citizenry. Here, we read and analyzed documentary films, news magazines, and a reality TV show, which represent recurrent themes and framings of outsourcing across representations.[9]

Two news magazines we examined were among the first to frame outsourcing for the U.S. public: these include episodes of *NOW: With Bill Moyers* and *60 Minutes*' "Out of India." In *The Other Side of Outsourcing*, journalist Thomas Friedman provides extensive commentary on the outsourcing debate. Friedman's documentary focuses on the global structures that shape the lives of Indian call center agents and their families in the wake of this burgeoning industry. PBS WideAngles' *1-800-INDIA* explores gender issues surrounding the empowerment of four women facing Westernizing processes working in one of India's first call centers, Geckis. *30 Days*' "Outsourcing" episode follows a U.S. American worker, Chris, who loses his job to outsourcing and goes to India to live and work with call center agents at "24/7," one of the giant call centers in Bangalore. Finally, Ashim Ahluwalia's *John and Jane Toll Free*, produced in India and aired on HBO in the United States, focuses on the ways the industry directly affects workers' lives, relations, dreams, and imaginaries.[10] These documentaries take a U.S. American vantage point and assume a national identity and perspective. The films attest to the "stubborn parochialism" of the documentary form,[11] while recasting the global primarily *through* the national. In the following sections we tease out the distinctions and convergences among these texts and the power temporalities that produce Western understanding and reception of the call center industry.

"Money, Money, Money, Money": Nation, Transnation, and Neoliberalism's Spatialized Logics

With offshore outsourcing, you have winners and losers in India; before offshore outsourcing, you only had losers.

—*1-800-INDIA*

In this section our rhetorical analysis defines the notion of the checkering of space.[12] Each of the texts we consider allows the viewer to travel between first and third world zones in India. Each depicts call center agents traveling back and forth between slums and skyscrapers in the course of daily life. While the call center agent's upward global mobility and ambition is presented as a threat to U.S. workers and their jobs, we argue that the visual emphasis on the checkered space in India functions to alleviate that threat by reassuring the viewer that India's progress (both spatially and relationally) remains temporally behind the United States. The juxtaposition of poverty in such close proximity to affluence places the viewer in an authority position to judge the viability of the industry and India's rising middle class: the hyper-visibility of slums signifies a recurrent colonialist trope of backwardness and lack of civilization and produces a contrast between slums and modern buildings that threaten to overtake them.

The rationale that the *60 Minutes* "Outsourcing" gives for the U.S. dependence on outsourcing is "Money, money, money, and money." This tautological claim provides the show an entry point for viewers to understand the politics of global employment and migration, and migration's shifting spatial and temporal terrain, both of which underwrite contemporary representations of outsourcing. At stake for the U.S. American viewer are the competing interests of production and consumption as they relate to the worker-consumer. "It may have cost hundreds of thousands of American jobs," the *60 Minutes* male voice-over explains, "but it's made American products more affordable." Likewise, *NOW with Bill Moyers* contends that the viewer learns that three million middle-class jobs will be lost in the United States over the next 15 years to students in India. The films expose the viewer to the dangerous possibility that India is overcoming the time-space divide that separates India from America. Thus, the tautological claim that "money" is why the United States depends on outsourced labor interpellates the viewers, aligning them with neoliberal logics and American exceptionalism: the market and the U.S. viewer are allied in determining the viability of the call center agent as neoliberal citizen, which, in turn, determines the extent to which Indians might become "Americans."

The exportation of "America," articulated as an evolution of labor and consumption practices in India, marks the checkered development of transnational America produced within documentary film. As the narrator in *1-800-INDIA* observes, "Shopping malls, previously unknown in India, are Gurgaon's temples to this new prosperity. And, the cash registers are ringing up the purchases of the industry's young affluent employees." The narrator's voice is heard over images of shopping malls with shiny floors and neon signs and young women toting large purses and browsing racks of merchandise. The figure of the call center agent, herself a consumer, is thus sutured into this first-world zone within India. As Pramod Bhasin, CEO of Geckis, explains to the viewer in *1-800-INDIA*, "These are young people, they're 22 to 25. They're earning often more than their parents did. And, these people are spending money. Unlike many other older employees who will necessarily save, this crowd goes out and spends everything it can." The young generation of call center agents is marked by their consumerism and the labor that enables it against the previous generation of the Indian laboring class. India is depicted through this generational divide, a temporal fracturing giving rise to a (trans)national identity that is rendered intelligible to American viewers through the shared cultural and classed terrain of consumption.

Indeed, the generational divide Bhasin references recursively marks a temporal distinction between old and new India: one aligned with the needs of transnational capital, the logics of neoliberalism, and the sensibilities of American consumerism; the other aligned with an outmoded economic practice that works against the needs of capitalism. Thus, the viewer is invited to discern between two Indias, both spatially distanced ("half way around the globe"), but one aligned with U.S. neoliberal and consumerist values. These alignments emerge through depictions of modern spaces and subjects marked by class privilege, youth, and hard work. The filmic techniques that move through spaces of poverty and wealth position the viewers as visual tourists of far-away places (that is, temporally and spatially distanced), even as they overcome that distance, both by bringing them into American living rooms and by landing on those far-away sites that resonate with American time/space. The documentary format, then, is particularly well equipped to wedge open time/space discontinuities, reassuring and confirming the viewers' privilege to validate the worth of the contemporary Indian worker-consumer.[13]

Osmond, one of the call center agents depicted in *John and Jane Toll-Free*, speaks directly to the camera, engaging the viewer in an uneasy conversation about the production of the transnational Americanized Indian. The film marks the contradictions and impossibilities that saturate the formation of his desire, imaginatively directed toward America, but spatially and temporally contained within India and his labor conditions as a call center worker. There are images of Osmond moving around his cramped, paint-chipped apartment, ardently listening to self-help tapes, as the camera follows him around. He hangs up clothes to dry, makes himself a breakfast of eggs and bacon, hums an Elvis Presley song, and optimistically talks about his dream of becoming a billionaire. His voice-over unfolds above a series of images that symbolize U.S. class privilege: wide freeways flowing with fast-moving cars, a Hollywood sign, upscale hotels, and parks. Osmond speaks with a steady confidence:

> So I do picturize myself as a billionaire. And that's very strong. But yes, you have to be [pause] in America. Indians, you know? Certain parts of India, they're not quite civilized. America has always been ahead of all the nations. Anyone and everyone who goes to the States [pause] becomes rich. That has registered in my mind.

Inanimate objects play a significant role in the film. Viewers are to understand the film through the strategic use of these objects, which position viewers inside of Osmond's home as a "participant in his visual coercion," as Silverman would describe it. "By privileging the point of view of an inanimate object," Silverman writes, this filmic technique makes the viewer "acutely aware of . . . the absent one—i.e. of the speaking subject." This framing "remains unmediated, unsoftened by the intervention of a human gaze"; it does not, however, "erase our perception of the cinematic apparatus," but rather "exploits it, playing on the viewing subject's own paranoia and guilt."[14] Thus, the viewer becomes implicated in Osmond's impossible desires through her/his encounter with the limits of transnational America. The ambition Osmond expresses of a bright future that he "*will* acquire," and the notion that the riches they imply are available to "everyone and anyone who goes to the States," could potentially produce a xenophobic anxiety in viewers already worried about immigrants coming to the United States.

Read intertextually, the object of Osmond's (self)hatred—Indian poverty—is a necessary condition of the power relations that constitute the outsourcing equation, which becomes a source of anxiety that must be negotiated within these texts. India is portrayed as a deeply divided economic zone, at once approximating America in its modernity and consumerism, and yet always also, and reassuringly, on the brink of chaos and collapse. *60 Minutes* features a narrator's voice-over over images of poverty, traffic, and chaos:

> India epitomizes the new global economy. A country that often looks on the edge of collapse, a background of grinding poverty, visually a mess, and yet [here the images

> switch to U.S.-style, corporate spaces], whether you know it or not, when you call
> Delta Airlines, American Express, Sprint, Citibank, IBM or Hewlett Packard technical
> support numbers, chances are, you'll be talking to an Indian.

The voice-over narrates the specter of India's postdevelopmentalist geography, placed over visual evidence of the uneasy commingling of first world and third world zones through the legible markers of American and capitalist normativity (Delta, American Express, Sprint) at the edge of markers of third world "chaos." India's zones of graduated sovereignty, in which transnational corporations generate spaces of hyper-capital alongside zones of neglect by both capital and the state, underscore the ambivalent quality of transnational America's mimetic function. If graduated sovereignty theorizes the spatialization of (extra)territorial national terrains, the viewer's access to the postdevelopmentalist spectacle of the call center industry's proximity to the Indian slum reasserts American supremacy by simultaneously exposing India both as an economic success (at the very sites of its capitulation to transnational capitalism) and as an economic failure in the slums. These are, in turn, the economic conditions and limited possibilities for its success. This failure registers as a sign of moral degradation assigned to the backward Indian nation, even though neoliberalism's graduated sovereignty relies upon "diverse categories of human capital" that generate "patterns of noncontiguous, differently administered spaces."[15] As the viewer is invited to tour these checkered zones of uneven development visually, s/he also tours a range of affectively charged temporal arrangements that s/he is empowered to assess, due to her/his secure temporal placement in the now and spatial location in the here. Thus, the audience gains control over the uneven formation of neoliberalism's noncontiguous spaces through the production of America's normative temporal placement. This position empowers the viewer to assess the viability of India's development from the point of arrival toward which that development narrative is directed.

"Geography Is History": Neoliberalism's Power Temporalities

> By day, the agents—as they're called—are dutiful Indian sons and daughters. By
> night, they take on phone names such as Sean, Nancy, Ricardo and Celine so they
> can sound like the girl or boy next door.
> —*60 Minutes*, Out of India

In this section, we attend to the ways power temporalities are constructed in, and enacted through, documentary films. The texts reassert the tradition/modernity temporal calculation in which the United States stands in for India's future, which is always and necessarily just beyond the reach of India. This is embodied in the ambitious, hard-working body of the call center agent. The documentary films on

Indian call centers work through an ambivalent convergence of colonial mimicry with emerging global temporalities and spatial relations.[16] The Indian call center agent emerges as a figure of colonial mimicry, articulated through temporal and spatial shifting: by day, a dutiful son or daughter; by night, the "girl or boy next door." That the agent is figured simultaneously as spatially and temporally distant *and* immediate marks the ambivalence. The immediacy that developments in global technologies make possible between such disparate geographical locations and temporalities (brought into viewers' living rooms through documentary film) creates social conditions in which the politics of passing take place.[17]

This time/space displacement compels us to rethink Homi Bhabha's claim that "the visibility of mimicry is always produced at the site of interdiction."[18] Here, it is the anxiety that the American consumer might not *know* to whom s/he is speaking: Thus, the visuality of the popular discourse serves to render the call center agent intelligible by creating a visual spectacle of the agent's formerly unseen body, placed ambiguously within ambivalent time/space: here *and* there, now *and* then. The authoritative voice of the journalist is coupled with the visual spectacle to accomplish narrative temporalization: while the "dutiful son or daughter" and the "boy or girl next door" both establish a familial relation of the laboring youth, "duty" is a concept linked with tradition and India while "next door" is an American colloquialism. The fracture of the Indian agents' familial and labor identities functions to place them in a liminal temporality that is neither fully here nor there. Thus, the documentary film exploits the agents' body to reestablish the politics of passing within a familiar visual register.

"Geography is history," explains Raman Roy in *60 Minutes*. Roy is considered the "father of Indian outsourcing," who is favorably compared to Bill Gates as one of the most significant global players of our time. With this bold claim, he names the contemporary collusion of time and space through the temporal depiction of space within the logic of a linear progress narrative. Roy's depiction resonates with Bauman's "liquid" conception of time, which emerges over and against the "solid" quality of space within modernity:

> In modernity, time has *history*, it has history because of the perpetually expanding "carrying capacity" of time—the lengthening of the stretches of space which units of time allow to "pass," "cross," "cover"—or *conquer*. Time acquires history once the speed of movement through space (unlike the eminently inflexible space, which cannot be stretched and would not shrink) becomes a matter of human ingenuity, imagination, and resourcefulness.[19]

Thus, for Bauman, technology generates time's "carrying capacity" to loosen its correspondence to space, ushering in a whole host of power relations marked by their "post-Panoptical" quality. This means that power has become extraterritorial: that rulers and ruled are no longer spatially bound to one another, but rather that rulers may escape into "sheer inaccessibility."[20] As with any historical accounting, the author narratively temporalizes and controls the direction of the story through his/her rhetoric. The Indian claim that "geography is history" destabilizes the temporal placement of India in the past as Indian and American modernities commingle, as time overcomes space. The films center the U.S. customer's temporal and spatial needs and, by extension, reassure the viewer through the assertion of power temporalities.

Thomas Friedman's documentary takes the audience into the video conferencing room of a call center, Infosys, where another high-ranking executive describes technology's capacity to overcome distance. He explains that he has the world at his fingertips through the 40 digital screens, while the camera reveals the control room that connects him to counterparts and clients all over the globe. The United States and other first world countries become spatially unbounded,[21] extending their tentacles into outsourcing service sectors at "half the cost" of conducting business "at home." According to *60 Minutes*, the Indian corporate elite gain a renewed sense of national identity that becomes articulated *through* transnational labor: "There is a huge amount of nationalistic pride," Roy claims. "Because we want to show that as a work force, as a labor pool, we are equivalent to, if not better than, anybody else. Anywhere in the world." Indian national identity becomes filtered through the nation's capacity to serve transnational capitalist interests by providing the immediacy of well-trained agents. The call center agents live temporally inverted lives, as "dutiful sons and daughters" by day and the "boy or girl next door" to U.S. consumers by night. "India" remains spatially and temporally tied to its territorial boundaries, even as it gains a competitive edge through the subordinated status of its workers. This subordination is a condition of possibility for the nation to emerge on the global stage within the hierarchy of simultaneous, yet uneven, modernities. The documentary film *shows* the viewer how technology eradicates space, while the Indian bodies conduct this labor. By doing so, the films reinscribe the politics of passing and the threat of commingling American and Indian modernities within a familiar, visual register.

"It's Like 1950s America": Gender, Heterosexuality, and Neoliberal Citizenship

Outsourcing impacts this family in more than one way. In America we used to have the husband going to work and the wife staying home. Indians right now are totally 1950s America. And Soni is that housewife–working woman turnaround that America went through in the '70s and '80s.
—Chris, *30 Days*

The previous sections demonstrate the ways in which Indian call center agents pose a certain, if distant, threat to U.S. workers. At the same time, outsourcing calibrates a particular acceleration of the time-space collapse. Through paternal narrative depictions that figure white male narrators (voice-over or authoritative presences) that secure the United States as the teleological point of arrival and mimicry, here power temporalities secure the pathway to India's development through the production of neoliberal subjects shaped through a gendered and heterosexed framework. The Indian female call center agent (and by extension India) is presented as a feminized figure in need of a white male (U.S.) savior to rescue her from both sexism and spatio-temporal backwardness in service of animating neoliberal progress. In this section, we examine how the embodied spectacle of Indian femininity and the bodily marking and rendering invisible of white masculinity converge with those discourses of heterosexuality that mediate empire's imperatives.

Embodied in the white male figures featured in each documentary[22]—Chris in *30 Days*, Thomas Friedman in *Outsourcing*, or the anonymous male voice featured in *1-800-INDIA*—U.S. America escapes its bodily and temporal contours over and against the gendered and racialized specificities of the Indian woman. Her intelligibility through heterosexuality to the Western viewer as "like us" mediates her Westernization.[23] The white male figures, who remain detached and rational, and whose action and interpretations often occur off-screen, help viewers overcome the anxiety they experience upon encountering both the form of the image (limited as it is through the camera) and the time-space upheavals addressed through the content of the film.

In this sense, the films help U.S. American audiences to apprehend their relationship to the call center industry affectively through the gendered and heterosexed figure of the Indian woman, whose relationship to the viewer is, in turn, mediated through her relationship to the white male gaze that apprehends her. Because the white male figure serves to suture the viewer to the film's narrative within the normative moment of the present, the progress narrative that mediates the relationship between this figure and the Indian woman temporally orients the audience in relation to her.

In the case of *30 Days*, the gendered dynamic of an Indian traditional heterosexual family is framed against the subtext of Chris's heterosexual family building. Chris's family is presumed to be the normative standard by the film's structure. The show begins and ends with Chris having dinner with his girlfriend, newborn son, and parents, which serves as a metonymy that enables modern heterosexual audiences in the United States (especially middle-class whites) to identify with him and to see his interpretations of life as normative. The erasure of Chris's body at key moments in the film is significant, because it allows us to re-trace the normalization of white heterosexual American-ness in Chris's role in the film. His movement in and out of the screen sutures the viewer into the action in his place, positioning Chris and the viewer (whose gaze his figure frames) as place-holders for modernity. The viewer can then decode the actions, intentions, and capacity for modernity of the Indian woman, who vacillates between tradition and modernity.

30 Days locates its tradition/modernity conflict in the relationship between Chris and his Indian host family, whose imperatives of Indian heterosexual family building collide with those who embrace transnational "capitalism and democracy." Chris is hosted by a young couple, Soni and Ravi, in their joint family home, a space Chris associates with tradition as distinct from the public sphere, which he associates with modernity: "When you go out, you're entering Americanized India, and when you enter the door, you're entering old India," Chris explains over scenes of a pooja ceremony featuring Soni and other women dressed in heavy saris, dancing around the living room for their male audience. Chris's description of the couple's home recalls Partha Chatterjee's insights into Indian anti-colonial nationalism; that is, the feminized "inner sphere" serves as the repository of India's refusal to take up fully the imperatives of Western nation-building. This symbolizes India's spiritual superiority over the West. By contrast, Westernized nation-building takes place in the realm of the "outer sphere" of public life.

Soni's "liberation," marked through her increasing capacity to move between the domestic and public spheres, serves as *30 Days'* primary narrative device to join and distinguish the disparate temporalities and spatialities at stake in the film. These temporal and spatial logics become localized on the contested site of Soni's body, as it moves between the public and private dimensions of the international division of labor.

As the men eat, Chris asks Soni if she prefers working inside or outside of the home; she admits that she likes to work outside of the house, but that she cannot because she cannot "manage such a big family and work outside." Ravi, decoding the critique within Chris's questioning, interrupts, explaining:

> When you have this kind of arranged marriage, you know that your wife [a twang of "Oriental" music begins] is going to come into your home. And she's gonna take care of the rest of the family. It's not an obligation actually, but you do that because that's how it has followed.

This domestic scene abruptly transitions into a voice-over, which orients the viewer to "India" through a temporal placement that moves from colonialism to neo-imperialism: "India's rich culture dates back tens of thousands of years," the *30 Days* narrator explains,

> But in the mid-1800s, India was colonized by the British, and all government business was conducted in English and today India has the third most English speakers in the

> world behind the United States and the United Kingdom. Although a lot of Indians
> speak English, if they want to sell products to Americans, they're gonna need to
> hone their accents.

This sequence underscores how gendered heterosexuality serves to bridge disparate temporalities in order to resuscitate colonialism's gendered and racialized rescue narrative for the contemporary moment of empire. Here, the local and intimate sphere of Soni and Ravi's home is mapped onto a condensed progress narrative spanning "tens of thousands of years," beginning with "India's rich culture" and moving toward a telos of transnational America in which "honing their accents" and "selling products to Americans" become the emphasized imperatives of nation and empire. The sequence positions Soni as the implicit object of this "honing" as her expressed desire to be released from the domestic to the public sphere becomes metonymic of the imperial progress narrative (from India's "rich" tradition to British colonization to U.S. and U.K. neo-imperialism) the narrator provides. The twang of music that underwrites Ravi's speech, coupled with the flow of the sequence from the home to the world, then to now, renders colonialism's trace palpable within empire, affixing the heteropatriarchal domestic spectacle to tradition, enabling Chris (and the viewer) to occupy modern time. The film recapitulates the economies of neoliberalism, affixing them seamlessly to former colonialism through the relations of ruling affirmed within a heterosexual frame.

Thomas Friedman serves a similar rhetorical function to Chris in *The Other Side of Outsourcing* as the embodiment of white heterosexual masculinity, providing the viewer with a normative point of entry through which to adjudicate India's progress through the gendered narrative of Indian women's Westernization. In this film, time gets mapped through the recurring theme of the "generation gap" arising through the class and cultural distinctions between the current generation, Westernized by their call center employment, and their parents, who invariably hold firmly to traditional Indian culture. This temporal narrative is also heterosexed through gendered relational tropes—dating and marriage, family duty and loyalty, spiritual purity and loose morals—locating the impact of call center work at the disjunctures between the increasingly Westernized public sphere and the shifting gender politics in the domestic sphere. Friedman tempers this generational tension, calling for a balance between these time/space contestations, imploring the youth to "balance new and old" by "taking the best of both worlds." This move positions Friedman, and by extension the viewer, as the arbiter not only between contested generations, but also the temporalities and (trans)national identities at stake as American multiculturalism becomes the fraught meeting ground for disparate temporal identifications. Indeed, his call for "balance" between the old and the new resonates with Grewal's insights into the global circulation of the American dream, which makes possible multiple and fragmented Indian identities as immigrant, Indian, ethnic, and American.

Because American multiculturalism is linked both to consumer culture and the production of American exceptionalism, Friedman's call for tolerance generates a framework for a transnational America in India. It creates an imperative for old and new India to tolerate one another, framing this contested temporal (trans) national project through a developmental frame that finds its telos in America, as a "civilizational discourse that identifies both tolerance and the tolerable with the West."[24] The scenes of generational and gendered contestation are placed in the private sphere and figured through the bodies of Indian women, whose meanings are decoded through Friedman's gaze, liberal American consciousness, and his authorized commentary.

Conclusion: Power Temporalities and Globalization

This chapter examines U.S. American outsourcing discourse as it is framed in popular documentary films to trace the contours of time, space, race, gender, and heterosexuality. These principles organize contemporary configurations of nation and transnation, empire, and neoliberalism. Within this sphere of representation, Indian national identity emerges alongside of and inseparable from transnational America, where "America" and "India" may be understood as simultaneously national and transnational discursive formations. This work extends recent theorization of globalization by adding an understanding of the way nation and transnation are mediated through temporal logics that naturalize U.S. American hegemony within contemporary geopolitics. Specifically, we explore the rhetorical forms through which the call center industry becomes intelligible within documentary films. The films suggest a space/time convergence between postdevelopmentalism's power geometries, which are inseparable from the power temporalities that organize these representations of the Indian call center industry. Quite broadly this suggests that studies of globalization may be productively extended through increased attention to representational practices that bind, structure, and enable capitalism's global reach.

Our efforts here show how time functions in documentary formats by inviting U.S. American viewers to see the call center agent as a potential global/American subject through a frame of temporal subordination. It reinforces viewers' investments simultaneously in the spread of global capitalism and American supremacy, which is a highly cultivated manifestation of it. Furthermore, the audience is drawn into the call center drama through the figures of a white male authority, which provide the telos toward which the Indian woman mimetically strives. Thus, the films not only orient viewers spatially, but position the audience temporally within the present, inviting them to gaze *back* in time at the call center agent.

These time/space forces are configured through raced and gendered heteronormativity, which circulates previous tropes of white masculinity and Indian femininity to conjoin disparate temporal registers of Indian imperial rule. If the white male figure functions as a telos in transnational America's progress narrative, the figure of the Indian woman marks India's movement toward that telos that is America. This orientation provides the ground on which heterosexual temporal struggles are staged through the relational positioning of the Indian woman: her responsibilities to keeping a home or capacity to work outside of the home, to date or build family within an arranged marriage, and to live in extended family homes or in apartments.

The white male figure, in turn, is rendered intelligible through the project of nuclear, heterosexual family building as his masculinity is domesticated and rendered sympathetic through his associations with these projects of nation- and empire-building. Thus, heteronormativity serves as the pivot around which disparate temporalities are conjoined: British imperialism is evoked as the precursor to American neo-imperialism through the well-worn narrative of "white men saving brown women from brown men."[25] As such, heterosexuality provides leverage for the American viewer to adjudicate the Indian woman's capacity for neoliberal, global, and American citizenship, providing the moral authority of the gaze that decodes her social position through the shared, although temporally distinct, relational terrain of heterosexual intimacies.

NOTES

The authors wish to thank individuals and institutions that have supported this chapter and the larger project, Answer the Call: Suspended Mobilities in Indian Call Centers, from which this chapter is culled. In particular, we thank the University of Iowa Obermann Interdisciplinary Research Center, the Center for Ethnic Studies and the Arts (CESA), the Project on the Rhetoric of Inquiry (POROI), the South Asian Studies Program (SASP), and the College of Humanities at California State University, Northridge, for their support of our project. We are especially grateful to Naomi Greyser, Daniel Gross, Meena Kandhewal, CESA faculty (Corey Creekmur, Deborah Whaley, Miriam Thaggert), and POROI faculty (Gigi Durham, David Depew, Russell Valentino, Les Margolin) who provided careful readings and insightful feedback on earlier versions of this chapter.

1. Safina Uberoi (Director), *1-800-INDIA* (A. Carter (Producer). USA: PBS WideAngle). Aired on August 15, 2006: PBS.

2. Ibid.

3. Thomas L. Friedman (Reporter), *The Other Side of Outsourcing*. (Thomas L. Friedman Reporting [Television broadcast]. Silverspring, MD: Discovery Communications Inc., 2004).

4. Bill Moyers, *NOW with Bill Moyers* (produced by Brenda Breslauer; Correspondent Keith Brown. Aired on August 29, 2003: PBS).

5. The rhetorical force of these debates from multiple political platforms functioned ironically in that they located the "problem" of outsourcing U.S. jobs elsewhere while simultaneously downplaying the heavy reliance on foreign labor in the United States.

6. See David Harvey, *The Condition of Postmodernity: An Enquiry into the Origins of Cultural Change* (Malden, MA: Blackwell, 1990) and Aiwha Ong, *Flexible Citizenship: The Cultural Logics of Transnationality* (Durham, NC: Duke University Press, 1999) for analyses of the "flexible" quality of late capital. Harvey argues that in the wake of Fordism's spatially bound relationship to production, flexible accumulation generates divisions among spatially disparate laboring classes as global capital's ability to move challenges traditional forms of resistance such as organizing labor (*The Condition of Postmodernity*, 147). Flexible accumulation works through a fluid relationship among labor processes and markets, products and patterns of consumption, enabling newly globalized sectors of production that is constitutive of the time-space compression. Ong examines this kind of global flexibility in relation to transnational subject formation (*Flexible Citizenship*). Her notion of "flexible citizenship" refers to the transnational practices and imaginaries of the "nomadic subject" (e.g., the Chinese citizen who holds multiple passports) to refute the notion that transnationalism does not displace nation-states but rather exists in complex relationships to them. This chapter extends these arguments in two ways. First, while both Harvey and Ong attend to the spatial components that enable this flexibility, they do not tease out the complexities of its temporalities. A second and related point is that by attending to the power temporalities through which contemporary flexible accumulation unevenly distributes and manages modern time, our chapter explores the disparate power relations at stake in broad claims of globalization's time-space compression.

7. Neoliberalism is a form of economic organization favoring a "free market" form of economic organization—one suspicious of government control. This economic form gained traction under the Reagan administration, in conjunction with the Thatcherite rule in Britain. Its practice combines the rollback of government services and spending with the strategic opening of developing markets in ways that tend to benefit wealthy nations at the expense of poorer nations through global agencies such as the World Bank and the IMF and policies such as "strategic adjustment lending"; see Walden Bello, *Dark Victory: The United States and Global Poverty* (Oakland, CA: Food First, 1999). Aihwa Ong underscores the ways neoliberalism reconfigures the relationship among governing, sovereignty, and territoriality (*Neoliberalism as Exception: Mutations in Citizenship and Sovereignty* [Durham, NC: Duke University Press, 2006]). "Neoliberalism can be conceived as an economic doctrine in negative relation to state power," Ong writes, "but it's also a new relationship between government and knowledge through which governing activities are recast as non political and non ideological problems in need of technical solutions" (*Neoliberalism as Exception*, 3). For our purposes, we attend to the ways in which neoliberalism, as a *representational practice* constituted through outsourcing documentary, reconfigures the relationship between the U.S. American imaginary of its global hegemony and the politics of territoriality that are destabilized by outsourcing.

8. See Doreen Massey, *For Space* (Thousand Oaks, CA: Sage, 2005).

9. Between 2003 and 2007, numerous documentaries, TV segments, feature films, and TV serials addressed and contributed to the outsourcing discussion in the United States. Space limitations here lead us to consider those with wide circulation through public and cable TV broadcasting.

10. This text departs from the others in its postmodern aesthetic and its critical politics, even as its uptake in the United States compels us to excavate the politics of its reception. See Lata Mani, "Multiple Mediations: Feminist Scholarship in the Age of Multinational Reception" (*Feminist Review* 35 [Summer 1990]: 24–41).

11. In *Realer than Real: Global Directions in Documentary* (Austin: University of Texas Press, 2006), 9, David Hogarth argues that the documentary's attachment to public service values tends to make it a stubbornly place-bound genre, a quality that tends to work against the "post-national" formation of television more broadly. And yet documentaries are increasingly "produced and exchanged for profit within and across borders," and so may be regarded as a "transnational commodity" (8). Worldwide documentary channels, such as the Discovery network (which distributes the Friedman video), may function as "duty" offerings (ibid., 9). And yet, the Friedman production was well-funded and circulated; the PBS film *1-800-INDIA* funded and relied upon a female director to get the "gendered" angle on the call center industry; *30 Days* is an FX-funded production; and *John and Jane* was a shoe-string, Indian production that now finds global and U.S. circulation through film festivals and HBO distribution. These components of the films' production and circulation, may be read with and against their U.S.-centered framing to suggest that while the genre goes global, it also remains bound to the domestic. That is, the global doesn't displace the national but merely recirculates it on a global scale. Indeed, our analysis suggests that these films fold the globalization of capital and the formation of neoliberal subjectivity into U.S. national identity.

12. Aihwa Ong's notion of "postdevelopmentalism" teases out the unevenness of "development" within Southeast Asia, not as a uniform phenomenon, but rather as a process of strategic, market-driven collaboration between nation-states and corporate interests that creates asymmetrical zones within the nation-state. Within this process, space becomes unevenly classed and developed according to neoliberal calculations in which some areas and populations are seen as advantageous to the global market, constituting a "checkered geography" (Ong, *Neoliberalism as Exception*, 77). Outsourcing documentaries capitalize on the checkering of space through depicting the close relationship between slums and modern spaces in India. While outsourcing documentaries depict the different zones that agents move through, that make up India, Leela Fernandes describes the ways in which these zones are part and parcel of India's rising middle class and the ways in which technological and class advancements are restructuring Indian cultural and spatial life (*India's New Middle Class: Democratic Politics in an Era of Economic Reform* [Minneapolis: University of Minnesota Press, 2006]).

13. As Kaja Silverman explains, suture is the cinematic work necessary to overcome the anxiety the viewer experiences upon encountering an image framed in the camera's reduced point of view by stitching images together into a reliable series, structured through the narrative expectations of the viewer (*The Subject of Semiotics* [New York: Oxford University Press, 1983]). This process of stitching provides the viewer a positionality through which to apprehend her/his *relationship* to the image by framing the point of view that constructs a subject position for the viewer. Suturing works through the "180° rule," which limits the range of a shot to the viewer's seeing capacity, leaving the visual field that the camera occupies unexplored. "Thus it derives from the imperative that the camera deny its own existence as much as possible, fostering the illusion that what it shows has an autonomous existence, independent of any technological interference, or any coercive gaze" (Silverman, *The Subject of Semiotics*, 201). While the viewer will temporarily adhere to this imperative, Silverman explains, he or she will soon "demand to know whose gaze controls what it sees" (202). This demand is met through a series of shot/reverse shots, which orient the viewer to the camera's gaze *through* the character or object from whose perspective the

viewer is invited to see. Thus, the filmic strategies through which this positioning is managed, produced, and crafted suture the viewer into the film's movement and look—and hence its time-space qualities—sometimes through fairly straightforward identifications and other times by generating multiple and even competing identifications, or structures of feeling.

14. Silverman, *The Subject of Semiotics*, 207–8.

15. Ong, *Neoliberalism as Exception*, 7.

16. Colonial mimicry is a term Homi Bhabha theorizes as the performative repetition (in body, language, affect, visibility) of a colonial presence (*The Location of Culture* [New York: Routledge, 1994/2003]). The force of the performance, of the internalization of colonial power relations, remains in the body and psyche of previously colonized populations even after colonial occupation. Though the performance references the colonial culture, it is, however, a fraught and anxious project marked by its inherent ambivalence—as mimicry "must continually produce its slippage, its excess, its difference" (Bhabha, *The Location of Culture*, 86). Though performances of colonial mimicry invoke a harnessing of progress narratives for Indians, they do so unevenly—depictions of the "third world" in relation to the West reassure the Western subject of her/his superiority through a temporal and spatial placement in the "developed world."

17. While U.S. "racial formation" (Michael Omi and Howard Winant, *Racial Formation in the United States: From the 1960s to the 1990s* [New York: Routledge, 1994]) has often been tied to embodied features associated with stereotyped racialization, call center labor reconfigures "a regime of visuality to aurality where the racism occurs through a control of language, voice, and accent all carried out under the label of 'cultural neutralization'" (Raka Shome, "Thinking Through the Diaspora: Call Centers, India, and a New Politics of Hybridity," *International Journal of Cultural Studies* 9, 1: 108). Documentaries circumvent the aural passing that takes place over the phone through the visual register of the medium.

18. Bhabha, *The Location of Culture*, 89.

19. Zigmunt Bauman, *Liquid Modernity* (Malden, MA: Blackwell, 2000), 9.

20. Ibid., 13.

21. Here we focus on the spatial reconfiguration of transnational America as opposed to other first world neo-imperial formations, as the films we examine are designed for the U.S. consumer/viewer. The influx of American cultural products and practices into India builds off of, even as it displaces, British imperialism as the privileged axis of imperialism within India at this historic moment.

22. *John and Jane Toll Free*, Ashim Ahluwalia (Director), Shumona Goel (Producer), India, 2005. Broadcast on HBO on November 13, 2007, this departs from the other documentaries under investigation in this and other regards: It is the only documentary that is Indian produced; the only white or American people that "appear" in the film are call center customers, aurally decoded, but visually absent. In this sense, *John and Jane* decenters whiteness and U.S. American-ness, representing these cultural forces as sources of struggle and negotiation without celebrating them.

23. This progress narrative also traffics in a 1950s nostalgia of unfettered white male control.

24. Wendy Brown, *Regulating Aversion: Tolerance in the Age of Identity and Empire* (Princeton: Princeton University Press, 2006), 6.

25. Gayatri Chakravorty Spivak, "Can the Subaltern Speak?" In *Marxism and the Interpretation of Culture*, ed. Cary Nelson and Lawrence Grossberg (Urbana: University of Illinois Press, 1988: 271–313), 297.

11 Inscribing Racial Bodies and Relieving Responsibility

Examining Racial Politics in *Crash*

Jamie Moshin and Ronald L. Jackson II

> The entire cultural system supports, reaffirms, and colludes with white males
> to keep them in power. Yet, most white males do not think of themselves
> as belonging to a powerful, elite group until others label them that way.
> —Anthony J. Isparo[1]

> We don't see things as they are; we see things as we are.
> —Anaïs Nin

Barack Obama's 2008 presidential campaign marked an immense cultural shift in the United States. For the first time, an African American candidate had a truly legitimate shot at the top office, and won. For many, Obama's achievement was indicative of even more: not only had American voters put aside age-old hatreds resulting from real inequalities when they entered the ballot booth, but they also had demonstrated what many consider to be true today—that race does not matter and that we now live in a "post-race" era. Of course, we find it shocking that anyone would proclaim we are living in a post-racial America.

Post-race has been defined as the belief that "despite the racialized and gendered nature of all aspects of American life, including media coverage, twenty-first-century U.S. culture is replete with the idea that we are beyond, past, or 'post-' notions of race-, gender-, and sexuality-based discrimination."[2] According to this thinking, America no longer rewards privilege; it is a meritocracy that only privileges success. Color, sexuality, and religion do not matter, because anyone can overcome these barriers and succeed, to such an extent that these barriers must surely be relics of the past. We have not only moved past race, the thinking goes, we have moved beyond *racism*—we are now a color-blind nation, a post-identity nation, where markers of difference and of Otherness are no longer consequential. Given that post-race refers to twentieth-century representations and experiences, Obama's presidential victory marks a shift, signpost, or temporal marker of racial progress. Some might argue that another important sign of progress was the 2005 cinematic release, and nearly instant popularity, of Paul Haggis's movie *Crash*.

We argue that this popular media text serves as both a counterpart and counterpoint to post-racial ways of thinking. This multi–Oscar winning film is unabashedly *not* post-race—in fact, we argue, race is the only word in this film that matters. But, because race matters, because it is so ubiquitous, it simultaneously does *not* matter: racism is such an important part of life and such a reflexive and perhaps instinctual way of acting and being in the world that it almost elides race. We argue in this chapter that the impulse to atone for racism reflects the contemporary milieu in the United States where racism is so pervasive that one's own race is diminished. It is your humanness, not your race, that guarantees your racism. This is the discursive move and practice at work in *Crash*, which goes beyond Aaron Gresson's idea of rhetorical reversals. *Crash* modifies the dominant racial hegemony to reaffirm both white privilege and multiculturalism.[3] Gresson would suggest that such a reversal aims to secure patriarchy and protect privilege by disguising White hegemony. But, white hegemony is not hidden in this film; it is overt. Everyday racism remains hidden. Closing our eyes, acting like it is not there, or even conflating bigotry with racism are not effective strategies for the eradication of racism or White privilege, both of which have material effects for non-White, racial Others in our society. Our fundamental aim in this chapter is to explore the well-meaning post-racial discourse, or the equally problematic "we all are racist, therefore racism does not really exist" discourse, which contravenes and interferes with meaningful White racial accountability.

Crash has been lauded for its educational, fair approach to race in America. In fact, the film purports to remove the veil of ignorance and show us how America *really is* by weaving an entire story about our diverse nation. For all its promises, we argue that *Crash* induces audiences to feel hopeless and indifferent about racial stereotypes and conflicts, reflecting a broader cultural paralysis about U.S. race relations. Moreover, we argue that there appears to be an escape from social responsibility, as well as an ineffectual representation of otherness, that only serves to facilitate the extant paralysis of race relations in the United States. The film reinscribes a particular White racial standpoint that strategically utilizes racial stereotypes of minorities (especially anti-black stereotypes) to downplay structural White racism. The film also excuses individual White racist acts and performances in an effort to argue that everyone is ultimately the same—*everyone is racist, everyone is to blame*. At a time in American history when we are celebrating America's first Black president, yet when racial profiling and hate crimes are still very prominent,[4] it is quite possible the film's pronouncement is correct: many of us do not have any idea of who we are. What it means to be American at this time is riddled with ontological questions; hence, the relationships among rhetoric, representation, and "real life" in the movie *Crash* are inextricably intertwined.

Crash was an enormous critical and popular success. It was nominated for 103 awards in 2005 and 2006, and won 41 of them, including Oscars for best film, original screenplay, and editing. The film also garnered awards for best picture from the Black Movie Awards and best film, best ensemble, and best supporting actor (Terrence Howard) from the Black Reel Awards. After a month in theaters, the film had grossed $54,557,348 in the United States, and as of 2006, had grossed over $1 billion worldwide.[5] Demonstrating the ideological reach of the film, *Crash* led to a TV series—of the same name—on the television network "Starz." Roger Ebert has proclaimed that no film "portrays the complexities of race relations in America any better."[6]

According to director and co-writer Paul Haggis, the film's genius stemmed from his own carjacking at the hands of two young Black men. Ten years later, thinking about the act, and about "white privilege," he decided to write the film.[7] *Crash* was hailed as a positive contemporary film about race that sheds a "most-chilling light on how sub-cultures inter-relate across class and color lines in present-day America."[8]

The movie is built on the presumption that everyone is racist. And, the selling point of the film, Ebert argues, is that "it shows the way we all leap to conclusions based on race—yes, all of us, of all races, and however fair-minded we may try to be—and we pay a price for that."[9] Similarly, Jonathan Rosenbaum notes, "Haggis wants to implicate us as well as many of his more sympathetic characters in the round-robin of prejudice, so he plays tricks with our expectations, making us retroactively aware of our own prejudices."[10] Eric Harrison adds, "The way some of the characters behave and the way good people get beat down is liable to anger you or break your heart. Those are some of the reactions Haggis wants. More than that, though, he wants you to leave the theater a little different—more aware, less close-minded—than when you went in."[11] While not every review of the film is positive—it has garnered a 75 percent "fresh" rating on *Rotten Tomatoes*—the positive takes on the film do tend to focus on its redemptive depiction of race relations in the United States.

Because of its popularity, critical acclaim, and handling of race in America in an even and enlightening manner, *Crash* is worthy of further analysis. But, does this film portray the complexities of race in America successfully? Does it escape the tendency of such films to place Whites on the pedestal and relegate Others to the pit?[12] We argue that *Crash* draws the blinders from our eyes by demonstrating how we are all implicated in America's long, problematic engagement with racism. As the film's tagline tells us: "You think you know who you are. You have no idea."[13]

Standpoint Theory, Racial Atonement, and Critical Rhetoric

Crash's ominous warning that, "You think you know who you are. You have no idea," is a statement about how racist we all are underneath our egalitarian skins. An important starting point to explain the significance of *Crash* is "Standpoint Theory," which contends that racial locations influence lives, and people achieve racial standpoints "through critical reflections on power relations."[14] Patricia Hill Collins notes that a racial standpoint must be one that is expressed via a political stance, which stands in opposition to a dominant cultural system.[15] Kinefuchi and Orbe observe that "In the U.S. society, the dominant worldview based on European American experience may be a location from which to see the world, but it cannot be a racial standpoint."[16]

From whence, then, does *Crash's* gaze emanate? In *America's Atonement*, Aaron David Gresson III argues that times are changing: an era of multiculturalism has made life particularly difficult for the White American male; there has been a boomerang effect such that the White man, long America's unquestioned symbol of morality, has become its figurehead of oppression.[17] This cathartic blame brings with it an uncomfortable tension and paradox: for, while White *men* are responsible for the structuration that relegated nonwhites to the margins of society, the White *man* is not necessarily complicit or responsible. Harkening back to Judith Butler and Stuart Hall, Gresson maintains that "White man" is not a homogenous identity marker; it is not a stable signifier; and it is a contemporary source of anxiety.[18]

Gresson argues that the cultural practices and ideologies that placed White men on the pedestal have had a "boomerang effect, resulting in popular culture representations and popular imagination that white males are all-powerful *and* all responsible for society's ills."[19] Gresson contends that articulating and/or foregrounding White racial pain is a strategic means of recovering from the reverse discrimination of policies such as affirmative action in which non-Whites, who previously complained of hegemony, seem to accept privileges associated with their skin color. This alteration of hegemony appears strange to Whites who choose not to recognize or remember the historical legacy of white supremacy, and contemporary effects of racial discrimination in schools, employment, home ownership, etc. since the late 1800s. As a result, strategies of recovery and reversal have emerged, in which some Whites are calling for their pain to be recognized, their discrimination to be acknowledged, and their experiences to be valued in the same way minorities' experiences have been valued. Obviously, this logic is absurd, but it reflects a "backlash" by Whites toward minorities' programmatic gains.

Our analysis differs from Gresson's in that Gresson suggests that all White racial recovery tends to be motivated by self-interested backlash. We believe it is sometimes just motivated by habit. Shannon Sullivan explains that Whites have trained themselves habitually to look for themselves as central characters in the American experience.[20] Despite the rich tapestry of diversity in the United States, Whites cannot imagine a story about America that does not center around their experiences.

Multiculturalism has produced newfound discomfort for Whites as the identity of the "oppressor" leading to what Gresson terms racial pain, which is created by a voluntary or forced identification with a "spoiled racial identity." This identification evokes a felt absence of power and the presence of guilt and shame in relation to projected feelings about race. Racial pain is as a result of social categories and structures created by White America, by those in power, Gresson argues; ironically, White men feel racial pain. Similarly, Butler argues that juridical systems of power *produce* the subjects they come to represent and have to operate within the requirements of those structures.[21]

Crash participates in the discourse of racial pain and atonement. Stuart Hall reminds us that "we should think . . . of identity as a 'production,' which is never complete, always in process, and always constituted within, not outside, representation."[22] Cultural identities are always undergoing social transformation; they are always subject to the whims of history, culture, and power. As communication scholars, an essential part of looking at this fluidity and creation of identity, of course, is language and discourse, for discourse "is language reflecting social order but also language shaping social order, and shaping individuals' interaction with society."[23] Language and representation, therefore, are never neutral mediums through which one transmits preexisting knowledge, but rather responsible for *constituting* knowledge—in this case, knowledge about race and society. As Fowler put it, "all knowledge, all objects are constructs . . . we might profitably conceive the world in some alternative way."[24]

An important distinction to make here, in discussing the linguistic construction of reality and the semioticization of the world, is between the imagined and the imaginary.[25] That is, while concepts such as race are unreal, human, linguistic, and imagined constructions, they are not *imaginary*. So, while we have *constructed* race as a dominant categorization device, one that does not have a true material referent, that does not mean race does not have real, felt effects.

This focus on the real-world impacts of language, and of the tangible potentialities of *Crash*, is one of the reasons why we have chosen critical rhetoric as our framework for this analysis. As Raymie McKerrow makes clear, "the task of a critical rhetoric is to undermine and expose the discourse of power in order to thwart its effects in a social relation."[26] Following this, a critic must attend to the "microphysics of power" in order to understand what sustains social practices. A critical rhetorician's job is to understand how *truth* is produced through discourse, and the processes that shape ideology. In so doing, the critical rhetorician pulls together scraps and fragments of discourse and interprets the meanings of the text that he or she has created.[27] From a critical rhetoric perspective, we argue that *Crash* demonstrates that the subject positions foisted upon both racial/gendered minorities within the film—and the audiences it interpellates—construct and maintain harmful stances that are inherent to a certain subject position.[28] The characters in *Crash* ostensibly mirror "real" Americans and exist only through an ideological discourse that constitutes them; that is, their identities are constituted *by* rhetoric and discourse. Critical rhetoric scholarship allows us to use an understanding of how intertextuality works to fill in lacunae, to read context, to envision interpellated audiences, to argue for change, to become embodied in the texts we interpret and thereby create.[29] As McKerrow notes, "A critical rhetoric ends in transformation of the conditions of domination or in the possibility of a revolt as the consequence of a critique of freedom."[30]

It is for this reason that we have chosen film—and this film in particular—as the "text" for our analysis. We follow from the notion that language and discourse *matter* to reiterate that discourse interpellates subject positions. It is *through* language, through discourse, that ideology—and identities—are constructed, manifested, and maintained. As Hall puts it, "Above all, cultural meanings are not only 'in the head.' They organize and regulate social practices, influence our conduct and consequently have real, practical effects."[31] To paraphrase Hall, popular culture *matters*, because it presents and confronts us with notions of power, identity, and the like. Hence, we contend that *Crash* was a blockbuster partly because of its rhetorical power, because of the convincing message it spread about race and racisms. It is not "just" a cultural manifestation of some larger material, then; it *is* material: "What cultural studies has helped me to understand is that the media play a part in the formation, in the constitution, of the things that they reflect. It is not that there is a world outside, 'out there,' which exists free of the discourses of representation. What is 'out there' is, in part, constituted by how it is represented. The reality of race in any society is, to coin a phrase, 'media-mediated.'"[32] *Crash* is not only entertainment; it is part of a larger cultural discourse that tells our stories, augments our conceptions of identities, and reifies stereotypes.

Crash

Crash looks at 36 hours in Los Angeles, California. This ensemble piece offers a diverse cast of characters, whose lives are all imbricated as they "crash" into each other, literally and figuratively. In all of these encounters, racial acts and prejudices occur. The plotline of the film unfolds through a series of intricately woven vignettes—a "random pattern movie"[33]—that generally draw attention to interactions among the various characters, reinforcing the notion that we are all touched by racism, on the part of both loved ones and strangers. By "random pattern movie," we mean one that does not rely on a conventional chronological progression to tell a story, instead jumping back and forth in time (akin to films such as *Pulp Fiction*, *Memento*, and *Magnolia*).

Crash is set in Los Angeles, California, which boasts a robust population of 9.5 million people, fewer than half of whom consider themselves to be White.[34] According to the latest census reports, White Americans will cease being the racial majority in the United States in 2050.[35] The city is rich with cultural heritage and tradition and has all of the problems common to large cities, not the least of which are crime, drugs, and illicit trading. *Crash* does not shy away from some of these ugly aspects of the city's landscape.

The film begins with a car crash, which involves a Latina, Ria (Jennifer Esposito), and an Asian woman, both of whom immediately use racial slurs to condemn each other for the accident. Ria then gets back in the car with her partner—and lover—Detective Graham Waters (Don Cheadle), whose life is complicated by his mother (Beverly Todd), who is addicted to drugs, and his criminal younger brother, Peter (Larenz Tate). Setting the theme for the film, Waters muses: "We're always behind this metal and glass. In any real city, people brush past people, bump into them . . . . I think we miss that touch so much that we crash into each other just so we can touch somebody."[36] The two then go about their business of investigating the murder of a young Black man, who we later find out is Graham's brother, Peter Waters.

Among the major players in the film is Jean Cabot (Sandra Bullock), a White housewife from Brentwood, whose racial paranoia and loneliness get the better of her when she and her husband are carjacked by two young Black males from the 'hood whose motives she begins to suspect. She voices stereotypes against them. The film asks us to sympathize with her as it does for all of the characters. Meanwhile, her husband, Rick Cabot (Brendan Fraser), the District Attorney, is attempting to play the political game by showing his sensitivity to people of all races.

Daniel (Michael Peña), the heavily tattooed Latino locksmith who is called to change the Cabot's locks, is a source of fear and subject of derision throughout the film. Jean Cabot is sure that he will give a copy of her new house key to his "homies" after he fixes her lock, and Farhad (Shaun Toub), an Iranian convenience store owner, becomes furious when Daniel tells him that, while he can supply a new lock, the store instead needs a new door—Farhad is sure he is being cheated. After unknown assailants loot his store and graffiti it with racial slurs, Farhad wrongly identifies Daniel as the cause of his downfall. Daniel, who has moved to the suburbs in order to protect his young daughter from the violent streets of inner city LA, is then confronted at his home with a gun by the enraged storeowner. Farhad pulls the trigger just as Daniel's daughter leaps into his arms; as an amazed Daniel looks down at his mercifully unharmed daughter, we learn that, unbeknownst to him, Farhad's gun has been loaded with blanks by his daughter, Dorri (Bahar Soomekh), the local medical examiner.

There are other strands in this multidimensional drama, however. Cameron Thayer (Terrence Howard) is a television director in Hollywood. Cameron is depicted as a Black man who feels uncomfortable in his own skin. As his wife, Christine (Thandie Newton) puts it, "You're worried that your friends will find out that you're actually Black."[37] We meet the Thayers when they are pulled over in their upscale SUV after attending a party, allegedly because Mrs. Thayer is performing fellatio on her husband. The lead officer, John Ryan (Matt Dillon), is portrayed here as a White racist more intent on pulling over Black people than in following the law; his younger partner, Tom Hansen (Ryan Philippe), is a young White rookie concerned with morality and egalitarianism. While Cameron attempts to cooperate with the police officers, Christine becomes enraged at being pulled over, calling Ryan a "pig" and telling him that they were only pulled over because he thought it was a "White woman blowing a Black man." Ryan is then overly aggressive with Christine, using a "search" as an excuse to grope her. The rest of the film follows Christine and Cameron as they attempt to come to terms with this sexual assault and their resulting anger. Christine is furious at Cameron for not stepping in to protect her from Ryan, criticizing her husband for being too weak in the face of White America, and for shucking and jiving. Cameron grapples with the ambivalence of the moment.

Using critical rhetoric, Crash can be seen as a reference for something that could potentially be experienced by an interpellated audience. The film seems to be directed toward black men and takes place during a time when racial profiling and police brutality are common and rampant. So, in this moment with the officers' guns drawn, we get to read all the anguish, emasculation, and helplessness on Cameron's face, as he, a black male, tries to make the right choice, which will not endanger him or his wife. He is livid (but incapacitated), but he has no other tool to respond other than being passive. Cameron calmly explains that he would like them to be given a warning and let go, reflecting an all too common experience for Black men in the United States.

Cameron Thayer also has his identity assaulted and compromised by his professional life as a TV director. We watch as he has to placate his White boss and swallow his pride by making sure that his Black actors don't speak English too well. The commentary implies that Black males are non-intellectual, inarticulate, and incompetent, with few exceptions, of which, of course, Cameron is one.

Other characters give us a sense of how complex racism can be in the contemporary United States. Officer John Ryan displays his racism throughout the film, from his assault on Christine Thayer to his repeated racial slurs directed at Shaniqua Johnson (Loretta Devine), the worker at the health insurance company where Ryan goes in an attempt to get his father better health care. Director Paul Haggis complicates the picture of Ryan by showing him to be a man who cares deeply for his elderly, sick father and who stays up with him at night when the old man is in pain. The arc of his story along with the Thayers' comes full circle when Christine is in a car accident and, as a result, becomes stuck in an overturned car that is about to explode. Ryan forsakes his own safety to extricate her from the car. We as an audience are extremely uncomfortable as we watch Christine, who is shaking in fear as much from her interaction with her racist oppressor as from her predicament, and has to give in and allow herself to trust Ryan. In his selfless act to rescue Christine, Ryan's character is transformed from racist into hero.

Many moments throughout the film are presented with a specifically masculine gaze, enabling us, as viewers, to forgive Ryan because he has atoned. The film downplays Ryan's assault on Christine Thayer from a feminist perspective, choosing not to read it through her experience. Not only do we forgive the perpetrator—partly because of his subject position, partly because he is male, and partly because he is white—we are never made to feel *badly* for Christine. Immediately after the assault, she is made to appear as the unreasonable spouse, the one who attacks Cameron for code switching. Lost in this vitriol is the acknowledgment that a woman has been sexually assaulted.

Other characters get a shot at transformation, such as the carjackers who rob the Cabots. Anthony (Chris "Ludacris" Bridges) is used as a prescient observer, uncritically articulating ways in which African Americans are dealt a bad hand in a racist society; at the same time, he acts as a carjacker and armed robber. So, his character is perhaps the most easily dismissed, both because of his inability to think through race with any sobriety and because of his ethically flawed character. He simply can't be taken seriously. He is an interesting iteration of an articulate young Black male, but one with a wasted intellect mired in conspiracy theories, preoccupied with criminal activity, chronically unemployed, topped off with a twisted sense of justice. It is not so much that this is a caricature we never see in real life, but that the danger is that the media have already inundated audiences with negative representations of Black males such as this. As Charland notes, such rhetoric constitutes subjects and perpetuates power structures: "Constitutive rhetorics are ideological not merely because they provide individuals with narratives to inhabit as subjects and motives to experience, but because they insert 'narrativized' subjects-as-agents into the world."[38] These rhetorics shape the characters within the film *and* the audiences that are interpellated by them. So, if we replace Peter (Detective Waters's brother) and Anthony with White males, their dialogue would have been unbelievable and unrealistic to these audiences who have been duped into believing this is just the way Black males are. In this way, the film sustains the extant stereotypes about Black males as incompetent, criminal, dangerous, non-intellectual, and innately incapacitated.[39]

After Anthony and Peter steal the Cabots' SUV, they accidentally run over a middle-aged Asian man, who we eventually discover is a slave-trader. Again, *Crash* relies on imbrications. Later in the film, Anthony and Peter attempt to carjack Cameron Thayer, mistakenly assuming that he is a White man (the film establishes that Anthony would never steal from African Americans). As they threaten Cameron with a gun, Anthony calls him a "nigger." Something within Cameron breaks, and he begins to beat up Anthony before seeing a police cruiser come toward them. Peter flees. Both Cameron and Anthony jump in the car and speed off, police cruisers in pursuit; and, they are eventually pulled over by a group of police officers, including Tom Hansen, who recognizes Cameron from his run-in with John Ryan. Cameron emerges from the car, as Anthony cowers in the front seat. Cameron's pent-up anger at his mistreatment—both legal and racial—reaches a climax, and he refuses to cooperate, despite the impending peril. Hansen steps in to save Cameron. After this incident is resolved and Cameron is let go with a warning, Cameron drives Anthony to the next block and, before letting him go, says: "Look at me. You embarrass me. You embarrass yourself."

The story comes full circle as we see Peter Waters fleeing from the scene of the failed carjacking, eventually being picked up by Tom Hansen (who is now off duty). Hansen misinterprets Waters movements in the passenger seat. Hansen panics and shoots Waters. This is the body that Detective Waters—his brother—is called upon to investigate at the beginning of the film.

As the movie comes to a close, we witness another car crash by people of two different races, who resort to racial epithets and stereotypes. Just when we thought the film's only good Black protagonist could escape from the film with her ethical character intact, we are shown that Shaniqua Johnson, the HMO manager who experienced racial slights by Detective John Ryan as he sought health care for his ailing father, is one of the characters involved in the car crash at the end of the movie, hurling racial slurs at the other driver. For an instant, if you are not careful, you may attribute this to the writers' intent to balance all characters and demonstrate how we are all complicit in racial hegemony. Of course, that only works logically if we rid hegemony of its most potent properties—collective dominance and power. Distilling racial hegemony by conflating it with racism, racial prejudice, bigotry, and racial inequity draws attention *away* from the ubiquity of power that is always already involved in racial relations. Inserting this necessary nuance does not allow the movie to function as intended.

Racial Pain and *Crash*

Crash centers on cars. We see multiple accidents, all of which cause the characters to use racial slurs: the Thayers are nearly torn apart after they are pulled over; the Cabots are thrown into turmoil after their car is stolen; Anthony and Peter make a living stealing the cars of others; a middle-aged Asian man is nearly killed after he is hit by a car and leaves behind a van full of slaves; Cameron Thayer is nearly shot down after he resists a carjacking; Peter is murdered in a car while attempting to demonstrate the sameness between himself and a White man. Interestingly, the vehicles carrying each individual to their racial *Crash* are either black or white.

What does this dichotomy tell us? While we must be careful to avoid falling into the trap of biological determinism ourselves, it seems important to draw some attention to the fact that the director and writer of this film, Paul Haggis, is a White man. Clearly, there is something to it that the person telling the story about discrimination in America is a member of the racialized majority (that usually gets to tell the story)—and therefore is not speaking from a marginalized racial standpoint. Haggis himself has noted, "Every day we sat down I said, 'Bobby [Moresco, co-writer], what the hell are we doing? We're two white guys. We're going to be killed. We don't have any right to say these things, do we?' He'd say 'Well, if it were true, no matter how ugly that truth is, yes.' I actually think that it was kind of ballsy for Bobby and me to do this."[40] Haggis explains: "It's easy to do if you do a lot of research. I read 20 or 30 nonfiction books [on the subject] to prepare myself and met with a lot of people. If you know all the given circumstances, it's easy to put yourself in that person's place, as long as you don't judge that person."[41]

Clearly, this initial "standpoint," if we can call it that, is problematic. Drawing back on Gresson's notion of racial pain, White men tend to feel guilt and shame as a result of the cultural trends toward multiculturalism. In response, they are often compelled, whether consciously or subconsciously, to do something to alter this problematic identity and image: "the fusion of white identity with power over several centuries and the continual renewing of this fusion through racism are the conditions that must be changed."[42]

Crash appears to be an expression of White pain, but it is not a *productive* expression of this pain. Throughout the film, we see people (e.g., Black people, Middle Eastern people, Asian people, White people) act in hateful, prejudiced ways. By showing us *everyone's* racism, *Crash* argues that Whites are not alone in their racism; we are all complicit. If we can get beyond the treatment of racism and prejudice as synonymous, in some ways, this is admirable. Every person has stereotypes about other races. However, making everyone complicit in racism is discomforting: because we are all the same, we do not *need* to feel racial guilt or pain. In this way, the film reads like an apologia. In his work on Holocaust memorialization, James Young notes, "To the extent that we encourage monuments to do our memory work for us, we become that much more forgetful. In effect, the initial impulse to memorialize events like the Holocaust may actually spring from an opposite and equal desire to forget them."[43] Is that what this film does? Is it an expression of White atonement and pain that allows the maker—and the viewer—to move on, to forget, to take a still snapshot of this live specimen of race that invades our social sphere?

Part of the reason why this notion of atoning and moving on appears accurate and problematic is that Haggis does not present race as a social creation, but as natural and biologically determined. The black and white cars clue us in to this, as do the constant crashing of people with different phenotypes. Whenever someone bumps into someone who looks different, the immediate reaction is a racist one. Again, assuming everyone is complicit in racism, racial reactions and hatred are made to seem the natural reaction. And, what makes them "natural"?: Phenotypical differences, accents, and race. The moral success of Haggis's film hinges on the reality he presents us. He makes it seem as if we cannot escape race and we cannot escape racism. He gets caught in the same notion of racial essentialism that he lambasts and gives us few, if any, alternatives to "you look different than me, therefore you are treated differently." "Biological conceptions of race," Stuart Hall tells us, "have greatly receded in importance."[44] Watching *Crash*, however, one would not know this.

Crash suggests not only that racism is inescapable because of biology, but also that racisms look alike. Conversation about race in *Crash* becomes, in effect, "because I'm Black, because I'm White, because I'm Latino, we cannot get beyond these conflicts." In Orbe and Kinefuchi's study of student responses to the film, many revealed that they were left with a feeling of helplessness and hopelessness. The authors indicate, "For this group of students, then, *Crash* showed that interracial relations could never improve."[45] And, why this sense of hopelessness? Because, as McKerrow puts it, all the conflict in *Crash* is distilled down to ego-ideologies versus alter-ideologies—who we *are*, as opposed to who we *are not*;[46] if one is different in one essential and unchangeable racial dimension, then one will always be diametrically opposed. This follows from Hall's argument that racial categorizations *always* trap us within binaries: "One aspect of racism is, certainly, that it occupies a world of manichean opposites: them and us, primitive and civilized, light and dark, a black and white symbolic universe."[47] The alter-ideology becomes the key component for both dominance and resistance: "In this sense, it is not so much how I see myself as how I see the Other—my appropriation of an alter-ideology for the Other defines the locus of our struggle."[48] Unfortunately, interpersonal conflict is ahistorically distilled purely to skin color in the movie. In the film, intracultural conflict is almost unexplored.

It is noteworthy that it is only Blackness that is viewed in gradations: Shaniqua Johnson, the HMO manager; Cameron Thayer, the racially conflicted TV producer; Anthony and Peter, the pariahs; Detective Graham Waters, the privately bigoted police officer caught between loving and supporting his drug-addicted mother and derelict brother Peter; a crooked FBI agent killed during a shooting exchange with another FBI agent while driving a stolen car with a stash of money tucked inside of a slit tire in the trunk; and voiceless Karen, the assistant to the District Attorney. The only race represented by more characters than African Americans are Whites. This is especially important, because Whiteness studies researchers have found that most Whites tend to claim no cultural identification other than American, despite knowledge of ancestral lineage in other countries. So, in some ways, they are cultureless. If that is true, then we are seeing only one dominant white culture in the film, while being exposed to Latino, Persian, Korean, and Chinese people.

As noted, Haggis introduces us to a mixed catalogue of Black characters. The previously mentioned description reads like a badly written novel, an endorsable television drama script, and even the Ghettopoly game board produced by Pennsylvania entrepreneur David Chang. On the one hand, perhaps we should be thrilled that all the characters are not stereotypical. On the other hand, it could be argued that they are. As noted earlier, these characters fulfill several stock stereotypes regarding U.S. Blacks: sexually charged Black men, the dichotomy of the militant and pacified Black male, the criminal delinquent, non-intellectual Black male, and the Black female named in fashion with other neologisms often devised in lower-income Black households (Shaniqua). Of the three Black women in the film, one has almost no dialogue (Karen), and one is always strung out on crack and barely comprehensible (Waters' mother). The other Black female character is Shaniqua Johnson, the HMO manager, whose role is fairly respectable up until the final scene. Before then, she appeared "normal." She did not feed any stereotype other than being a Black woman with an accent, having a unique name and an indignant attitude. Black viewers are not presented with an array of positive representations.

Beyond the Black characters, it is worth noting others in the film who are constructed via the White gaze, maintaining a relatively strict black/white dichotomy, rendering Others existent but unimportant in their unidimensionality. To begin with, there are only two characters in this film that are unequivocally good.

The most empathetic character in the film is Daniel, the Latino locksmith. We never see the worst of Daniel, despite the fact that he is at the receiving end of two vicious racist attacks. Instead, Haggis portrays Daniel as a loving father who will go to any length to protect his daughter and make her feel safe, and who never sinks to the level of those around him.[49] The second character, Dorri, is the Iranian daughter of Farhoud; she also happens to be the medical examiner who examines Peter Waters. Dorri, too, does not engage in any bigotry throughout the film; instead, she is the reasonable voice who, unbeknownst to her permanently angry father, fills his gun with blanks. By dint of good fortune she saves the life of Daniel's daughter.

What makes these "good" characters particularly noticeable is how they compare to all of the other characters in the film. They stand above a swirling sea of racism that surges below them; *every other character in the film* is racist, and it seems *all* they talk about is race and racism. Haggis highlights this notion through his storytelling device; in his dark fairytale Los Angeles, everyone's life is interconnected with one another's, and it becomes clear that it is race/racism that is the catalyst for this imbrication, and for this *crashing*. This is problematic and unbelievable, because it is clearly unreasonable that a city of the scale of Los Angeles can be distilled to a constantly colliding cast of 20 or so people, who cross each other's paths.

In addition, Daniel and Dorri's infallibility is noticeable in the film because of the stark dualism with which every other character in the film is constructed. That is, while we see moments of racism, ignorance, hatred, and violence, we also see these same characters exhibit love and kindness. While, of course, humans necessarily have both good and bad dimensions, the distance between these two poles is remarkable: from the Asian man's kindness to his wife to his selling of slaves, from Farhoud's desire to see his family succeed in America to his attempted murder of Daniel, and so on. Haggis explores none of these polarities with the same attention to detail as he does with Officer Ryan. Ryan risks life and limb to extricate Christine from a car that is about to explode and, as she is led away by paramedics, she looks back over her shoulder at her antagonist/savior, giving him a nebulous smile.

What are we, as an audience, meant to feel about this turn of events? It seems that Haggis does multiple things to make us feel for Ryan: he has an aging father whom he cares for, and he saves a desperate woman. But, even beyond that, we are made to feel ambivalent about Christine because of the abuse that she levels upon him just for pulling them over. We must question if this is a device to make us feel that his sexual assault and racism are *okay*, are *justified*. And, if this is so, is Ryan blameless? One gets the discomfiting feeling that a common reaction, upon walking away from this film, is not that Ryan is a bad person who has moments of goodness, but rather that he is a *hero* who has moments of weakness. Sadly, and uncomfortably, the film forgives Ryan his racism, and we forgive him for his sexual assault of Christine—while these are moments of fallibility, his essence is that of a compassionate hero. It is indeed a problem that *Crash* could lead us to believe that actions speak louder than words. On the flip side of this, we also argue that *Crash* makes a rhetorical move that demonstrates that we should not be overly concerned with our racism; if *everyone* is racist, then either we are all bad or none of us is bad. In the case of the Asian slave trader, in fact, *Crash* argues rhetorically that we should not feel bad about our stereotypes or our racism, because at least *we* do not act on them.

The racist language and stereotypes that shape the rest of the film thus pale in comparison to those times when people actually harm someone else. Here, we harken back to Hall's reminder that language and representation are not empty vessels, but rather are responsible for *constituting* knowledge. Therefore, in contrast to the message that *Crash* provides, language is as important—or more important—than action.

Extremely problematic aspects of the film that directly project the White gaze and White pain are the roles into which Haggis funnels actors of certain ethnicities and races. The Black actors in *Crash* portray carjackers, an Uncle Tom, a shrewish wife, a crack-head, and a police officer. Latino actors play a housekeeper, a locksmith, and a police officer. The Iranian characters in the film are a convenience store owner, who attempts to commit murder, and a medical examiner. The Asians in the film are either slave-traders or slaves. For the most part, to be certain, it is an ignominious list. Let us now look at the White characters for sake of comparison: a District Attorney, a privileged wife, an assistant District Attorney, multiple police officers, a retiree who was a successful entrepreneur, a TV producer . . . *There is not one White criminal on this list*. In fact they are all in positions of authority. Three of the characters (the district attorneys and the father) are portrayed very sympathetically, and, in fact, are portrayed as being very conscious of race relations and egalitarianism (in fact, Cabot's role was originally scripted from Haggis's own point of view). Jean Cabot is the only character in the film we actually see come to terms with her own racism, and who actually acts in a caring manner toward someone of another race. And, even Ryan, who is responsible for some of the most virulent racism in the film, walks away a hero. Haggis, if he is indeed attempting to show a film that takes us beyond race and racialism, fails here. The weight and value given to White characters as opposed to those who are not White is clearly not equal. Audrey Thompson notes:

> Rearticulating whiteness is an emergent project. We know the racism of our white-
> ness in part through recourse to particular methods of inquiry but in part also by

our own resistances to change and by our temptations to see ourselves in particular racialized terms. A temptation for progressive whites is to not only be a good white but to be *recognized* as a good white. Identifying oneself as an anti-racist ally or aspiring to a final stage of moral white development, however, evades the problematic character of whiteness. In a racist society, whiteness is an inherently problematic position.[50]

The problematic nature of this position is demonstrated by the roll call of characters in *Crash*. The standpoint from which Haggis delivers his observations is a privileged one, and the film does not escape this White-Other dichotomy. Unfortunately it leaves us with our own preconceived notions.[51]

Implications

In writing and directing *Crash*, Paul Haggis made a noble attempt to provide a contemporary commentary on race and racism in the United States. And there were many ways the film succeeded. He shows that the world is not perfect: neither members of racially marginalized groups nor Whites are always right. This invites us to look at a pastiche of who we sometimes can be in hopes that we might take part in a productive dialogue. For this, he should be applauded.

However, the film is unable to escape the deeply rooted history of White dominance and a White-Black racial dichotomy. Haggis appears to approach the film from a standpoint that acknowledges the problems of racism, without considering its causes or history. This is an area in which *Crash* fails—*it treats race and racism as if everyone is equally affected by them, as if different races each have an equal footing in America.* While we wish this were the case, it is not; Haggis whitewashes history to have us believe that all racisms are and have been equal. Audrey Thomson notes,

> a healthy white racial identity will not become possible until whites confront and accept their whiteness (abandoning colorblindness), acknowledge the privileges of whiteness, and take a consistently anti-racist stance. The keys to developing a healthy white identity, then, are (1) developing an *awareness* of whiteness, including white privilege; and (2) acting in ways that makes use of that knowledge to challenge personal and institutional racism.[52]

This is something that does not occur in *Crash*—rather than taking on the onus of shouldering the blame, Haggis points the finger at everyone around him. *Crash* does not succeed as a message against racism, because it does not question its own privilege and assumes that its audiences are equally powerful and privileged.

Crash operates as an apologia, seemingly taking some responsibility for racism, and then sloughing it off like a second skin, to relieve us of guilt, and as a memorial to racism. However, this memorial is not one that is yet ready to be built. Before a memorial to racism is erected, a call to action must be sounded. *Crash* tells us that racism is redeemable by our actions, which mean more than our racist language or viewpoints. Racism is also redeemed by the fact that we are *each* racist; if *everyone* is racist, then either we are all bad or none of us is bad. And, in either case, this encourages quiescence, not action. Stuart Hall argues that we must "speak of identity as constituted not outside but within representation; and hence of cinema, not as a second-order mirror held up to reflect what already exists, but as that form of representation which is able to constitute us as new kinds of subjects, and thereby enable us to discover who we are."[53] While we applaud Haggis for what he tried to achieve, we do not want this to be what and who we become. We want to become something better. Yes we can.

NOTES

1. Anthony J. Ipsaro, *White Men, Women and Minorities in the Changing Work Force* (Denver: Meridian Associates, 1997), 14.

2. Ralina L. Joseph, "'Tyra Banks Is Fat': Reading (Post-)Racism and (Post-) Feminism in the New Millennium," *Critical Studies in Media Communication* 26, 3 (2009): 237–54.

3. Aaron David Gresson III, *America's Atonement: Racial Pain, Recovery Rhetoric, and the Pedagogy of Healing* (New York: Peter Lang, 2005).

4. According to the FBI, there were 7,780 reported hate crime incidents in 2008, of which 51.3 percent were racially motivated, 19.5 percent were motivated by religious bias, 16.7 percent stemmed from sexual-orientation bias, 11.5 percent resulted from ethnicity/national origin bias, and 1.0 percent were motivated by disability bias. Additionally, in his 2010 "State of the Union," President Barack Obama called for an extension of hate crime laws.

5. Internet Movie Database, "Crash."

6. In Roland Atkinson, "Agitation in the City of Angels," *Clinical Psychiatry News*, 33, 10 (2005): 20–21.

7. Paul Haggis, "On the Origins of *Crash*," Landmark Theatres website. Accessed online at http://www.landmarktheatres.com/mn/crash.html.

8. Kam Williams, "Movie Reviews: Crash." *Blacknews.com* (2005). Accessed online at http://www.blacknews.com/pr/crash101.html.

9. Ibid.

10. Jonathan Rosenbaum, "A Critic Examines His Path to Judgment," *Chicago Reader*. Accessed online at http://www.chicagoreader.com/movies/archives/2005/0505/050513.html.

11. Eric Harrison, "Crash." *Houston Chronicle Online* (September 30, 2005). Accessed online at http://www.chron.com/disp/story.mpl/ae/movies/reviews/3169528.html.

12. Kelly J. Madison, "Legitimation Crisis and Containment: The 'Anti-Racist-White-Hero' Film." *Critical Studies in Mass Communication* 16 (1999): 399–416.

13. Internet Movie Database, "Crash." Accessed online at http://www.imdb.com/title/tt0375679/.

14. Julia Wood, "Feminist Standpoint Theory and Muted Group Theory: Commonalities and Divergences," *Women and Language* 28, 2 (2005): 61–64, 61.

15. Patricia Hill Collins, "Comment on Heckman's 'Truth and Method: Feminist Standpoint Theory Revisited': Where's the Power? *Signs: Journal of Women in Culture and Society* 22 (1997): 375–81.

16. Kinefuchi and Orbe, "Situating Oneself," 73.

17. Gresson, *America's Atonement.*

18. Judith Butler, *Gender Trouble* (New York: Routledge, 1990).

19. Ibid., 4.

20. Shannon Sullivan, *Revealing Whiteness: The Unconscious Habits of Racial Privilege* (Bloomington: Indiana University Press, 2006).

21. Ibid.

22. Stuart Hall, "Cultural Identity and Cinematic Representation," in *Black British Cultural Studies: A Reader*, ed. Houston A. Baker, Jr., Manthia Diawara, and Ruth H. Lindeborg (Chicago: University of Chicago Press, 1996), 210–22, 210.

23. Adam Jaworski and Nikolas Coupland, "Introduction: Perspectives on Discourse Analysis," in *The Discourse Reader*, ed. Adam Jaworski and Nikolas Coupland (London: Routledge, 1999), 3.

24. Ibid., 33.

25. This idea has been appropriated from Akhil Gupta and James Ferguson, "Beyond 'Culture': Space, Identity, and the Politics of Difference," *Cultural Anthropology* 7 no. 1 (Feb. 1992): 6–23. Thanks to Dr. Crispin Thurlow for bringing this idea to our attention.

26. Raymie McKerrow, "Critical Rhetoric: Theory and Praxis," *Communication Monographs* 56 (1989): 91–111.

27. Michael Calvin McGee, "Text, Context, and the Fragmentation of Contemporary Culture," *Western Journal of Communication* 54 (1990): 274–89.

28. McKerrow, "Critical Rhetoric."

29. Celeste Condit, "Rhetorical Criticism and Audiences: The Extremes of McGee and Leff," *Western Journal of Speech Communication* 54 (1990): 330–45.

30. McKerrow, *Critical Rhetoric*, 104.

31. Stuart Hall, "Introduction," in *Representation: Cultural Representations and Signifying Practice*, ed. Stuart Hall (Thousand Oaks, CA: Sage, 1997), 1-11, 3.

32. Hall, "Race, Culture, and Communications," 340.

33. Stephen Hunter, "'Crash': The Clash of Human Contradictions," *Washingtonpost.com* (May 6, 2005). Accessed online at http://www.washingtonpost.com/wpdyn/content/article/2005/05/06/AR2005062901114.html.

34. U.S. Census Bureau, 2008. Accessed online at http://quickfacts.census.gov/qfd/states/06/06037.html on January 29, 2010.

35. Nicole Santa Cruz, "White Americans' Majority to Continue Until 2050, Report Says," *Los Angeles Times* (December 17, 2009).

36. *Crash*, directed by Paul Haggis (Hollywood, CA: Lions Gate Films, 2005).

37. Ibid.

38. Maurice Charland, "Constitutive Rhetoric: The Case of the Peuple Québécois," *Quarterly Journal of Speech* 72, 2 (1994):143.

39. Ronald Jackson, *Scripting the Black Masculine Body: Identity, Discourse, and Racial Politics in Popular Media* (Albany: SUNY Press, 2006).

40. Stephen Appelbaum, "Interview with Paul Haggis." *BBC*. Accessed online at http://www.bbc.co.uk/films/2005/07/29/paul_haggis_crash_interview.shtml.

41. Greg Ursic, "Crashing with Paul Haggis: An Interview with Hollywood's New Go-to Drama Guy." Accessed online at http://efilmcritic.com/feature.php?feature=1470.

42. Gresson, *America's Atonement*, 41.

43. James E. Young, *The Texture of Memory: Holocaust Memorials and Meaning* (New Haven: Yale University Press, 1993), 5.

44. Stuart Hall, "Race, Articulation, and Societies Structure in Discourse," in *Black British Cultural Studies: A Reader*, ed. Houston A. Baker, Jr., Manthia Diawara, and Ruth H. Lindeborg (Chicago: University of Chicago Press, 1996), 18.

45. Kinefuchi and Orbe, "Situating Oneself," 73.

46. McKerrow, "Critical Rhetoric."

47. Stuart Hall, "Race, Culture, and Communications: Looking Backward and Forward at Cultural Studies," in *What Is Cultural Studies: A Reader*, ed. John Storey (London: Arnold, 1996), 341.

48. Ibid., 95.

49. In one of the film's most effective moments, Haggis elicits a racist supposition on the part of the audience; after Jean Cabot tells her husband that the locksmith must be in a gang, we see his beeper go off as hip-hop begins playing on the soundtrack. As we realize we've been had—he is a gang member and her racist tirade was on the mark—we find out that in actuality he is being called to an emergency job. Of course, the fact that Haggis uses hip-hop to elicit this reaction is problematic on multiple levels. In a similar vein, Haggis seemingly allows the audience to go through a large portion of the film assuming that Farhad and his family are Arab, until we actually find out that they are Iranian. Here, again, this does a nice job of making the audience realize how much they must question their own assumptions.

50. Audrey Thompson, "[Essay Review of] Off White, edited by Michelle Fine, Lois Weis, Linda C. Powell, and L. Mun Wong," Education Review (12 November, 1999) [online journal] http://coe.asu.edu/edrev/reviews/rev76.htm.

51. One other aspect of othering in Crash worth noting is the homogenization of religion in the film. We would argue that despite Haggis's explicit goal of portraying the racism intrinsic in everyone, the problems with that racism, and the possibilities of getting past it, he makes a large miscue by using symbols of Christianity as his symbol of moral correctness, unity, and acceptance. Not only are these symbols *not* inclusive of other religious/ethnic groups in the United States, they are also markers of difference and, often, oppression. Haggis unquestioningly conflates Christianity with rightness and morality.

52. Thompson, "Review," 2.

53. Stuart Hall, "Cultural Identity," 221.

Cinematic Representation and Cultural Critique

The Deracialization and Denationalization of the African Conflict Diamond Crises in Zwick's *Blood Diamond*

Marouf Hasian, Jr., Carol W. Anderson, and Rulon Wood

> If it had been filmed in Sierra Leone, imagine the benefit for the people . . . By our people not being used for casting, accommodations, food, and such, we felt raped once again.[1]

On first impression, it seems unfair to complain about some of the local micropolitics that can be linked to various cultural or economic facets of Western filmmaking that tries to render visible "curses"[2] that are sometimes associated with regional "resource wars."[3] After all, doesn't Ed Zwick, the director of the film *Blood Diamond*, deserve credit for enlightening the world about the horrors of the West African "conflict" diamond trades that ravaged the lives of millions during the 1990s?

In this chapter, we contend that Zwick, Leonardo DiCaprio, and others involved in the filming of *Blood Diamond* should be credited with having helped complicate the ways that we think about diamond industries and the funding of regional conflicts, but this credit needs to be qualified. In spite of the fact that Zwick and others might sincerely believe they are telling "a story" (with a budget of some $40 million) that belongs to "the people" of Africa whom they film, they have nevertheless produced representations that marginalize "the other." *Blood Diamond* rendered invisible the thoughts and feelings of the very Sierra Leoneans' "story" which was supposed to be the film's *raison d'être*.

Today's diamond trading industries involve a host of countries—from Canada to Russia—but given the fact that Zwick's *Blood Diamond* is supposed to be about the story of Sierra Leone's bloody conflicts during the 1990s, this chapter focuses attention on the deracializaton and denationalization involved when filmmakers try to tell a globalized "story" through a selective lens. For example, when one of us interviewed Ann Norman,[4] a national consultant for the government of Sierra Leone, we learned that President Tejan Kabbah had offered the filmmakers of *Blood Diamond* a tour of the country, so that the actors could get some experiential idea of how diggers and other Sierra Leoneans made a living. Surprisingly, their offer was turned down by the filmmakers. Later on, in May 2007, Warner Brothers arranged for one of the first public screenings of *Blood*

Diamond in Sierra Leone, and the U.N. World Food Programme (WFP) was given credit for providing relief for more than 300,000 victims of decade-long civil wars.[5] Sierra Leoneans—who on average earn $1–$3 a day—thus played cameo roles in globalization tales that were told about the beneficence of nongovernmental organizations (NGOs) feeding the hungry.

In this chapter, we show how Western representations of the diamond controversies have aided or hindered national and international consciousness-raising efforts. Our criticism follows analytical work by critical race theorists[6] focusing on the role that narrative form and characters play in public controversies. We examined and analyzed the ethnic and national stereotypes embedded in the film *Blood Diamond*. We also conducted and analyzed interviews to understand how Sierra Leoneans think about the presences and absences that shadow this cinematic representation.

Specifically, one of our research team members (Carol Anderson) traveled to Sierra Leone in January and February 2008 and conducted interviews that revealed how local populations felt about Zwick's *Blood Diamond*. We also examined newspaper articles, film reviews, and personal interviews with presidents and paupers. This multi-faceted approach allowed us to peek behind the scenes and critique Zwick's story about Sierra Leone.

In this chapter, we argue that the abstract deracialized and denationalized images presented in Zwick's *Blood Diamond* present us with flawed—yet heuristically valuable—cultural vehicles for grappling with concrete African social, political, and economic problems. In order to foreground and expose the racial and ethnic characterizations and narrative strategies, our chapter is divided into three major segments. First, we explain the major plot lines and figurations that appear in Zwick's *Blood Diamond*. Second, we shift our gaze to focus on what some local and indigenous "others" in Sierra Leone think about the film's imaging. Finally, we assess how this type of cultural critique can inform the ways that we think about national and international resource controversies.

Cultural Critique and Post(colonial) Characterizations in *Blood Diamond*

Near the end of 2006, Edward Zwick directed the movie *Blood Diamond*, a film meant to provide audiences with a consciousness-raising vehicle about the horrors associated with the collection and circulation of uncertified blood diamonds. Warner Brothers used a tale set in the Sierra Leone of 1999 as the backdrop for illustrating how the collection of some types of diamonds could be linked to the loss of thousands of lives, the loss of limbs, and other human tragedies. The film's narrative focuses on the social agency of three major characters: Danny Archer

(Leonardo DiCaprio), a white "Rhodesian" smuggler; Maddy Bowen (Jennifer Connelly), an American reporter; and Solomon Vandy (Djimon Hounsou), a fisherman from Sierra Leone. When Vandy is forced at gunpoint to mine diamonds for the rebel Revolutionary Front (RUF) in Sierra Leone, he finds and hides a priceless "pink" diamond. The rest of the movie uses the search for that buried rock as a way of commenting on the need for more regulatory control of the African diamond industry.

Blood Diamond is considered to be a political action melodrama that covers everything from white racism in Rhodesia to the cutting off of hands by the RUF. Several of the plots that are sutured together in this movie try to provide viewers with some sense of social agencies working in international contexts, alongside communities of civilians, soldiers, relief workers, and journalists who witnessed some of the brutality that took place during the civil war in Sierra Leone (1991–2002).

The movie ostensibly highlights some of the horrific details surrounding the mining and distribution of gemstones in Sierra Leone. The film was marketed as a celluloid vehicle for consciousness-raising in the West, where people of all colors could learn about the trials and tribulations of the people of West Africa. In theory, as the logic of the film's production and distribution suggested, if audiences from around the world could become vicarious witnesses to the violence and carnage resulting from the global sale of conflict diamonds, then the economic demand for diamonds might go down. Publics would no longer be duped by the false scarcity created by distributors, and this in turn would cut down on the resources of warlords and terrorists who profit from this illicit trade. One of the key characters in *Blood Diamond*, the journalist Maddy Bowen, becomes a vocal messenger for the movie's producers when she claims that people "back home wouldn't buy a diamond if they knew it cost someone a hand."[7]

Yet, we believe *Blood Diamond* manifests latent racial and ethnic tensions that reproduce material and symbolic disparities, which directly affect the residents of Sierra Leone. One of the potential difficulties the producers faced derives from the form of the Hollywood action blockbuster, a genre that often dictates adherence to stock character types. In the remainder of this section, we describe how the protagonists, antagonists, and other supporting characters symbolically reinforce ethnic and nationalist stereotypes that sometimes tell us more about international perceptions about Africa than about legitimate indigenous concerns.

Solomon Vandy: The Noble Savage

Blood Diamond opens as Solomon Vandy playfully instructs his son Dia about the importance of school and also conveys his own desire for Dia to live a virtuous life. Solomon hopes for a brighter future for his son than the hand-to-mouth existence he, himself, has faced as a local fisherman. Solomon is a physically and morally impressive character. He frequently appears shirtless, with his dark, muscular physique glistening in the African sun. He moves slowly, with an air of quiet nobility, his head held high as he looks across the African savannah. Yet, Solomon also exhibits naiveté. In an early scene, he questions his son about the meaning of the word "utopia." Apparently, Solomon lacks an extensive English vocabulary as well as demonstrates a propensity for incongruous Western values. Throughout the film, other characters press Solomon to "stretch the truth" by posing as a journalist—a necessary deception for him to be able to cross into enemy territory. He appears uncomfortable with the other characters' dubious ethics, even if these "white lies" are necessary to achieve his altruistic goals. Unlike the other characters in the film, Solomon is devoid of any character flaws. His naiveté could be construed to be a character flaw; however, he is only naïve to the unethical practices of the white man. In other respects, Solomon is an ethical character, pure in his intentions and close to nature, as demonstrated by his profession as a fisherman.

Solomon's characterization may appear to be a modern figuration that illustrates the multiracial nature of *Blood Diamond* and the specific concerns of West Africans. In fact, however, his characterization functions as a rhetorical trope that has a much earlier origin within the Western literary tradition: the noble savage. Like James Fenimore Cooper's Uncas in *the Last of the Mohicans*, Solomon represents an idealized version of the "savage" in which "primitive human beings are naturally good and whatever evil they develop is the product of the corrupting action of civilization and society."[8] In Solomon's case, the Mendi communities of Sierra Leone become innocent victims caught up in the maelstrom of economic resource exploitation.

As Kent Ono and Derek Buescher note,[9] by placing indigenous characters on a narrative pedestal, sometimes producers reinforce racial stereotypes and remove agency from the individual. For example, in *Blood Diamond*, we get precious little historical information about the cultural, social, economic, or political legacies to help us understand the rise of what Greg Campbell calls the "RUF war."[10] Rather than a three-dimensional character, Solomon Vandy becomes a mere foil—a bundle of idealized traits that represents Enlightenment innocence. On first impression this may not appear to be such a dangerous narrative practice, but throughout the film, if we view Solomon as representative of an ethnic or racial group, it becomes clear that serious issues arise. Solomon represents "the good African" who lacks the skills necessary to make quick tactical decisions. When Freetown comes under attack by rebel forces, Solomon screams out and covers his head like a frightened child. His only salvation comes from

Danny, a Rhodesian mercenary, who, by his own admission, considers himself Solomon's "master."

What is to be made of Solomon's love of the "simple life"? Is this supposed to be emblematic of nationalistic simplicity, where Solomon stands in metaphorically for a Sierra Leone that lays prostrate at the feet of regional powers or Western exploiters? Solomon wishes for a better life for his son, but, at the same time, the hundred-carat "pink" means little to him beyond monetary aid for his family and country. In one of the film's most poignant scenes, Solomon questions Danny about what he will ultimately do with his money. Perhaps "find a wife and raise a family?" Solomon inquires—the obvious answer for the African. Danny responds, "probably not." Solomon says nothing, but shakes his head in disbelief. Again, Solomon's selfless desires are commendable, but, at the same time, if we think of Solomon as a character type, he then appears to stand in for the idea that the removal of voracious external forces will return West Africa to a pristine state of nature. This, in turn, provides a rationale for Western humanitarian intervention or investigative journalism. Western neocolonizers who deal with the likes of Solomon Vandy are faced with a dichotomous choice: either continue or stop the pillaging of the African continent. Solomon, positioned here as a representative of his race/ethnic group, reflects the West Africans' desire to be free from the trauma that comes with digging for diamonds, accumulated wealth, or social privilege.

In short, *Blood Diamond* is an action movie that masquerades as a social justice picture. It is a permutation of a genre that has been around since the Enlightenment, in which abolitionists, reporters, and beneficent Westerners have looked after their innocent wards. Viewers become vicarious witnesses to a process that pits virtuous whites and their allies against rapacious Rhodesians and other villains. The support of diamond cleansing is directly tied to the future of Africans like Solomon Vandy. However, movie producers and financiers who have invested time and tens of millions of dollars into making the film found a way to recoup their investment by making *Blood Diamond* into an action movie, which relies more on high-tech explosions, violence, and chase sequences than it does on a truly transformative message.

The Rebel Leader: The Villain

The role of the antagonist is to stand in direct opposition, or juxtaposition, to the protagonist and her or his overall goals and desires.[11] In *Blood Diamond*, there are essentially two antagonists. The first, and most powerful, is a composite character representing the entire diamond industry. There is also a more tangible character who confronts Solomon throughout the film, the nameless leader of the guerilla forces. He, like Solomon, is well muscled, and appears wearing dark sunglasses throughout the film; but unlike Solomon, who represents goodness, he represents evil. The nameless leader is the image of the modern African slaver, an immoral creature who cares nothing about tradition, honor, or virtue. If Solomon plays the role of the "good" African, the leader is the epitome of regional evil, the rapacious neighbor who arbitrarily loots whatever he can find.

For example, early in the film, when Solomon has been captured by the RUF, the rebel leader holds a machete over his head and spouts political rhetoric. His men hold each prisoner by the wrists, asking them if they want a short sleeve or a long sleeve, a euphemism for the act of cutting limbs with the swift blow of the machete. Later, he threatens to kill Solomon's son unless he finds the diamond for him. As an extreme antagonist, he is ruthless, and his men are without feeling. In every scene, they are shown against a backdrop of violence, while loud rap music plays in the background. They live amidst continued meaningless killing, drug use, and brutality against their own people.

We are not shown a variety of three-dimensional African types, who may have hybrid, contested, or ambivalent feelings. Instead, moviegoers are offered a choice between two types through which to experience the Sierra Leone diamond industry: the good African, as represented by Solomon, or the evil African, who leads a life of drugs and violence and represents the RUF forces.

Danny Archer: The Protagonist

Blood Diamond opens with a central character or protagonist as he or she faces a problem that drives the narrative forward, what some call "the setup."[12] It begins with a touching scene between Solomon and his son, but we quickly learn that the main character in this film is not Solomon; rather, it is Danny Archer, a racist mercenary. If Solomon had truly played the main or central role in the film, viewers would then see Sierra Leone's diamond trade through his perspective, which might have provided more narrative space for social agency and development of a three-dimensional representation of Sierra Leoneans or African characters. Unfortunately, however, an action film requires an action star, and Leonardo DiCaprio, with his long pedigree of award-winning performances, commands the screen like no other.

The central character in the film provides a point of view, a means by which we, as audience, may view the filmic world.[13] Danny Archer is cut from the same cloth as other action stars: he is savvy, strong, persistent, wisecracking, and possesses Rambo-like reflexes. Danny first appears on screen as a smuggler, confronting a group of gun-wielding guerilla thugs outside of an aviation hangar. He shows no fear in this first meeting, swatting away enemy guns that are trained on his chest. In this early scene, the guerillas refuse to let Danny talk to the "man in charge," but, undaunted, he pushes past the guerilla lackeys to talk to "the big boss." Inside a darkened hangar, he dickers in Krio (the local dialect) with a character known only as Commander Zero, a dangerous guerilla. Danny knows his way around the continent and has a keen knowledge of local customs. In later scenes, he demonstrates physical prowess. When Danny's driver is killed by stray enemy fire, he thinks quickly—grabbing the wheel, kicking the driver's lifeless body from the vehicle, and maneuvering it to safety.

Danny represents a prototypical, Western action hero. Nevertheless, he has a "fatal flaw." According to Robin Tobin, writing in a popular screenwriting text, "The hero most often views his flaw as a defense mechanism he needs for his survival. The hero does not view his flaw as a flaw, but as a way of coping with life, as a behavior that protects his life metaphorically or perhaps even literally."[14] Surprisingly, in *Blood Diamond*, Danny's central flaw runs much deeper than we might expect: he is a white racist. In one of the most compelling scenes in the film, Danny physically attacks Solomon Vandy, throwing him to the ground and calling him "kaffer," a term that for those living in southern Africa is more inflammatory than the "n" word in the United States. He later reinforces this bigoted comment by telling Solomon that he is his master. These slurs might be expected from an antagonist, but not from a central, heroic character.

Danny is the likable, wisecracking Schwarzenegger-esque character who we have come to expect from Hollywood blockbusters; yet, his flaw runs deeper than Han Solo's arrogance or John McClane's recklessness (characters from *Star Wars* and *Die Hard*, respectively). Danny represents a recognizable colonial or imperial trope: the recalcitrant white South African who has trouble coping with social change. During the apartheid years, we received constant media exposure to the evils of the degenerate white South African—a despicable character who refused to see his fellow humans as equals.

Zwick's *Blood Diamond*, however, provides viewers with a slightly different variation of this traditional figuration—Danny Archer, like South Africa itself, understands the importance of reform and regeneration. Throughout the film, Archer appears to lose some of his racism as he learns more about Solomon Vandy, and his materialist pursuit of diamonds becomes tinged with some transcendent idealism as he learns more about the life of this Mendi fisherman. At the conclusion of the film, racial differences are put aside, and Danny experiences a conversion on his deathbed. Danny, who has been fatally wounded, holds Solomon's hand and gives him the "pink," telling him to take care of his son. Amidst what must have been muffled tears in the theater, we, as audience members, are invited to accept Danny's redemptive act. In terms of the overall message, it seems that under the right circumstances, reform is possible. A likable action hero, even a racist, can sacrifice his life for a good cause, and, in turn, the evil specter of bigotry once again goes away.

Some may wonder why this representation is problematic. Conclusions to Hollywood films are often tidy, devoid of either ethnic or national complication. As such, in *Blood Diamond* we are not asked to wrestle with the ambiguities, ambivalences, and contestations that are a part of life in Sierra Leone. Rather, we are provided with a redemptive act in which all has been made right with the world. The racist hero has become a saint. The problems with conflict-ridden diamond trades are a thing of the past. This is in spite of the fact that one Sierra Leonean, Walton Paul, told one of us that miners in that country are still "very poor," and that the "Kimberley Process has not made a difference and is not working."[15]

We believe the problem is similar to what Havens and other critics have noted in other Hollywood productions that attempt to explore issues of race.[16] While addressing racial issues in a cursory way, the difficult questions are left untouched. The multicultural presence of people of color on the screen is taken as illustrative proof of race neutrality and progressive interventionism.

Maddy Bowen: The Hero's Ally

Solomon Vandy appears in *Blood Diamond* to be an African who hates exploitation and has moral scruples, but he is not the only uplifting character in the film who represents redemptive hope. Solomon has an ally in Maddy Bowen, a U.S. reporter who hopes to uncover the evils of the diamond industry. Bowen's investigative journalism symbolizes Zwick's liberalism, embracing a type of activism that relies on multinational and multiracial alliances. Maddy plays what Tobin calls the "hero's ally." The hero's ally functions to "help the hero overcome his flaw."[17] Maddy repeatedly rebukes Danny for his pessimistic, materialistic view of the world, hoping to transform this racist "Rhodesian" into the man he is destined to become. At the same time, Maddy, like Danny, is fearless. As presented in a long exposition by a fellow reporter, Maddy has traveled into the most treacherous corners of the world, never once fearing for her life. And like so many of Hollywood's well-groomed leading female protagonists, she returns from these war-torn countries looking as beautiful as ever, which emphasizes the film's understanding of the importance of image over the materiality of political struggles.

Maddy Bowen uses moral suasion as a tool in her redemptive quests, and an on-screen example of her heroics takes center stage when she is confronted by a local militia. Maddy is able to save the entire group of travelers by convincing the guerillas to pose with her in several photographs. She appears to have the ethics of Solomon, coupled with Danny's savvy. Unlike Solomon, however, Maddy possesses a degree of selfishness. When asked to help Solomon, her first reaction is to state that "the world is full of people in need, why should I help this one man?" Immediately following this revelation of her ethical flaw, she corrects herself by stating, "I can't believe I just said that." If not for this lapse, she, too, could be perceived as a nearly flawless character.

Maddy's role as reporter is supposed to show us narrative details that ordinarily we might not have noticed. This is accentuated visually with a unique cinematic device. As Maddy photographs the trauma of war, we see a freeze frame image (a black and white photograph) accompanied by the sound of an SLR (single-lens reflex) shutter sound effect. This momentarily interrupts the narrative flow by presenting a different mediated representation, one more commonly seen in print media. This device serves to disrupt the codified narrative structure and create a unique moment of reflexivity, a space in which the film implies consideration of the "actual" events in Sierra Leone. These visual flashes are not part of what has come to be known as the classic Hollywood style. Instead, they are part of a more adaptive and ostensibly realistic presentation, in which we become privy to some complex concerns of the investigative photojournalist. The use of these hybrid flashes operates very much like the hand-held camera, making the filmic world appear more real through the materiality of the visual artifact. We note, for example, that, after seeing one of these images, Maddy's comments appear to represent more of an authorial statement by the film: She states that if people back home (USA) knew about the violence in Sierra Leone, they wouldn't buy any conflict diamonds. In essence, Maddy may be signaling the transcendent message of the film, where revelation of wrongdoing might become the paramount concern of all types of witnesses.

As with many in the United States, Maddy, as foreign outsider, seems to be the only character who, in her words, gives a "shit." In spite of the fact that she tells us very little about daily life in Sierra Leone, we applaud Maddy's international efforts, as she opens doors for Americans and other Westerners who we might want to applaud for taking the time to think about the sources of the conflicted diamond wars. Maddy, like the Anglo-American women who once funded a host of abolitionist causes in the eighteenth and nineteenth centuries, is waging her own form of noble reformation. We might feel better upon leaving the theater knowing that because of Maddy, the American, the world is a safer place, but outside of the local Cineplex, things are not nearly so rosy.

Narrative Patterns of the Anti-Racist Hero

To some degree, the narrative characterizations found in *Blood Diamond* follows a familiar pattern also noted by rhetorical critics of films such as *Mississippi Burning, Cry Freedom*, and *Amistad*. According to Madison, this pattern includes the following four elements:

> 1) white hero experiences some extreme form of racism vicariously through some black contact, 2) white hero develops a relatively radical anti-racist consciousness, 3) white hero sacrifices a great deal at the hands of white racists to further the cause of the black people's struggle (usually in some type of leadership capacity), and 4) white hero suffers terribly for his or her efforts but manages to somehow prevail in the end.[18]

This pattern functions rhetorically to relieve the guilt that many white viewers feel about institutionalized forms of racism. As a means of containing these feelings of guilt, according to John Gabriel, these films "distance the racism of the here and now" by situating it in the past or a remote geographical location,[19] which, it could be argued, is the case with *Blood Diamond*. The end result is a kind of "white innocence," Michael Lacy observes, in which audiences see racism as a largely remedied problem, rather than the continuing pernicious and embedded practice we know it to be.[20]

We believe, however, that *Blood Diamond* deviates from this standard pattern in several important and interesting ways. First and foremost, rather than distancing the American viewer from the institutionalized practice of racist violence, *Blood Diamond* implicates the viewer. The point becomes clear (as the film progresses) that any American who purchases a diamond engagement ring indirectly contributes to a cycle of pain for Sierra Leoneans. This is certainly an over-simplification of Sierra Leone's diamond industry, but as Maddy put it: people "back home wouldn't buy a diamond if they knew it cost someone a hand."

Maddy's portrayal also deviates from types found in classical anti-racist white hero films. In those films, Maddy would be seen as the protagonist who would have come into contact with extreme white racists in the diamond industry—such as Danny, would have faced insurmountable obstacles and, by putting her own life in jeopardy, would eventually have eliminated the perpetrator of that racism, thereby suggesting racism is a thing of the past. Yet, consider the fact that the perpetrator of the most visceral violence is not a white character but, instead, African slave traders who enact violence against other Africans. Certainly, the capitalist system is equally culpable, yet violence stemming from capitalism receives very little screen time. By the same token, the racist character as represented by Danny is not eliminated by force or violence. Instead, he is convinced by Maddy to change his ways, to become a better man, and to give up his life for a greater good.

Blood Diamond alleviates guilt for white audiences through Maddy's and Danny's portayals, but it also becomes a call to action for audiences. Yet, even in this somewhat improved representation over previous films, the colonized, again, face extreme violence, both from outsiders (the diamond industry) and from within. Perhaps in this new pattern there are degrees of guilt white people may share, but at the same time, the paternalistic representations of the past remain intact as white Americans retain a sense of moral superiority, and the South African gives up his life for a greater good.

When Subjects Talk Back—Critiques of *Blood Diamond* from Sierra Leone

While many folks in Sierra Leone are appreciative of the fact that filmmakers have taken an interest in representing some of the horrors committed by the RUF and other participants in the conflict diamond wars, they often lament the fact that even those who play anti-racist characters, like DiCaprio; Zwick, himself; and the other promoters of this film did not take the time to visit Sierra Leone so they could see the struggles of impoverished divers and other workers who play key roles in the diamond trade. This was a world on the ground filled with Lebanese middle men and gavel shakers, "miners" who made up a part of what the *Concord Times* of Sierra Leone called the "diamond chain."[21] A more realistic portrayal of the blood diamond industries would have noted that the diamonds passed through Koindu to Monrovia. In this way, the producers could also have commented on the involvement of Charles Taylor of Liberia (on trial at The Hague) or Sam Bockarie (*aka* Mosquito).

Moreover, what bothered many Sierra Leoneans was the fact that *Blood Diamond* was filmed elsewhere. This meant a loss of employment opportunities for locals and also meant access to the movie by viewers would be limited. A movie that was supposed to tell "the story" of Sierra Leone and was receiving rave international reviews for consciousness raising seemed to be devoid of materialist *praxis* and had little positive impact on local politics or economies. Josette Sheeran, the executive director of the U.N. World Food Program, reminded audiences who viewed the film in 2007 that "Sierra Leoneans can take pride in the immense achievements since the end of the war,"[22] but it was unclear how *Blood Diamond* was conveying any of this pride.

One member of our critical research team, Carol Anderson, observed that the average person in Sierra Leone cannot afford to spend money on a DVD, but there were some Sierra Leoneans who had seen the film and had quite vocal opinions about this cinematic representation. Victor Lewis, for example, the publisher of the *Spectator*, opined that the producers of *Blood Diamond* seemed to be "more concerned with making money than portraying the real Sierra Leone."[23] Nauvo, a politician and a businessman, argued that this celluloid representation provided an "improper portrayal of Sierra Leone." He explained that the absence of local actors, musicians, and businesses made it unreal, which was highly problematic when the "subject matter" of the film involved "a country."[24]

Some interviewees suggested that if these filmmakers really cared about the people of Sierra Leone, then DiCaprio and the others should think about sequels that might provide more constructive and complete pictures of these affairs. It was bad enough that the film did not take into account the fact that this country was in the middle of registration for presidential elections—now this nation's history was being poached as well. One local journalist, Sorious Samura, has made his own documentary, *Blood On the Stone*, which tries to trace the trials and tribulations of workers who travel to Kono. In some ways, Samura's work is a critique of the very certification process that is valorized in *Blood Diamond*, because he shows that getting a Kimberley certificate and smuggling diamonds into Guinea was "as easy as drinking cool water."[25]

Carol Anderson's synthesis of the interviews revealed a common sentiment about *Blood Diamond*: by not involving the leadership or the people of Sierra Leone, and by not employing local actors, these filmmakers seemed to have lost some valuable opportunities. They failed to take advantage of local business and musicians, which in turn contributed to the poor usage of the Krio language.

In sum, while many moviegoers in the West were flocking to theaters so that they could see the characters in *Blood Diamond*, one of the poorest nations in the world had exasperated denizens wondering about appropriation of a history of the bloody 1990s.

Conclusion

After accumulating and analyzing all of this information, we understandably have mixed feelings about Zwick's movie *Blood Diamond*. While we applaud the choice of topics and the attempted use of diverse characters, we are bothered by both the film's use of stereotypes and the film's implied realist depiction of the Sierra Leoneans. It is one thing to claim that filmmakers have creative cinematic license that allows them to engage in liberal consciousness-raising through film, but it is quite another to claim that that filmic representation is also an accurate portrayal of the trials and tribulations of the people of Sierra Leone. At a time when the infusion of just hundreds of thousands of dollars would have markedly helped many communities in that nation, Western nations were trumpeting the fact that this movie was making tens of millions of dollars.

We argue that the use of familiar movie plot lines that rely on hegemonic audience expectations about multiculturalism create enthymematic situations that allow for the domestication of filmic critiques—by the end of Zwick's *Blood Diamond* we are invited to believe that the Kimberley Process has helped "end" the abusive use of much of this mineral wealth, and that the instantiation of this procedure depended on the alliances that were created between white journalists and African workers. We learn precious little about some of the histories of Sierra Leone, the multiple causes of economic dislocation, or the needs of the average worker in these regions.

NOTES

1. Junior Nauvo, in interview with one of the authors (Carol W. Anderson), January 2008.

2. Lujala Paivi, Nils Gleditsch, and Elisabeth Gilmore, "A Diamond Curse?: Civil War and a Lootable Resource," *Journal of Conflict Resolution* 49 (2005): 538–62.

3. Michael T. Klare, *Resource Wars: the New Landscape of Global Conflict* (New York: Metropolitan, 2001).

4. Ann Norman, in interview with one of the authors (Carol W. Anderson), January, 2008.

5. "U.N. Agency Holds First-Ever Screening of Film 'Blood Diamond' in Sierra Leone," States News Service, 4 May 2007, http:www.lexisnexis.com.

6. Richard Delgado, *Critical Race Theory: The Cutting Edge* (Philadelphia: Temple University Press, 2001).

7. David Edelstein, "They Cut Glass, and Hands," *New York Magazine*, December 11, 2006, paragraph 1.

8. Hugh Holman and William Harmon, *A Handbook to Literature*, 5th ed. (New York: Macmillan, 1986), 333.

9. Kent Ono and Derek Buescher, "Deciphering Pocahontas: Unpacking the Commodification of a Native American Woman," *Critical Studies in Mass Communication* 18, no. 1 (2001): 23–43.

10. Greg Campbell, *Blood Diamonds: Tracing the Deadly Path of the World's Most Precious Gems* (Boulder, CO: Westview Press, 2002), xiv.

11. Darsie Bowden, *Writing for Film: the Basics of Screenwriting* (Mahwah, NJ: Lawrence Erlbaum, 2006), 59.

12. Linda Aronson, *Screenwriting Updated: New (and Conventional) Ways of Writing for the Screen* (Los Angeles: Sillman-James, 2000), 57.

13. Linda Seger, *Making a Good Script Great*, 2nd ed. (Hollywood: Samuel French, 1994), 149.

14. Robin Tobin, *The Screenwriting Formula* (Cincinnati: Writer's Digest Books, 2007), 19.

15. Paul Walter, in interview with one of the authors (Carol W. Anderson), January 2008.

16. Timothy Havens, "'The Biggest Show in the World': Race and the Global Popularity of the Cosby Show," *Media, Culture, and Society* 22 (2000): 371–91.

17. Tobin, *The Screenwriting*, 35.

18. Kelly Madison, "Legitimation Crisis and Containment: The "Anti-Racist-White-Hero" Film," *Critical Studies in Mass Communication* 16 (1999): 405.

19. John Gabriel, *Whitewash: Racialized Politics and the Media* (London: Routledge, 1998), 61.

20. Michael Lacy, "White Innocence Heroes: Recovery, Reversals, Paternalism, and David Duke," *Journal of International and Intercultural Communication*, 3, no. 3 (2010): 206–27.

21. "Diamond Tales." *Concord Times*, 31 May 2007, http://www.lexisnexis.com.

22. "U.N. Agency Holds First-Ever Screening of Film '*Blood Diamond*' in Sierra Leone," *States News Service*, 4 May 2007, paragraph 7, http://www.lexisnexis.com.

23. Victor Lewis, in interview with one of the authors (Carol W. Anderson), January 2008.

24. Junior Nauvo, in interview with one of the authors (Carol W. Anderson), January 2008.

25. Clare Heal, "Paying for Diamonds with Child's Blood," *Sunday Express*, 28 January 2007, paragraphs 18-20, http://www.lexis.nexis.

13 Abstracting and De-Racializing Diversity

The Articulation of Diversity in the Post-Race Era

Rona Tamiko Halualani

Articulated in a newspaper near you:

Thousands of busy commuters drive in and out of the bustling metropolitan city of Anytown without noticing the large suburban community—Centerville—they pass through everyday. With its "small neighborhood" feel, Centerville is a historic bedroom community filled with 1970s tract homes and a quaint, distinctive downtown district that was created in the 1960s. Twenty years ago, Centerville was a predominantly White, middle-class community. Today it is "home" to a multicultural mix of Asians, Hispanics, Samoans, and immigrants from all over the world, which is emblematic of the major changes in diversity that are sweeping through the region. Twenty years ago, Whites comprised 86 percent of Centerville's population, while Hispanics made up only 7 percent. According to Census 2000, only 40 percent of Centerville's 165,017 residents are White while Asians account for 20 percent and Hispanics, 22 percent. These changes are especially evident when you walk through the downtown district's row of Korean markets, Chinese shops, Japanese and Mexican restaurants, and Afghan bakeries. Centerville has emerged as the quintessential melting pot.

Sheila Ma, a Chinese American resident, also highlights the city's demographic changes: "Look at all the cultures here. You can meet someone from a different culture just by walking down the street. This is the cross-section of the United States in Centerville."

Centerville's mayor, Daniel Williamson, a White resident who moved to the area 15 years ago, claims that Centerville is such a thriving multicultural place that "it shows that race doesn't matter" and "lots of different groups can come and live here without worrying about the baggage of race."

Not all residents of Centerville share the optimism of their neighbors. Several express concern that the city would no longer be home to a great number of Centerville's oldest families as in the past. Harry Lincoln, a White contractor in the city, asks: "Where would all the longtimers—the ones who built Centerville—go? Who do we become with all these groups shuffling in and out?" Several residents reminisce about what life used to be like in Centerville. Others bring up how some groups, such as the Asian immigrants, seem to be "moving quickly" through the city, buying up several property tracts and igniting an influx of Asians into Centerville. It seems Centerville will never be quite the same.[1]

"Centerville" can be one of many towns across the United States, a place that was once historically White and racially/ethnically homogenous and is now thriving with an influx of cultural groups. The Census 2000 figures show that demographic changes have instead occurred. Compared to 20 years ago, there are more racial, ethnic, and immigrant residents living in "Centerville" than ever before. Census projections predict even more dramatic shifts for the future: the percentage of Latinos and Asians will increase three-fold in that area. There seems to be little doubt that we are witnessing a groundbreaking intercultural transformation of the U.S. populace. "Centerville" residents are living witnesses to such change and personally attest to the demographic shifts and the positive cultural climate among the residents. The city proclaims it has already accomplished integration and tolerance, and points to minority residents' satisfaction and happiness levels as evidence.

Indeed, Centerville does sound too good to be true, but this is precisely because of the representational power of the dominant media and the cultural work they do.[2] Centerville is not a specific place per se; yet, it is similar to many places in the western United States in the post-race era. By post-race era, I refer to the period from the late 1990s to the present during which U.S. society invoked a neoliberal stance through which race, in all social and political matters, was to be avoided, shunned, and discarded.[3] In this light, Centerville is not some fictional account, but a power-laden representation brought to life in newspaper discourses, a representation that signifies what diversity is and looks like, and whom it benefits and costs.

In this chapter, I use critical articulation theory and methods to examine 100 regional newspaper texts from Silicon Valley, California. These media texts articulate a specific ideological representation of diversity in the post-race era in two ways: First, diversity signifies an abstract, idealized, and/or raceless representation and reality, in which cultural communities are collocated, while simultaneously emptied of any particular histories, social structures, or structural inequalities. Instead, racial and ethnic groups are taken to be *present* and thus *equal* in the same city spaces. Second, diversity and difference are depicted as universal. Each cultural group is deemed to be the *same* and *equal* precisely because they are all equally *different*. The universalization of difference in media discourses works to inscribe a set of intercultural relations that is nonthreatening, without reference to race, and equal. Above all, such a universalizing move recuperates the normative role of the state as the neutral, fair, rational, and race-less arbiter of society.

This "abstract or raceless diversity" articulation is made possible through two discursive constructions. First, compelling narratives, city profiles, and bold headlines document and establish diversity as real, present, and a significant kind of change that is markedly different from the past ("the way it once was"). In featured profiles, cities are deemed more demographically diverse, inclusive, and open, as residents highlight the "variety" of cultures in their communities and reflect upon the "racially/ethnically homogenous yesterday" through narrative flashbacks. Thus, personal and private memories of residents about how their city *once was* compared to *what it is now* powerfully illustrate the notion that society is advancing, progressing, and moving away from the "way it used to be" during, for example, the nation's historical period of segregation that ran from the late 1800s through the 1950s.[4] In its second construction, diversity is made abstract through a "minority majority" construction in which the numerical census counts of minority groups are deployed to obliterate the notion of a White majority. By this, the demographic presence of all racialized (minority) groups is encoded to underscore the point that no majority reigns in the post-race era and that racism and intolerance are things of the past.

Through an abstract or raceless diversity, I contend that regional newspaper media advance the dominant interests of the racial state, or the structural apparatus composed of local, state, and federal governmental structures, backed by the courts of law, military power, public policy, public educational institutions, and local, regional, and national media.[5] With such power to support and enforce it, the racial state invisibly legislates and mandates specific race definitions—and racial inclusions and exclusions—without referring to "race," and structurally frames intercultural relations between and among ethnic and racial groups.[6]

Dominant Discourses around Diversity and Multiculturalism

Communication Studies scholars have examined the rhetorical discourses around immigration,[7] race,[8] and ethnicity.[9] While they have uncovered the discursive operations of dominant and oppositional meanings that surround these social issues, missing are the larger encodings of "diversity" and "multiculturalism" in media texts and public communication.

Critical cultural studies scholars Avery Gordon and Christopher Newfield and David Theo Goldberg do unpack the governmental, educational, and mediated representations of multiculturalism at a time when "multiculturalism" was hailed as the ideal goal of U.S. society.[10] Gordon and Newfield trace how, in the 1970s, educators initiated a vision of multiculturalism that "sought to dismantle White majority control of schools and use of White backgrounds and values as yardsticks."[11] Over the next 20 years, multiculturalism pervaded the political, institutional, and social realms of U.S. society and eventually lost touch with its original anti-racist and politically-edged focus of the 1970s.[12] In the 1990s, the focus on "multiculturalism" encompassed "diversity," or the embracing of cultural differences between and among groups. Diversity discourse contained a spirit of cultural pluralism and presumed equality and even became corporatized as "diversity management" to organize cultural difference productively for business success.

Critical race scholars Michael Omi and Howard Winant and Goldberg further theorize that discourses around multiculturalism and diversity are always intertwined with meanings of race and racism.[13] These scholars argue that dominant discourses that surround multiculturalism and diversity are particularly important to interrogate, because they advance the interests of the racial state. According to Goldberg,[14] the racial state is a structural apparatus made up of local, state, and federal governmental structures and backed by the courts of law, military power, public policy, public educational institutions, local, regional, and national media.[15] Indeed, society has come to view the state not as primarily subjective or racial, but as an impartial and disinterested body that oversees and delimits social order according to a set of neutral rules, conditions, and procedures. Such a guise illustrates the ideological power of the state and the central role it plays in our lives. For instance, the modern racial state creates, modifies, and reifies racial expressions, inclusions, and exclusions and thereby demonstrates how groups are situated in relation to one another. Moreover, the racial state legally and administratively defines non-racial admissions and employment criteria for public institutions of learning and business and class-based criteria for residential districting, thus shaping which groups—by race and class—will occupy specific contexts. Through these acts, with racial effects that are disguised, the state "manages and oversees what individuals can do, where they can go, what educational institution they can access, with whom they can interact, and where they can reside."[16]

More specifically, the racial state establishes its predominance by reproducing *racial power* and *racial order*.[17] Racial power is defined as "the cumulative and interactive political, economic, social, and cultural processes that jointly reproduce racial categories and distribution and perpetuate a system of White dominance."[18] The state comes into existence in part through the systemic nature of its racial power, or the continuous reproduction and distribution of racial categories and meanings that serve to maintain a racial status quo. But, the racial state also remains dominant through its racial ordering of cultural groups. The racial categories and meanings are reproduced in a distinct order as groups are positioned relative to one another. In her analysis of Black-Korean relations in New York City, Claire Jean Kim explains that U.S. society is not merely a vertical hierarchy but is also a racially ordered field constructed of at least two axes (i.e., superior/inferior, insider/foreigner).[19] She argues that this racial order "stands at the intersection of the discursive-ideational and social-structural realms; it is a discursively constructed, shared cognitive map that serves as a normative blueprint for who should get what in American society."[20] The state, therefore, racially classifies groups in specific relation to one another, all the while maintaining a "colorless" authority. All in all, the racial state promotes its hidden and unspoken power interests, including economic power and legal/political supremacy, underneath a cloak of neutrality, fairness, and racelessness.

While communication scholars have examined rhetorical discourse surrounding specific political initiatives and acts from the state,[21] I follow Ono and Sloop's example by examining dominant newspaper discourse that ideologically constitutes and shapes diversity from the vantage point of the racial state.[22] Ono and Sloop underscore the point that dominant media discourse (especially news media) frame and reify social issues in a way that proffers the dominant status quo perspective and carries social and political consequences for individuals.[23] Given this, it is imperative that we critically analyze the dominant media discourses through which the racial state delimits and shapes the meanings and stakes of diversity for the public.

Articulation

I employed the theory and method of articulation (derived from cultural studies) to analyze 100 mainstream, or dominant, regional newspaper texts. Ono and Sloop make a case that mainstream local, regional, and national media texts "fundamentally shape what issues become salient, the way issues come to have meaning, and the audiences who participate in learning about issues, as well as what responses ultimately become possible."[24] Likewise, despite the claim of fair and objective journalism, I argue that mainstream regional newspaper discourses are extensions of the racial state and promote dominant state interests of hegemonic capitalism, nationalism, and "colorblindness" to the general public.[25] Moreover, these discourses powerfully circulate and reproduce ideology as a form of common sense (doxa) at a societal level and at an individual, private level.[26]

I selected five major regional newspaper outlets that represent Bay Area-Silicon Valley Northern California and its diverse constituency and studied them from 1994 to 2003. Then, in order to collect a manageable number of meaningful texts for my sample, I collected Bay Area and Silicon Valley newspaper texts searching for one key word: "diversity." I analyzed each text using the theory and method of articulation.

Although my sample is derived from one specific region (the western United States—California, which has its own unique political and social characteristics, in particular), my analysis proffers both regionally specific and nationally relevant insights. I unpacked the distinct dominant representations of diversity in a region (Northern California), known for its supposed political progressivism, economic volatility, and explosive cultural heterogeneity. My study sheds light on how such regionally specific and dominant articulations of diversity cut across several regions and perhaps constitute a larger discursive formation about U.S. diversity generally.

According to the key works of Ernest Laclau, Chantal Mouffe, and Stuart Hall,[27] articulation is a theory and method used by cultural analysts to examine discourses and texts and trace these texts' meanings to larger ideological forces, power interests, and social groups. Through articulation, a scholar can identify and analyze the social/ideological forces behind, and/or that benefit from, a discourse's meanings and significations such as capitalism, nationalism, patriarchy, state neutrality, sexism, Whiteness, and heterosexism, among others.[28] Hall explains further that "the theory of articulation is both a way of understanding how ideological elements come, under certain conditions, to cohere together within a discourse, and a way of asking how they do or do not become articulated, at specific conjunctures, to certain political subjects."[29] In a similar vein, Lawrence Grossberg emphasizes that articulation "links this practice to that effect, this text to that meaning to that reality, these experiences to those politics. And these links are themselves articulated into larger structures."[30] Thus, articulation is more than just a method for textual analysis; it stands as a microscopic *and* wide-focus lens through which to track and chase down the political operations of a discourse's meanings, or how meanings benefit and advance specific structures of power and ideologies and negatively valorize social groups in a specific historical and sociopolitical moment/context.[31]

While articulation theory informed my approach, for this study, I searched for articles that featured the term "diversity" as the main topic or byline. I then traced how the articles each portrayed, described, and valorized (positively, negatively, or ambivalently) the term "diversity," and I coded these as significant themes. Lastly, I searched for specific racial/ethnic groups that were discussed in relation to the topic of "diversity." My main research questions were: How is diversity depicted in the media texts in terms of overall framing (as positive celebrations or de-emphasized as conflicts) and key terms? What social forces, structural interests, and ideologies are promoted through these articulations of diversity?

Articulating Diversity

Though I found a range of significant articulations around diversity, this chapter highlights two major themes that dominated the sample of texts. The first theme foregrounds the dramatic demographic shifts via compelling narratives, city profiles, and bold headlines. It elevates the burgeoning diversity by erasing identifiable power differences and social inequalities between groups using census counts, demographic predictions, and city profiles. The second theme highlights how diversity is abstracted through a "minority majority" construction, in which the numerical census counts of minority groups are deployed to obliterate the notion of a White majority. The demographic presence of all minority groups is de-racialized to illustrate that no majority reigns in the post-race era and that racism and intolerance are things of the past. My analysis highlights several key representative examples.

Signifying an Abstract and Raceless Diversity

Documenting the Presence of Diversity

Featured on the front page of "The Majority of None" Newspaper Series are the following:

> A magnified photograph of six high school couples made up of young females and males from various racial and ethnic backgrounds, dancing together at a high school event. The caption underneath the photo reads: "1998 – Prospect High: The ethnically diverse mix of students at Prospect High in Saratoga reflects Santa Clara County's new demographic makeup. Prospect students, shown at the first dance of the school year, come from dozens of countries."
>
> Below the photo, is a much smaller image of a group of White students dancing together at a high school event. The caption underneath the photo reads: "1971 – Prospect High: A yearbook picture captures students at a Sadie Hawkins Day dance almost 30 years ago when the student body was largely white."
>
> The opening paragraph of the article reads: "The precise moment is anybody's guess. But sometime this year, the population meter will click—and for the first time Santa Clara County's white residents will no longer be the majority. In a nation forged from majority rule, in an age obsessed with race, the shift drives home the magnitude of the changes that have transformed the county for the past 30 years."[32]

The dominant regional newspaper texts articulate diversity by first establishing and documenting its widespread presence in the Bay Area. Newspaper texts (31%, 25) highlight the extraordinary shifts in demographic diversity through compelling narratives, testimonials from residents, and bold headlines. For example, the *San Jose Mercury News* featured a week-long series entitled, "Majority of None," in which several compelling narratives delineate the dramatic changes in demographic diversity in the Silicon Valley. One narrative reads:

> Silicon Valley's allure in the 1990s has been so great that the Asian population, boosted by immigration and domestic migration, is growing at a pace that exceeds any forecasts prepared as recently as a decade ago. Denis Fong, a 47-year-old Chinese-American developer, said that when he was growing up in San Jose in the

1960s, he knew most of the other Asians by name: "Back then you ran into another Asian randomly once or twice a year. Now they're all over the place."[33]

This same article continued to feature exoticized descriptions of the influx of cultures: "And for every workplace or mall filled with a collage of black, White, Latino and Asian faces, there are other pockets of the county where immigrant culture and custom have dug in. At the twin Pacific Rim plazas in North San Jose, Chinese grocers hawk squid and shark fin to people who live nearby on Taipei Drive, Shanghai Circle, Hong Kong Drive. At East Side taqueria and mercados, practically everyone speaks 'Spanglish.'"[34] Such narratives, among others, present a changing portrait of racial and ethnic groups through descriptions of how such change has personally affected individual Silicon Valley residents.

The newspaper texts (10) also featured personal accounts of community residents who have witnessed dramatic changes in diversity. These individual testimonials serve as "witnesses" of changes in regional diversity, seeing firsthand the shift from "the way it once was" to "what it is now and what it will become." For instance, about 20% (20) of the newspaper texts analyzed featured city spotlights or profiles of specific cities that mention diversity growth rates and trends. The article profiles read very much like descriptions of communities experiencing groundbreaking shifts from once White majority towns to bustling, cosmopolitan, and culturally rich ones. The narrative sound bites include an array of resident types: White residents who grew up in the city, local city officials, and newly arriving residents, many of whom are recent immigrants. For example, one article that highlights a rapidly changing city highlights the testimony of one longtime resident who grew up in the area: "When I was a kid we were pretty much isolated. We didn't have daily interaction with other people except those who were just like us . . . It's a lot different for my children and grandchildren. They see a community today that is vibrant and economically viable. They can intermix with pretty much the cross section of the United States, which is essentially here in Concord."[35] This same article powerfully profiles the local city area and focuses on the reach diversity has made and the personal impact diversity has had on its community members.

> For decades, Concord was the ultimate bedroom community—middle-class, boring, and overwhelmingly white. But Contra Costa's largest city is now emblematic of the changes sweeping through Bay Area suburbs such as Milpitas, San Leandro, and Redwood City—onetime white bastions that are now home to a vibrant multicultural stew of Samoans, Iranians, Latin Americans, and immigrants from every nation of the world. Larry Azevedo, a former mayor and longtime businessman in the city, has seen the changes firsthand. When he moved with his parents from Richmond to Concord in 1949, there were almost no members of minority groups in his class at Mount Diablo High School.[36]

Another article highlights several personal accounts of several residents in a changing city, two of which are as follows:

> Harvey Matthews has watched more than a dozen new faces and families move onto his block in the Bayview over the past 10 years. One has a Star of David hanging in the window, but most of the others regularly carry home bags of Asian vegetables and baked goods from nearby markets. It's become a familiar scene in many San Francisco neighborhoods, largely because of an influx of Asian immigrants, reflected in newly released Census 2000 statistics. [37]
>
> David Lee, director of the city's Chinese American Voters Education Committee said, "When we're registering voters, 10 years ago, we very rarely ran into Mandarin (speakers) . . . Now, it's one of the fastest-growing dialects in San Francisco . . . Neighborhoods like the Sunset have become much more Asian, having really matured from 10 years ago, when it was first recorded that Asian settlement was just beginning."[38]

These depictions typically frame "the way it once was" as a reflection of predominantly White residential composition, and the "what it is now" as a reflection of the arrival and settlement of racial and ethnic groups not recorded before in the city. Personal testimony, such as this, works to concretize a sense of change as evident in people's stories and outlooks on their own growing neighborhoods and communities. City profiles imply that integration and cultural progress have already been achieved and are currently in motion in designated areas.

In addition, the "Majority of None" newspaper series featured several photographic images that illustrate the far reach of diversity in everyday life. There was an image of culturally different residents (Asians, Latino/as, and Whites) walking down a city street as well as images of a visibly diverse high school class and student body in the school hallways and at a school dance. Other images captured the racially and ethnically different persons interacting in workplaces, local government offices, and on neighborhood streets. Newspaper accounts also presented the following as front page headlines: "New Demographics Changing Everything," "Who We Are: Vibrant Mix of Newcomers Transforms Suburbs into a Burgeoning Multiethnic Haven," "A Majority of None: Shift to Foreshadow Changes in State, U.S."; "Multicultural Mingling Helps Enrich Daily Life."[39] The vast diversity of people, ethnic communities, neighborhoods, and businesses is therefore amply highlighted throughout all the articles analyzed; in this way these texts establish a clear message: Diversity is real and present in the region.

Verifying the Presence of Diversity: The Minority-Majority Construction

"The Bay Area and California are rapidly approaching the point where no racial group will be in the majority, according to new federal statistics being released today."

"By 2020, there will be no racial majority."

"By 2040, only 31 percent of Californians will be White."

"Experts, responding to census data showing the rise to dominance of minority groups over non-Latino White Californians, anticipate that the shift will change the state's political makeup, its economic balance, its educational institutions—even people's perceptions of themselves."[40]

Dominant newspaper texts (40%, 32) prominently featuring population growth charts, census count figures, and population projections abound throughout regional media. These data serve as powerful vehicles to verify once and for all that diversity exists. More specifically, newspaper texts underscore the census counts and projections and inscribe a minority-majority construction, or a representation that claims there will be no racial/ethnic majority in the region (or the majority will consist of minority groups). Such a construction reifies the portrait of diversity articulated by the state: a form of social life in which every group is present, equal, and no one group dominates.

Over half (20) of the newspaper texts focused on demographic changes in the Silicon Valley's racial/ethnic make-up and highlighted the "exploding growth" and "spilling over of diversity" via census counts and county figures.[41] These "figures" are much more than numerical indicators of a state's diversity index; these figures are taken-for-granted representations that structure and constitute such measures all at once.[42] Seemingly objective, census estimates mask the subjective ways in which census enumerators record their commonsensical perceptions of physical appearance as racial fact, thereby structurally determining racial categories and racial assignment which, in turn, organizes the racial body politic.[43] According to Goldberg, census figures and population projections, which emanate from the state, "purport to count without judging, to photograph without transforming . . . in the name of an objectivity that claims simply to document or to reflect."[44] Hence, population projections mask politicized constructions that predetermine and fix state-preferred racial compositions and intercultural relations. For example, one newspaper account suggests that "The Bay Area and California are rapidly approaching the point where no racial group will be in the majority, according to new federal statistics being released today."[45] In addition, the following population projection appears on the front page, with a visual image of African Americans and Latinos walking on a downtown street:

Assuming that the trends in the new federal statistics continue, California will become a "minority majority" state within five years. The new federal numbers show that about 51 percent of the state is White. Formal projections for the Bay area are out of date, but state analysts said that the region will no longer have a White majority sometime around 2008.[46]

This widely circulated projection—"by the year 20__, there will be no majority"—assumes a peculiar state formation when combined with the aforementioned narratives that celebrate demographic growth ("they're all over the place"). These examples consistently refer to "California's transformation into a minority-majority state," "meaning that no one ethnic/racial group will constitute more than 50 percent of a state with significant increases in the Latino and Asian populations."[47] Here, the key words "minority" and "majority" appear in a way that highlights the conceptual erasure of a powerful racial "majority" and the rise and predominance of all minority groups, especially Asians and Latinos, who stand out with the most explosive growth patterns. A minority-majority construction ultimately frames diversity as about the demographic increase and representational growth of specific groups in a particular area. It provides an illusion, backed up with concrete data (numerical figures, the objectivist language of demography), of a predominant White majority as a thing of the past. Now, however, racial and ethnic groups have grown in number and gained entry into specific residential locations. The assumption here is that the groups that have grown in number do experience social, structural, and material equality with one another.

While seemingly celebrating and reveling in diversity, the dominant newspaper discourses articulate diversity in a way that is pointedly different from discourses of the late 1980s, during which multiculturalism was hailed as the remedy for the racial conflicts of the 1960s and 1970s.[48] Instead, diversity is a contradictory formation, signifying demographic diversity but one that is *raceless*, lacking power differentiation, and without any cultural hierarchy. For instance, the "Majority of None" newspaper series observes that, with such diversity, "there is a high number of residents who said race just doesn't matter in matters of work, politics, their neighbors—and even love."[49] Yet another example can be seen in the following quotation: "Jeff Moe looks forward to a day when a person's race simply won't matter. Moe, who grew up in a Wisconsin town that was all White, has married a Filipino woman and is the father of two mixed race kids. He has taken on a leadership role in Cupertino's Asian American Parent Association and lives on a Cupertino street that couldn't be more diverse."[50] What is interesting in this example is that the article argues race does not matter by detailing all the aspects of diversity in this resident's life. Other articles feature Bay Area students' responses to the question: "What will race be like in 2020?" These teenagers comment that "I really don't think there will be set types of race. Everybody's going to be mixed. It won't matter. We'll be colorblind," and "There will be less hate. Race will matter less. We'll realize it was silly to make such a big deal out of it."[51] Thus, the logic of this comment is that with so much diversity around, one can more easily overlook the racial and ethnic specificity of the individual. Diversity is therefore highlighted at the very same moment as it is abstracted away from race or difference. This specific articulation of diversity is used to eradicate race, the much publicized divider of cultural groups, in the public sphere.

Given these examples, then, a raceless diversity is an encoding that operates by first demarcating unprecedented diversity growth (i.e., the rise in births, arrivals, and settlement patterns of different racial/ethnic groups) and, thus, is solidified through the specification of the ethnic and racial composition of such diversity. Then, as the next move, the articulation works in opposition by taking such racial specificity and abstracting/emptying "race" (which, in this vein, only separates groups) of its historical, political, and economic significance. I contend that diversity becomes abstract and raceless, as modeled after Lisa Lowe's notion of the abstract citizen in which citizenship is made general and nonspecific against the contradicting historical, social, racial, and situated particularities of such citizenship (from and through embodied national borders, cultural identities, and social positionalities).[52] Here, in this argument, diversity is also abstracted as a general set of social relations between groups that are "present" and "different," thereby glossing over the specific inequalities and power differentials, historical and structural positionings, and racial ordering of these groups. These latter details fall to the wayside, thereby ideologically separating diversity from power, inequality, and racialization.

An abstract or raceless diversity suddenly becomes transformed through demographic increases into a positive equalizer among cultural groups. For example, one article notes: "So far, Santa Clara County seems to have thrived in its exploding diversity, largely free of the backlash and racial violence that have erupted in other parts of California and the nation."[53] In this same vein, several articles cite a poll of Santa Clara County residents in which 77 percent believed race relations are generally good and about 60 percent predicted race relations will remain good or will get better when Whites are no longer the majority.[54] Thus, according to these texts, the new demographic of diversity stands as a "role model for America," but not in terms of embracing diversity (and difference) in and of itself. Instead, diversity becomes resignified as a vehicle that can eradicate race altogether and equalize relations among all groups. There is the presumption that dramatic demographic shifts can de-emphasize and strip diversity of any reference to or reliance on race. This move, however, may seem without race but still works in line with the structural inequalities and status quo of the current White racial hierarchy and formation in the United States.[55]

Thus, a minority-majority construction refers to demographic diversity in name only, and not in terms of actual political/socioeconomic equality achieved among groups. According to this articulation, if there are no majorities or, rather, there is only a "minority majority" in which every group is a minority, race relations and historical/economic inequalities can, in one fell swoop, be abstracted out of existence under the guise of diversity appeals. This representation is dangerous, according to Leslie Roman, because it "celebrates diversity without adequately analyzing power differentials among groups positioned by racial categorizations and inequalities."[56] Instead, diversity in this newspaper discourse "reduces all groups to a nonexistent level playing field" and "de-culturalizes economic and political structures, treating the latter as transparent objective forces."[57]

An abstract or raceless diversity is particularly interesting, given that the discourses are created during the aftermath of the post–affirmative action era in California and that the state needs to locate a different way of subtly exerting its interests and authority via a re-made diversity (a diversity that erases race). New census counts are invoked in newspaper texts as evidence of racial/ethnic group settlement and growth and presumed to be achieved through state mechanisms and values, such as democratic capitalism, equal rights, fair state agencies, and proceduralities. The state erases its steps so as to reflect objectively, in pure and untainted form, the conditions, policies, and procedures that led to the societal ideals of positive diversity and race(less) relations. This encoded raceless diversity does great political work for the racial state; the astounding diversity reflects the openness and workability of the state and demonstrates the finished success of past affirmative action programs, thereby creating an impetus for the outdated nature and necessary obliteration of such programs that privilege race. In effect, these newspaper discourses signify an abstract or raceless diversity but one that is not necessarily without racial reference. Rather, racelessness becomes an encoded position of Whiteness, since the interests of a hegemonic White-centered racial state are promoted, advanced, and strengthened.

Conclusions

According to dominant newspaper discourse in the Bay Area, diversity has emerged as a positive social force. Diversity is no longer about conflict, division, or race; it is about the formation of a society in which cultural minorities are present and there is no larger majority. Integration is occurring, as high schools, communities, workplaces, and local politics are reconstituted with new cultural group members and dynamics. By virtue of their presence, groups surely must have access to and opportunity for new residential spaces, economic classes and lifestyles, and political power.

This portrait of diversity, as signified through personalized stories and census counts, is what dominant regional newspaper discourse constructs and promises for the public. It is an image promised to us to appease our fears and anxieties about an ever-changing U.S. populace and to ensure a "coming together" of cultural groups typically understood to be in conflict with one another. The articulation of diversity discussed in this chapter enables the racial state to rally support for itself as well as its color-neutral or race-neutral state procedural mechanisms and redefine the problematic of diversity and race relations away from race and power and yet solidly in line with the White status quo.

We see the signification of an abstract or raceless diversity in the post-race era and specifically during a period when color neutrality is not only being promoted but vigilantly mandated and enforced. The state has worked hard to stamp out any trace of race or racial exclusion or inclusion, ripping it out of the public sphere once and for all. This is especially true for the state of California with its still reigning mandate (Proposition 209) that prohibits any state or local affirmative action programs; taking the logic of this mandate further, many attempt to rid race from any public context (i.e., Ward Connerly's past efforts, most notably the California Racial Privacy Act). Thus, dominant discourses in California seem especially critical to unpack for the ideological articulations and encodings of diversity as these discourses may spread throughout the country. In the post-race era, the focus has been on affirming the demographic trends spreading throughout the country but in a way that does not highlight, discuss, or rely on the signifier of race, namely through the moniker of "diversity" as found in university, higher education, governmental, and corporate discourses.[58] This analysis illustrates that there is much to be gained from flattening, abstracting, de-racializing, and removing diversity from any vestige of power or state influence. In this way, diversity stands as an achievement of the state, the direct result of a system that unquestionably works for all in the same way while undergirding and reinscribing a White racial status quo system of power.

Similar to Lowe, I find simply heightening, glorifying, and viewing diversity as positive to be problematic, because doing so does not recognize or address power differentials among groups produced in large part by larger macro-structural conditions and apparatuses.[59] The discourse around diversity found in higher education and institutional apparatuses, therefore, becomes limited to "flat" and seemingly objective demographic trends and growth patterns. There is far too celebratory or prideful a tone in these newspaper texts when pointing out that cultural groups "are here" in groundbreaking fashion and that such presence is proof that the racial state system works, that the status quo structures attempt to address social, economic, and political inequalities and transform our society to be more inclusive, supportive, and just. An abstract or raceless diversity is particularly dangerous because, as Lowe states, it "levels the important differences and contradictions within and among racial and ethnic minority groups according to the discourse of pluralism that asserts the American culture is a democratic terrain to which every variety of constituency has equal access and in which all are represented while simultaneously masking the existence of exclusions by recuperating dissent, conflict, and otherness through the promise of inclusion."[60] We must vigorously contest this articulation of abstract or raceless diversity, because it severs the signified links between culture and power, between inclusion and presence and exclusion and positioning, and presumes that, with the presence of all groups "at the table," racial inequalities and the historical legacy of White privilege will magically and swiftly disappear. Disarticulating diversity from power can bring about drastic consequences for marginalized groups, while at the same time reaffirming the hegemonic power of the White racial state in framing diversity without confronting the structural exclusions and inequalities it sets into motion.

NOTES

1. I created the opening excerpt that features "Centerville" by incorporating key elements that I found in studied newspaper texts around the theme of abstract and raceless diversity. The Centerville excerpt represents the overall articulation of diversity that I found in my analysis.

2. Stuart Hall, "Ideology and Communication Theory," in *Rethinking Communication, 1, Paradigm Issues*, ed. B. Dervin, L. Grossberg, B. J. O'Keefe, and E. Wartella (Newbury Park, CA: Sage, 1989), 40–52; Stuart Hall, "On Postmodernism and Articulation: An Interview with Stuart Hall," *Journal of Communication Inquiry* 10, no. 2 (Summer 1986): 45–60; Stuart Hall, "The Whites of Their Eyes: Racist Ideologies and the Media," in *Gender, Race, and Class in Media: A Text Reader*, ed. G. Dines and J. McMahon Humez (Thousand Oaks, CA: Sage, 1995), 89–93.

3. David Theo Goldberg, *Racist Culture: Philosophy and the Politics of Meaning* (Oxford: Blackwell, 1993); David Theo Goldberg, *The Racial State* (Malden, MA: Blackwell, 2002); Michael Omi and Howard Winant, *Racial Formation in the United States: From the 1960s to the 1990s*, 2nd ed. (New York: Routledge, 1994).

4. Goldberg, *Racist Culture*.

5. Goldberg, *Racial State*; Omi and Winant, *Racial Formation*.

6. Goldberg, *Racist Culture*.

7. Marouf Hasian, Jr. and Fernando Delgado, "The Trials and Tribulations of Racialized Critical Rhetorical Theory: Understanding the Rhetorical Ambiguities of Proposition 187," *Communication Theory* 8, no. 3 (1998): 245–70; Kent A. Ono and John M. Sloop, *Shifting Borders: Rhetoric, Immigration, and California's Proposition 187* (Philadelphia: Temple University Press, 2002).

8. Carrie Crenshaw, "Colorblind Rhetoric," *Southern Communication Journal* 63, no. 3 (Spring 1998): 244–57; Lisa A. Flores and Dreama G. Moon, "Rethinking Race, Revealing Dilemmas:

Imagining a New Racial Subject in Race Traitor," *Western Journal of Communication* 66, no. 2 (Spring 2002): 181–207; Lisa A. Flores, Dreama G. Moon, and Thomas K. Nakayama, "Dynamic Rhetorics of Race: California's Racial Privacy Initiative and the Shifting Grounds of Racial Politics," *Communication and Critical/Cultural Studies* 3, no. 3 (2006): 181–201; Ronald L. Jackson and Thurmon Garner, "Tracing the Evolution of 'Race,' 'Ethnicity,' and 'Culture' in Communication Studies," *Howard Journal of Communications* 9, no. 1 (January 1998): 41–55; Aaron David Gresson, *The Recovery of Race in America* (Minneapolis: University of Minnesota Press, 1995); Ronald L. Jackson, Chang In Shin, and Keith B. Wilson, "The Meaning of Whiteness: Critical Implications of Communicating and Negotiating Race," *World Communication* 29, no. 1 (2000): 69–86; Ronald L. Jackson and Katherine Simpson, "White Positionalities and Cultural Contracts: Critiquing Entitlement, Theorizing, and Exploring the Negotiation of White Identities," in *Ferment in the Intercultural Field: Axiology/value/praxis*, ed. W. J. Starosta and G. M. Chen (Thousand Oaks, CA: Sage, 2003), 177–210; Mark Lawrence McPhail, "The Politics of Complicity: Second Thoughts about the Social Construction of Racial Equality," *Quarterly Journal of Speech* 80, no. 3 (1994): 343–81; Mark Lawrence McPhail, *The Rhetoric of Racism* (Lanham, MD: University Press of America, 1994); Mark Lawrence McPhail, "The Politics of Complicity: Second Thoughts about the Social Construction of Racial Equality," *Quarterly Journal of Speech* 80, no. 3 (1998): 343–81; Dreama G. Moon, "White Enculturation and Bourgeois Ideology," in *Whiteness: The Communication of Social Identity*, ed. T. K. Nakayama and J. N. Martin (Thousand Oaks, CA: Sage, 1999), 177–97.

9. Fernando P. Delgado, "Chicano Ideology Revisited: Rap Music and the (Re)articulation of Chicanismo," *Western Journal of Communication* 62 (1998): 95–113; Wenshu Lee, "In the Names of Chinese Women," *Quarterly Journal of Speech* 84 (1998): 283–302; Thomas Nakayama, "Dis/orienting Identities: Asian Americans, History and Intercultural Communication," in *Our Voices: Essays in Culture, Ethnicity, and Communication*, ed. A. González, M. Houston, and V. Chen (Los Angeles: Roxbury, 1994), 12–17; Thomas K. Nakayama, "Show/Down Time: 'Race,' Gender, Sexuality, and Popular Culture," *Critical Studies in Mass Communication* 11, no. 2 (1996): 162–79; Thomas K. Nakayama and Robert L. Krizek, "Whiteness: A Strategic Rhetoric," *Quarterly Journal of Speech* 81, no. 3 (1995): 291–309. Thomas K. Nakayama and Judith N. Martin, *Whiteness: The Communication of Social Identity* (Thousand Oaks, CA: Sage, 1999); Kent A. Ono, "Re/signing 'Asian American': Rhetorical Problematics of Nation," *Amerasia Journal* 21, no. 1 (1995): 67–78.

10. Avery Gordon and Christopher Newfield, eds., *Mapping Multiculturalism* (Minneapolis: University of Minnesota Press, 1996); David Theo Goldberg, *Multiculturalism: A Critical Reader* (Oxford: Blackwell, 1994).

11. Gordon and Newfield, *Mapping Multiculturalism*, 77.

12. Ibid.

13. Omi and Winant, *Racial Formation*; Goldberg, *Racial State*.

14. Goldberg, *Racial State*.

15. Lisa C. Bower, David Theo Goldberg, and Michael C. Musheno, *Between Law and Culture: Relocating Legal Studies* (Minneapolis: University of Minnesota Press, 2001); Omi and Winant, *Racial Formation*.

16. Goldberg, *Racial State*, 108.

17. Claire Jean Kim, *Bitter Fruit: The Politics of Black-Korean Conflict in New York City* (New Haven: Yale University Press, 2000).

18. Ibid., 9.

19. Ibid.

20. Ibid., 10.

21. Hasian and Delgado, "Rhetorical Ambiguities"; Flores, Moon, and Nakayama, "Dynamic Rhetorics."

22. Ono and Sloop, *Shifting Borders*.

23. Ibid.

24. Ibid., 6.

25. Stuart Hall, "Race, Articulation and Societies Structured in Dominance," in *Sociological Theories: Race and Colonialism* (Paris: UNESCO, 1979), 305–45; Goldberg, *Racial State*.

26. Ono and Sloop, *Shifting Borders*.

27. Ernesto Laclau and Chantal Mouffe, *Hegemony and Socialist Strategy: Towards a Radical Democratic Politics* (London: Verso, 1985); Hall, "Race, Articulation and Societies."

28. Robert S. Hanczor, "Articulation Theory and Public Controversy: Taking Sides Over NYPD Blue," *Critical Studies in Mass Communication* 14, no. 1 (1997): 1–30.

29. Hall, "Postmodernism," 53.

30. Lawrence Grossberg, *We Gotta Get Out of This Place: Popular Conservatism and Postmodern Culture* (New York: Routledge, 1992), 54.

31. Hanczor, "Articulation Theory"; Jennifer D. Slack, "The Theory and Method of Articulation in Cultural Studies," in *Stuart Hall: Critical Dialogues in Cultural Studies*, ed. D. Morley and K. H. Chen (London: Routledge, 1996), 112–27.

32. A. E. Cha and Ken McLaughlin, "Shift to Foreshadow Changes in State, U.S.," *San Jose Mercury News*, April 14, 1999.

33. Ibid.

34. Ibid.

35. Erin Hallissy, "Census 2000: Who we are—Concord's Melting Pot—Vibrant Mix of Newcomers Transforms Suburb into a Burgeoning Multiethnic Haven," *San Francisco Chronicle*, April 19, 2001.

36. Ibid.

37. Anastasia Hendrix, "Census 2000—Who we are—S.F. Grew by 7.3% since '90 Census—Asian Influx Accounts for most of Change," *San Francisco Chronicle*, 2001.

38. Ibid.

39. Tanya Schevitz, Lori Olszewski, and John Wildermuth, "New Demographics Changing Everything: Experts Examine Rise of State's Minorities," *San Francisco Chronicle*, August 31, 2000; Hallissy, "Census 2000"; Cha and McLaughlin, "Shift"; Mike Antonucci, "Multicultural Mingling Helps Enrich Daily Life in Bay Area, Interaction with Varied Cultures Every Day Eases Tensions between People," *San Jose Mercury News*, June 20, 2001.

40. Schevitz et al., "New Demographics."

41. Cha and McLaughlin, "Shift"; R. G. McLeod, "'Minority Majority' Well on Way in State: Striking Changes in New Census Data," *San Francisco Chronicle*, September 4, 1998.

42. Goldberg, *Racial State*.

43. David Theo Goldberg, "Taking Stock: Counting by Race," in *Racial Subjects: Writing on Race in America*, ed. David Theo Goldberg (New York: Routledge, 1997), 27–58; Rona Tamiko Halualani, *In the Name of Hawaiians: Native Identities and Cultural Politics* (Minneapolis: University of Minnesota Press, 2002).

44. Goldberg, "Taking Stock," 39.

45. McLeod, "'Minority Majority.'"

46. Ibid.

47. Schevitz et al., "New Demographics."

48. Gordon and Newfield, *Mapping Multiculturalism.*

49. Cha and McLaughlin, "Shift."

50. Barbra Stocking, "County's Whites Enter Unknown Territory," *San Jose Mercury News,* April 14, 1999.

51. *San Jose Mercury News,* "What Will Race be Like in 2020?" April 18, 1999.

52. Lisa Lowe, "Immigration, Citizenship, Racialization: Asian American Critique," in *Immigrant Acts: On Asian American Cultural Politics* (Durham, NC: Duke University Press, 1996), 1–36.

53. Cha and McLaughlin, "Shift."

54. McLeod, "'Minority Majority.'"

55. Omi and Winant, *Racial Formation.*

56. Leslie G. Roman, "White Is a C! White Discursiveness, Postmodernism, and Anti-racist Pedagogy," in *Race, Identity, and Representation in Education,* ed. C. McCarthy and W. Crichlow (New York: Routledge, 1993), 279–378.

57. Gordon and Newfield, *Mapping Multiculturalism,* 79.

58. Goldberg, *Racial State.*

59. Lisa Lowe, "Imagining Los Angeles in the Production of Multiculturalism," in *Mapping Multiculturalism,* ed. A. Gordon and C. Newfield (Minneapolis: University of Minnesota Press, 1996), 238–502.

60. Ibid., 415.

Bibliography

30 days: "Outsourcing." Season 2, Episode 2. Aired August 2, 2006. Todd Lubin (Executive Producer). USA: FX.

60-minutes. "Out of India" [Television segment]. Aired January 11, 2004. A. Bourne (Producer): CBS, 2004.

ABC. *Nightline*, January 13, 2010, http://www.abcnews.go.com/nightline.

Abdul-Jabbar, Kareem, and Peter Knobler. *The Autobiography of Kareem Abdul-Jabbar*. New York: Bantam, 1983.

"About Us." http://www.jimgilchrist.com (accessed January 3, 2006).

Adams, Josh, and Vincent J. Roscigno. "White Supremacists, Oppositional Culture and the World Wide Web." *Social Forces* 84 (2005): 759–73.

African American Market in the U.S. New York: Packaged Facts, 2008.

Ahluwalia, Ashim (Director). 2005. *John and Jane Toll-Free*. Shumona Goel (Producer). India. Broadcast on HBO on November 13, 2007.

Alcoff, Linda. "What Should White People Do?" *Hypatia* 13, no. 3 (1998): 6–26.

Alexander, M. Jacqui. *Pedagogies of Crossing. Meditations on Feminism, Sexual Politics, Memory, and the Sacred.* Durham and London: Duke University Press, 2005.

Altheide, David L. *Qualitative Media Analysis*. Thousand Oaks, CA: Sage Publications, 1996.

Amaya, Hector. "Dying American or the Violence of Citizenship: Latinos in Iraq." *Latino Studies* 5 (2007): 3–24.

Ampadu, Lena. "Maria W. Stewart and the Rhetoric of Black Preaching: Perspectives on Womanism and Black Nationalism." In *Black Women's Intellectual Traditions: Speaking Their Minds*, edited by Kristin Waters and Carol B. Conaway, 38–54. Burlington: University of Vermont Press, 2007.

Andrews, David L. "The Fact(s) of Michael Jordan's Blackness: Excavating a Floating Signifier." *Sociology of Sport Journal* 12 (1996): 125–58.

Antonucci, Mike. "Multicultural Mingling Helps Enrich Daily Life in Bay Area, Interaction with Varied Cultures Every Day Eases Tensions between People." *San Jose Mercury News*, June 20, 2001.

Appadurai, Arjun. "Putting Hierarchy in Its Place." *Cultural Anthropology* 3 (1988): 36–49.

Appelbaum, Stephen. "Interview with Paul Haggis." BBC. http://www.bbc.co.uk/films/2005/07/29/paul_haggis_crash_interview.shtml.

Argetsinger, Amy. "In Ariz.,'Minutemen' Start Border Patrols." *Washington Post*, April 5, 2005.

Aristotle. *On Rhetoric: A Theory of Civic Discourse.* Edited by George A. Kennedy. New York: Oxford University Press, 1991.

Aronson, Linda. *Screenwriting Updated: New (and Conventional) Ways of Writing for the Screen.* Los Angeles: Sillman-James, 2000.

Asante, Molefi Kete. *The Afrocentric Idea*. Philadelphia: Temple University Press, 1987.

———. *The Afrocentric Idea*. Revised and expanded edition. Philadelphia: Temple University Press, 1998.

———. *Race, Rhetoric, and Identity: The Architecton of Soul.* Amherst, NY: Humanity Books, 2005.

Ashe, Arthur. *A Hard Road to Glory: A History of African American Athletes Since 1946*. New York: Warner Books, 1988.

Associated Press. "Golf Channel Anchor Suspended for Tiger Woods 'Lynch' Comment." http://www.foxnews.com.

Atkinson, Roland. "Agitation in the City of Angels." *Clinical Psychiatry News* 33, no. 10 (2005): 20–21.

Aucoin, Don, and Drew Jubera. "Colorado School Massacre: Children Killing Children; Television: An 'Interactive Siege' Unfolds." *Atlanta Journal and Constitution*, April 21, 1999, home edition, http://www.lexis-nexis.com/.

Austin American-Statesman. "Puzzling Search for Answers," April 22, 1999, http://www.lexis-nexis.com/.

Babb, Valerie. "'The Joyous Circle': The Vernacular Presence in Frederick Douglass's Narratives." *College English* 67 (2005): 365–77.

Bacon, Jacqueline. *The Humblest May Stand Forth: Rhetoric, Empowerment, and Abolition*. Columbia: University of South Carolina Press, 2002.

———. "Reading the Reparations Debate." *Quarterly Journal of Speech* 89 (2003): 171–95.

———. "'Acting as Freemen': Rhetoric, Race, and Reform in the Debate over Colonization in *Freedom's Journal*, 1827–1828." *Quarterly Journal of Speech* 93 (2007): 58–83.

———. *Freedom's Journal: The First African-American Newspaper*. Lanham: Lexington Books, 2007.

Bacon, Jacqueline, and Glen McClish. "Descendents of Africa, Sons of '76: Exploring Early African-American Rhetoric." *Rhetoric Society Quarterly* 36 (2006): 1–29.

Bajaj, Vikas, and Ford Fessenden. "The Subprime Landscape, from Detroit to Ithaca." *New York Times*, November 4, 2007, 16.

Baker, Houston, Jr. "Critical Memory and the Black Public Sphere." In *Cultural Memory and the Construction of Identity*, edited by Dan Ben-Amos and Lillian Weissberg, 264–96. Detroit: Wayne State, 1999.

Barkley, Charles, and Michael Wilbon. *I May Be Wrong: But I Doubt It*. New York: Random House, 2003.

Bauman, Zigmunt. *Liquid Modernity*. Malden, MA: Blackwell, 2000.

BBC News Magazine. "Jay-Z Boycotts Cristal Champagne." June 19, 2006. http://news.bbc.co.uk/2/hi/entertainment/5086482.stm.

BBC World Service. *Newshour*, January 14, 2010, http://www.bbc.co.uk/programmes/p005rcox#-.

Bell, Derrick. *Faces at the Bottom of the Well: The Permanence of Racism*. New York: Basic Books, 1992.

Bello, Walden. *Dark Victory: The United States and Global Poverty*. Oakland, CA: Food First, 1999.

Beltran, Mary, and Camilla Fojas, eds. *Mixed Race Hollywood*. New York: New York University Press, 2008.

Berlant, Lauren. "National Brands/National Body: Imitation of Life." In *The Phantom Public Sphere*, edited by Bruce Robbins, 173–208. Minneapolis: University of Minnesota Press, 1993.

Bhabha, Homi K. *The Location of Culture*. New York: Routledge, 1994/2003.

Billig, Michael and others. *Ideological Dilemmas: A Social Psychology of Everyday Thinking*. London: Sage Publications, 1988.

Birrell, Susan, and Mary. G. McDonald. *Reading Sport: Critical Essays on Power and Representation*. Boston: Northeastern University Press, 2000.

Biskind, Peter. *Down and dirty pictures: Miramax, Sundance and the Rise of Independent Film.* London: Bloomsbury, 2004.

Blair, Carole, Julie R. Brown, and Leslie A. Baxter. "Disciplining the Feminine." *Quarterly Journal of Speech* 80, no. 4 (1994): 383–409.

Bohman, James. *Public Deliberation: Pluralism, Complexity, and Democracy.* Cambridge, MA and London: MIT Press, 1996.

Bonilla-Silva, Eduardo. *Racism Without Racists: Color-Blind Racism and the Persistence of Racial Inequality in the United States.* Lanham, MD: Rowman and Littlefield, 2003.

———. *Racism Without Racists: Color-Blind Racism and the Persistence of Racial Inequality in America.* New York: Rowman & Littlefield, 2009.

Booker, Christopher B. *"I Will Wear No Chain!" A Social History of African American Males.* Westport: Praeger, 2000.

Boston Globe, "Something Wrong, Nothing Done." April 20, 2007, first edition, http://www.lexis-nexis.com/.

Bourdieu, Pierre. *Practical Reason: On Theory of Action.* Cambridge, UK: Polity, 1998.

Bowden, Darsie. *Writing for Film: The Basics of Screenwriting.* Mahwah, NJ: Lawrence Erlbaum, 2006.

Bower, Lisa C., David Theo Goldberg, and Michael C. Musheno. *Between Law and Culture: Relocating Legal Studies.* Minneapolis: University of Minnesota Press, 2001.

Bowers, Detine L. "When Outsiders Encounter Insiders in Speaking: Oppressed Collectives on the Defensive." *Journal of Black Studies* 26 (1996): 490–503.

Bowers, John W., and Donovan J. Ochs. *The Rhetoric of Agitation and Control.* Reading, MA: Addison-Wesley, 1971.

Boyd, Herb. "Amadou Diallo's Homecoming: Sharpton and Cochran to Lead Case Against PBA." *New York Amsterdam News,* March 3, 1999.

———. "New York's Honor Role." *New York Amsterdam News,* March 24, 1999.

Boyd, Todd, ed. *Out of Bounds: Sports, Media and the Politics of Identity.* Bloomington: Indiana University Press, 1997.

Boyd, Todd. *The New H.N.I.C. (Head Niggas in Charge): The Death of Civil Rights and the Reign of Hip Hop.* New York: New York University Press, 2003.

Boyd, Todd, and Kenneth L. Shropshire. "Basketball Jones: A New World Order?" In *America Above the Rim: Basketball Jones,* edited by Todd Boyd and K. L. Shropshire. New York: New York University Press, 2001.

Bradenton (FL) Herald. "Black Monday: A Senseless Massacre—and No Easy Answers." April 18, 2007, http://www.lexis-nexis.com/.

Brandzel, Amy, and Jigna Desai. "Race, Violence, and Terror: The Cultural Defensibility of Heteromasculine Citizenship in the Virginia Tech Massacre and the Don Imus Affair." *Journal of Asian American Studies* 11, no. 1 (2008): 61–85.

Breed, Allen G., and Aaron Beard. "AP Exclusive: Cho Family Is 'Hopeless.'" Associated Press Online, April 20, 2007, http://www.lexis-nexis.com/.

Brown, H. Rap. "Street Talk." In *Rappin' and Stylin' Out: Communication in Urban Black America,* edited by Thomas Kochman, 205–7. Urbana: University of Illinois, 1972.

Brown, Michael K. et al. *Whitewashing Race: The Myth of a Color-Blind Society.* Berkeley: University of California Press, 2004.

Brown, Timothy. "Allan Iverson as America's Most Wanted: Black Masculinity as a Cultural Site of Struggle." *Journal of Intercultural Communication Research* 34 (2005): 65–87.

Brown, Wendy. *States of Injury: Power and Freedom in Late Modernity.* Princeton, NJ: Princeton University Press, 1995.

———. *Regulating Aversion: Tolerance in the Age of Identity and Empire.* Princeton, NJ: Princeton University Press, 2006.

Browne, Stephen Howard. "Counter-Science: African American Historians and The Critique of Ethnology in Nineteenth-Century America." *Western Journal of Communication* 64 (2000): 268–84.

Browne, Zambga J. "Communities of Color Unite over Slaughter." *New York Amsterdam News,* February 17, 1999.

Brummett, Barry. "How to Propose a Discourse." *Communication Studies* 41, no. 2 (1990): 128–35.

———. *Rhetoric in Popular Culture.* New York: St. Martin's Press, 1994.

———. *The World and How We Describe It: Rhetorics of Reality, Representation, Simulation.* Westport, CT: Praeger, 2003.

———. *Rhetorical Homologies: Form, Culture, Experience.* Tuscaloosa: University of Alabama Press, 2004.

———. *Rhetoric in Popular Culture.* 2nd ed. Tuscaloosa: University of Alabama Press, 2006.

Bumiller, Elizabeth (w/ Ginger Thompson). "Giuliani Cancels Political Trip Amid Protest Over Shooting." *New York Times,* February 10, 1999.

Burgess, Parke. "The Rhetoric of Black Power: A Moral Demand?" *Quarterly Journal of Speech* 54 (April 1968): 122–33.

Burke, Kenneth. *A Grammar of Motives.* Berkeley: University of California Press, 1969.

Burke, Ronald K. *Samuel Ringgold Ward: Christian Abolitionist.* New York: Garland, 1995.

Butler, Judith. *Gender Trouble.* New York: Routledge, 1990.

Butterworth, Michael L. "Ritual in the 'Church of Baseball': Suppressing the Discourse of Democracy After 9/11." *Communication and Critical/Cultural Studies* 2 (2005): 107–29.

———. "Race in 'the Race': Mark McGuire, Sammy Sosa, and the Heroic Construction of Whiteness." *Critical Studies in Media Communication* 24 (2007): 228–44.

———. "The Politics of the Pitch: Claiming and Contesting Democracy through the Iraqi National Soccer Team." *Communication and Critical/Cultural Studies* 4 (2007): 184–203.

Calafell, Bernadette Marie, and Fernando P. Delgado. "Reading Latina/o Images: Interrogating Americanos." *Critical Studies in Media Communication* 21 (2004): 1–21.

Calhoun, Craig. "The Privatization of Risk." *Public Culture* 18 (2006): 257–63.

Campbell, Greg. *Blood Diamonds: Tracing the Deadly Path of the World's Most Precious Gems.* Boulder, CO: Westview Press, 2002.

Campbell, Joseph. *The Hero with a Thousand Faces.* 2nd ed. Princeton, NJ: Princeton University Press, 1968.

Campbell, Karlyn Kohrs. "The Rhetoric of Black Nationalism: A Case Study in Self-conscious Criticism." *Central States Speech Journal* 22 (1971): 151–60.

Campbell, Kermit E. "We Is Who We Was: The African/American Rhetoric of Amistad." In *African American Rhetoric(s): Interdisciplinary Perspectives,* edited by Elaine B. Richardson and Ronald L. Jackson II, 204–20. Carbondale: Southern Illinois University Press, 2004.

Capital (Anapolis, MD). "Gunman Mailed Manifesto Between Attacks," April 19, 2007, http://www.lexis-nexis.com/.

Carbado, Devon W. "Black Rights, Gay Rights, Civil Rights: The Deployment of Race/Sexual Orientation Analogies in the Debates about the "Don't Ask, Don't Tell" Policy." In *Black Men on Race, Gender and Sexuality,* edited by Devon W. Carbado, 283–302. New York: New York University Press, 1999.

Carney, Jim. "Portage Student Recounts Day at Virginia Tech." *Akron (OH) Beacon Journal*, April 16, 2007, http://www.lexis-nexis.com/.

Carrington, Ben. "Sport, Masculinity, and Black Cultural Resistance." *Journal of Sport and Social Issues* 22 (1998): 275–98.

Carter, Richard. "NBA's New Dress Code: Racist or Just Smart Business?" *New York Amsterdam News*, 17.

Carton, Evan. *Patriotic Treason: John Brown and the Soul of America*. New York: Free Press, 2006.

Cashmore, Ernest. *Black Sportsmen*. London: Routledge, 1982.

Cassidy, Mike. "Cassidy: Digital Tools Were Potential Life Savers During Virginia Tech Massacre." *San Jose Mercury News*, April 16, 2007, http://www.lexis-nexis.com/.

Cha, A. E., and K. McLaughlin. "Shift to Foreshadow Changes in State, U.S." *San Jose Mercury News*, April 14, 1999.

Chambers, Jason. "Equal in Every Way: African Americans, Consumption and Materialism from Reconstruction to the Civil Rights Movement." *Advertising and Society Review* 7, no. 1 (Spring 2006).

Chaney, Michael A. "Coloring Whiteness and Black Voice Minstrelsy: Representations of Race and Place in *Static Shock, King of the Hill,* and *South Park.*" *Journal of Popular Film and Television* 31, no. 4 (2004): 167–75.

Charland, Maurice. "Constitutive Rhetoric: The Case of the Peuple Québécois." *Quarterly Journal of Speech* 72, no. 2 (1994).

Chatterjee, Partha. *The Nation and Its Fragments. Colonial and Postcolonial Histories*. Princeton, NJ: Princeton University Press, 1993.

Cho, David, and Amy Gardner. "An Isolated Boy in a World of Strangers: Cho's Behavior Alarmed Some Who Knew Him; Family Humbled by 'This Darkness.'" *Washington Post*, April 21, 2007, Met 2 edition, http://www.lexis-nexis.com/.

Chonin, Neva. "Permanent Resident, Alienated." *San Francisco Chronicle*, April 22, 2007, final edition, http://www.lexis-nexis.com/.

Cisneros, J. David. "Contaminated Communities: The Metaphor of 'Immigrant as Pollutant' in Media Representations of Immigration." *Rhetoric and Public Affairs* 11 (2008): 569–601.

Clayton, John. "Smith, Dungy Will Make This a Classy Super Bowl." http://sports.espn.go.com/espn.

Cloud, Dana. "Hegemony or Concordance? The Rhetoric of Tokenism in 'Oprah' Winfrey's Rags-t-Riches Biography." *Critical Studies in Mass Communication* 13 (1996): 115–37.

CNN. "Activist Bay Buchanan Supports Minuteman Project." *Lou Dobbs Tonight*, April 1, 2005. http://www.lexisnexis.com (accessed April 24, 2005).

———. "Minuteman Project Highlights Problems with US Border Policy." *Lou Dobbs Tonight*, April 4, 2005. http://www.lexisnexis.com (accessed April 24, 2005).

———. "Project Minuteman Continues in Southwest." *Lou Dobbs Tonight*, April 11, 2005. http://www.lexisnexis.com (accessed April 24, 2005).

Cohen, Cathy. *The Boundaries of Blackness*. Chicago: University of Chicago Press, 1999.

Cohen, Joshua. "Deliberation and Democratic Legitimacy." In *The Good Polity: Normative Analyses of the State*, edited by Alan Hamlin and Philip Pettit, 17–34. London: Basil Blackwell, 1989.

Cohen, Lizabeth. *A Consumers' Republic: The Politics of Mass Consumption in Postwar America*. New York: Alfred A. Knopf, 2003.

Cole, Elizabeth, and Nesha Haniff. "Building a Home for Black Women's Studies." *Black Women, Gender, and Families* 1 (2007): 27.

Collins, Patricia Hill. "Comment on Heckman's 'Truth and Method: Feminist Standpoint Theory Revisited': Where's the Power?" *Signs: Journal of Women in Culture and Society* 22 (1997): 375–81.

———. *Black Feminist Thought: Knowledge, Consciousness, and the Politics of Empowerment.* 2nd ed. New York: Routledge, 2000.

———. *Black Sexual Politics: African Americans, Gender, and the New Racism.* New York: Routledge, 2004.

Communipaw [James McCune Smith]. "Frederick Douglass in New York." *Frederick Douglass' Paper,* February 2, 1855.

———. "From Our New York Correspondent." *Frederick Douglass' Paper,* January 26, 1855.

———. "From Our New York Correspondent." *Frederick Douglass' Paper,* February 16, 1855.

———. "From Our New York Correspondent." *Frederick Douglass' Paper,* May 11, 1855.

Conaway, Carol. "Crown Heights: Politics and Press Coverage of the Race War that Wasn't." *Polity* 32, no. 1 (1999): 93–118.

Concord Times, "Diamond Tales." May 31, 2007. http://www.lexisnexis.com.

Condit, Celeste. "Rhetorical Criticism and Audiences: The Extremes of McGee and Leff." *Western Journal of Speech Communication* 54 (1990): 330–45.

Condit, Celeste Michelle, and John Louis Lucaites. *Crafting Equality: America's Anglo-African Word.* Chicago: University of Chicago Press, 1993.

Connell, R. W. *Gender and Power: Society, the Person and Sexual Politics.* Stanford, CA: Stanford University Press, 1987.

Conquergood, Dwight. "Performance Studies: Interventions and Radical Research." *The Drama Review* 46 (2002): 145–56.

Consalvo, Mia. "The Monsters Next Door: Media Constructions of Boys and Masculinity." *Feminist Media Studies* 3, no. 1 (2003): 27–45.

Cooper, Helene. "Meet the New Elite, Not Like the Old." *New York Times,* July 26, 2009, Week in Review, 1.

Cosby, Bill, and Alvin F. Poussaint. *Come On People: On the Path from Victims to Victors.* Nashville, TN: Thomas Nelson, 2007.

Crawford, Clinton. "The Multiple Dimensions of Nubian/Egyptian Rhetoric and Its Implications for Contemporary Classroom Instructions." In *African American Rhetoric(s): Interdisciplinary Perspectives,* edited by Elaine B. Richardson and Ronald L. Jackson II, 111–35. Carbondale: Southern Illinois University Press, 2004.

Crenshaw, Carrie. "Resisting Whiteness' Rhetorical Silence." *Western Journal of Communication* 61 (1997): 253–78.

———. "Colorblind Rhetoric." *Southern Communication Journal* 63, no. 3 (Spring 1998): 244–56.

Crenshaw, Kimberle. "Mapping the Margins: Intersectionality, Identity Politics, and Violence Against Women of Color." *Stanford Law Review* 43, no. 6 (1991): 1241–99.

Crimp, Douglas (with Adam Rolston). *AIDS Demographics.* Seattle: Bay Press, 1990.

Crittenden, Jules. "High School Horror: Reign of Terror Inside Colo. High School." *Boston Herald,* April 21, 1999, third edition, http://www.lexis-nexis.com/.

Cross, Gary. *An All-Consuming Century: Why Commercialism Won in Modern America.* New York: Columbia University Press, 2000.

Cunningham, Michael. "NBA's New Rules on Apparel are a Good Fit for Most Players." *The Collegian Online.* November 14, 2005. http://blue.utb.edu/collegian/2005/fall (accessed February 11, 2007).

Curry, George E. "Walking Billboards." *Emerge* 9 (December 1997): 8.

Custred, Glen. "Where Wre My Juice and Crackers?: Citizens along America's Southwestern Border Have Organized a Neighborhood Watch." *American Spectator* (July–August 2005): 20–25.

Daniel, Jack L. *Changing the Players and the Game: A Personal Account of the Speech Communication Association Black Caucus Origins.* Speech Communication Association, 1995.

Daniel, Jamie Owen. "Rituals of Disqualification: Competing Publics and Public Housing in Contemporary Chicago." In *Masses, Classes, and the Public Sphere*, edited by Mike Hill and Warren Montag, 62–82. New York: Verso Books, 2000.

Danzinger, Pamela. *Luxury Report 2006: Who Buys Luxury, What They Buy, Why They Buy.* Stevens, PA: Unity Marketing, 2006. http://www.unitymarketingonline.com/reports2/luxury/luxury1.html.

Dargis, Manohla. "West looks east: City on Fire and Reservoir Dogs." *L.A. Weekly*, March 17–23, 1995.

Davis, Mark. "Victims Were Cross-Section of School's Student Body." *Philadelphia Inquirer*, April 23, 1999, http://www.lexis-nexis.com/.

Davis, Olga. "Vigilance and Solidarity in the Rhetoric of the Black Press: The Tulsa Star." *Journal of Intergroup Relations* 32, no. 3 (2005): 9–31.

DeCaro, Louis A. *"Fire from the Midst of You": A Religious Life of John Brown.* New York: New York University Press, 2002.

De Certeau, Michel. *The Practice of Everyday Life.* Berkeley: University of California Press, 1984.

DeChaine, D. Robert. "Bordering the Civic Imaginary: Alienization, Fence Logic, and the Minuteman Civil Defense Corps." *Quarterly Journal of Speech* 95 (2009): 43–65.

Delgado, Fernando Pedro. "Major League Soccer: The Return of the Foreign Sport." *Journal of Sport and Social Issues* 21 (1997): 287–99.

———. "Chicano Ideology Revisited: Rap Music and the (Re)articulation of Chicanismo." *Western Journal of Communication* 62 (1998): 95–113.

———. "The Fusing of Sport and Politics: Media Constructions of U.S. Versus Iran at France 98." *Journal of Sport and Social Issues* 27 (2003): 293–307.

———. "Golden But Not Brown: Oscar De La Hoya and the Complications of Culture, Manhood, and Boxing." *International Journal of the History of Sport* 22 (2005): 194–210.

Delgado, Richard. *Critical Race Theory: The Cutting Edge.* Philadelphia: Temple University Press, 2001.

Delgado, Richard, and Jean Stefancic. *Critical Race Theory: An Introduction.* New York: New York University Press, 2001.

DeLombard, Jeannine Marie. *Slavery on Trial: Law, Abolitionism, and Print Culture.* Chapel Hill: University of North Carolina Press, 2007.

DelVecchio, Rick, and Benjamin Pimentel. "Asians Changing Fremont, Milpitas—Census Figures Show Impact of High-Tech Immigration Wave." *San Francisco Chronicle*, March 26, 2001.

Detweiler, Frederick. *The Negro Press in the United States.* College Park, MD: McGrath, 1922.

Dillard, Angela D. *Guess Who's Coming to Dinner Now? Multicultural Conservatism in America.* New York: New York University Press, 2001.

———. *Guess Who's Coming to Dinner Now? Multicultural Conservatism in America.* New York: New York University Press, 2004.

Dines, Gail, and Jean M. Humez, eds. *Gender, Race and Class in Media: A Text-Reader.* Thousand Oaks, CA: Sage Publications, 1994.

———, eds. *Gender, Race and Class in Media: A Text-Reader.* 2nd ed. Thousand Oaks, CA: Sage Publications, 2003.

Doane, Ashley Woody. "What Is Racism? Racial Discourse and Racial Politics." *Critical Sociology* 32 (2006): 255–74.

Doty, William G. *Myth: A Handbook*. Westport, CT: Greenwood Press, 2004.

Douglas, Mary, and Baron Isherwood. *The World of Goods: Towards an Anthropology of Consumption*. New York: Routledge, 1996.

Douglass, Frederick. "Fifth Volume." *Frederick Douglass' Paper*, December 17, 1852.

———. *Narrative of the Life of Frederick Douglass, an American Slave*. New York: Penguin, 1845 [1986].

Drake, St. Clair. *Black Folk Here and There: An Essay in History and Anthropology*. 2 vols. Los Angeles: Center for Afro-American Studies, University of California, Los Angeles, 1987.

Dryzek, John. *Deliberative Democracy and Beyond*. Oxford: Oxford University Press, 2000.

Drzewiecka, Jolanta, and Kay Wong. "The Dynamic Construction of White Ethnicity in the Context of Transnational Cultural Formations." In *Whiteness: The Communication of Social Identity*, edited by Tom Nakayama and Judith N. Martin, 198–216. Thousand Oaks, CA: Sage Publications, 1999.

Du Bois, W. E. B. *Dusks of Dawn: An Essay Toward an Autobiography of a Race Concept*. New York: Harcourt, Brace & Co., 1940.

Duncan, Margaret Carlisle, and Barry Brummett. "The Mediation of Spectator Sport." *Research Quarterly for Exercise and Sport* 58 (1987): 168–77.

———. "Types and Sources of Spectating Pleasure in Televised Sports." *Sociology of Sport Journal* 6 (1989): 195–211.

———. "Liberal and Radical Sources of Female Empowerment in Sport Media." *Sociology of Sport Journal* 10 (1993): 57–72.

DuPree, David. "NBA Drug Use: High-Risk Recreation." *Washington Post*, March 21, 1982.

Durkin, Erin. "Minorities Hit Hard in Mortgage Crunch." *New York Daily News*, October 28, 2008, 6.

Dyer, Richard. *Heavenly Bodies: Film Stars and Society*. London: Macmillan, 1986.

———. *Stars*. London: British Film Institute, 1979.

———. *White*. New York: Routledge, 1997.

Ebert, Roger. *Roger Ebert's Movie Yearbook 2005*. Kansas City: Andrews McMeel Publishing, 2004.

Edelstein, David. "They Cut Glass, and Hands." *New York Magazine*, December 11, 2006: paragraph 1.

Edinger, Edward F. *Archetype of the Apocalypse: Divine, Vengeance, Terrorism, and the End of the World*. Chicago: Open Court, 1999.

Edwards, Harry. *The Revolt of the Black Athlete*. New York: Free Press, 1969.

Egan, Timothy. "Wanted: Border Hoppers. And Some Excitement, Too." *New York Times*, April 1, 2005.

Eligon, John. "Dressing Up Basketball? Been There, Done That." *New York Times*, October 27, 2005. http://select.nytimes.com/search/restricted/article (accessed December 26, 2005).

Eliot, T. S. *The Waste Land*. Edited by Michael North. New York: W.W. Norton, 1922/2000.

Embry, Wayne, and Mary S. Boyer. *The Inside Game: Race, Power, and Politics in the NBA*. Akron, OH: University of Akron Press, 2004.

Entman, Robert M. "Framing: Toward Clarification of a Fractured Paradigm." *Journal of Communication* 43, no. 4 (1993): 51–58.

Ernest, John. *Liberation Historiography: African American Writers and the Challenge of History, 1794–1861*. Chapel Hill: University of North Carolina Press, 2004.

ESPN. "One-Size-Fits-All Dress Code Draws Divergent Views." October 18, 2005. http://sports.espn.go.com/espn/print (accessed February 11, 2007).

Essed, Philomena. *Understanding Everyday Racism: An Interdisciplinary Theory.* Thousand Oaks, CA: Sage Publications, 1991.

Evans, Christine, and Douglas Kalajian. "How Can You Tell When Your Kid Is Headed for Real Trouble?" Cox News Service, April 22, 1999, http://www.lexis-nexis.com/.

"Facts about Katrina." *Surviving Katrina.* The Discovery Channel, 2008.

Faludi, Susan. *The Terror Dream: Myth and Misogyny in an Insecure America.* New York: Picador Publishers, 2007.

Fanon, Frantz. *Black Skin, White Masks.* New York: Grove Press, 1967.

Federal Deposit Insurance Corporation. "Bank Performance After Natural Disasters: A Historical Perspective." January 16, 2006.

Fernandes, Leela. *India's New Middle Class: Democratic Politics in an Era of Economic Reform.* Minneapolis: University of Minnesota Press, 2006.

Fernandez, Manny, and Marc Santora. "In Words and Silence, Hints of Anger and Isolation." *New York Times,* April 18, 2007, late edition-final, http://www.lexis-nexis.com/.

Fishkin, Shelley Fisher, and Carla Peterson. "'We Hold These Truths to Be Self-Evident': The Rhetoric of Frederick Douglass's Journalism." In *The Black Press: New Literary and Historical Essays,* edited by Todd Vogel, 71–83. New Brunswick, NJ and London: Rutgers, 2001.

Flagg, Barbara J. "'Was Blind, But Now I See': White Race Consciousness and the Requirement of Discriminatory Intent." In *Critical White Studies: Looking Behind the Mirror,* edited by Richard Delgado and Jean Stefancic, 629–31. Philadelphia: Temple University Press, 1997.

Flake, Floyd, "The Road to Columbine High." *New York Post,* April 23, 1999, http://www.lexis-nexis.com/.

Flores, Lisa A., and Dreama G. Moon. "Rethinking Race, Revealing Dilemmas: Imagining a New Racial Subject in Race Traitor." *Western Journal of Communication* 66, no. 2 (Spring 2002): 181–207.

Flores, Lisa A., Dreama G. Moon, and Thomas K. Nakayama. "Dynamic Rhetorics of Race: California's Racial Privacy Initiative and the Shifting Grounds of Racial Politics." *Communication and Critical/Cultural Studies* 3, no. 3 (2006): 181–201.

Flynn, Kevin. "8 Arrested Near City Hall in Protest of Police Shooting." *New York Times,* February 23, 1999.

Forbes, Ella. "Every Man Fights for His Freedom: The Rhetoric of African American Resistance in the Mid-Nineteenth Century." In *Understanding African American Rhetoric: Classical Origins to Contemporary Innovations,* edited by Ronald L. Jackson II and Elaine B. Richardson, 155–70. New York: Routledge, 2003.

Forman, Murray, and Mark A. Neal, eds. *That's the Joint: The Hip Hop Studies Reader.* New York: Routledge, 2004.

Foster, Frances Smith. *Written by Herself: Literary Production by African American Women, 1746–1892.* Bloomington: Indiana University Press, 1993.

Foster, Hal. "The Problem of Pluralism." *Art in America* 70 (January 1982): 9–15.

Foucault, Michel. *Discipline and Punish: The Birth of the Prison.* Translated by Alan Sheridan. New York: Random House, 1977/1995.

——. *The History of Sexuality: Volume I.* Translated by Robert Hurley. New York: Vintage, 1978/1990.

Fox, James Alan. "Why They Kill: Mass Shooters Tend to Be Alienated Loners with Access to High-Powered Weapons." *Pittsburgh Post-Gazette*, April 18, 2007, Sooner edition, http://www.lexis-nexis.com/.

Fox Gotham, Kevin. "Critical Theory and Katrina: Disaster, Spectacle and Immanent Critique." *City* 11, no. 1 (April 2007): 81–99.

Frankenberg, Ruth. *White Women, Race Matters: The Social Construction of Whiteness.* Minneapolis: University of Minnesota Press: 1992.

Frankenberg, Ruth, ed. *Displacing Whiteness: Essays in Social and Cultural Criticism.* Durham, NC: Duke University Press, 1997.

Franklin, John Hope. *Mirror to America.* New York: Farrar, Straus, and Giroux, 2005.

Franklin, John Hope, and Alfred A. Moss, Jr. *From Slavery to Freedom: A History of African Americans.* 8th ed. New York: Alfred A. Knopf, 2000.

Fraser, Nancy. "Rethinking Recognition." *New Left Review* (May–June 2000): 107–20.

Freeman, Elizabeth. "Introduction." *GLQ: A Journal of Lesbian and Gay Studies* 13, 2–3 (2007): 159–76.

Friedman, Monroe. *Consumer Boycotts: Effecting Change Through the Marketplace and the Media.* London and New York: Routledge, 1999.

Friedman, Thomas L. (Reporter). *The Other Side of Outsourcing.* Thomas L. Friedman Reporting. [Television broadcast]. Silverspring, MD: Discovery Communications Inc, 2004.

Fusco, Caroline. "Cultural Landscapes of Purification: Sports Spaces and Discourses of Whiteness." *Sociology of Sports Journal* 22 (2005): 283–310.

Gabler, Neal. *Life: The Movie: How Entertainment Conquered Reality.* New York: Vintage, 2000.

Gabriel, John. *Whitewash: Racialized Politics and the Media.* London: Routledge, 1998.

Galbraith, John Kenneth. *The Affluent Society.* Boston and New York: Houghton Mifflin, 1958/1998.

Gallagher, Charles. "White Racial Formation: Into the Twenty-First Century." In *Critical White Studies: Looking Behind the Mirror*, edited by Richard Delgado and Jean Stefancic, 6–11. Philadelphia: Temple University Press, 1997.

García Canclini, Néstor. *Consumers and Citizens: Globalization and Multicultural Conflicts.* Translated by George Yúdice. Minneapolis: University of Minnesota Press, 2001.

Gardner, Charles. "NBA's Dress Code; Clothes Call; Dress Code Doesn't Suit All Players." *Milwaukee Journal Sentinel*, October 19, 2005. http:// www.findarticles.com/p/articles/mi_qn4196 (accessed February 11, 2007).

Gardner, Jared. *Master Plots: Race and the Founding of an American Literature, 1787–1845.* Baltimore: Johns Hopkins University Press, 1998.

Garofalo, James, and Maureen McLeod, "The Structure and Operations of Neighborhood Watch Programs in the United States." *Crime and Delinquency* 35 (1989): 326–44.

Gates, Henry Louis, Jr. *Figures in Black: Words, Signs and the "Racial" Self.* New York and London: Oxford University Press, 1987.

———. *The Signifying Monkey: A Theory of Afro-American Literary Criticism.* New York and London: Oxford University Press, 1988.

Gavin, Alice. "Reading Katrina: Race, Space and an Unnatural Disaster." *New Political Science* 30, no. 3 (September 2008): 325–46.

Gelzinis, Peter. "Campus Massacre: Random Violence Reminds Us Evil Lurks Everywhere." *Boston Herald*, April 17, 2007, http://www.lexis-nexis.com/.

Gencarella, Stephen O. "Constituting Folklore: A Case for Critical Folklore Studies." *Journal of American Folklore* 122, no. 484 (2009): 172–96.

Gibson, Campbell, and Kay Jung. "Historical Census Statistics on Population Totals By Race, 1790 to 1990, and By Hispanic Origin, 1970 to 1990, For The United States, Regions, Divisions, and States." United States Census Bureau. September 2002. http://www.census.gov/population/www/documentation/twps0056.html (accessed July 8, 2008).

Gibson, Robert. "The Negro Holocaust: Lynching and Race Riots in the United States, 1880–1950." Yale–New Haven Teachers Institute. http://www.yale.edu/ynhti/curriculum/units/1979/2/79.02.04.x.html

Gilens, Martin. *Why Americans Hate Welfare: Race, Media and the Politics of Anti-Poverty Policy.* Chicago: University of Chicago Press, 1999.

Gilroy, Paul. *Against Race: Imagining Political Culture Beyond the Color Line.* Cambridge, MA: Harvard University Press, 2000.

Giroux, Henry. "Racism and the Aesthetic of Hyper-real Violence: *Pulp Fiction* and Other Visual Tragedies." *Social Identities* 1, no. 2 (1995): 333–54.

Gitlin, Todd. *The Whole World is Watching: Mass Media in the Making and Unmaking of the New Left.* Berkeley: University of California Press, 2003.

Glaude, Eddie S., Jr. *Exodus! Religion, Race, and Nation in Early Nineteenth-Century Black America.* Chicago: University of Chicago Press, 2000.

Glickman, Lawrence B. "Introduction: Born to Shop? Consumer History and American History." In *Consumer Society in American History: A Reader,* edited by Lawrence B. Glickman, 1–14. Ithaca, NY: Cornell University Press, 1999.

Goldberg, David Theo. *Racist Culture: Philosophy and the Politics of Meaning.* Oxford: Blackwell, 1993.

———. *Multiculturalism: A Critical Reader.* Oxford: Blackwell, 1994.

———. "Taking Stock: Counting by Race." In *Racial Subjects: Writing on Race in America,* edited by David Theo Goldberg, 27–58. New York: Routledge, 1997.

———. *The Racial State.* Malden, MA: Blackwell, 2002.

Goldiner, Dave. "If Only We Could See 'Our' Tapes, Say Littleton Kin." *Daily News* (New York), April 20, 2007, city final edition, http://www.lexis-nexis.com/.

Goldzwig, Steven R., and Patricia A. Sullivan. "Narrative and Counternarrative in Print-Mediated Coverage of Milwaukee Alderman Michael McGee." *Quarterly Journal of Speech* 86 (2000): 215–31.

Gonzalez, Alberto, Marsha Houston, and Victoria Chen, eds. *Our Voices: Essays in Culture, Ethnicity, and Communication.* Los Angeles: Roxbury Press, 1994.

Goodwin, Michael. "CBS Dismisses Snyder." *New York Times,* in Penrose Library Nexus Lexus, http://o-www/lexisnexis.combianca.penlib.du.edu (accessed February 17, 2008).

Gordon, Avery, and Christopher Newfield, eds. *Mapping Multiculturalism.* Minneapolis: University of Minnesota Press, 1996.

Gordon, Dexter B. *Black Identity: Rhetoric, Ideology, and Nineteenth-Century Black Nationalism.* Carbondale: Southern Illinois University Press, 2003.

Gordon, Ted, and Wahneema Lubiano. "The Statement of the Black Faculty Caucus." In *Debating P.C.: The Controversy Over Political Correctness on College Campuses,* edited by Paul Berman. New York: Dell-Laurel, 1992.

Gormley, Paul. "Trashing Whiteness: *Pulp Fiction, Se7en, Strange Days,* and Articulating Affect." *Angelaki: Journal of the Theoretical Humanities* 6, no. 1 (2000): 155–71.

Gotanda, Neil. "Multiculturalism and Racial Stratification." In *Mapping Multiculturalism,* edited by Avery Gordon and Christopher Newfield, 238–502. Minneapolis: University of Minnesota Press, 1996.

Grano, Danial A. "Ritual Disorder and the Contractual Morality of Sports: A Case Study in Race, Class, and Agreement." *Rhetoric and Public Affairs* 10, no. 3 (2007): 445–74.

Green, Rodney D., Beverly Wright, and Tiffany Hamelin. "Strategies for Recovery from Katrina: Corporate Capitalism, NGOs, Racism, and Class." Paper presented at the meetings of the National Economic Association, 2008.

Greene, Ronald W. "Another Materialist Rhetoric." *Critical Studies in Mass Communication* 15, no. 1 (1998): 21–40.

Greene, Susan, and Bill Briggs. "World of Darkness: Comfortable Suburbs Harbor Troubled Teens." *Denver Post*, April 22, 1999, http://www.lexis-nexis.com/.

Gregg, Richard B. "The Ego-Function of the Rhetoric of Protest." *Philosophy & Rhetoric* 4, no. 2 (1971): 71–91.

Gregg, Richard B., Jackson A. McCormack, and Douglas J. Pedersen. "The Rhetoric of Black Power: A Street-Level Interpretation." *Quarterly Journal of Speech* 55, no. 2 (1969): 151–60.

Gresson, Aaron David, III. *The Recovery of Race in America*. Minneapolis: University of Minnesota Press, 1995.

———. *America's Atonement: Racial Pain, Recovery Rhetoric, and the Pedagogy of Healing*. New York: Peter Lang, 2004.

———. *Racial Pain, Recovery Rhetoric, and the Pedagogy of Healing*. New York: Peter Lang, 2004.

———. *America's Atonement: Racial Pain, Recovery Rhetoric, and the Pedagogy of Healing*. New York: Peter Lang, 2005.

Grewal, Inderpal. *Transnational America. Feminisms, Diasporas, Neoliberalisms*. Durham and London: Duke University Press, 2005.

Greyser, Naomi. "Affective Geographies: Sojourner Truth's Narrative, Feminism, and the Ethical Bind of Sentimentalism." *American Literature* 79, no. 2 (2007): 275–305.

Gronbeck, Bruce E. "The Rhetoric of Social-Institutional Change: Black Action at Michigan." In *Explorations in Rhetorical Criticism*, edited by Gerald P. Mohrmann, Charles J. Stewart, and Donovan J. Ochs, 96–123. University Park: Pennsylvania State University Press, 1973.

Gross, Jane. "N.B.A.'s Rebuilding Program is Showing Results." *New York Times*, December 23, 1984.

Grossberg, Lawrence. *We Gotta Get Out of This Place: Popular Conservatism and Postmodern Culture*. New York: Routledge, 1992.

Grosz, Elizabeth. *Time Travels: Feminism, Nature, Power (Next Wave: New Directions in Womens Studies)*. Durham and London: Duke University Press, 2005.

Guerrero, Edward. "Interview." *BaadAsssss Cinema: A Bold Look At 70s Blaxploitation Films*, DVD. Directed by Isaac Julian. New York: IFC Entertainment, 2002.

Gupta, Akhil, and James Ferguson. "Beyond 'Culture': Space, Identity, and the Politics of Difference. *Cultural Anthropology* 7, no. 1, Space, Identity, and the Politics of Difference (February 1992): 6–23.

Gutierrez-Jones, Carl. *Critical Race Narratives*. New York: New York University Press, 2001.

Gutmann, Amy, and Dennis Thompson. *Why Deliberative Democracy?* Princeton, NJ: Princeton University Press, 1996.

Haberman, Charles. "A Shooting, and Shooting from the Hip." *New York Times*, February 12, 1999.

Habermas, Jurgen. *Communication and the Evolution of Society*. Boston: Beacon, 1979.

———. "A Reply to My Critics." In *Habermas: Critical Debates*, edited by John Thompson and David Held, 219–83. Cambridge, MA: MIT Press, 1982.

———. *The Theory of Communicative Action, Vol. 1. Reason and Rationalization of Society.* Boston: Beacon, 1984.

———. "On the Distinction Between Poetic and Communicative Uses of Language." In *On the Pragmatics of Communication*, edited by Maeve Cooke. Cambridge, MA: MIT Press, 1988.

———. "Political Communication in Media Society: Does Democracy Still Enjoy an Epistemic Dimension? The Impact of Normative Theory on Empirical Research." *Communication Theory* 16, no. 4 (2006): 411–26.

Haggis, Paul. "On the Origins of Crash." Landmark Theatres website. http://www.landmarktheatres.com/mn/crash.html.

Halberstam, Judith. *In a Queer Time and Place: Transgender Bodies, Subcultural Lives (Sexual Cultures).* New York: New York University Press, 2005.

Hale, Grace Elizabeth. *Making Whiteness: The Culture of Segregation in the South, 1890–1940.* New York: Vintage, 1999.

Hall, Ronald E. "Entitlement Disorder: The Colonial Traditions of Power as White Male Resistance." *Journal of Black Studies* 34 (2004): 562–79.

Hall, Stuart. "Race, Articulation and Societies Structured in Dominance." In *Sociological Theories: Race and Colonialism*, 305–45. Paris: UNESCO, 1979.

———. "Encoding, Decoding." In *Culture, Media, Language*, edited by Stuart Hall, Dorothy Hobson, Andrew Lowe, and Paul Willis, 128–39. London: Hutchinson, 1980.

———. "The Whites of Their Eyes: Racist Ideologies and the Media." In *Silver Lining: Some Strategies for the Eighties*, edited by George Bridges and Rosalind Brunt, 28–52. London: Lawrence and Wishart, 1981.

———. "On Postmodernism and Articulation: An Interview with Stuart Hall." *Journal of Communication Inquiry* 10, no. 2 (Summer 1986): 45–60.

———. "Ideology and Communication Theory." In *Rethinking Communication, 1, Paradigm Issues*, edited by Brenda Dervin, Lawrence Grossberg, Barbra J. O'Keefe, and Ellen Wartella, 40–52. Newbury Park, CA: Sage Publications, 1989.

———. "The Whites of Their Eyes: Racist Ideologies and the Media." In *Gender, Race, and Class in Media: A Text Reader*, edited by Gail Dines and Jean McMahon Humez. Thousand Oaks, CA: Sage Publications, 1995.

———. "Cultural Identity and Cinematic Representation." In *Black British Cultural Studies: A Reader*, edited by Houston A. Baker, Jr., Manthia Diawara, and Ruth H. Lindeborg, 210–22. Chicago: The University of Chicago Press, 1996.

———. "Race, Articulation, and Societies Structure in Discourse." In *Black British Cultural Studies: A Reader*, edited by Houston A. Baker, Jr., Manthia Diawara, and Ruth H. Lindeborg, 16–60. Chicago: University of Chicago Press, 1996.

———. "Race, Culture, and Communications: Looking Backward and Forward at Cultural Studies." In *What is Cultural Studies: A Reader*, edited by John Storey, 336–43. London: Arnold, 1996.

———. "Introduction." In *Representation: Cultural Representations and Signifying Practices*, edited by Stuart Hall, 1–11. London: *Sage Publications*, 1997.

———. "The Whites of Their Eyes: Racist Ideologies and the Media." In *Gender, Race, and Class in Media*. 2nd ed., edited by Gail Dines and Jean M. Humez, 89–93. London: Sage Publications, 2003.

Hallissy, Erin. "Census 2000: Who We Are—Concord's Melting Pot—Vibrant Mix of Newcomers Transforms Suburb into a Burgeoning Multiethnic Haven." *San Francisco Chronicle*, April 19, 2001.

Halualani, Rona Tamiko. *In the Name of Hawaiians: Native Identities and Cultural Politics*. Minneapolis: University of Minnesota Press, 2002.

Hanczor, Robert S. "Articulation Theory and Public Controversy: Taking Sides Over NYPD Blue." *Critical Studies in Mass Communication* 14, no. 1 (1997): 1–30.

Haney López, Ian F. *White by Law: the Legal Construction of Race*. New York: New York University Press, 1996.

Harris, Cheryl I. "Review Essay: Whitewashing Race: Scapegoating Culture." *California Law Review* 94 (2006): 907–43.

Harrison, Eric. "Crash." *Houston Chronicle Online*, September 30, 2005. http://www.chron.com/disp/story.mpl/ae/movies/reviews/3169528.html.

Harrold, Stanley. *American Abolitionists*. Harlow, UK: Pearson Education Limited, 2001.

Hartigan, Patti. "To Stop the Violence, the Play's the Thing: Cyberlinks." *Boston Globe*, April 23, 1999, city edition, http://www.lexis-nexis.com/.

Hartmann, Douglass. "The Politics of Race and Sport: Resistance and Domination in the 1968 African American Olympic Protest Movement." *Ethnic and Racial Studies* 19, no. 3 (1996): 548–66.

Harvey, David. *The Condition of Postmodernity: An Enquiry into the Origins of Cultural Change*. Malden, MA: Blackwell, 1990.

Hasian, Marouf, Jr., and Fernando Delgado. "The Trials and Tribulations of Racialized Critical Rhetorical Theory: Understanding the Rhetorical Ambiguities of Proposition 187." *Communication Theory* 8, no. 3 (1998): 245–70.

Hassell, John. "Pair Were Bright But Odd, and Teasing Never Stopped." *Star Ledger* (Newark, NJ), April 22, 1999, final edition, http://www.lexis-nexis.com/.

Hauser, Gerard A. *Vernacular Voices: The Rhetoric of Publics and Public Spheres*. Columbia: University of South Carolina Press, 1999.

Havens, Timothy. "'The Biggest Show in the World': Race and the Global Popularity of the *Cosby Show*." *Meida, Culture, and Society* 22 (2000): 371–91.

Heal, Clare. *Paying for Diamonds with Child's Blood*. January 28, 2007. http://www.lexisnexis.com.

Hebdige, Dick. *Subculture: The Meaning of Style*. London and New York: Routledge, 1979.

Hecht, Michael L., ed. *Communicating Prejudice*. Newbury Park, CA: Sage Publications, 1998.

Hendren, John. "Detailed Diary Discloses Plans, Motives of Gunmen in Massacre." Associated Press, April 24, 1999, AM cycle, http://www.lexis-nexis.com/.

Hendrix, Anastasia. "Census 2000—Who We Are—S.F. Grew by 7.3% since '90 Census—Asian Influx Accounts for most of Change." *San Francisco Chronicle*, 2001.

Hill Collins, Patricia. *Black Feminist Thought: Knowledge, Consciousness, and the Politics of Empowerment*. New York: Routledge, 2000.

Hine, Darlene Clark, and Ernestine Jenkins. "Introduction: Black Men's History: Toward a Gendered Perspective." In *A Question of Manhood. Vol. 1: "Manhood of Rights": The Construction of Black Male History and Manhood, 1750–1870*, edited by Darlene Clark Hine and Ernestine Jenkins, 1–58. Bloomington: Indiana University Press, 1999.

Ho, Pensri. "Performing the 'Oriental': Professionals and the Asian Model Minority Myth." *Journal of Asian American Studies* 6, no. 2 (2003): 149–75.

Hoerl, Kristen. "Monstrous Youth in Suburbia: Disruption and Recovery of the American Dream." *Southern Communication Journal* 67, no. 3 (2002): 259–75.

Hogarth, David. *Realer than Real: Global Directions in Documentary*. Austin: University of Texas Press, 2006.

Holman, Hugh, and William Harmon. *A Handbook to Literature.* 5th ed. New York: Macmillan, 1986.

Holthouse, David. "Minute Mess: Minuteman Leader Ousted, Forms New Group." *Intelligence Report,* Summer 2007. http://www.splcenter.org/intel/intelreport (accessed January 3, 2010).

———. "Nativists to 'Patriots': Nativist Vigilantes Adopt 'Patriot' Movement Ideas." *Intelligence Report,* Fall 2009. http://www.splcenter.org/intel/intelreport (accessed January 3, 2010).

hooks, bell. *Teaching Community: A Pedagogy of Hope.* New York: Routledge, 2003.

Hoon, Song. "Seeing Oneself Seeing Oneself: White Nihilism in Ethnography and Theory." *Ethnos* 71, no. 4 (2006): 470–88.

Horton, James Oliver, and Lois E. Horton. "Violence, Protest, and Identity: Black Manhood in Antebellum America." In *Free People of Color: Inside the African American Community,* edited by James Oliver Horton, 80–96. Washington, DC: Smithsonian Institution Press, 1993.

———. *In Hope of Liberty: Culture, Community, and Protest Among Northern Free Blacks, 1700–1860.* New York: Oxford University Press, 1997.

———. *Black Bostonians: Family Life and Community Struggle in the Antebellum North.* 20th anniversary edition. New York: Holmes & Meier, 1999.

House, Billy. "Hayworth Says Bush insulted Minutemen." (April 28, 2005). http://www.azcentral.com/arizonarepublic/news/articles/0428minuteman-dc28.html (accessed July 6, 2008).

Humphreys, Jeffrey M. "The Multicultural Economy." *Georgia Business and Economic Conditions* 67, no. 3. Athens: Selig Center for Economic Growth/University of Georgia, 2007.

Hunter, Stephen. "'Crash': The Clash of Human Contradictions." *Washingtonpost.com,* May 6, 2005. http://www.washingtonpost.com/wpdyn/content/article/2005/05/06/AR2005062901114.html.

Huntzicker, William. *The Popular Press, 1833–1865.* Westport, CT and London: Greenwood Press, 1999.

Hurtado, Aida. *The Color of Privilege: Three Blasphemies on Race and Feminism.* Ann Arbor: University of Michigan Press, 1996.

Huspek, Michael. "Black Press, White Press, and Their Opposition: The Case of the Police Shooting of Tyisha Miller." *Social Justice* 31, no. 1/2 (2004): 217–41.

———. "'From the Standpoint of the White Man's World': The Black Press and Contemporary White Media Scholarship with Emphasis upon the Work of W. Lance Bennett." *Journal of Intergroup Relations* 32, no. 3 (2005): 67–88.

———. Habermas and Oppositional Public Spheres: A Stereoscopic Analysis of Black and White Press Practices. *Political Studies* 55, no. 6 (2007): 821–43.

———. "Normative Potentials of Rhetorical Action within Deliberative Democracies." *Communication Theory* 17, no. 4 (2007): 356–67.

———. "Untamed Rhetoric in the Public Sphere: Beyond Communicative and Strategic Action." Forthcoming. Unpublished manuscript.

Hutchison, Earl Ofari. "Black Capitalism: Self-Help or Self-Delusion?" In *African Americans in the U.S. Economy,* edited by Cecilia A. Conrad et al., 271–77. Lanham, MD: Rowman & Littlefield, 2005.

Hutton, Frankie. "Democratic Idealism in the Black Press." In *Outsiders in 19th Century Press History: Multicultural Perspectives,* edited by Frankie Hutton and B.S. Reed, 5–20. Bowling Green, OH: Bowling Green University Popular Press, 1995.

Intelligence Report. "Anti-Immigration Groups: Second Minuteman Group in Bitter Split." Fall 2007, http://www.splcenter.org/intel/intelreport (accessed January 3, 2010).

Ipsaro, Anthony J. *White Men, Women and Minorities in the Changing Work Force.* Denver: Meridian Associates, 1997.

Jackson, John L. Jr. *Harlemworld: Doing Race and Class in Contemporary Black America.* Chicago: University of Chicago Press, 2001.

Jackson, Ronald L., II. "White Space, White Privilege: Mapping Discursive Inquiry into the Self." *Quarterly Journal of Speech* 85, no. 1 (1999): 38–54.

———. *Scripting the Black Masculine Body: Identity, Discourse, and Racial Politics in Popular Media.* Albany: State University of New York Press, 2006.

Jackson, Ronald, and Sonja M. Brown, eds. *Black Pioneers in Communication Research.* Thousand Oaks, CA: Sage Publications, 2006.

Jackson, Ronald, and Celnisha Dangerfield. "Defining Black Masculinity as Cultural Property: Toward an Identity Negotiation Paradigm." In *Intercultural Communication: A Reader.* 10th ed., edited by Larry Samovar and Richard Porter, 120–30. Belmont, CA: Wadsworth. 2002.

Jackson, Ronald L., and Thurmon Garner. "Tracing the Evolution of 'Race,' 'Ethnicity,' and 'Culture' in Communication Studies." *Howard Journal of Communications* 9, no. 1 (January 1998): 41–55.

Jackson, Ronald L., Chang In Shin, and Keith B. Wilson. "The Meaning of Whiteness: Critical Implications of Communicating and Negotiating Race." *World Communication* 29, no. 1 (2000): 69–86.

Jackson, Ronald L., and Katherine Simpson. "White Positionalities and Cultural Contracts: Critiquing Entitlement, Theorizing, and Exploring the Negotiation of White Identities." In *Ferment in the Intercultural Field: Axiology/value/praxis,* edited by William J. Starosta and Guo-Ming Chen, 177–210. Thousand Oaks, CA: Sage Publications, 2003.

Jacobs, Meg. *Pocketbook Politics: Economic Citizenship in Twentieth-Century America.* Princeton, NJ: Princeton University Press, 2005.

Jacobson, Matthew Frye. *Whiteness of a Different Color: European Immigrants and the Alchemy of Race.* Cambridge, MA: Harvard University Press, 1998.

James, Michael Rabinder. *Deliberative Democracy and the Plural Polity.* Lawrence: University of Kansas Press, 2004.

Jasinski, James. "Constituting Antebellum African American Identity: Resistance, Violence, and Masculinity in Henry Highland Garnet's (1843) 'Address to the Slaves.'" *Quarterly Journal of Speech* 93 (2007): 27–57.

Jaworski, Adam, and Nikolas Coupland. "Introduction: Perspectives on Discourse Analysis." In *The Discourse Reader,* edited by Adam Jaworski and Nikolas Coupland, 1–44. London, Routledge, 1999.

Jefferson, Thomas. *Notes on the State of Virginia.* 1787. Reprint, ed. David Waldstreicher. New York: Bedford/St. Martin's, 2002.

Johnson, Scott. "The Border War." *Newsweek,* April 4, 2005, 29, http://www.lexisnexis.com (accessed July 3, 2008).

Johnston, Hank, and John A. Noakes, ed. *Frames of Protest: Social Movements and The Framing Perspective.* Lanham, MD: Rowman and Littlefield, 2005.

Joseph, Ralina L. "'Tyra Banks Is Fat': Reading (Post-)Racism and (Post-) Feminism in the New Millennium." *Critical Studies in Media Communication* 26, no. 3 (2009): 237–54.

Kachun, Mitch. *Festivals of Freedom: Memory and Meaning in African American Emancipation Celebrations, 1808–1915.* Amherst: University of Massachusetts Press, 2003.

"Katrina Timeline," http://www.thinkprogress.org/2005/09/07/the-katrina-timeline/ (July 29, 2007).

Kawai, Yuko. "Stereotyping Asian Americans: The Dialectic of the Model Minority and the Yellow Peril." *Howard Journal of Communication* 16, no. 2 (2005): 109–30.

Keating, Christine. *Decolonizing Democracy: Transforming the Social Contract in India.* State College: Penn State Press, forthcoming.

Keating, Cricket. *Decolonizing Democracy: The Social Contract in Transition.* Unpublished book manuscript, 2008.

Kelley, Robin D. G. "Untitled Essay." *Social Text* 42 (Spring 1995): 2–5.

Kelley, Venita. "'Good Speech': An Interpretive Essay Investigating an African Philosophy of Communication." *Western Journal of Black Studies* 26 (2002): 44–54.

Keough, Peter. "Independents' Daze: Quentin Tarantino and Gus Van Sant on Playing Hollywood's Game." *Worcester Phoenix,* January 2, 1998. http://worcesterphoenix.com/archive/movies/98/01/02/VAN_SANT_TARANTINO.html (accessed January 24, 2008).

Kim, Claire Jean. *Bitter Fruit: The Politics of Black-Korean Conflict in New York City.* New Haven, CT: Yale University Press, 2000.

Kinefuchi, Etsuko, and Mark P. Orbe. "Situating Oneself in Racialized World: Understanding Student Reactions to Crash through Standpoint Theory and Context-positionality Frame. *Journal of International and Intercultural Communication* 1.1 (2008): 70–90.

King, J. L., and Karen Hunter. *On the Down Low: A Journey into the Lives of Black Men Who Sleep With Men.* New York: Random House, 2004.

King, Richard C. "Cautionary Notes on Whiteness and Sports Studies." *Sociology of Sports Journal* 22 (2005): 397–408.

King, Richard C., David J. Leonard, and Kyle W. Kusz. "White Power and Sport: An Introduction." *Journal of Sport and Social Issues* 31, no. 1 (2007): 3–10.

Kish, Zenia. "'My FEMA People': Hip-Hop as Disaster Recovery in the Katrina Diaspora." *American Quarterly* (2009): 671–92.

Kitch, Carolyn. "Twentieth-Century Tales: Newsmagazines and American Memory." *Journalism and Communication Monographs* 1, no. 2 (1999): 119–55.

Kizla, Mark. "Sons of Columbine as Different as Good and Evil." *Denver Post,* April 22, 1999, http://www.lexis-nexis.com/.

Klare, Michael T. *Resource Wars: The New Landscape of Global Conflict.* New York: Metropolitan, 2001.

Knighton, Gloria. "Get the Racist Nuts Off the Squad." *New York Amsterdam News,* March 3, 1999.

Kobayashi, Audrey, and Linda Peake. "Racism Out of Place: Thoughts on Whiteness and an Antiracist Geography in the New Millennium." *Annals of the Association of American Geographers* 90, no. 2 (2000): 392–403.

Krieger, Zvika. "Time's Up: The Minutemen Turn on Each Other." *The New Republic,* November 19, 2008, http://www.tnr.com (accessed December 1, 2008).

Kurtz, Howard. "For Virginia Tech Killer's Twisted Video, Pause But No Rewind." *Washington Post,* April 23, 2007, http://www.lexis-nexis.com/.

Kwan, Allen. "Seeking New Civilizations: Race Normativity in the Star Trek Franchise." *Bulletin of Science, Technology and Society* 27, no. 1 (2007): 59–70.

Laclau, Ernesto. *Politics and Ideology in Marxist Theory: Capitalism, Fascism, Populism.* London: New Left Books, 1977.

Laclau, Ernesto, and Chantal Mouffe. *Hegemony and Socialist Strategy: Towards a Radical Democratic Politics.* Translated by W. Moore and P. Cammack. London: Verso, 1985.

Lacy, Michael G. "Exposing the Spectrum of Whiteness: Rhetorical Conceptions of White Absolutism." *Communication Yearbook* 32 (2008): 277–311.

————. "White Innocence Myths in Citizen Discourse, The Progressive Era (1974–1988)." *Howard Journal of Communications* 21 (2010a): 20–39.

————. "White Innocence Heroes: Recovery, Reversals, Paternalism, and David Duke." *Journal of International and Intercultural Communication* 3, no. 3 (2010b): 206–27.

Lage, Larry. "Indiana 97, Detroit 82." Associated Press. November 20, 2004. http://sports.yahoo.com/nba/recap (accessed February 13, 2008).

Lamont, Michèle, and Virág Molnár. "How Blacks Use Consumption to Shape Their Collective Identity: Evidence from Marketing Specialists." *Journal of Consumer Culture* 1, no. 1 (2001): 31–45.

Lampe, Gregory P. *Frederick Douglass: Freedom's Voice, 1818–1845*. East Lansing: Michigan State University Press, 1998.

Lancaster (PA) New Era. "What Can We Do To Prevent More Horrors Like Littleton?" April 21, 1999, http://www.lexis-nexis.com/.

Lane, Jeffrey. *Under the Boards: The Cultural Revolution in Basketball*. Lincoln: University of Nebraska Press, 2007.

Lapchick, Richard. *Smashing Barriers: Race and Sport in the New Millennium*. Lanham: Madison Books, 2001.

Lapchick, Richard, Marina Bustamante, and Horacio Ruiz. "The 2006-07 Season Racial and Gender Report Card: National Basketball Association." www.bus.ucf.edu/sport (accessed July 1, 2007).

Lapsansky, Phillip. "Graphic Discord: Abolitionist and Antiabolitionist Images." In *The Abolitionist Sisterhood: Women's Political Culture in Antebellum America*, edited by Jean Fagan Yellin and John C. Van Horne, 201–30. Ithaca, NY: Cornell University Press, 1994.

Larson, Stephanie Greco. *Media and Minorities: The Politics of Race in News and Entertainment*. Lanham, MD: Rowman & Littlefield, 2006.

Lee, Spike. "Interview: Getting Spikey: *The Context* interviews Spike Lee, director of *Bamboozled*," *The Context*, 2001. http://www.thecontext.com/docsi/2942.html (accessed June 11, 2007).

Lee, Wenshu. "In the Names of Chinese Women." *Quarterly Journal of Speech* 84 (1998): 283–302.

Leonard, David J. "The Real Color of Money: Controlling Black Bodies in the NBA." *Journal of Sport and Social Issues* 30, no. 2 (2006): 158–79.

Levine, Robert S. *Martin Delany, Frederick Douglass, and the Politics of Representative Identity*. Chapel Hill: University of North Carolina Press, 1997.

Lipscomb, Drema R. "Sojourner Truth: A Practical Public Discourse." In *Reclaiming Rhetorica: Women in the Rhetorical Tradition*, edited by Andrea A. Lunsford, 227–45. Pittsburgh: University of Pittsburgh Press, 1995.

Lipsitz, George. "'Swing Low, Sweet Cadillac': White Supremacy, Antiblack Racism, and the New Historicism." *American Literary History* 7, no. 4 (Winter 1995): 700–25.

————. *The Possessive Investment in Whiteness: How White People Profit from Identity Politics*. Philadelphia: Temple University Press, 1998.

Lite, Jordan. "Some Mass Murderers Aim to Be 'More Sensational Than the Last.'" *New York Daily News*, April 16, 2007, http://www.lexis-nexis.com/.

Logan, Shirley Wilson. *"We Are Coming": The Persuasive Discourse of Nineteenth-Century Black Women*. Carbondale: Southern Illinois University Press, 1999.

————. *Liberating Language: Sites of Rhetorical Education in Nineteenth-Century Black America*. Carbondale: Southern Illinois University Press, 2008.

Logue, Cal. "Rhetorical Ridicule of Reconstruction." *Quarterly Journal of Speech* 62 (1976): 400–409.

Lowance, Mason I., ed. *Against Slavery: An Abolitionist Reader*. New York: Penguin Books, 2000.

Lowe, Lisa. "Imagining Los Angeles in the Production of Multiculturalism." In *Mapping Multiculturalism*, edited by Avery Gordon and Christopher Newfield, 238–502. Minneapolis: University of Minnesota Press, 1996.

———. "Immigration, Citizenship, Racialization: Asian American Critique." Chapter 1 in *Immigrant Acts: On Asian American Cultural Politics*. Durham, NC: Duke University Press, 1996.

Lubiano, Wahneema. "Like Being Mugged by a Metaphor: Multiculturalism and State Narratives." In *Mapping Multiculturalism*, edited by Avery F. Gordon and Christopher Newfield, 64–75. Minneapolis: University of Minnesota Press, 2008.

Machiyama, Tomohiro. "Tarantino Interview," *Japattack*, August 28, 2003. http://japattack.com/japattack/film/tarantino.html (accessed February 10, 2010).

MacKenzie, Ross. "Littleton Puts Needed Light on the Abject Condition of Our Boys." *Richmond (VA) Times Dispatch*, April 25, 1999, city edition, http://www.lexis-nexis.com/.

Maddox, Alton, Jr. "No Justice! No Peace!" *New York Amsterdam News*, February 24, 1999.

Madison, Kelly J. "Legitimation Crisis and Containment: The 'Anti-Racist-White-Hero' Film." *Critical Studies in Mass Communication* 16 (1999): 399–416.

Magazine Publishers of America. *African American/ Black Market Profile*. New York: Magazine Publishers of America Information Center, 2008.

Maharaj, Gitaniali. "Talking Trash: Late Capitalism, Black (Re)Productivity, and Professional Basketball." In *Sportcult*, edited by Randy Martin and Toby Miller, 227–40. Minneapolis: University of Minnesota Press, 1999.

Mandziuk, Roseann M. "Commemorating Sojourner Truth: Negotiating the Politics of Race and Gender in the Spaces of Public Memory." *Western Journal of Communication* 67 (2003): 271–91.

Mani, Lata. "Multiple Mediations: Feminist Scholarship in the Age of Multinational Reception." *Feminist Review* 35 (Summer 1990): 24–41.

Mansbridge, Jane. "Everyday Talk in the Deliberative System." In *Deliberative Politics: Essays on Democracy and Engagement*, edited by Stephen Macedo, 211–38. New York: Oxford University Press, 1999.

Marable, Manning. "History and Black Consciousness: The Political Culture of Black America." *Monthly Review* 47, no. 3 (July–August 1995): 71–89.

———. "History of Black Capitalism." In *African Americans in the U.S. Economy*, edited by Cecilia A. Conrad et al., 231–36. Lanham, MD: Rowman & Littlefield, 2005.

Marqusee, Mike. "Sport and Stereotype: From Role Model to Muhammad Ali." *Race & Class* 36, no. 4 (1995): 1–29.

Martin, Randy, and Toby Miller. *Sportcult*. Minneapolis: University of Minnesota Press, 1999.

Marty, Debian. "White Antiracist Rhetoric as Apologia." In *Whiteness: The Communication of Social Identity*, edited by Tom Nakayama and Judith N. Martin, 51–68. Thousand Oaks, CA: Sage Publications, 1999.

Massey, Doreen. *Space, Place, and Gender*. Minnesota: University of Minnesota, 1994.

———. *For Space*. Thousand Oaks, CA: Sage Publications, 2005.

McCallum, Jack. "The Ugliest Game: An NBA Brawl Exposes the Worst Player and Fan Behavior and Serves as a Frightening Wake-Up Call." *Sports Illustrated*. November 29, 2004. http://o-find.galegroup.com.bianca.penlib.du.edu (accessed March 3, 2005).

McClish, Glen. "William G. Allen's 'Orators and Oratory': Inventional Amalgamation, Pathos, and the Characterization of Violence in African-American Abolitionist Rhetoric." *Rhetoric Society Quarterly* 35 (2005): 47–72.

———. "'New Terms for the Vindication of Our Rights': William Whipper's Activist Rhetoric." *Advances in the History of Rhetoric* 9 (2006): 97–127.

———. "'The Spirit of Human Brotherhood,' 'The Sisterhood of Nations,' and 'Perfect Manhood': Frederick Douglass and the Rhetorical Significance of the Haitian Revolution." In *African Americans and the Haitian Revolution: Selected Essays and Historical Documents*, edited by Maurice Jackson and Jacqueline Bacon, 123–39. New York: Routledge, 2010.

McCosky, Chris. "Some Pistons Are Unhappy about Talk of a Dress Code." *Detroit News*. October 9, 2005. http:www.detnews.com/2005/pistons (accessed February 11, 2007).

McDonald, Mary G. "Mapping Whiteness and Sport: An Introduction." *Sociology of Sports Journal* 22 (2005): 245–55.

McFeely, William S. *Frederick Douglass*. New York: W. W. Norton, 1991.

McGee, Michael Calvin. "The 'Ideograph': A Link Between Rhetoric and Ideology." *Quarterly Journal of Speech* 66 (1980): 1–16.

———. "Text, Context, and the Fragmentation of Contemporary Culture." *Western Journal of Communication* 54 (1990): 274–89.

McKeon, Richard. "Dialectic and Political Thought and Action." *Ethics* 65, no. 1 (1954): 1–33.

McKerrow, Raymie E. "Critical Rhetoric: Theory and Praxis." *Communication Monographs* 56, no. 2 (1989): 91–111.

———. "Critical Rhetoric in a Postmodern World." *Quarterly Journal of Speech* 77, no. 1 (1991): 75–78.

McLeod, R. G. "'Minority Majority' Well on Way in State: Striking Changes in New Census Data." *San Francisco Chronicle*, September 4, 1998.

McPhail, Mark Lawrence. "The Politics of Complicity: Second Thoughts about the Social Construction of Racial Equality." *Quarterly Journal of Speech* 80, no. 3 (1994): 343–81.

———. *The Rhetoric of Racism*. Lanham, MD: University Press of America, 1994.

———. *The Rhetoric of Racism Revisited*. Maryland: University Press of America, 2002.

McPhee, Mike. "Remembering the Slain: Isaiah Shoels Son Killed by 'Hatred,' Father Says." *Denver Post*, April 23, 1999, 2nd edition, http://www.lexis-nexis.com/.

McWhorter, John. "Obama and the Black Elite." *Forbes*, January 20, 2009. http://www.forbes.com/2009/01/20/obama-inauguration-race-oped-cx_jm_0120mcwhorter_print.html.

———. *Winning the Race: Beyond the Crisis in Black America*. New York: Gotham, 2006.

Means Coleman, Robin R., and Jasmine Cobb. "No Way of Seeing: Mainstreaming and Selling the Gaze of Homo-thug Hip Hop." *Popular Communication* 5 (2007): 89–108.

Melish, Joanne Pope. *Disowning Slavery: Gradual Emancipation and "Race" in New England, 1780–1860*. Ithaca, NY: Cornell University Press, 1998.

Mendelberg, Tali. *The Race Card: Campaign Strategy, Implicit Messages, and the Norm of Equality*. Princeton, NJ: Princeton University Press, 2001.

Miller, Toby. *Sportsex*. Philadelphia, PA: Temple University Press, 2001.

Minh-Ha, Trinh T. "Documentary Is/Not a Name." *October* 52, (Spring, 1990): 76–98.

MinutemanHQ. "MinuteManHQ On Patrol: In Four States All Month In October." http://www.minutemanhq.com (accessed June 19, 2005).

Mishra, Raja, and Marcella Bombardieri. "Closer Look Reveals Cho's Isolation: Hard Working Student Let Few Inside His World." *Boston Globe*, April 22, 2007, http://www.lexis-nexis.com/.

Mitchell, Elvis. "Interview." *BaadAsssss Cinema: A Bold Look at 70s Blaxploitation Films*, DVD. Directed by Isaac Julian. New York: IFC Entertainment, 2002.

Montero, Douglas. "What Pushed Outcasts Over the Edge?" *New York Post*, April 26, 1999, http://www.lexis-nexis.com/.

Moon, Dreama G. "White Enculturation and Bourgeois Ideology." In *Whiteness: The Communication of Social Identity*, edited by Thomas K. Nakayama and Judith N. Martin, 177–97. Thousand Oaks, CA: Sage Publications, 1999.

Moon, Dreama, and Thomas K. Nakayama. "Strategic Social Identities and Judgments: A Murder in Appalachia." *Howard Journal of Communications* 16, no. 2 (2005): 87–107.

Mooney, Joshua. "Interview with Quentin Tarantino." *Movieline*, August, 1994.

Morgan, Marcyliena. "More than a Mood or an Attitude: Discourse and Verbal Genres in African-American Culture. In *African-American English: Structure, History and Use*, edited by Salikoko Mufwene, John Rickford, Guy Bailey, and John Baugh, 251–81. London: Routledge, 1998.

Moses, Wilson Jeremiah. *Afrotopia: The Roots of African American Popular History*. Cambridge: Cambridge University Press, 1998.

Moyers, Bill. 2003. *NOW with Bill Moyers*. Produced by Brenda Breslauer. Correspondent Keith Brown: Aired on August 29, 2003: PBS.

Mukherjee, Roopali. "The Ghetto Fabulous Aesthetic in Contemporary Black Culture: Class and Consumption in the Barbershop Films." *Cultural Studies* 20, no. 6 (2006): 599–629.

———. *The Racial Order of the Things: Cultural Imaginaries of the Post-Soul Era*. Minneapolis: University of Minnesota Press, 2006.

Mullins, Paul R. *Race and Affluence: An Archaeology of African America and Consumer Culture*. New York: Kluwer Academic/Plenum Publishers, 1999.

———. "Race, Racism and Archaeology." *World Archaeology* 38, no. 1 (2006): 60–71.

Nakayama, Thomas K. "Dis/orienting Identities: Asian Americans, History and Intercultural Communication." In *Our Voices: Essays in Culture, Ethnicity, and Communication*, edited by Alberto González, Marsha Houston, and Victoria Chen, 12–17. Los Angeles: Roxbury, 1994.

———. "Show/Down Time: 'Race,' Gender, Sexuality, and Popular Culture." *Critical Studies in Mass Communication* 11, no. 2 (1994): 162–79.

Nakayama, Thomas K., and Robert L. Krizek. "Whiteness: A Strategic Rhetoric." *Quarterly Journal of Speech* 81, no. 3 (1995): 291–309.

———. "Whiteness as a Strategic Rhetoric." In *Whiteness: The Communication of Social Identity*, edited by Thomas K. Nakayama and Judith N. Martin, 87–106. Thousand Oaks, CA: Sage Publications, 1999. Originally published as Nakayama, Thomas K., and Judith N. Martin. "Whiteness: A Strategic Rhetoric." *Quarterly Journal of Speech* 81, no. 3 (1995): 291–309.

Nakayama, Thomas K., and Judith N. Martin, eds. *Whiteness: The Communication of Social Identity*. Thousand Oaks, CA: Sage Publications, 1999.

Nance, Roscoe. "Hudson Helped Pave the Way for Other Referees." *USA Today*. February 18, 2003. http://usatoday.printthis.clickability.com/pt/cpt?action=cpt&title=USATODAY (accessed March 3, 2006).

National Center for Education Statistics. "Indicators of School Crime and Safety: 2007." http://nces.ed.gov/programs/crimeindicators/crimeindicators2007/tables/table_01_2. asp?referrer=report.

National Crime Prevention Council. "Neighborhood Watch." http://www.ncpc.org (accessed July 7, 2008).

NBA Media Ventures. "David J. Stern." November 7, 2007. http://www.nba.com/nba101/
david_j_stern_bio.html.

NBA Press Conference. "David Stern NBA Press Conference." November 22, 2004. http://www.
insidehoops.com/conferene-transcript.shtml (accessed December 21, 2007).

Nero, Charles I. "'Oh, What I Think I Must Tell This World!' Oratory and Public Address of
African-American Women." In *Black Women in America*, edited by Kim Marie Vaz, 261–75.
Thousand Oaks, CA: Sage Publications, 1995.

Ness, Carol. "Big Disparities among Races, New Study Shows." *San Francisco Chronicle*, February
22, 2001.

Ness, Carol, and Ryan Kim. "Census Reveals Fast-Growing Diversity in U.S." *San Francisco
Chronicle*, March 13, 2001.

Ness, Carol, and Erin McCormick. "33,871,648— Hispanics Now Make Up Third of Californians: Race—Whites no Longer a Majority." *San Francisco Chronicle*, March 13, 2001.

Newkirk, Pamela. *Within the Veil: Black Journalists, White Media*. New York: New York University Press, 2000.

Newman, Andy. "Prayer in New York, Protest in Washington." *New York Times*, February 16,
1999.

Newman, Kathy M. *Radio Active: Advertising and Consumer Activism, 1935–1947*. Berkeley and
Los Angeles: University of California Press, 2004.

News & Observer (North Carolina). "Testimony to Evil: Tapes and Writings Make Clear the
Breadth and Depth and Violence within Young Cho Seung-Hui," editorial, April 20, 2007,
final edition, http://www.lexis-nexis.com/.

News Services. "Campanis Apologizes for His Racial Remarks." *Washington Post*, 1987, B2.

New York Times Manual of Style and Usage. New York: Random House, 1999.

New York Times, Editorial [untitled]. February 27, 1895.

Oates, Thomas P. "The Erotic Gaze in the NFL Draft." *Communication and Critical/Cultural
Studies* 4 (2007): 74–90.

O'Kelly, Charlotte. "Black Newspapers and the Black Protest Movement: Their Historical Relationship, 1827–1945." *Phylon* 43, no. 1 (1982): 1–14.

Omi, Michael, and Howard Winant. *Racial Formation in the United States: From the 1960s to the
1990s*. 2nd ed. New York: Routledge, 1994.

Ong, Aiwha. *Flexible Citizenship: The Cultural Logics of Transnationality*. Durham, NC: Duke
University Press, 1999.

———. *Neoliberalism as Exception: Mutations in Citizenship and Sovereignty*. Durham, NC: Duke
University Press, 2006.

Ono, Kent A. "Re/signing 'Asian American': Rhetorical Problematics of Nation." *Amerasia Journal* 21, no. 1 (1995): 67–78.

———. *Contemporary Media Culture and the Remnants of a Colonial Past*. New York: Peter Lang,
2009.

Ono, Kent, and Derek Buescher. "Deciphering Pocahontas: Unpacking the Commodification of a
Native American Woman." *Critical Studies in Mass Communication* 18, no. 1 (2001): 23–43.

Ono, Kent A., and John M. Sloop. "Commitment to 'Telos'—A Sustained Critical Rhetoric."
Communication Monographs 59, no. 1 (1992): 48–60.

———. "The Critique of Vernacular Discourse." *Communication Monographs* 62, no. 1 (1995):
19–46.

———. *Shifting Borders: Rhetoric, Immigration, and California's Proposition 187*. Philadelphia, PA:
Temple University Press, 2002.

Osborn, Michael. "In Defense of Broad Mythic Criticism." *Communication Studies* 41 (1990): 121–27.

Owens, Reginald. "Entering the 21st Century: Oppression and the African-American Press." In *Mediated Messages and African-American Culture*, edited by Venise T. Berry and Carmen L. Manning-Miller, 96–116. Thousand Oaks, CA: Sage, 1999.

Paivi, Lujala, Nils Gleditsch, and Elisabeth Gilmore. "A Diamond Curse?: Civil War and a Lootable Resource." *Journal of Conflict Resolution* 49 (2005): 538–62.

Palczewski, Catherine Helen. "Cyber-movements, New Social Movements, and Counterpublics." In *Counterpublics and the State*, edited by Robert Asen and Daniel C. Brouwer, 161–86. Albany: State University of New York Press, 2001.

Pareles, Jon. "An All-American Striver Keeps Things in Perspective." *New York Times*, November 4, 2005, E3.

Patton, Tracey O. "In the Guise of Civility: The Complicitous Maintenance of Inferential Forms of Sexism and Racism in Higher Education." *Women's Studies in Communication* 27 (2004): 60–87.

Peiss, Kathy. "Making Up, Making Over: Cosmetics, Consumer Culture, and Women's Identity." In *The Sex of Things: Gender and Consumption in Historical Perspective*, edited by Victoria de Grazia (with Ellen Furlough), 311–36. Berkeley and Los Angeles: University of California Press, 1996.

Peterson, Carla L. *"Doers of the Word": African-American Women Speakers and Writers in the North, 1830-1880*. New York: Oxford University Press, 1995.

Peterson, Frederick A., and John E. Stone. "Results and Implications of the Minuteman Project." *A Field Report Submitted to the Congressional Immigration Reform Caucus* (2005): 1–30.

Pew Research Center for the People and the Press. "Huge Racial Divide Over Katrina and its Consequences." September 8, 2005. http://people-press.org/reports/pdf/255.pdf.

Peyser, Andrea. "Blaming Parents a Shameless Cop-Out." *New York Post*, April 27, 1999, http://www.lexis-nexis.com/.

Phillips, Kendall R. "Rhetorical Maneuvers: Subjectivity, Power, and Resistance." *Philosophy and Rhetoric* 39, no. 4 (2006): 310–32.

Pimental, B. "Diversity Goals Are Surpassed: San Mateo County Workforce Now Short of Whites, Men." *San Francisco Chronicle*, May 10, 1996.

Pollack, Andrew. "2 Illegal Immigrants Win Arizona Ranch in Court Fight." *The New York Times*, August 19, 2005, http://lexisnexis.com (accessed July 3, 2008).

Poniewozik, James. "Who Can Say What?" *Time Magazine*, April 23, 2007, 32–38.

Postman, Neil. *Amusing Ourselves to Death: Public Discourse in the Age of Show Business*. New York: Penguin, 1985, 2005.

Projansky, Sarah, and Kent Ono. "Strategic Whiteness as Cinematic Racial Politics." In *Whiteness: The Communication of Social Identity*, edited by Thomas Nakayama and Judith Martin, 149–74. Thousand Oaks, CA: Sage Publications, 1999.

Pryce, Vinette. "Women's Scorn Lands on City Hall." *New York Amsterdam News*, March 17, 1999.

Pulley, Brett. "He's Got Game," *Forbes Magazine*, 171, no. 4, 46.

Quarles, Benjamin. *Black Abolitionists*. New York: Oxford University Press, 1969.

———. *Black Mosaic: Essays in Afro-American History and Historiography*. Amherst: University of Massachusetts Press, 1988.

Ramlow, Todd. "Bad Boys: Abstractions of Difference and the Politics of Youth 'Deviance.'" *GLQ: A Journal of Lesbian and Gay Studies* 9, no. 1–2 (2003): 107–32.

Randolph, Eleanor. "A Long Day of Venting about the City's Police." *New York Times*, May 28, 1999.

Reed, Adolph L., Jr. "The Real Divide." In *After the Storm: Black Intellectuals Explore the Meaning of Hurricane Katrina*, edited by David Dante Troutt, 63–70. New York: New, 2006.

Reisigl, Martin, and Ruth Wodak. Discourse and Discrimination: Rhetorics of Racism and Antisemitism. London: Routledge, 2001.

Reyes, Belinda I., ed. *A Portrait of Race and Ethnicity in California: An Assessment of Social and Economic Well-being*. San Francisco: Public Policy Institute of California, 2001.

Reyes, Damasco. "Protests Follow Diallo Funeral." *New York Amsterdam News*, February 24, 1999.

Rhoden, William C. *Forty Million Dollar Slaves: The Rise, Fall, and Redemption of the Black Athlete*. New York: Crown Publishers, 2006.

Ripley, C. Peter et al., eds. *The Black Abolitionist Papers*. 5 vols. Chapel Hill: University of North Carolina Press, 1985–92.

Robinson, Cedric J. *Black Marxism: The Making of the Black Radical Tradition*. Chapel Hill: University of North Carolina Press, 2000.

Roediger, David R. *Towards the Abolition of Whiteness: Essays on Race, Politics, and Working Class History*. New York: Routledge, 1994.

Rogin, Michael. *Blackface, White Noise: Jewish Immigrants in the Hollywood Melting Pot*. Berkeley: University of California Press, 1998.

Rohrer, Finlo. "Taking the Shine Off Cristal." *BBC News Magazine*, June 8, 2006. http://news.bbc.co.uk/2/hi/uk_news/magazine/5056744.stm.

Roman, Leslie G. "White Is a C! White Discursiveness, Postmodernism, and Anti-racist Pedagogy." In *Race, Identity, and Representation in Education*, edited by C. McCarthy and W. Crichlow 279–378. (New York: Routledge, 1993.

Romano, Andrew, Aku Ammah-Tagoe, and Brian No. "Black in the Age of Obama." *Newsweek*, April 27, 2009, 42–45.

Rooks, Noliwe M. *Hair Raising: Beauty, Culture, and African American Women*. New Brunswick, NJ: Rutgers University Press, 1996.

Root, Deborah. *Cannibal Culture: Art, Appropriation and the Commodification of Difference*. Boulder, CO: Westview, 1996.

Rosenbaum, Jonathan. "A Critic Examines his Path to Judgment." *Chicago Reader*. http://www.chicagoreader.com/movies/archives/2005/0505/050513.html.

Rovell, Darren. "Stern Sure Players Will Comply With New Dress Code." October 18, 2005. http://sports.espn.go.com/espn/print (accessed December 21, 2007).

Roy, Abhik, and Robert C. Rowland. "The Rhetoric of Hindu Nationalism: A Narrative of Mythic Redefinition." *Western Journal of Communication* (2003): 225–48.

Ruane, Michael E. "A List of 'Little Incidents': Former Roommate of Cho Recalls Odd Behavior; 'Who Does This?' He Thought." *Richmond Times Dispatch*, April 22, 2007, final edition, http://www.lexis-nexis.com/.

Rushing, Janice H. "On Saving Mythic Criticism—A Reply to Rowland's Rejoinder." *Communication Studies* 41, no. 2 (1990): 136–49.

Rushing, Janice H., and Thomas S. Frentz. "The Frankenstein Myth, in Contemporary Cinema." *Critical Studies in Mass Communication* 6 (1989): 61–80.

———. "Integrating Ideology and Archetype in Rhetorical Criticism." *Quarterly Journal of Speech* 77 (1991): 385–406.

Russell, Bill, and William McSweeny. *Go Up for Glory*. New York: Coward McCann, 1996.

Ryan, Joan. "Requiem for Lost Boys—and Their Victims." *San Francisco Chronicle*, April 21, 1999, final edition, http://www.lexis-nexis.com/.

Ryan, Susan M. *The Grammar of Good Intentions: Race and the Antebellum Culture of Benevolence.* Ithaca, NY: Cornell University Press, 2003.

Sachs, Susan. "Anger and Protest at Rite for African Killed by Police." *New York Times*, February 13, 1999.

Sanchez, Casey. "Blunt Force: San Diego Nativist Group Faces Troubles." *Intelligence Report*, Summer 2007. http://www.splcenter.org (accessed January 28, 2009).

San Francisco Chronicle. "Census 2000: Who We Are-Poll Finds Positive View of State's Diversity." May 14, 2001.

San Francisco Examiner. "California's Changing Face." December 20, 1998.

San Jose Mercury News. "What Will Race Be Like in 2020?" April 18, 1999.

San Jose Mercury News. "Unfathomable Violence." April 21, 1999, http://www.lexis-nexis.com/.

Santa Cruz, Nicole. "White Americans' Majority to Continue Until 2050, Report Says." *Los Angeles Times*, December 17, 2009.

Saporito, Bill. "Why Fans and Players Playing So Rough: The Worst Brawl in NBA History Highlights the Combustible Mix of Rabid Spectators and Strutting Athletes. Is the Game Itself Losing Out?" *Time Magazine*, December 6, 2004. http://0-find.galegroup.com.bianca. penlib.du.edu (accessed February 22, 2008).

Sartre, J. P. *Anti-Semite and Jew.* New York: Schocken Book, 1986.

Sauer, Rachel. "Shootings Bring Up Memories of Past School Horrors." Cox News Service, April 20, 1999, http://www.lexis-nexis.com/.

Schevitz, Tanya, Lori Olszewski, and John Wildermuth. "New Demographics Changing Everything: Experts Examine Rise of State's Minorities." *San Francisco Chronicle*, August 31, 2000.

Schwartz, Jerry. "Looking for Explanations for Schoolhouse Massacres." Associated Press, April 21, 1999, http://www.lexis-nexis.com/.

Scott, James C. *Domination and the Arts of Resistance: Hidden Transcripts.* New Haven, CT: Yale University Press, 1990.

Searle, John. *Expression and Meaning: Studies in the Theory of Speech Acts.* Cambridge and New York: Cambridge University Press, 1979.

Security on Campus, Inc. "College & University Campus Crime Statistics (1999–2001)." Last accessed: Dec. 14, 2010; http://www.securityoncampus.org/images/pdf/99/co_murder.pdf.

———. "College & University Campus Crime Statistics, 1998–2000." http://www.securityon-campus.org/images/pdf/98/1998_2000.pdf.

Seger, Linda. *Making a Good Script Great.* 2nd ed. Cincinnati, OH: Writer's Digest Books, 2007.

Sekora, John. "Black Message / White Envelope: Genre, Authenticity, and Authority in the Antebellum Slave Narrative." *Callaloo* 10 (1987): 482–515.

———. "'Mr. Editor, If You Please': Frederick Douglass, My Bondage and My Freedom, and the End of the Abolitionist Imprint." *Callaloo* 17 (1994): 608–26.

Selby, Gary S. "The Limits of Accommodation: Frederick Douglass and the Garrisonian Abolitionists." *Southern Communication Journal* 66 (2000): 52–66.

Shade, William G. "'Though We Are Not Slaves, We Are Not Free': Quasi-Free Blacks in Antebellum America." In *Upon These Shores: Themes in the African-American Experience, 1600 to the Present*, edited by William R. Scott and William G. Shade, 118–38. New York: Routledge, 2000.

Shah, Hemant, and Michael C. Thornton. *Newspaper Coverage of Interethnic Conflict: Competing Visions of America.* Thousand Oaks, CA: Sage Publications, 2004.

Shapiro, Ann-Louise. "How Real Is the Reality in Documentary Film? Jill Godmilow, in Conversation with Ann-Louise Shapiro." *History and Theory* (Blackwell Publishing) 36, no. 4 (1997): 80–101.

Sheridan, Earl. "The New Accommodationists." *Journal of Black Studies* 27 (1996), 152–71.

Shohat, Ella, and Stam Robert. *Eurocentrism: Multiculturalism and the Media*. New York: Routledge, 2000.

Shome, Raka. "Race and Popular Cinema: The Rhetorical Strategies of Whiteness in City of Joy." *Communication Quarterly* 44, no. 4 (1996): 502–18.

———. "Outing Whiteness." *Critical Studies in Mass Communication* 17(3) (2000): 366–71.

———. "Space Matters: The Power and Practice of Space." *Communication Theory* 13 (2003): 39–56.

———. "Thinking Through the Diaspora: Call centers, India, and a New Politics of Hybridity." *International Journal of Cultural Studies* 9, no. 1 (2006): 105–24.

Siegel, Robert. "A New, 'Post-Racial' Political Era in America." *All Things Considered*. Washington, DC: National Public Radio, January 28, 2008.

Siegman, Joseph. *Jewish Sports Legends: The International Jewish Sports Hall of Fame*. 2nd ed. Washington, DC: Brassey's, 1997.

Silverman, Kaja. *The Subject of Semiotics*. New York: Oxford University Press, 1983.

Simmons, Charles. *The African-American Press: With Special References to 4 Newspapers, 1827–1965*. Jefferson, NC: McFarland, 1998.

Simpson, Kevin, and David Blevins. "Germany Lured Harris But Pal Klebold Not as Fascinated with the Culture." *Denver Post*, April 24, 1999, 2nd edition, http://www.lexis-nexis.com/.

Slack, Jennifer D. "The Theory and Method of Articulation in Cultural Studies." In *Stuart Hall: Critical Dialogues in Cultural Studies*, edited by David Morley and Kuan-Hsing Chen, 112–27. London: Routledge, 1996.

Smith, James M'Cune [McCune]. Introduction to *My Bondage and My Freedom*, by Frederick Douglass. New York, 1857.

Smith, James McCune, George B. Wilson, and William H. Topp. "Report by the Committee on a National Press of the National Convention of Colored People and Their Friends, Presented at the Liberty Street Presbyterian Church, Troy, New York, 6 October 1847." In *The Black Abolitionist Papers*, volume 4, edited by C. Peter Ripley et al., 7–15. Chapel Hill: University of North Carolina Press, 1991.

Solomon, Martha, "The Rhetoric of Dehumanization: An Analysis of Medical Reports of the Tuskegee Syphilis Project." *Western Journal of Speech Communication* 49 (1985): 233–47.

Song, Min Hyoung, "Communities of Remembrance: Reflections on the Virginia Tech Shootings and Race." *Journal of Asian American Studies* 11, no. 1 (2008): 1–26.

Spears, Marc J. "First Black Player Recalls NBA Days." *Boston Globe*, January 24, 2008. http://www.iht.com/bin/printfriendly.php (accessed February 9, 2008).

Spencer, Jim. "Horrifying Deeds Can Inspire Twisted Kindred." *Denver Post*, April 20, 2007, final edition, http://www.lexis-nexis.com/.

Spivak, Gayatri Chakravorty. "Can the Subaltern Speak?" In *Marxism and the Interpretation of Culture*, edited by Cary Nelson and Lawrence Grossberg, 271–313. Urbana and Chicago: University of Illinois Press, 1988.

Sports Briefing. "Pro Basketball: Dress Code Called Racist." *New York Times*, October 20, 2005. http://select.nytimes.com/search/restricted/article (accessed December 26, 2005).

Squires, Catherine R. "The Black Press and the State: Attracting Unwanted(?) Attention." In *Counterpublics and the State*, edited by Robert Asen and Daniel Brouwer. Albany: State University of New York Press, 2001.

———. *Dispatches from the Color Line: The Press and Multiracial Identity*. Albany: State University of New York Press, 2007.

Stabile, Carol A. *White Victims, Black Villains: Gender, Race, and Crime News in U.S. Culture*. New York: Routledge, 2006.

Starr, Mark. "Starr Gazing: NBA Brawl Shouldn't Surprise Anyone." *Newsweek* (Web Exclusive), November 26, 2004. http://www.newsweek.com/id/55463 (accessed February 22, 2008).

State News Service. "U.N. Agency Holds First-Ever Screening of Film 'Blood Diamond' in Sierra Leone." May 4, 2007. http:www.lexisnexis.com.

Stauffer, John, ed. *The Works of James McCune Smith: Black Intellectual and Abolitionist*. Oxford: Oxford University Press, 2006.

Steinberg, Neil. "Media Can't Look Away: Sharing Gunman's Rants With World Was the Right Thing to Do." *Chicago Sun Times*, April 22, 2007, final edition, http://www.lexis-nexis.com/.

Steinberg, Stephen. *Turning Back: The Retreat from Racial Justice in American Thought and Policy*. Boston: Beacon Press, 1995.

Stewart, James B. "Civil Rights and Organized Labor: The Case of the United Steelworkers of America, 1948–1970." In *African Americans in the U.S. Economy*, edited by Cecilia A. Conrad et al., 66–80. Lanham, MD: Rowman & Littlefield, 2005.

Stocking, Barbra. "County's Whites Enter Unknown Territory." *San Jose Mercury News*, April 14, 1999.

Stormfront. http://www.stormfront.org/forum/showthread.php?s=4d11da9a1f1479fca51a4eedd ee3cad5&t=609089.

Strauss, Bob. "Five Questions with the King of Pulp." *E! Online*, 1997. http://www.angelfire.com/movies/tarantinoconnection/Quentin_Tarantino_QandA.html (accessed February 10, 2010).

Sullivan, Patricia A. "Signification and African-American Rhetoric: A Case Study of Jesse Jackson's 'Common Ground and Common Sense' Speech." *Communication Quarterly* 41 (1993): 1–15.

Sullivan, Shannon. *Revealing Whiteness: The Unconscious Habits of Racial Privilege*. Bloomington: Indiana University Press, 2006.

Sunstein, Cass. *Designing Democracy: What Constitutions Do*. Oxford: Oxford University Press, 2001.

Swift, E. M. "From Corned Beef to Caviar; NBA Commissioner David Stern." *Sports Illustrated* 74, no. 21 (1991): 74–87.

Talese, Gay. *The Kingdom and the Power*. Cleveland, OH: World Publishing, 1969.

Tarantino, Quentin. "I'm Proud of My Flop." *Telegraph*, April 27, 2007. http://www.telegraph.co.uk/arts/main.jhtml?xml=/arts/2007/04/27/bfquentin27.xml&page=1 (accessed January 20, 2008).

———. "Tarantino Embraces Past Lives." *Contactmusic.com*, May 2, 2008. http://www.contact-music.com/news.nsf/article/tarantino embraces past lives_1029799 (accessed July 11, 2008).

———. "Playboy Interview 2003." The Quentin Tarantino Archives. http://www.tarantino.info/wiki/index.php/Playboy_Interview_2003 (accessed March 18, 2010).

Target Market News. *Annual Report on the Buying Power of Black America*. Chicago: Target Market News Inc., 2007.

Tatum, Wilbert. "Giuliani: A Monster in Our Midst." *New York Amsterdam News*, February 24, 1999.

———. "It's Only a Matter of Time: Giuliani's Political Demise." *New York Amsterdam News*, March 3, 1999.

Taubin, Amy. "The Men's Room." *Sight and Sound* 2, no. 8 (December 1992): 2–5.

Tedeschi, Bob. "Subprime Loans' Wide Reach," Real Estate, New York Times, August 3, 2008, 10.

Thomas, Ron. They Cleared the Lane: The NBA's Black Pioneers. Lincoln: University of Nebraska Press, 2002.

Thompson, Audrey (1999). Essay Review of Off White, edited by Michelle Fine, Lois Weis, Linda C. Powell, and L. Mun Wong. Education Review (online journal).

Thompson, Ginger. "1,000 Rally to Condemn Shooting of Unarmed Man by Police." New York Times, February 8, 1999.

Thomsen, Ian. "Why Fans Are Tuning Out the NBA." Sports Illustrated, February 2005, 70.

Tierney, Sean. "Themes of Whiteness in Bulletproof Monk, Kill Bill, and The Last Samurai." Journal of Communication 56, no. 3 (2006): 607–24.

Tobin, Robin. The Screenwriting Formula. Cincinnati, OH: Writer's Digest Books, 2007.

Tomlinson, Tommy. "Shattered by a Chilling Blow." Charlotte Observer, April 16, 2007, http://www.lexis-nexis.com/.

Toobin, Jeffrey. "The Unasked Question." New Yorker, March 6, 2000: 38–44.

Torreiro, E. A., and James Janega. "Parallel Paths of Victim, Killer." Chicago Tribune, April 23, 2007, http://www.lexis-nexis.com/.

Toure, Ahati N. N. "Nineteenth Century African Historians in the United States: Explorations of Cultural Location and National Destiny." In Black Cultures and Race Relations, edited by James L. Conyers, Jr., 16–50. Chicago: Burnham, 2002.

Trotter, Joe W., Jr. "Introduction: Pennsylvania's African American History: A Review of the Literature." In African Americans in Pennsylvania: Shifting Historical Perspectives, edited by Joe William Trotter Jr., and Eric Ledell Smith, 1–39. University Park: Pennsylvania Historical and Museum Commission and the Pennsylvania State University Press, 1997.

Trujillo, Nick. "Hegemonic Masculinity at the Mound: Media Representations of Nolan Ryan and American Sports Culture." Critical Studies in Mass Communication 8 (1991): 290–308.

Trujillo, Nick, and Leah Vande Berg. "Sportswriting and American Cultural Values: The 1984 Chicago Cubs." Critical Studies in Mass Communication 2 (1985): 262–82.

Tucker, Linda. "Blackballed: Basketball and Representations of the Black Male Athlete." American Behavioral Scientist 47 (2003): 306–28.

Turner, Graeme. Understanding Celebrity. Thousand Oaks, CA: Sage Publications, 2004.

Twine, France Widdance. "Brown Skinned White Girls: Class, Culture, and the Construction of White Identity in Suburban Communities," In Displacing Whiteness: Essays in Social and Cultural Criticism, edited by Ruth Frankenberg, 238–61. Durham, NC: Duke University Press, 1997.

Uberoi, Safina. (Director) 2006. 1-800-INDIA. A. Carter (Producer). USA: PBS WideAngle. Aired on August 15, 2006: PBS.

Ursic, Greg. "Crashing with Paul Haggis: An Interview with Hollywood's New Go-to Drama Guy." http://efilmcritic.com/feature.php?feature=1470.

U.S. Department of Education and U.S. Department of Justice Office of Justice Programs. "Indicators of School Crime and Safety, 2009." Washington, DC: Government Printing Office, 2009. http://www.securityoncampus.org/images/pdf/doe2001.pdf.

U.S. Department of Education Office of Postsecondary Education. "The Incidence of Crime on the Campuses of U.S. Postsecondary Education Institutions: A Report to Congress." Washington, DC: Government Printing Office, 2001. http://www.securityoncampus.org/images/pdf/doe2001.pdf.

Accessed Dec. 14, 2010. U.S. Department of Education. "Criminal Offenses: Murder/Non-negligent Manslaughter (2001–2003)." http://www.ed.gov/admins/lead/safety/crime/criminaloffenses/edlite-murder.html.

Utley, Ebony A. "A Woman Made of Words: The Rhetorical Invention of Maria W. Stewart." In *Black Women's Intellectual Traditions: Speaking Their Minds*, edited by Kristin Waters and Carol B. Conaway, 55–71. Burlington: University of Vermont Press, 2007.

Valdivia, Angharad, ed. *Feminism, Multiculturalism, and the Media: Global Diversities*. Thousand Oaks, CA: Sage Publications, 1995.

Van Dijk, Teun A. *Communicating Racism: Ethnic Prejudice in Thought and Talk*. Newbury Park, CA: Sage Publications, 1987.

———. *Elite Discourse and Racism*. Newbury Park, CA: Sage Publications, 1993.

Van Graber, M. "Functional Criticism: A Rhetoric of Black Power" In *Explorations in Rhetorical Criticism*, edited by Gerald P. Mohrmann, Charles J. Stewart, and Donovan J. Ochs, 207–22. University Park: Pennsylvania State University Press, 1973

Verrengia, Joseph B. "Families Mourn Innocent Victims Caught in Wrong Place at Wrong Time." Associated Press, April 21, 1999, http://www.lexis-nexis.com/.

Von Frank, Albert J. *The Trials of Anthony Burns: Freedom and Slavery in Emerson's Boston*. Boston: Harvard University Press, 1998.

Walker, Jim. "NBA Drug Use Up, Says Study." *Chicago Tribune*, August 20, 1980.

Wall, Melissa A. "Social Movements and Email: Expressions of Online Identity in the Globalization Protests." *New Media and Society* 9 (2007): 258–77.

Ward, Samuel Ringgold. Letter to editor. *National Anti-Slavery Standard*, July 2, 1840.

———. "Origin, History and Hopes of the Negro Race." *Pennsylvania Freeman*, December 29, 1853.

———. "Editorial Correspondence." *Provincial Freeman*, June 10, 1854.

———. *Autobiography of a Fugitive Negro: His Anti-Slavery Labours in the United States, Canada, & England*. London, 1855.

Watkins, S. Craig. "Framing Protest: News Media Frames of the Million Man March." *Critical Studies in Media Communication* 18 (2001): 83–102.

Watkins, William J. "Extracts from a Speech, Delivered at the Celebration of West India Emancipation by the Colored Citizens of New Bedford, by Wm. J. Watkins, of Boston." *Frederick Douglass' Paper*, August 26, 1853.

———. "One Thing Thou Lackest." *Frederick Douglass' Paper*, February 10, 1854.

———. "What Are We Doing?" *Frederick Douglass' Paper*, February 2, 1855.

———. "Are We Ready for the Conflict?" *Frederick Douglass' Paper*, February 9, 1855.

Waymer, Damion, and Robert L. Heath. "Emergent Agents: The Forgotten Publics in Crisis Communication and Issues Management Research." *Journal of Applied Communication Research* 35 (2007): 88–108.

Wedge, Dave, and Jessica Heslam. "Campus Massacre: 'No One Deserved to Die'; Police Probe for Motive as University Mourns." *Boston Herald*, April 18, 2007, http://www.lexis-nexis.com/.

Weems, Robert E., Jr. *Desegregating the Dollar: African American Consumerism in the Twentieth Century*. New York: New York University Press, 1998.

———. "Consumerism and the Construction of Black Female Identity in Twentieth-Century America." In *The Gender and Consumer Culture Reader*, edited by Jennifer Scanlon, 166–78. New York: New York University Press, 2000.

———. "Bling Bling and Other Recent Trends in African American Consumerism." In *African Americans in the U.S. Economy*, edited by Cecilia A. Conrad et al., 252–57. Lanham, MD: Rowman & Littlefield, 2005.

Weichselbaum, Simone. "He Knew Cho 8 Yrs., But Killer Never Said a Word to Him." *Philadelphia Daily News*, April 21, 2007, http://www.lexis-nexis.com/.

West, Cornel. *Race Matters*. Boston: Beacon Press, 1993.

———. "On Black-Jewish Relations." In *Readings for Diversity and Social Justice: An Anthology on Racism, Antisemitism, Sexism, Heterosexism, Ableism, and Classism*, edited by Maurianne Adams, Warren J. Blumenfield, Rosie Castaneda, Heather W. Hackman, Madeline L. Peters, and Ximena Zuniga, 177–81. New York: Routledge, 2000.

West, Kanye. "George Bush Doesn't Care About Black People." September 5, 2005. www.YouTube.com.

West, Thomas R. *Signs of Struggle: The Rhetorical Politics of Cultural Difference*. Albany: State University of New York Press, 2002.

Wiegman, Robyn. "Whiteness Studies and the Paradox of Particularity." *Boundary 2* 26, no. 3 (1999): 115–51.

Wilbon, Michael. "Misplaced Fury Over Racism." *Washington Post*, October 29, 2005. http://www.lexisnexis.com/us/Inacademic/delivery (accessed March 10, 2008).

Wilder, Craig Steven. *In the Company of Black Men: The African Influence on African American Culture in New York City*. New York: New York University Press, 2001.

Wilgoren, Jodi. "Diallo Rally Focuses on Call for Strong Oversight of Police." *New York Times*, April 16, 1999.

Williams, Juan. "Obama's Color Line." *New York Times*, November 30, 2007, A23.

Williams, Kam. "Movie Reviews: *Crash*." *Blacknews.com*, 2005. http://www.blacknews.com/pr/crash101.html.

Williams, Melissa. *Voice, Trust and Memory: Marginalized Groups and the Failings of Liberal Representation*. Princeton, NJ: Princeton University Press, 1998.

Williams, Mike. "Father's Agony: African-American Son Slain for Race." Cox News Service, April 22, 1999, http://www.lexis-nexis.com/.

———. "Harsh Reality Hits Shocked Littleton, Colo." Cox News Service, April 21, 1999, http://www.lexis-nexis.com/.

Williams, Patricia J. "Alchemical Notes: Reconstructing Ideals from Deconstructed Rights." *Harvard Civil Rights--Civil Liberties Law Review* 22, no. 1 (1987): 401–34.

———. *Alchemy of Race & Rights*. Cambridge, MA: Harvard University Press, 1991.

Williamson, Larry. "Racism, Tolerance and Perfected Redemption: A Rhetorical Critique of the Dragging Trial." *Southern Communication Journal* 67 (2002): 245–58.

Wilson, Bobby M. "Race in Commodity Exchange and Consumption: Separate But Equal." *Annals of the Association of American Geographers* 95, no. 3 (2005): 587–606.

Wilson, Carol. *Freedom at Risk: The Kidnapping of Free Blacks in America, 1780–1865*. Lexington: University Press of Kentucky, 1994.

Wilson, Clint C., II, and Felix Gutierrez, eds. *Minorities and the Media: Diversity and the End of Mass Communication*. Beverly Hills: Sage Publications, 1985.

———, eds. *Race, Multiculturalism, and the Media: From Mass to Class Communication*. 2nd ed. Thousand Oaks, CA: Sage Publications, 1995.

Wilson, Clint C., II, Felix Gutierrez, and Lena M. Chao. *Racism, Sexism, and the Media: The Rise of Class Communication in Multicultural America*. 3rd ed. Thousand Oaks, CA: Sage Publications, 2003.

Wilson, Kirt H. "The Racial Politics of Imitation in the Nineteenth Century." *Quarterly Journal of Speech* 89 (2003): 89–108.

Wilson, William Julius. *The Declining Significance of Race: Blacks and Changing American Institutions*. Chicago: University of Chicago Press, 1980.

Wise, Mike. "Opinions on NBA's Dress Code Are Far From Uniform." *Washington Post*, October 23, 2005. http://www.washingtonpost.com/wp-dyn/content/article/2005 (accessed January 29, 2008).

Wolseley, Roland. *The Black Press, U.S.A.* Ames: Iowa State University Press, 1971.

Wong, Edward. "Parkview: Two Views of Diallo Case." *New York Times*, February 25, 1999.

Wood, Julia. "Feminist Standpoint Theory and Muted Group Theory: Commonalities and Divergences. *Women and Language* 28, no. 2 (2005): 61–64.

Woods, Clyde Adrian. "Do You Know What It Means to Miss New Orleans? Katrina, Trap Economics, and the Rebirth of the Blues." *American Quarterly* 57, no. 4 (December 2005): 1005–18.

Woodson, Robert L., Sr. "Obama and a Post-Racial America." *Washington Times*, April 12, 2008, A11.

Wootton, Adrian. "Quentin Tarantino interview (I) with Pam Grier, Robert Forster and Lawrence Bender." *Guardian*, January 5, 1998. http://www.guardian.co.uk/film/1998/jan/05/quentintarantino.guardianinterviewsatbfisouthbank1 (accessed February 10, 2010).

Young, Iris Marion. *Inclusion and Democracy*. Oxford: Oxford University Press, 2000.

Young, James E. *The Texture of Memory: Holocaust Memorials and Meaning*. New Haven, CT: Yale University Press, 1993.

Young, R. J. *Antebellum Black Activists: Race, Gender, and Self*. New York: Garland, 1996.

About the Contributors

Carol W. Anderson is an independent researcher and film producer. She is interested in issues of colonization, specifically on the African continent. Her past projects have dealt with the colonization of the Congo, and she is currently interested in the post–civil war reconstruction of Sierra Leone.

Jacqueline Bacon is the author of the books *Freedom's Journal: The First African-American Newspaper* (Lexington Books, 2007) and *The Humblest May Stand Forth: Rhetoric, Empowerment, and Abolition* (University of South Carolina Press, 2002); as well as articles on a variety of topics, including African American history and rhetoric, media criticism, and historical and contemporary issues of race and discourse. She is also the co-editor, with Maurice Jackson, of *African Americans and the Haitian Revolution: Selected Essays and Historical Documents* (Routledge, 2010). An independent scholar, Bacon lives in San Diego, California.

Bernadette Marie Calafell is Associate Professor of Communication Studies at the University of Denver. Her research lies at the intersection of performance, rhetoric, and feminist studies, focusing particularly on Chicana/o and Latina/o identities in popular culture and everyday life. In addition to her book *Latina/o Communication Studies: Theorizing Performance* (Peter Lang, 2007), she has published articles in various journals, including *Critical Studies in Media Communication*, *Text and Performance Quarterly*, *Cultural Studies—Critical Methodologies*, and *The Communication Review*.

Aimee Carrillo Rowe is Associate Professor of Rhetoric and GWSS (Gender, Women's and Sexuality Studies) and is executive director of POROI (Project on the Rhetoric of Inquiry) at the University of Iowa. Her teaching and writing address the politics of representation and feminist alliances, third world feminism, and whiteness and anti-racism. Her book, *Power Lines: On the Subject of Feminist Alliances* (Duke University Press, 2008), offers a coalitional theory of subjectivity as a bridge to difference-based alliances. Her writing appears primarily in interdisciplinary outlets such as *Hypatia* (Summer 2007), *Radical History Review* (Summer 2004), and *NWSA Journal* (Summer 2005).

Rachel Alicia Griffin is Assistant Professor of Intercultural Communication at Southern Illinois University at Carbondale in the Department of Speech Communication. Her research interests include critical race theory, black feminist thought, black masculinity, popular culture, and gender violence. All of her current research projects speak strongly to notions of power, privilege, and voice. She has presented keynote addresses at national conferences, and has led diversity training sessions. Recently, Dr. Griffin published in *Interracial Communication: Contexts, Communities, and Choices* and *Communication Teacher*. She also delivered the keynote for the 2010 Men Against Violence conference in Tacoma, Washington, and earned a Top Paper award at the 2010 National Communication Association conference.

Rona Tamiko Halualani is Professor in the Department of Communication Studies at San Jose State University in California, specializing in the linguistic and cultural dimensions of imperial hegemony and native identity in Pacific regions such as Hawai'i and the Philippines, as well as intercultural contact relations and critical intercultural communication studies. Dr. Halualani has published one university press book; 14 refereed academic journal articles in *International Journal of Intercultural Relations, Journal of International and Intercultural Communication, International and Intercultural Communication Annual*, and *The Review of Communication*, among others; six academic book chapters; and is currently finalizing three books (one for the University of Hawai'i Press, one for Sage Publications, and the other for Blackwell Publications). Her research interests include the following: intercultural contact, intercultural communication patterns, cultural competence in applied settings, race/ethnicity, diversity, prejudice, critical intercultural communication studies, identity and cultural politics, diasporic identity, and Hawaiians/Pacific Islanders.

Marouf Hasian, Jr., is Professor in the Department of Communication at the University of Utah. His areas of interest include law and rhetoric, critical rhetorical theory, postcolonial studies, and critical memory studies. He is currently at work on several projects involving the study of how different international communities cope with the remembering and forgetting of colonial atrocities.

Kathleen C. Haspel is Associate Professor of Communication Studies at Fairleigh Dickinson University. Her research examines narrative communication practices of ordinary citizens in public and institutional contexts. Her work has been published in the *Journal of Communication*, the *American Communication Journal*, and in edited volumes. She is currently studying local constructions and uses of identity of citizens' voices in public discourse.

Michelle A. Holling is Associate Professor in the Department of Communication and coordinator of the Ethnic Studies program at California State University San Marcos. Her scholarly interests include the politics embedded in and generated through the discursive construction of particular subject/ivities, Chicana/o self-inscriptions, and issues of identity and agency. She works at the intersection of rhetorical and Chicana/o studies as a means to examine discourse produced by, about, and implicating Chicana/os and Latina/os. In 2009, she was awarded Scholar of the Year by the Latina/o Communication Studies Division of the National Communication Association and, in 2007, she earned the B. Aubrey Fisher award from the Western States Communication Association. In addition to editing *Latina/o Discourse in Vernacular Spaces: Somos de Una Voz?* with B. M. Calafell and publishing book chapters, Holling has published in *The Communication Review* (2008), *Text & Performance Quarterly* (2007), *Western Journal of Communication* (2006), *Communication and Critical/Cultural Studies Journal* (2006), and *Journal of Latinos and Education* (2006).

Michael Huspek is Professor of Communication at California State University, San Marcos. His most recent research, which involves the scope and contours of rational discourse as related to ideas of deliberative democracy, has appeared in *Political Studies, Social Justice*, and *Communication Theory*. Other recent work includes his editorship of *Oppositional Discourses and Democracies* (2009), which appears in the Routledge Series on Social and Political Thought. He is currently completing a book-length manuscript on the uses and limits of Jurgen Habermas's theory of communicative action as it relates to the participation of historically marginalized groups within actually existing democracies.

Ronald L. Jackson II is Professor and head of African American Studies and professor of Media and Cinema Studies at the University of Illinois at Urbana-Champaign and co-editor (with Kent Ono) of the national communication association journal *Critical Studies in Media Communication*. Jackson is a leading scholar of the social construction and negotiation of masculinity, culture, and identity. He is the author or editor of ten books, including *Scripting the Black Masculine Body in Popular Media* (SUNY Press, 2006) and the recently released *SAGE Encyclopedia of Identity*. He is also co-editor (with Murali Balaji) of the forthcoming *Culturing Manhood: Global Perspectives on Manhood and Masculinity* (University of Illinois Press).

Michael G. Lacy is an independent scholar and visiting associate professor of Communication at DePaul University in Chicago. His special interests are race, rhetoric, culture, and politics. He has received several teaching awards, including being listed in *Who's Who among American Teachers*. His research has been published by the *Communication Yearbook 32*, the *Howard Journal of Communications*, the *Journal of Intercultural and International Communication*, and by the Education Communication of the States. In addition to reviewing research grants for the U.S. Department of Education, he has presented research at several international and national conferences and delivered public lectures at several colleges and universities.

Sheena Malhotra is Chair of Gender and Women's Studies at California State University, Northridge. Her academic research and articles explore the intersections of gender, media, technology, and global culture, with a particular focus on Indian films and television, as well as the Indian diaspora. Her current book project, co-authored with Aimee Carrillo Rowe and Kimberlee Perez, is entitled *Answer the Call: Suspended Mobilities in Indian Call Centers*. She is also co-editing an anthology on silence with Dr. Carrillo Rowe entitled, *Still the Silence: Feminist Reflections on the Edges of Sound*.

Raymie E. McKerrow is the Charles E. Zumkehr Professor of Speech Communication, School of Communication Studies at Ohio University. A past president of both NCA and ECA, he is the current editor of the *Quarterly Journal of Speech*. He has received the Lifetime Achievement Award from the National Communication Association's Critical and Cultural Studies Division, and NCA's Douglas Ehninger Distinguished Rhetorical Scholar Award. His research focuses on the intersection of postmodernism, rhetoric, and culture. He teaches graduate seminars in feminist rhetoric, rhetoric and culture, and Foucault and social change.

Jamie Moshin is Assistant Professor of Communication Studies and Co-Director of Forensics at Marietta College. A scholar who works at the intersection of race, identity, whiteness, ethnicity, and discourse. Jamie's work focuses on the representation of American Jewishness, and aims to reinvigorate critical investigations of Jewishness within rhetorical and cultural studies. His most recent work—and current book project—is on the "New Jew," the Jew who "queers" common conceptions of Jewish identity, largely via the appropriation of what are considered to be "authentic" African American discourses.

Roopali Mukherjee is Associate Professor of Media Studies at the City University of New York/Queens College. She writes on issues of race within contemporary public culture in the United States. She is the author of *The Racial Order of Things: Cultural Imaginaries of the Post-Soul Era* (University of Minnesota Press,

2006) and co-editor of *Commodity Activism: Cultural Resistance in Neoliberal Times* (New York University Press, 2011).

Kent A. Ono is Professor of Asian American Studies and Media and Cinema Studies at the University of Illinois at Urbana-Champaign. He is author of *Contemporary Media Culture and the Remnants of a Colonial Past* (2009, Peter Lang) and co-author of *Asian Americans and the Media* with Vincent Pham (2009, Polity Press) and *Shifting Borders: Rhetoric, Immigration, and California's Proposition 187* with John Martin Sloop (2002, Temple University Press). He has edited *Asian American Studies after Critical Mass* (2005, Blackwell) and *A Companion to Asian American Studies* (2005, Blackwell) and has co-edited *Enterprise Zones: Critical Positions on Star Trek* (1996, Westview Press). He is currently writing a book with Etsuko Kinefuchi entitled, *Critical Intercultural Communication* (under contract with Pearson Allyn & Bacon).

Kimberlee Pérez is a doctoral student in the Hugh Downs School of Human Communication at Arizona State University. Her writing and teaching are at the intersections of performance, queer, and cultural studies.

Catherine R. Squires is the inaugural John and Elizabeth Bates Cowles Professor of Journalism, Diversity, and Equality at the University of Minnesota's School of Journalism and Mass Communication. Her work focuses on the interactions between racial groups, mass media, and the public sphere. Squires is the author of *Dispatches from the Color Line* and *African Americans and the Media* (Polity, 2009), and co-editor of *The Obama Effect: Multidisciplinary Renderings of the 2008 Campaign* (SUNY 2010). She has published articles on media and identity in *Critical Studies in Media Communication, Communication Theory,* and the *Harvard International Journal of Press/Politics.* Squires's work has been included in the books *Counterpublics and the State* (SUNY, 2001), *Say It Loud! African American Audiences,* and *Media and Identity* (Routledge, 2002), and *African American Communication and Identities: Essential Readings* (Sage, 2004). She received her PhD from Northwestern University's School of Speech in 1999. She was an assistant professor at the University of Michigan, Ann Arbor, from 2000 to 2007.

Sean Tierney was Assistant Professor in the School of Journalism and Communication at the Chinese University of Hong Kong. He earned his Bachelor's degree at the University of Rhode Island and earned his Master's and PhD in critical intercultural communication at Howard University in Washington, DC. His major research interests are Hong Kong cinema and critical intercultural studies, with an emphasis on whiteness research. His previous publications include "Themes of Whiteness in *Bulletproof Monk, Kill Bill,* and *The Last Samurai*," which was awarded the 2006 Outstanding Journal Article Award by the International and Intercultural Communication Division of the National Communication Association.

Cynthia Willis-Chun is Assistant Professor in the Department of Communication at Hiram College, after spending three years as a visiting assistant professor in the Department of Rhetoric and Media Studies at Willamette University. Her work examines the intersection of race/ethnicity, gender, sexuality, and nation in both political and popular texts. She has published a co-authored piece in *New Media and Society* on cultural memory and digital technology in NPR's Sonic Memorial; has a chapter in the book *Bitten by Twilight: Youth Culture, Media, and the Vampire Franchise* on the tourism industry that has arisen on the Olympic Peninsula because of the series, with particular attention given to the role of the LaPush reservation as a tourist destination; and book reviews in the *Review of Communication* and the *Quarterly Journal of Speech.*

Rulon Wood is a filmmaker and doctoral student in the Communication Department at the University of Utah. He also teaches at Westminster College. Currently, he is interested in multi-method research, that combines ethnographic and rhetorical methods.

Index

Multiculturalism, 99, 105; 106, 215, 217, 218, 224, 245, 249, 257; American multiculturalism, 208, 209; discourse around, 250; and MMP, 105

My Bondage and My Freedom (book), 143, 146, 156n23

Myrdal, Gunnar, 40n25

NAACP (National Association for the Advancement of Colored People), 71; President, 29

NAFTA (North American Free Trade Agreement), 101

Nagin, C. Ray, 22, 30, 35

Nakayama, Thomas K., 14n6, 49, 61n14, 66, 69, 76n13, 121, 134n40

Narrative, 21; apocalyptic, 23, 34; 36; diffuse textual, 21; dystopian, 23; logic, 146; mythic, 21, 36; metonymic, 28, 203; paternal, 206

National Anti-Slavery Standard, 148

National Basketball Association (NBA), 117; and race, 133n36; and racism, 133n36. *See also* NBA

National Convention of Colored People and Their Friends, 144

National Guard, 35; as civilizing agents, 35; as superheroes, 35; troops, 22, 31, 35

National Hurricane Center, 22. *See also* NHC

National Public Radio, 31

Nationality, 48, 53, 55, 165; Nationalists, 103

Nativism, 105; nativists, 99, 101

Natural Hazards Center: Director, 31

Naturalize (in nature), 55, 59

NBA (National Basketball Association), 128, 129, 133n31; and blackness, 119; capitalistic desire, 126; commissioner, 118, 120, 122; discourses, 117; and dress code, 126, 127; and hip hop, 128; and hip hop styles of dress, 128; and new racism, 121; and race, 118, 119, 120, 123, 130; as racial equalizer, 121; as racialized space, 120; and racism, 118, 119, 120, 127, 130; and whiteness, 119, 128, 130. *See also* National Basketball Association

NBC, 48, 57, 58, 187

Neocolonialism, 12, 37; neocolonizer, 237

Neoliberalism, 180, 187, 189, 201, 208, 211n7; and space, 199, 200, 203

New Hegelian, 172; and justice, 172

New Orleans, 8, 21, 22, 24, 25, 35, 36; Convention Center, 25, 26, 188; Mayor, 22, 30; population, 23, 43n77; Superdome, 22, 25, 26, 34, 188

New Right, 179

New York Amsterdam News, 162, 172; *New York Amsterdam News*'s coverage, 165–167

New York City, 163

New York Post, 1, 6

New York Times Manual of Style and Usage, 164–165, 167

New York Times, 25, 26, 28, 30, 31, 34, 38n4, 162; absence of inclusion of black press rhetoric, 173; challenge of, 168; public outcry towards, 164; *New York Time*'s coverage, 163–165, 176n38

Newfield, Christopher, 249

News Now, 72

Newsweek, 98

NHC (National Hurricane Center), 22; Director, 22. *See also* National Hurricane Center

Nietzsche, 189

Nigger: appropriation of, 89; in *Crash*, 223; versus kike, 92; power of the word, 88; and social power, 93; used by Tarantino, 88, 89, 91, 92; N-word, 71

Nonwhites, 143, 215, 217

Norman, Ann, 233

Norms: heterosexual, 210; normative blueprint, 250; racialized, 151; of rational discourse, 160, 167–168; violation of, 160, 167; whiteness, 122, 128

Notes on the State of Virginia (book), 143, 155n14

NOW with Bill Moyers, PBS, 198, 199; *NOW with Bill Moyers*'s rhetoric on outsourcing, 200–201

NPR (National Public Radio), 71, 72, 73

N-word (nigger), 69, 71, 73, 78n35; power of, 72; used among blacks, 72, 74

O'Donnell, Rosie: as lesbian, 73

Obama, Barack: as ape, 1; as first black president, 1, 4; as mixed race, 1; Obama's race, 4; as the President, 78n47, 93,179, 214;

as presidential candidate, 157n24; racist songs about, 74

Omi, Michael, 250

Ong, Aihwa, 211n6, 211n7, 212n12

Ono, Kent A., 8, 11, 12, 17n20, 107, 110, 121, 134n42, 140, 236, 251

O'Reilly Factor, Fox News, 71

O'Reilly, Bill, 71

Orientalism, 36; Orientalist gaze, 199; Orientialist tropes, 27, 198; and Quentin Tarantino, 94, 95n2

Otherness, 59, 165, 214, 215

Others, 37, 107, 110, 111, 216, 226; characterizations of, 110; colonization, 112; and criminalization, 110, 111; as criminals, 122; and dehumanization, 110, 111; ethnic, 59; and externalization, 110, 111; foreign, 105; as "illegal aliens," 100; local, 234; the marginalization of, 233; non-American, 27; racial, 21, 23, 27, 30, 69, 165, 215; religious, 380; primitive, 27; and whiteness, 121, 122

"Out of India" (documentary film), 199

Outsourcing, 198

Owens, Jesse, 119

Palin, Sarah, 4; and whiteness, 4

Paternalism, 8, 123; father-figure thesis, 125; paternalistic 243; patriarchy, 215; white, 10, 128; white paternalistic ideologies, 118

Patriotism, 99, 105; and MMP, 103; "patriotic nationalists," 103; patriots, 102; "revolutionary patriotism," 101; and white supremacy, 103; xenophobic, 109

PBS, 197, 199, 212n11

Peake, Linda, 51, 55, 61n25, 63n56

Pendejo games, 66, 70, 72, 73, 74, 75

Pepsi Cola Company, 184

Pérez, Kimberlee, 12

Phenotypes, 225

Philadelphia Inquirer, 54

Phillips, Kendall R., 63n71

Pittsburgh Post-Gazette, 52

Popular culture, 21, 117; black popular culture, 179, 185

Post-affirmative action, 259

Post-civil rights, 178, 180, 185

Postdevelopmentalism, 203, 209, 212n12

Postmodernism, 8, 94, 180

Post-Panopticon, 204

Postrace, ix, 1, 4, 130, 178, 179, 214, 248; post-racial hegemony, 181; post-racial subjects 180

Powell, Colin, 179

Power geometry, 199, 209

Power temporalities, 199, 200, 203, 205, 206, 209, 211n6

Power, 7, 218, 219, 223

Projansky, Sarah, 121, 134n42

Provincial Freeman, 142, 144

Public sphere, 146, 147, 207, 258; exclusion of minority, 160, 161, 167; westernized, 208

Public, 159, 160

Pulitzer Prize, 40n20

Pulp Fiction (film), 81, 88, 92, 95n1

Q-word (queer), 72

R. J. Reynolds Tobacco Company, 184

Race, 14n1, 48, 83, 90, 215, 218, 258; biological conception of, 225; and Columbine massacre, 54, 55; and communication studies, 7, 14n10; and consumption, 181, 184; denials of, 26, 86; discourse of, 4, 5, 6, 8; effectivity and materiality of, 8; essentializing, ix, 8; and ethnicity, 130n1; and freedom, 92, 93; images of, 1; inferential, 2, 3, 5; mixed race, 1, 14n1; and Barack Obama, 1; and National Basketball Association, 133n36; and NBA, 118, 119, 120, 123, 130; overt, 5; racial privilege, 83; and rhetoric, 15n11; sexualized, 75; and sports, 122; in sports, 117, 130, 130n2

Raceless, 251, 259

Racial: racial body polic, 256; racial formation, 3, 6; racial neutrality, 84; racial order, 179, 180, 181, 188, 250; racial power, 250; racial realism, 180; racial state, 189, 249, 250, 251, 259, 260, 261

Racial and Gender Report Card, 128

Racial pain, 15n11, 106, 218, 224; "a form of racial pain," 112; white masculine pain, 15n11, 100, 112; white pain, 99, 109, 112, 224, 225, 228; white racial pain, 217

Racial slurs, 68, 72, 74, 92, 93, 222, 223

Racism, ix, 1, 3, 72, 123, 215; analogies, 67; and black gays and lesbians, 67; colorblind racism, 178; and Columbine massacre, 55; and communication studies, 7; denials of, 26, 42n65; discourse of, 5, 6; in entertainment industry, 69, 73; and gay blacks, 74; and individual behaviors, 68; inferential, 2, 3, 4, 5, 26, 42n65; institutional, 2, 72, 229; institutionalized, 242; modern, 66; and MMP, 101, 106; and National Basketball Association, 133n36; and NBA, 118, 119, 120, 127, 130; new, 121, 129, 135n70; overt, 3, 4, 5; personal, 90; racism without racists, 121, 178; reverse racism, 2; and rhetoric, 15n11; in sports, 117, 130, 130n2; structural, 30, 33, 36, 38, 215; and use of racist language, 72, 90

Ramlow, Todd, 53, 62n43

Rational, and discourse, 159; irrational and blacks, 4, 36

Refugee, 27, 28, 34, 42n70, 43n92

Representation, 2, 214, 217, 218, 228, 230, 240; of African American, 86; of blacks, 222, 226; of otherness, 215; paternalistic, 243

Republican Party, 179

Request: hyperbolic request, 171; insulting request, 172; ironic request, 171; standard request, 171, 172; transgressive request, 172

Reservoir Dogs (film), 81, 92, 95n1

Ressentiment, 189

Revere, Paul, 102

Rhetoric, 4, 139; Afrocentric, 150, 152; black, 82; black press, 161, 162, 166, 169; black (righteous or radical) rage, 147; constitutive, 222; dehumanization, 23, 24; Habermas's view of, 169; of immigration, 116n43; and race, 15n11; racial, 139, 178, 180; and racism, 15n11; rhetorical criticism, 5; rhetorical reversals, 215; rhetorical theory, 5; rhetorics, 4; self-produced, 58; tactical, 57, 63n71, 86; transgressive rhetoric, 159–160, 161, 167, 169–170, 170, 171, 176n38; of whiteness, 120

Rhetorical trope, 166, 167, 236: colonialist, 200; colonial/imperial, 239; gendered, 208, 210; Orientalist, 27; hyperbole (as elements of transgressive rhetoric) 160, 161, 162; hyperbolic request, 171; against

truthfulness, 168; the use of hyperbole in *Amsterdam News*, 166–167

Rhoden, William C., 120

Rice, Condoleezza, 33

Richards, Michael, 68, 77n25

Rodman, Dennis, 119

Rodriguez, Robert, 81

Rosewood (film), 183

Rotten Tomatoes, 216

Rowe, Aimee Carillo, 12

Roy, Raman, 204, 205

RUF (The Revolutionary United Front), 235, 236, 238, 243

Russell, Bill, 119

Safir, Howard, 163

Samura, Sorious, 244

San Jose Mercury News, 51, 253

Sartre, J.P., 91

Savage, 235, 236

Searchers, The, 35

Searle, John, 168

Sexism, 206, 252; and Black leaders, 76n6; institutional, 72; and sports, 126

Sexuality: deviant, 52, 53

Sheeran, Josette, 243

Shome, Raka, 129, 136n101

Shropshire, Kenneth L., 118, 132n16

Sierra Leone, 233, 234

Sierra Leoneans, 233, 234, 238, 242; as audience, 243–244; Lewis, Victor, the interviewee, 244; Nauvo, the interviewee, 244; Paul, Walton, the interviewee, 240; stereotype of, 244

Silicon Valley, California, 248, 251, 253, 254, 256

Simcox, Chris, 98, 101, 104, 113, 113n3, 114n8

Sincerity: as norms of rationality, 159, 160, 167–168

Singleton, John (film director), 183

Slavery, 123, 157n30, 182; appropriation of, 85; chattel, 128

Slaves, 119, 172

Sloop, John M., 8, 11, 17n20, 107, 110, 140, 251

Smith, James McCune, 142, 143, 144, 146, 149

Social justice, 1, 2

Solomon, Martha, 23, 40n24

Song, Hoon, 97n64